CSS

THE MISSING MANUAL

*The book that
should have been
in the box®*

Other resources from O'Reilly

Related titles

FrontPage 2003: The Missing Manual

Dreamweaver 8: The Missing Manual

Flash 8: The Missing Manual

Google: The Missing Manual

eBay: The Missing Manual

Yahoo! Hacks™

Google Hacks™

Web Site Measurement Hacks™

Internet Annoyances

---

oreilly.com

oreilly.com is more than a complete catalog of O'Reilly books. You'll also find links to news, events, articles, weblogs, sample chapters, and code examples.

---

oreillynet.com is the essential portal for developers interested in open and emerging technologies, including new platforms, programming languages, and operating systems.

Conferences

O'Reilly brings diverse innovators together to nurture the ideas that spark revolutionary industries. We specialize in documenting the latest tools and systems, translating the innovator's knowledge into useful skills for those in the trenches. Visit *conferences.oreilly.com* for our upcoming events.

Safari Bookshelf (*safari.oreilly.com*) is the premier online reference library for programmers and IT professionals. Conduct searches across more than 1,000 books. Subscribers can zero in on answers to time-critical questions in a matter of seconds. Read the books on your Bookshelf from cover to cover or simply flip to the page you need. Try it today for free.

CSS

David Sawyer McFarland

POGUE PRESS™
O'REILLY®

Beijing • Cambridge • Farnham • Köln • Paris • Sebastopol • Taipei • Tokyo

CSS: The Missing Manual
by David Sawyer McFarland

Published by O'Reilly Media, Inc., 1005 Gravenstein Highway North, Sebastopol, CA 95472.

O'Reilly books may be purchased for educational, business, or sales promotional use. Online editions are also available for most titles (*safari.oreilly.com*). For more information, contact our corporate/institutional sales department: (800) 998-9938 or *corporate@oreilly.com*.

Printing History:

August 2006:   First Edition.

RepKover™ This book uses RepKover™, a durable and flexible lay-flat binding.

ISBN-10: 0-596-52687-3
ISBN-13: 978-0-596-52687-0

[C]   [1/07]

Table of Contents

Part Two: Applied CSS

Chapter 6: Formatting Text 99

Chapter 7: Margins, Padding, and Borders 133

The Missing Credits

About the Author

 **David Sawyer McFarland** is president of Sawyer McFarland Media, Inc., a Web development and training company in Portland, Oregon. He's been building Web sites since 1995, when he designed his first Web site: an online magazine for communication professionals. He's served as the Webmaster at the University of California at Berkeley and the Berkeley Multimedia Research Center, and oversaw a complete CSS-driven redesign of Macworld.com.

In addition to building Web sites, David is also a writer, trainer, and instructor. He's taught Web design at UC Berkeley Graduate School of Journalism, the Center for Electronic Art, the Academy of Art College, Ex'Pressions Center for New Media, and Portland State University. He's written articles about the Web for *Practical Web Design, MX Developer's Journal, Macworld* magazine, and *CreativePro.com*.

He welcomes feedback about this book by email: *missing@sawmac.com*. (If you're seeking technical help, however, please refer to the sources listed in Appendix C.)

About the Creative Team

Nan Barber (editor) has worked with the Missing Manual series since its inception—long enough to remember booting up her computer from a floppy disk. Email: *nanbarber@oreilly.com*.

Peter Meyers (editor) works as an editor at O'Reilly Media on the Missing Manual series. He lives with his wife in New York City. Email: *peter.meyers@gmail.com*.

Michele Filshie (copy editor) is O'Reilly's assistant editor for Missing Manuals and editor of *Don't Get Burned on eBay*. Before turning to the world of computer-related books, Michele spent many happy years at Black Sparrow Press. She lives in Sebastopol. Email: *mfilshie@oreilly.com*.

Mark Levitt (tech reviewer) is a Senior Web Producer for O'Reilly Media's Online Publishing Group. His background includes Computer Science, Interactive & Educational Media, and Web Development. He's known to eat cereal at all hours of the day. Email: *mark@levittation.com*.

Justin Watt (tech reviewer) is currently an author-services engineer for Federated Media Publishing, a blog advertising company based in Sausalito, California. He blogs at justinsomnia.org, where you can read about his adventures in Northern California. Email: *jwatt@federatedmedia.net*.

Rose Cassano (cover illustration) has worked as an independent designer and illustrator for 20 years. Assignments have ranged from the nonprofit sector to corporate clientele. She lives in beautiful Southern Oregon, grateful for the miracles of modern technology that make working there a reality. Email: *cassano@highstream. net.* Web: *www.rosecassano.com.*

Acknowledgements

Many thanks to all those who helped with this book, including my students, who always help me see technical issues through beginners' eyes. Thanks to my technical editors, Mark Levitt and Justin Watt, who saved me from any embarrassing mistakes, Zoe Gillenwater for her valuable advice, and all of the generous souls on the CSS-Discuss mailing list who share their hard one wisdom about CSS. Also, we all owe a big debt of gratitude to the many Web designers who have broken new ground by using CSS in creative ways, and shared their discoveries with the Web design community.

Finally, thanks to David Pogue whose unflagging enthusiasm and endurance is inspiring; Nan Barber for refining my writing; Peter Meyers for polishing my prose and keeping me on track; my wife, Scholle, for motivating me to get this project done; and my son, Graham, who doesn't know what I do for a living and doesn't care.

The Missing Manual Series

Missing Manuals are witty, superbly written guides to computer products that don't come with printed manuals (which is just about all of them). Each book features a handcrafted index and RepKover, a detached-spine binding that lets the book lie perfectly flat without the assistance of weights or cinder blocks.

Recent and upcoming titles include:

Access for Starters: The Missing Manual by Kate Chase and Scott Palmer

AppleScript: The Missing Manual by Adam Goldstein

AppleWorks 6: The Missing Manual by Jim Elferdink and David Reynolds

Creating Web Sites: The Missing Manual by Matthew MacDonald

Digital Photography: The Missing Manual by Chris Grover and Barbara Brundage

Dreamweaver 8: The Missing Manual by David Sawyer McFarland

eBay: The Missing Manual by Nancy Conner

Excel: The Missing Manual by Matthew MacDonald

Excel for Starters: The Missing Manual by Matthew MacDonald

FileMaker Pro 8: The Missing Manual by Geoff Coffey and Susan Prosser

Flash 8: The Missing Manual by Emily Moore

FrontPage 2003: The Missing Manual by Jessica Mantaro

GarageBand 2: The Missing Manual by David Pogue

Google: The Missing Manual, Second Edition by Sarah Milstein, J.D. Biersdorfer, and Matthew MacDonald

Home Networking: The Missing Manual by Scott Lowe

iLife '05: The Missing Manual by David Pogue

iMovie 6 & iDVD: The Missing Manual by David Pogue

iPhoto 6: The Missing Manual by David Pogue

iPod & iTunes: The Missing Manual, Fourth Edition by J.D. Biersdorfer

iWork '05: The Missing Manual by Jim Elferdink

Mac OS X Power Hound, Panther Edition by Rob Griffiths

Mac OS X: The Missing Manual, Tiger Edition by David Pogue

Office 2004 for Macintosh: The Missing Manual by Mark H. Walker and Franklin Tessler

PCs: The Missing Manual by Andy Rathbone

Photoshop Elements 4: The Missing Manual by Barbara Brundage

QuickBooks 2006: The Missing Manual by Bonnie Biafore

Quicken for Starters: The Missing Manual by Bonnie Biafore

Switching to the Mac: The Missing Manual, Tiger Edition by David Pogue and Adam Goldstein

The Internet: The Missing Manual by David Pogue and J.D. Biersdorfer

Windows 2000 Pro: The Missing Manual by Sharon Crawford

Windows XP for Starters: The Missing Manual by David Pogue

Windows XP Home Edition: The Missing Manual, Second Edition by David Pogue

Windows XP Pro: The Missing Manual, 2nd Edition by David Pogue, Craig Zacker, and Linda Zacker

Windows Vista: The Missing Manual by David Pogue

Introduction

Cascading Style Sheets—CSS for short—give you creative control over the layout and design of your Web pages. Using them, you can dress up your text with eye-catching headings, drop caps, and borders, just like the ones you see in glossy magazines. You can also arrange images with precision, create columns and banners, and highlight your text links with dynamic rollover effects.

Anything that can do all that must be pretty complicated, right? Au contraire! The purpose of CSS is to streamline the process of styling Web pages. In the next few pages, you'll learn about the basics of CSS. In Chapter 1, you'll get right to work creating your first Web page.

How CSS Works

If you've used styles in word processing programs like Microsoft Word or page layout programs like Adobe InDesign, CSS will feel familiar. A *style* is simply a rule describing how to format a particular portion of a Web page. A style *sheet* is a set of these canned styles.

CSS is *not* HTML. HTML provides structure to a document by organizing information into headers, paragraphs, bulleted lists, and so on. CSS is another language altogether. It works hand-in-hand with the Web browser to make HTML *look* good.

For example, you might use HTML to turn a phrase into a top-level heading, indicating that it introduces the content on the rest of the page. However, you'd use CSS to format that heading with, say, big and bold red type and positioned 50 pixels from the left edge of the window. CSS is all about changing (and improving) the appearance of the HTML.

You can also create styles specifically for working with images. For instance, a style can align an image along the right edge of a Web page, surround the image with a colorful border, and place a 50-pixel margin between the image and the surrounding text.

Once you've created a style, you can apply it to text, images, headings, or other elements on a page. For example, you could select a paragraph of text and apply a style to instantly change the text's size, color, and font. You can also create styles for specific HTML tags, so that, for example, all first-level headings (<h1> tags) in your site are displayed in the same style, no matter where they appear.

The Benefits of CSS

Before CSS, Web designers were limited to the layout and styling options of HTML. And if you surfed the Web in 1995, then you understand the emphasis on *limited*. HTML, as you'll see later in this introduction, still forms the foundation of all pages on the World Wide Web, but it's simply not a design tool. Sure, HTML provides basic formatting options for text, images, tables, and other Web page elements and patient, meticulous Web masters can make pages look pretty good using only HTML. But the result's often sluggish, unpredictable Web pages laden with clunky code.

CSS, in contrast, offers the following advantages:

- Style sheets offer far more formatting choices than HTML. With CSS, you can format paragraphs as they appear in a book or newspaper (the first line indented and no space between each paragraph, for example) and control the *leading* (the space between lines of type in a paragraph).

- When you use CSS to add a background image to a page, you get to decide how (and whether) it tiles (repeats). HTML can't even begin to do that.

- Even better, CSS styles take up much less space than HTML's formatting options, such as the much-hated <font> tag. You can usually trim a lot of kilobytes from text-heavy Web pages using CSS. As a result, your pages look great *and* load faster.

- Style sheets also make updating your site easier. You can collect all of your styles into a single external style sheet that's linked to every page in your site. When you edit a style, that change immediately ripples through your site *wherever* that style appears. You can completely change the appearance of a site just by editing a single style sheet.

Note: HTML is so long in the tooth design-wise that the World Wide Web Consortium (W3C), the organization responsible for defining standards for the Web, has already *deprecated* (phased out) many HTML tags used solely for formatting the look of HTML (the <font> tag, for example). (For a list of other obsolete tags, see *www.codehelp.co.uk/html/deprecated.html*.)

What You Need to Know

This book assumes you've already got some knowledge of HTML (and perhaps some CSS experience as well); you've built a site or two (or at least a page or two) and have some familiarity with the sea of tags—<html>, <p>, <h1>, <table>, and so on—that make up the Hypertext Markup Language. CSS doesn't do anything without HTML, so to move forward you need to know how to create a Web page using basic HTML.

If you have used HTML to create Web pages, but feel like your knowledge is a bit rusty, the next section provides a basic refresher.

Note: If you're just getting your feet wet learning HTML, then check out these free online tutorials: HTML Dog (*www.htmldog.com/guides/htmlbeginner/*) and W3Schools (*www.w3schools.com/html/*). If you're a printed page fan, then you may want to pick up a copy of *Creating Web Sites: The Missing Manual*, or *Head First HTML with CSS & XHTML* (O'Reilly).

HTML: The Barebones Structure

HTML (Hypertext Markup Language) uses simple commands called *tags* to define the various parts of a Web page. For example, this HTML code creates a simple Web page:

```
<html>
<head>
<title>Hey, I am the title of this Web page.</title>
</head>
<body>
Hey, I am some body text on this Web page.
</body>
</html>
```

It may not be exciting, but this example has all the basic elements a Web page needs. You'll notice *html* (between brackets) at the very beginning and very end of the code, a header, a body, and some stuff—the actual page contents—inside the body.

How HTML Tags Work

In the above example, as in the HTML code of any Web page you look at, you'll notice that most commands appear in pairs that surround a block of text or other commands. Sandwiched between brackets, these *tags* are instructions that tell a Web browser how to display the Web page. Tags are the "markup" part of the Hypertext Markup Language.

The starting (*opening*) tag of each pair tells the browser where the instruction begins, and the ending tag tells it where the instruction ends. Ending or *closing* tags always include a forward slash (/) after the first bracket symbol (<).

For a Web page to work, you must include at least these three tags:

- The <**html**> tag appears once at the beginning of a Web page and again (with an added slash) at the end. This tag tells a Web browser that the information contained in this document's written in HTML, as opposed to some other language. All of the contents of a page, including other tags, appear between the opening and closing <html> tags.

  If you were to think of a Web page as a tree, the <html> tag would be its trunk. Springing from the trunk are two branches that represent the two main parts of any Web page: the *head* and the *body*.

- The *head* of a Web page, surrounded by <**head**> tags, contains the title of the page. It may also provide other, invisible information (such as search keywords) that browsers and Web search engines can exploit.

  In addition, the head can contain information that's used by the Web browser for displaying the Web page and for adding interactivity. You put Cascading Style Sheets, for example, in the head of the document. In addition, JavaScript scripts, functions, and variables can be declared in the head of the document.

- The *body* of a Web page, as set apart by its surrounding <**body**> tags, contains all the information that appears inside a browser window—headlines, text, pictures, and so on.

Within the <body> tag, you commonly find the following tags:

- You tell a Web browser where a paragraph of text begins with a <**p**> (opening paragraph tag), and where it ends with a </p> (closing paragraph tag).

- The <**strong**> tag emphasizes text. When you surround some text with it and its partner tag, </strong>, you get boldface type. The HTML snippet <strong> Warning!</strong> tells a Web browser to strongly emphasize the word "Warning!"

- The <**a**> tag, or anchor tag, creates a *hyperlink* in a Web page. When clicked, a hyperlink—or link—can lead anywhere on the Web. You tell the browser where the link points by putting a Web address inside the <a> tags. For instance, you can type *<a href="http://www.missingmanuals.com/">Click here!</a>*.

  The browser knows that when your visitor clicks the words "Click here!" it should go to the Missing Manual Web site. The *href* part of the tag is called an *attribute* and the URL (the Uniform Resource Locator or Web address) is the *value.* In this example, *http://www.missingmanuals.com* is the *value* of the *href* attribute.

Like any technology, HTML's showing its age. Although it's served its purpose well, it's always been a somewhat sloppy language. Among other things, it allows uppercase, lowercase, or mixed case letters in tags (<body> and <BODY> are both correct, for example), and permits unclosed tags (so that you can use a single <p> tag without the closing </p> to create a paragraph). While this flexibility may make page writing easier, it also makes life more difficult for Web browsers, PDAs, and other places you want to display your pages. Furthermore, HTML doesn't work with one of the hottest up-and-coming Internet languages: *XML* or Extensible Markup Language.

XML is a tag-based language, somewhat like HTML, that's used to organize data in a clear, easy to understand way so that different computers, operating systems, and programs can quickly and easily exchange data. However, unlike HTML, XML isn't limited to a handful of tags, In fact, XML provides a set of rules for defining your own tags. XHTML, which you'll read about next, is one example of XML—but there are many others: from RSS feeds to iTunes playlists.

XHTML: HTML for the New Era

To keep pace with the times, an "improved" version of HTML, called XHTML is finding its way into more and more Web sites. If you already understand HTML, don't worry—XHTML isn't a revolutionary new language that takes years to learn. It's basically HTML, but with stricter guidelines.

The hot debate's whether HTML or XHTML is the best approach. To judge by some of the online discussions, you'd think HTML and XHTML are completely different languages. They aren't. You can build snazzy and functional Web sites with HTML now and will probably be able to continue in the future. If you continue using HTML, the most important thing is that you follow the guidelines discussed in Chapter 1: in particular, an HTML page must use the correct "Doctype" (page 24) or your CSS will fall apart in certain browsers, and it must "validate" (page 22) so that you know for sure there aren't any typos or other mistakes that can mess up how your HTML displays.

You need to do those same things for XHTML, but because it's stricter than HTML it enforces rules that make sure the page works (for example, a Doctype isn't absolutely required in HTML; it *is* with XHTML).

XHTML's the future of Web page languages: there won't be any future versions of HTML, but there's a lot of work being put into creating the next generation of XHTML. (Don't hold your breath, though—it'll be years before there's wide support in browsers for it.)

Note: If you really want to delve into the innards of XHTML, then check out W3Schools XHTML Tutorial at *www.w3schools.com/xhtml/default.asp*

The HTML page code shown on page 3 would look like *this* in XHTML:

```
<!DOCTYPE html PUBLIC "-//W3C//DTD XHTML 1.0 Transitional//EN"
"http://www.w3.org/TR/xhtml1/DTD/xhtml1-transitional.dtd">

<html xmlns="http://www.w3.org/1999/xhtml">

<head>
<title>Hey, I am the title of this Web page.</title>
<meta http-equiv="Content-Type" content="text/html; charset=iso-
8859-1" />
</head>

<body>
<p>Hey, I am some body text on this Web page. </p>
</body>
</html>
```

As you can see, this code looks a lot like HTML. To make an XHTML file comply with XML, however, there are a few strict rules to keep in mind:

- **Begin the page with a document type declaration.** That's the first few lines in the code above, starting with *<!DOCTYPE*. The document type declaration is the most important part of an XHTML page, as you'll see in the next section.

- **Tags and tag attributes must be lowercase.** Unlike with HTML, typing the tag <BODY> is a no-no; when you're writing XHTML, capitalized tags aren't invited to the party.

- **Quotation marks are required for tag attributes.** For example, a link written like this: <a href=http://www.missingmanuals.com> is valid in HTML, but won't work in XHTML. You have to enclose the value of the Href property in quotes: <a href="http://www.missingmanuals.com">.

- **All tags (even empty tags) must be closed.** To create a paragraph in XHTML, for example, you must begin with <p> and end with </p>. Trouble is, some tags don't come in pairs. These tags, called *empty tags* have no closing tag. The line break tag's one example. To close an empty tag, include a backslash at the end of the tag, like this: <br />.

What the Doctype Does

In the example XHTML code, everything below the <head> is *exactly* the same as the HTML page you looked at earlier. The information that *begins* the page, however, is very different. Each XHTML page begins with a few lines that state what type of document the page is and which standard it conforms to. This *document type declaration*—doctype for short—also points the Web browser to files on the Internet that contain definitions for that type of file.

In this case, it merely says that the page is a type of XML document, in particular, an XHTML document. The doctype plays a key role in how a Web browser displays CSS—in fact a missing or incorrect doctype's enough to make Internet Explorer completely mishandle the presentation of a CSS-heavy Web page. You'll learn much more about doctypes—and their importance to CSS—in Chapter 1.

Note: This may seem like a lot to take in if you're relatively new to building Web pages. Don't worry–it is. In Chapter 1, you'll also learn a cool tool for making sure you're creating correct XHTML–the W3C Validator. It checks your page and lets you know if everything's OK. Even more importantly, you'll learn how to create CSS-friendly XHTML.

Software for CSS

To create Web pages made up of HTML and CSS you need nothing more than a basic text editor like Notepad (Windows) or Text Edit (Mac). But after typing a few hundred lines of HTML and CSS you may want to try a program better suited to working with Web pages. This section lists some common programs; some of them are free and some you have to buy.

Note: There are literally hundreds of tools that can help you create Web pages, so the following isn't a complete list. Think of it as a greatest hits-style tour of the most popular programs that CSS fans are using today.

Free Programs

There are plenty of free programs out there for editing Web pages and style sheets. If you're still using Notepad or Text Edit, then give one of these a try. Here's a short list to get you started:

HTML-Kit (Windows, *www.chami.com/html-kit/*). This powerful HTML/XHTML editor includes lots of useful features like the ability to preview a Web page directly in the program (so you don't have to switch back and forth between browser and editor), shortcuts for adding HTML tags, and a lot more.

TextWrangler (Mac, *www.barebones.com/products/textwrangler/*). This free software's actually a paired down version of BBEdit, the sophisticated, well-known text editor for the Mac. TextWrangler doesn't have all of BBEdit's built-in HTML-tools, but it does include syntax-coloring (meaning that tags and properties are highlighted in different colors so it's easy to scan a page and identify its parts), FTP support (so you can upload files to a Web server), and more.

Commercial Software

Commercial Web site development programs range from inexpensive text editors to complete Web site construction tools with all the bells and whistles:

EditPlus (Windows, *www.editplus.com*) is an inexpensive ($30) text editor that includes syntax-coloring, FTP, auto-completion and other wrist-saving features.

skEdit (Mac, *www.skti.org*) is a cheap ($25) Web page editor, complete with FTP/SFTP support, code hints and other useful features.

BBEdit (Mac, *www.barebones.com/products/bbedit*). This much-loved Mac text editor ($199) has plenty of tools for working with HTML, XHTML, CSS and more. Includes many useful Web building tools and shortcuts.

Dreamweaver (Mac and Windows, *www.macromedia.com/software/dreamweaver*) is a visual Web page editor ($399.) It lets you see how your page looks in a Web browser. The program also includes a powerful text-editor and excellent CSS creation and management tools. Check out *Dreamweaver: The Missing Manual* for the full skinny on how to use this powerful program.

Expression Web Designer (Windows, *www.microsoft.com*) is Microsoft's new entry in the Web design field. It replaces FrontPage and includes many professional Web design tools including very good support for creating CSS.

Note: The various types of software discussed in this section are general purpose programs that let you edit both HTML/XHTML and CSS. With them, you need to learn only one program for your Web development needs. But if you've already got a beloved HTML/XHTML editor that doesn't do CSS, then you may want to check out one of the CSS-specific editing programs covered in Appendix C.

About This Book

The World Wide Web is really easy to use. After all, grandmothers in Boise and first graders in Tallahassee log onto the Web every day. Unfortunately, the rules that govern how the Web *works* aren't so easy to understand. The computer scientists and other techie types who write the official documentation aren't interested in explaining their concepts to the average Joe (or Joanne). Just check out *www.w3. org/TR/CSS21/* to get a taste of the technical mumbo-jumbo these geeks speak.

There's no manual for Cascading Style Sheets. People just learning CSS often don't know where to begin. And the finer points regarding CSS can trip up even seasoned Web pros. The purpose of this book, then, is to serve as the manual that should have come with CSS. In this book's pages, you'll find step-by-step instructions for using CSS to create beautiful Web pages.

CSS: The Missing Manual is designed to help readers at every technical level. To get the most out of this book, you should know a sampling of HTML and maybe even CSS. So if you've never built a Web page before, then check out the tutorial that starts on page 34. The primary discussions in these chapters are written for

UP TO SPEED

The Different Flavors of CSS

Like operating systems and iPods, CSS spins off new versions continuously. CSS 1, introduced in 1996, laid the groundwork for Cascading Style Sheets. The basic structure of a style, the selector concept (Chapter 3), and most of the CSS properties in this book were all in that very first version.

CSS 2 added new features, including the ability to target your CSS to different printers, monitors, and other devices (page 365). CSS 2 also added new selectors and the ability to precisely position elements on a Web page.

This book covers CSS 2.1, which is the current accepted standard for Cascading Style Sheets. It incorporates all of CSS 1, adds several new properties, and corrects a few problems with the CSS 2 guidelines.

CSS 2.1 isn't a radical change from version 2, and most Web browsers have adapted to the new rules just fine, thank you. (A notable exception is Internet Explorer 6 for Windows—that's why you'll find helpful workarounds for dealing with browser differences sprinkled throughout this book. Thankfully, Internet Explorer 7 has fixed most of the hair-pulling bugs of its ancestors.)

CSS 3 is just around the corner. Although the W3C still has to finalize this standard, some Web browsers are already adopting a few of its new guidelines and features. Safari's ability to add multiple images to the background of a single element, for example, is thanks to CSS 3. However, since CSS 3 is still evolving, most browsers don't deal with it much—and neither does this book.

advanced-beginners or intermediates. But if you're new to building Web pages, special boxes called "Up to Speed" provide the introductory information you need to understand the topic at hand. If you're an advanced Web page jockey, on the other hand, then keep your eye out for similar shaded boxes called Power Users' Clinic. They offer more technical tips, tricks, and shortcuts for the experienced computer fan.

Note: This book periodically recommends *other* CSS books, covering topics that are too specialized or tangential for a manual. Sometimes the recommended titles are from Missing Manual series publisher O'Reilly Media—but not always. If there's a great book out there that's not part of the O'Reilly family, we'll let you know about it.

About the Outline

CSS: The Missing Manual is divided into four parts, each containing several chapters:

- Part 1, **CSS Basics,** shows you how to create style sheets and provides an overview of key CSS concepts, like inheritance, selectors, and the cascade. Along the way, you'll learn the best HTML/XHTML writing practices when working with CSS. Four tutorials reinforce the part's main concepts and give you a good taste of the power of CSS.

- Part 2, **Applied CSS,** takes you into the real world of Web design. You'll learn the most important CSS properties and how to use them to format text, create useful navigation tools, and enhance your page with graphics. This section also provides advice on how to make Web pages look better when printed and how to make attractive tables and forms.

• Part 3, **CSS Page Layout,** helps you with one of the most confusing, but most rewarding, aspects of CSS: controlling the placement of elements on a page. You'll learn how to create common designs (like 2 and 3-column layouts) and how to add sidebars. You'll also learn about floats and positioning—two common CSS techniques for controlling page layout.

• Part 4, **Advanced CSS,** teaches you how to make web pages look good when printed and covers advanced techniques for using CSS more effectively and efficiently.

• Part 5, **Appendixes,** provides three sets of resources. The CSS Property Reference summarizes each CSS Property in small, easy-to-digest, chunks so you can casually brush-up on what you already know, or quickly learn about other useful CSS properties that you may not remember. The last two appendices cover tools and resources for creating and using CSS, from how to create CSS in Dreamweaver to lists of helpful Web sites and books.

Living Examples

This book is designed to get your work onto the Web faster and more professionally. It's only natural, then, that half the value of this book lies on the Web.

As you read the book's chapters, you'll encounter a number of *living examples—* step-by-step tutorials that you can build yourself, using raw materials (like graphics and half-completed Web pages) that you can download from *www.sawmac. com/css/.* You may not gain very much by simply reading these step-by-step lessons while relaxing in your porch hammock. But if you take the time to work through them at the computer, you'll discover that these tutorials give you insight into the way professional designers build Web pages.

You'll also find, in this book's lessons, the URLs of the finished pages, so that you can compare your work with the final result. In other words, you won't just see pictures of how the Web pages *should* look: You'll find the actual, working Web pages on the Internet.

About MissingManuals.com

At the Missing Manuals Web site (*www.missingmanuals.com*), you'll find articles, tips, and updates to the book. In fact, we invite and encourage you to submit such corrections and updates yourself. In an effort to keep the book as up-to-date and accurate as possible, each time we print more copies of this book, we'll make any confirmed corrections you've suggested. We'll also note such changes on the Web site, so that you can mark important corrections into your own copy of the book, if you like. (Click the book's name, and then click the Errata link, to see the changes.)

In the meantime, we'd love to hear your suggestions for new books in the Missing Manual line. There's a place for that on the Web site, too, as well as a place to sign up for free email notification of new titles in the series.

The Very Basics

To use this book, and indeed to use a computer, you need to know a few basics. You should be familiar with these terms and concepts:

- **Clicking.** This book gives you three kinds of instructions that require you to use your computer's mouse or trackpad. To *click* means to point the arrow cursor at something on the screen and then—without moving the cursor at all—to press and release the clicker button on the mouse (or laptop trackpad). To *double-click,* of course, means to click twice in rapid succession, again without moving the cursor at all. And to *drag* means to move the cursor *while* pressing the button.

    When you're told to ⌘-*click* something on the Mac, or *Ctrl-click* something on a PC, you click while pressing the ⌘ or Ctrl key (both of which are near the Space bar).

- **Menus.** The *menus* are the words at the top of your screen or window: File, Edit, and so on. Click one to make a list of commands appear, as though they're written on a window shade you've just pulled down.

- **Operating-system basics.** This book assumes that you know how to open a program, surf the Web, and download files. You should know how to use the Start menu (Windows) and the Dock or menu (Macintosh), as well as the Control Panel (Windows), or System Preferences (Mac OS X).

If you've mastered this much information, you have all the technical background you need to enjoy *CSS: The Missing Manual.*

About → These → Arrows

Throughout this book, and throughout the Missing Manual series, you'll find sentences like this one: "Open the System → Library → Fonts folder." That's shorthand for a much longer instruction that directs you to open three nested folders in sequence, like this: "On your hard drive, you'll find a folder called System. Open that. Inside the System folder window is a folder called Library; double-click it to open it. Inside *that* folder is yet another one called Fonts. Double-click to open it, too."

Similarly, this kind of arrow shorthand helps to simplify the business of choosing commands in menus, as shown in Figure I-1.

Figure I-1:
In this book, arrow notations help simplify menu instructions. For example, View → Text Size → Increase is a more compact way of saying, "From the View menu, choose Text Size; from the submenu that then appears, choose Increase.

Safari® Enabled

When you see a Safari® Enabled icon on the cover of your favorite technology book, that means it's available online through the O'Reilly Network Safari Bookshelf.

Safari offers a solution that's better than e-books: it's a virtual library that lets you easily search thousands of top tech books, cut and paste code samples, download chapters, and find quick answers when you need the most accurate, current information. Try it for free at *http://safari.oreilly.com.*

Part One:
CSS Basics

1

Rethinking HTML for CSS

To get the most out of CSS, your HTML code needs to provide a solid, well-built foundation. This chapter shows you how to write better, more CSS-friendly HTML. The good news is that when you use CSS throughout your site, HTML actually becomes *easier* to write. You no longer need to worry about trying to turn HTML into the design maven it was never intended to be; instead, CSS offers all the graphic design touches you'll likely ever want. And your job becomes simpler since HTML pages written to work with CSS require less code, less typing, and are easier to create. They'll also download faster—a welcome bonus your site's visitors will appreciate (see Figure 1-1).

HTML: Past and Present

As discussed in the Introduction, HTML and its successor, XHTML, provide the foundation for every page you encounter on the World Wide Web. When you add CSS into the mix, the way you use HTML changes. Say goodbye to repurposing awkward HTML tags merely to achieve certain visual effects. Some HTML tags and attributes—like the <font> tag—you can forget completely. The following sections explain why.

Note: Throughout this chapter, everything you read about HTML applies equally to XHTML. There are as many variants of HTML and XHTML as there are colors in the rainbow, though, and in the end you must pick a type and make sure your Web page identifies which one you're using. Otherwise, your visitors' browsers may gunk up your painfully crafted page. You'll learn how to tell CSS which flavor of HTML/XHTML you're using later in this chapter.

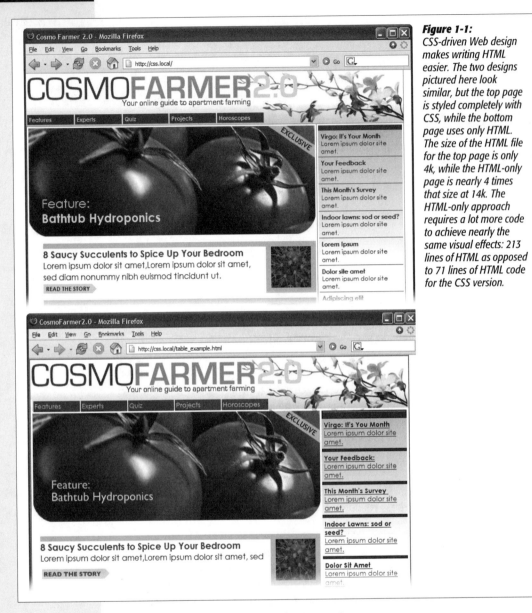

Figure 1-1:
CSS-driven Web design makes writing HTML easier. The two designs pictured here look similar, but the top page is styled completely with CSS, while the bottom page uses only HTML. The size of the HTML file for the top page is only 4k, while the HTML-only page is nearly 4 times that size at 14k. The HTML-only approach requires a lot more code to achieve nearly the same visual effects: 213 lines of HTML as opposed to 71 lines of HTML code for the CSS version.

HTML Past: Whatever Looked Good

When a bunch of scientists created the Web to help share and keep track of techni-cal documentation, nobody called in the graphic designers. All the scientists needed HTML to do was to clearly structure information for easy comprehension. For example, the <h1> tag indicates an important headline, while the <h2> tag represents a lesser heading, usually a subheading of the <h1> tag. Another favor-ite, the <ol> (ordered list) tag, creates a numbered list for things like "Top 10 rea-sons not to play with jellyfish."

But as soon as people besides scientists started using HTML, they wanted their Web pages to look good. So Web designers started to use tags to control appearance rather than structure information. For example, you can use the <blockquote> tag (intended for material that's quoted from another source) on any text that you want to indent a little bit. You can use heading tags to make any text bigger and bolder—regardless of whether it functions as a heading.

In an even more elaborate workaround, designers learned how to use the <table> tag to create columns of text, and to accurately place pictures and text on a page. Unfortunately, since that tag was intended to display spreadsheet-like data— research results, train schedules, and so on—designers had to get creative by using the <table> tag in unusual ways, sometimes nesting a table within a table within a table in order to make their pages look good.

Meanwhile, browser makers introduced new tags and attributes for the specific purpose of making a page look better. The <font> tag, for example, lets you specify a font color, typeface, and one of seven different sizes. (If you're keeping score at home, that's about 100 fewer sizes than you can get with, say, Microsoft Word.)

Finally, when designers couldn't get exactly what they wanted, they often resorted to using graphics. For example, they'd use a very large graphic as background for a Web page or slice it up into smaller graphic files and piece them back together inside tables to recreate the original image.

While all of the above techniques—using tags in creative ways, taking advantage of design-specific tag attributes, and making extensive use of graphics—provide design control over your pages, they also add a lot of additional HTML code (and more wrinkles to your forehead than a lifetime in the sun).

HTML Present: Scaffolding for CSS

No matter what content your Web page holds—the fishing season calendar, driving directions to the nearest IKEA, or pictures from your kid's last birthday party—it's the page's design that makes it look like either a professional enterprise or a part-timer's hobby. Good design enhances the message of your site, helps visitors find what they're looking for and determines how the rest of the world sees your Web site. That's why Web designers went through the contortions described in the previous section to force HTML to look good. By taking on those design duties, CSS lets HTML go back to doing what it does best—structure content (more on what *that* means in a moment).

Using HTML to control the look of text and other Web page elements is obsolete. Don't worry if HTML's <h1> tag is too big for your taste or bulleted lists aren't spaced just right. You can take care of that later using CSS. Instead, think of HTML as a method of adding structure to the content you want up on the Web. Use HTML to organize your content, and CSS to make that content look great.

Writing HTML for CSS

If you're new to Web design, you may need some helpful hints to guide your for-ays into HTML (and to steer clear of well-intentioned, but out-of-date HTML techniques). And if you've been building Web pages for a while, then you may have picked up a few bad HTML-writing habits that you're better off forgetting. The rest of this chapter introduces you to some HTML writing habits that will make your mother proud—and help you get the most out of CSS.

Think Structure

HTML adds meaning to text by logically dividing it and identifying the role that text plays on the page: for example, the <h1> tag's the most important introduc-tion to a page's content. Other headers let you divide up the content into other, less important, but related sections. Just like the book you're holding, for example, a Web page should have a logical structure. Each chapter in this book has a title (think <h1>); and several sections (think <h2>), which in turn contain smaller subsections. Imagine how much harder it would be to read these pages if every word just ran together as one long paragraph.

Note: For a good resource on HTML/XHTML check out *HTML & XHTML: The Definitive Guide* (O'Reilly) by Chuck Musciano and Bill Kennedy, or visit *www.w3schools.com* for online HTML and XHTML tutorials. For a quick list of all available HTML and XHTML tags, visit *www.w3schools.com/tags/*.

HTML provides many other tags besides headers for *marking up* (that's the M in HTML) content to identify its role on the page. Among the most popular are the <p> tag for paragraphs of text, and the <ul> tag for creating bulleted (non-num-bered) lists. Lesser-known tags can indicate very specific types of content, like <abbr> for abbreviations and <code> for computer code.

When writing HTML for CSS, use a tag that comes close to matching the role the content plays in the page, not the way it looks (see Figure 1-2). For example, a bunch of links in a navigation bar isn't really a headline and it isn't a regular para-graph of text. It's most like a bulleted list of options, so the <ul> tag is a good choice. If you're saying "but items in a bulleted list are stacked vertically one on top of the other, and I want a horizontal navigation bar where each link sits next to the previous link," don't worry. With CSS magic you can convert a vertical list of links into a stylish horizontal navigation bar as described in Chapter 9.

Two New HTML Tags to Learn

HTML's motley assortment of tags doesn't cover the wide range of content you'll probably add to a page. Sure, <code> is great for marking up computer program code, but most folks would find a <recipe> tag handier. Too bad there isn't one. Fortunately, HTML provides two generic tags that let you better identify content, and, in the process, provide "handles" that let you attach CSS styles to different elements on a page.

```
<p>
<strong>
<font color="#0066FF" size="5" face="Verdana,
Arial, Helvetica, sans-serif">Urban Agrarian
Lifestyle</font></strong>
<br />
<font color="#FF3300" size="4" face="Georgia,
Times New Roman, Times, serif">
<em>
<strong>A Revolution in Indoor Agriculture
<br /></strong></em></font>
Lorem ipsum dolor sit amet...</p>
```

Figure 1-2:
Old School, New School. Before CSS, designers had to resort to the <font> tag and other extra HTML to achieve certain visual effects (top). You can achieve the same (and often better) look with a lot less HTML code (bottom.) In addition, by using CSS to format your Web pages, you're free to write HTML that follows the logical structure of the page's content.

The Urban Agrarian Lifestyle
A Revolution in Indoor Agriculture
Lorem ipsum dolor sit amet, consectetuer adipiscing elit, sed diam nonummy nibh euismod tincidunt ut laoreet dolore magna aliquam erat volutpat. Ut wisi enim ad minim veniam, quis nostrud exerci tation ullamcorper suscipit lobortis nisl ut aliquip ex ea commodo consequat. Duis autem vel eum iriure.

```
<h1>The Urban Agrarian Lifestyle</h1>
<h2>A Revolution in Indoor Agriculture</h2>
<p>Lorem ipsum dolor sit amet...</p>
```

GEM IN THE ROUGH

Simple HTML Is Search Engine Friendly

Once you take the mental leap of picturing HTML as the way to structure a document's content, and CSS as the tool for making that content look good, you'll discover additional benefits to writing lean, mean HTML. For one thing, you may boost your search engine ranking as determined by sites like Google, Yahoo, and MSN. That's because when search engines crawl the Web, indexing the content on Web sites, they must go through *all* the HTML on a page to discover the actual content. The old HTML-way of using special tags (like <font>) and lots of tables to design a page, gets in the way of a search engine's job. In fact, some search engines stop reading a page's HTML after a certain number of characters. When you use a lot of HTML just for design, the search engine may miss important content on the page, or even fail to rank it at all.

By contrast, simple, structured HTML is easy for a search engine to read and index. Using an <h1> tag to indicate the most important topic of the page (as opposed to just making the text big and bold) is smart strategy: Search engines give greater weight to the contents inside that tag while indexing the page.

To see Google's suggestions for building search-friendly Web sites, visit *www.google.com/webmasters/guidelines. html*.

You can also hear a podcast of an excellent speech on SEO (search engine optimization) from the 2005 Web Visions conference at *http://www.webvisionsevent.com/podcasts/ WV05_Alan_Knecht.mp3* and read an article by that speaker covering the same topic at: *www.digital-web.com/ articles/seo_and_your_web_site/*.

The <div> tag and the <span> tag are like empty vessels that you fill with content. Since they have no inherent visual properties, you can use CSS to make them look any way you want. The <div> (for *division*) tag indicates any discrete block of content, much like a paragraph or a headline. But you can also use it to surround any number of *other* elements, so you can insert a headline, a bunch of paragraphs, and a bulleted list inside a single <div> block. The <div> tag is a great way to subdivide a page into logical areas, like a banner, footer, sidebar, and so on. Using CSS, you can later position each area to create sophisticated page layouts (a topic that's covered in Part Three of this book).

The <span> tag is used for *inline* elements; that is, words or phrases that appear inside of a larger paragraph or heading. Treat it just like other inline HTML tags such as the <a> tag (for adding a link to some text in a paragraph) or the <strong> tag (for emphasizing a word in a paragraph). For example, you could use a <span> tag to indicate the name of a company, and then use CSS to highlight the name using a different font, color, and so on. Here's an example of those tags in action, complete with a sneak peek of a couple of attributes—*id* and *class*—frequently used to attach styles to parts of a page.

```
<div id="footer">
<p>Copyright 2006, <span class="bizName">CosmoFarmer.com</span></p>
<p>Call customer service at 555-555-5501 for more information</p>
</div>
```

This brief introduction isn't the last you'll see of these tags. They're used frequently in CSS-heavy Web pages, and in this book you'll learn how to use them in combination with CSS to gain creative control over your Web pages (page 47).

HTML to Forget

CSS lets you write simpler HTML for one big reason: You can stop using a bunch of tags and attributes that only make a page better looking. The <font> tag is the most glaring example. Its sole purpose is to add a color, size and font to text. It doesn't do anything to make the structure of the page more understandable.

Here's a list of tags and attributes you can easily replace with CSS:

- Ditch <font> for controlling the display of text. CSS does a much better job with text. (See Chapter 6 for text-formatting techniques.)

- Stop using <b> and <i> to make text bold and italic. CSS can make any tag bold or italic, so you don't need these formatting-specific tags. However, if you want to *really* emphasize a word or phrase, then use the <strong> tag (browsers display <strong> text as bold anyway). For slightly less emphasis, use the <em> tag to emphasize text (browsers italicize content inside this tag).

Note: To italicize a publication's title, the <cite> tag kills two birds with one stone. It puts the title in italics *and* tags it as a cited work for search engines' benefit. This one's a keeper.

- Skip the <table> tag for page layout. Use it only to display tabular information like spreadsheets, schedules, and charts. As you'll see in Part 3 of this book, you can do all your layout with CSS for much less time and code than the table tag tango.

- Eliminate the awkward <body> tag attributes that enhance only the presentation of the content: **background, bgcolor, text, link, alink,** and **vlink** set colors and images for the page, text, and links. CSS gets the job done better (see Chapter 7 and Chapter 8 for CSS equivalents of these attributes). Also trash the browser-specific attributes used to set margins for a page: **leftmargin, topmargin, marginwidth, marginheight.** CSS handles page margins easily (see Chapter 7).

- Don't abuse the <br /> tag. If you grew up using the <br /> tag (
 in HTML) to insert a line break without creating a new paragraph, then you're in for a treat. (Browsers automatically—and sometimes infuriatingly—insert a bit of space between paragraphs, including between headers and <p> tags. In the past, designers used elaborate workarounds to avoid paragraph spacing they didn't want, like replacing a single <p> tag with a bunch of line breaks and using a <font> tag to make the first line of the paragraph *look like* a headline.) Using CSS's margin controls you can easily set the amount of space you want to see between paragraphs, headers and other block-level elements (see page 135).

As a general rule, adding attributes to tags that set colors, borders, background images, or alignment—including attributes that let you format a table's colors, backgrounds, and borders—is pure old-school HTML. So is using alignment properties to position images and center text in paragraphs and table cells. Instead, look to CSS to control text placement (see page 114), borders (page 141), backgrounds (page145), and image alignment (page 172).

Tips to Guide Your Way

It's always good to have a map for getting the lay of the land. If you're still not sure how to use HTML to create well-structured Web pages, then here are a few tips to get you started:

- Use only one <h1> tag per page, and use it to identify the main topic of the page. Think of it as a chapter title: you only put one title per chapter. Using <h1> correctly has the added benefit of helping the page get properly indexed by search engines (see the box on page 19).

- Use headings to indicate the relative importance of text. Again, think outline. When two headings have equal importance in the topic of your page, use the same level header on both. If one is less important or a subtopic of the other, then use the next level header. For example, follow a <h2> with a <h3> tag (see Figure 1-4). In general, it's good to use headings in order and try not to skip heading numbers. For example, don't follow a <h2> tag with a <h5> tag.

Validate Your Web Pages

HTML follows certain rules: For example, the <html> tag wraps around the other tags on a page and the <title> tag needs to appear within the <head> tag. XHTML provides an even more strict set of rules to follow. It's easy to forget these rules, or simply make a typo. Incorrect (or *invalid*, as the geeks would say) HTML causes problems like making your page look different in different Web browsers. More importantly, you can't create valid CSS with invalid HTML. Fortunately, there are tools for checking whether the HTML in your Web pages is correctly written.

The easiest way to check—that is, *validate*—your pages is on the W3C's Web site at *http://validator.w3.org/* (see Figure 1-3).

The W3C, or World Wide Web Consortium, is the organization responsible for determining the standards for many of the technologies and languages of the Web, including HTML, XHTML, and XML.

If the W3C validator finds any errors in your page, it tells you what those errors are. If you use Firefox, you can download an extension that lets you validate a Web page directly in that browser, without having to visit the W3C site. It can even attempt to fix any problems it encounters. You can get the extension here: *http://users.skynet.be/mgueury/mozilla/*. A similar tool is available for the Safari browser as well: *www.zappatic.net/safaritidy/*.

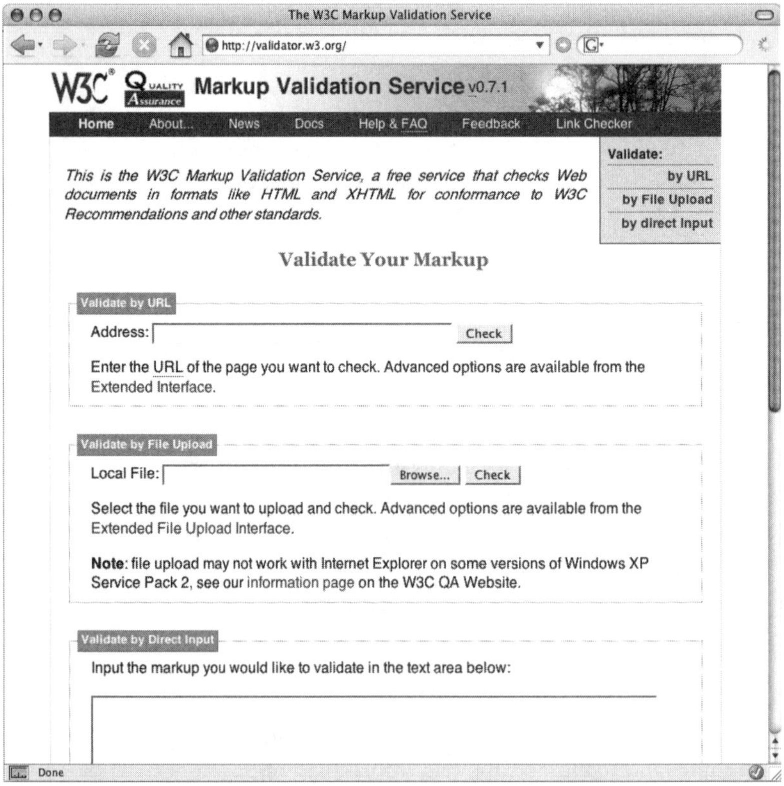

Figure 1-3:
The W3C HTML validator located at http:// validator.w3.org lets you quickly make sure the HTML in a page is sound. You can either point the validator to an already existing page on the Web, upload an HTML file from your computer, or just type or paste the HTML of a Web page into a form box and press the submit button to check it.

- Use the <p> tag for, duh, paragraphs of text.

- Use unordered lists when you've got a list of several related items, such as navigation links, headlines, or a set of tips like these.

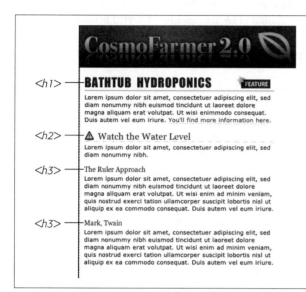

Figure 1-4:
Use the headline tags (<h1>, <h2> and so on) like you would if you were outlining a school report: put them in order of importance, beginning with an <h1> tag, which should shout "Listen up! This is what this whole page is about."

- Use numbered lists to indicate steps in a process, or define the order of a set of items. The tutorials in this book (see page 123) are a good example, as is a list of rankings like "Top 10 Web sites popular with Monks."

- To create a glossary of terms and their definitions or descriptions, use the <dl> (definition list) tag in conjunction with the <dt> (definition term) and <dd> (definition description) tags. (For an example of how to use this combo visit *www.w3schools.com/tags/tryit.asp?filename=tryhtml_list_definition.*)

- If you want to include a quotation like a snippet of text from another Web site, a movie review, or just some wise saying of your grandfather's, try the <blockquote> tag for long passages, or the <q> tag for one-liners.

- Take advantage of obscure tags like the <cite> tag for referencing a book title, newspaper article or Web site, and the <address> tag to identify and supply contact information for the author of a page (great for a copyright notice).

- As explained in full on page 20, steer clear of any tag or attribute aimed just at changing the appearance of a text or image. CSS, as you'll see, can do it all.

- When there just isn't an HTML tag that fits the bill, but you want to identify an element on a page or a bunch of elements on a page so that you can apply a distinctive look, use the <div> and <span> tags (see page 18). You'll get more advice on how to use these in later chapters (for example, page 47).

- Remember to close tags. The opening <p> tag needs its partner in crime (the closing </p> tag), as do all other tags, except the few self-closers like <br /> and <img />.

- Validate your pages with the W3C validator (see Figure 1-3 and the box on page 22). Poorly written or typo-ridden HTML causes many weird browser errors.

The Importance of the Doctype

As discussed in the box on page 22, HTML follows certain rules—these rules are contained in a *Document Type Definition* file, otherwise known as a DTD. A DTD is an XML document that explains what tags, attributes, and values are valid for a particular type of HTML. And for each version of HTML, there's a corresponding DTD. By now you may be asking, "But what's all this got to do with CSS?"

Everything, if you want your Web pages to appear correctly and consistently in Web browsers. You tell a Web browser which version of HTML or XHTML you're using by including what's called a *doctype declaration* at the beginning of a Web page. This doctype declaration is the first line in the HTML file and not only defines what version of HTML you're using (such as HTML 4.01 transitional) but also points to the appropriate DTD file out on the Web. When you mistype the doctype declaration, you can throw most browsers into an altered state called *quirks mode.*

Quirks mode is browser manufacturers' attempts to make their software behave like browsers did circa 1999 (in the Netscape 4 and Internet Explorer 5 days). If a modern browser encounters a page that's missing the correct doctype, then it thinks "Gee, this page must have been written a long time ago, in an HTML editor far, far away. I'll pretend I'm a really old browser and display the page just as one of those buggy old browsers would display it." That's why, without a correct doctype, your lovingly CSS-styled Web pages may not look as they should, according to current standards. If you unwittingly view your Web page in quirks mode when checking it in a browser, you may end up trying to fix display problems that are related to an incorrect doctype and not the incorrect use of HTML or CSS.

Note: For more (read: technical) information on quirks mode, visit *www.quirksmode.org/index.html?/ css/quirksmode.html* and *http://hsivonen.iki.fi/doctype/.*

Fortunately, it's easy to get the doctype correct. All you need to know is what version of HTML you're using. In all likelihood, you're already creating Web pages using HTML 4. You may even have started using XHTML for your Web sites (page 5).

The most popular versions of HTML and XHTML these days are HTML 4.01 Transitional and XHTML 1.0 Transitional. These types of HTML still let you use presentational tags like the <font> tag, thereby providing a *transition* from older HTML to the newer, stricter types of HTML and XHTML. Although it's best not to use these tags at all, they still work in the Transitional versions, so you can phase out these older tags at your own pace. In the strict versions of HTML and XHTML, some older tags don't work at all.

Note: In general, the strict versions of both HTML and XHTML disallow tags and attributes aimed at making a page look good, like the <font> tag and a paragraph's center attribute. They also disallow a number of once-popular properties like a link's target property, which let you make a link open in a new window.

If you're using HTML 4.01 Transitional, type the following doctype declaration at the very beginning of every page you create:

```
<!DOCTYPE HTML PUBLIC "-//W3C//DTD HTML 4.01 Transitional//EN" "http://www.
w3.org/TR/html4/loose.dtd">
```

The doctype declaration for XHTML 1.0 Transitional is similar, but it points to a different DTD. It's also a good idea to add a little code to the opening <html> tag that identifies the language the page is in, like this:

```
<!DOCTYPE html PUBLIC "-//W3C//DTD XHTML 1.0 Transitional//EN" "http://www.
w3.org/TR/xhtml1/DTD/xhtml1-transitional.dtd">
<html xmlns="http://www.w3.org/1999/xhtml" xml:lang="en" lang="en">
```

Note: If you're using frames for your Web pages, then you need to use a doctype intended for framesets. See the W3C site for a list of proper doctypes: *www.w3.org/QA/2002/04/valid-dtd-list.html*.

If this entire discussion is making your head ache and your eyes slowly shut, just make sure you use the proper doctype listed above, and *always* make it the first line of your HTML file (before even the opening <html> tag). If you want a basic template to use when building either HTML or XHTML pages, visit this book's Web site at *www.sawmac.com/css/*. In fact, it's a good idea to have a blank HTML page with the proper doctype somewhere on your computer, so you can make a copy of it whenever you need to create a new Web page. Using an HTML validator, like the one described in the box on page 22, is also a great way to ensure you've typed the doctype declaration correctly.

Note: Most visual Web page tools like Dreamweaver, GoLive, and FrontPage, automatically add a doctype declaration whenever you create a new Web page, and many HTML-savvy text editors have shortcuts for adding doctypes.

Now that your HTML ship is steering in the right direction, it's time to jump into the fun stuff (and the reason you bought this book): Cascading Style Sheets.

Creating Styles and Style Sheets

Even the most complex and beautiful Web sites, like the one in Figure 2-1, start with a single CSS style. As you add multiple styles and style sheets, you can develop fully formed Web sites that inspire designers and amaze visitors. Whether you're a CSS novice or a Style Sheet Samurai, you need to obey a few basic rules about how to create styles and style sheets. In this chapter you'll start at square one, learning the basics of creating and using styles and style sheets.

Tip: Some people learn better by doing rather than reading. If you'd like to try your hand at creating styles and style sheets first and then come back here to read up on what you just did, then turn to page 34 for a hands-on tutorial.

Anatomy of a Style

A single style defining the look of one element on a page is a pretty basic beast. It's essentially just a rule that tells a Web browser how to format something on a Web page—turn a headline blue, draw a red border around a photo, or create a 150-pixel-wide sidebar box to hold a list of links. If a style could talk it would say something like, "Hey Browser, make *this* look like *that*." A style is, in fact, made up of two elements: The Web-page element that the browser formats (the *selector*) and the actual formatting instructions (the *declaration block*). For example, a selector can be a headline, a paragraph of text, a photo, and so on. Declaration blocks can turn that text blue, add a red border around a paragraph, position the photo in the center of the page—the possibilities are endless.

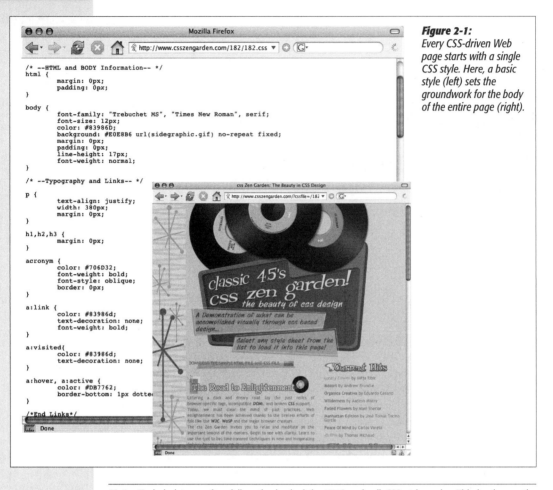

Figure 2-1:
Every CSS-driven Web page starts with a single CSS style. Here, a basic style (left) sets the groundwork for the body of the entire page (right).

Note: Technical types often follow the lead of the W3C and call CSS styles *rules*. This book uses the terms "style" and "rule" interchangeably.

Of course, CSS styles can't communicate in nice clear English like the previous paragraph. They have their own language. For example, to set a standard font color and font size for all paragraphs on a Web page, you'd write the following:

```
p { color: red; font-size: 1.5em; }
```

This style simply says, "Make the text in all paragraphs—marked with <p> tags—red and 1.5 ems tall." (An *em* is a unit of measurement that's based on a browser's normal text size. More on that in Chapter 6.) As Figure 2-2 illustrates, even a simple style like this example contains several elements:

- **Selector.** As described earlier, the selector tells a Web browser which element or elements on a page to style—like a headline, paragraph, image, or link. In Figure 2-2, the selector (p) refers to the <p> tag, which makes Web browsers format all <p> tags using the formatting directions in this style. With the wide range of selectors that CSS offers and a little creativity, you'll master your pages' formatting. (The next chapter covers selectors in depth.)

- **Declaration Block.** The code following the selector includes all the formatting options you want to apply to the selector. The block begins with an opening brace ({) and ends with a closing brace (}).

- **Declaration.** Between the opening and closing braces of a declaration block, you add one or more *declarations*, or formatting instructions. Every declaration has two parts, a *property* and a *value,* and ends with a semicolon.

- **Property.** CSS offers a wide range of formatting options, called *properties.* A property is a word—or a few hyphenated words—indicating a certain style effect. Most properties have straightforward names like *font-size, margin-top,* and *background-color.* For example, the *background-color* property sets—you guessed it—a background color. You'll learn about oodles of CSS properties throughout this book.

Tip: Appendix A has a handy glossary of CSS properties.

- **Value.** Finally, you get to express your creative genius by assigning a *value* to a CSS property—by making a background blue, red, purple, or chartreuse, for example. As upcoming chapters explain, different CSS properties require specific types of values—a color (like *red*, or *#FF0000*), a length (like *18px, 2in,* or *5em*), an URL (like *images/background.gif*), or a specific keyword (like *top, center,* or *bottom*).

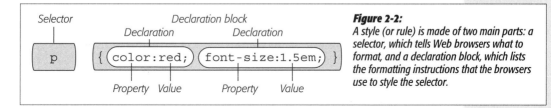

Figure 2-2:
A style (or rule) is made of two main parts: a selector, which tells Web browsers what to format, and a declaration block, which lists the formatting instructions that the browsers use to style the selector.

You don't need to write a style on a single line as pictured in Figure 2-2. Many styles have multiple formatting properties, so you can make them easier to read by breaking them up into multiple lines. For example, you may want to put the selector and opening brace on the first line, each declaration on its own line, and the closing brace by itself on the last line, like so:

```
p {
    color: red;
    font-size: 1.5em;
}
```

It's also helpful to indent properties, with either a tab or a couple of spaces, to visibly separate the selector from the declarations, making it easy to tell which is which. And finally, putting one space between the colon and the property value is optional, but adds to the readability of the style. In fact you can put as much white space between the two as your want. For example *color:red*, *color: red* and *color: red* all work.

Understanding Style Sheets

Of course, a single style won't transform a Web page into a work of art. It may make your paragraphs red, but to infuse your Web sites with great design, you need many different styles. A collection of CSS styles comprises a *style sheet*. A style sheet can be one of two types—*internal* or *external,* depending on where the style information's located: in the Web page itself, or in a separate file linked to the Web page.

Internal or External—How to Choose

Most of the time, external style sheets are the way to go, since they make building Web pages easier and updating Web sites faster. They contain all your style information in a single file. With just a line of code, you attach the external style sheet to an HTML page and completely alter that page's appearance. You can revamp the look of an entire site by editing a single text file: the style sheet.

On the receiving end, external style sheets help Web pages open faster. When you use an external style sheet, your Web pages can contain only basic HTML—no byte-hogging HTML tables or <font> tags, and no internal CSS style code. Furthermore, when a Web browser downloads an external style sheet, it stores the file on your visitor's computer (in a behind-the-scenes folder called a *cache*) for quick access. When your visitor hops to other pages on the site that use the same external style sheet, there's no need for the browser to download the style sheet again. The browser simply pulls the external style sheet from its cache—a significant savings in download time.

Note: When you're working on your Web site and previewing it in a browser, the cache can work against you. See the box on page 35 for a workaround.

Internal Style Sheets

An internal style sheet is a collection of styles that's part of the Web page's code, always between opening and closing HTML <style> tags in the page's <head> portion. Here's an example:

```
<style type="text/css">
h1 {
    color: #FF7643;
```

```
        font-face: Arial;
    }
    p {
        color: red;
        font-size: 1.5em;
    }
    </style>
    </head>
    <body>

    /* The rest of your page follows... */
```

Note: You can place the <style> tag and its styles after the <title> tag in the head of the page, but Web designers usually place them right before the closing </head> tag as shown here.

The <style> tag is HTML, not CSS. But its job is to tell the Web browser that the information contained within the tags is CSS code and not HTML. Creating an internal style sheet's as simple as typing one or more styles between the <style> tags.

Internal style sheets are easy to add to a Web page, and provide an immediate visual boost to your HTML. But they aren't the most efficient method for designing an entire Web site composed of many Web pages. For one thing, you need to copy and paste the internal style sheet into each page of your site—a time consuming chore that adds bandwidth-hogging code to each page.

But internal style sheets are even more of a hassle when you want to update the look of a site. For example, say you want to change the <h1> tag, which you originally decided should appear as large, green, bold type. But now you want small, blue type using the Courier type face. Using internal style sheets, you'd need to edit *every* page. Who has that kind of time? Fortunately, there's a simple solution to this dilemma—external style sheets.

Note: It's also possible (though rarely advisable) to add styling information to an individual HTML tag without using a style sheet. The tutorial on page 35 shows you how to perform that maneuver using an *inline* style.

External Style Sheets

An external style sheet is nothing more than a text file containing all your CSS rules. It never contains any HTML code—so don't include the <style> tag—and always ends with the extension .css. You can name the file whatever you like, but it pays to be descriptive. Use *global.css,* for example, to indicate a style sheet used by every page on the site, or use *form.css* to name a file containing styles used to make a Web form look good.

Validate Your CSS

Just as you should make sure you've correctly written the HTML in your Web pages using the W3C HTML validator (see the box on page 22), you should also check your CSS code to make sure it's kosher. The W3C provides an online tool for CSS checking as well: *http://jigsaw.w3.org/css-validator/*. It operates just like the HTML validator: You can type the URL of a Web page (or even just the address to an external CSS file), upload a CSS file, or copy and paste CSS code into a Web form and submit it for validation.

It's easy to make a typo when writing CSS, and one small mistake can throw all of your carefully planned designs out of whack. When your CSS-infused Web page doesn't look as you expect, a simple CSS error may be the cause. The W3C CSS Validator's a good first stop, when troubleshooting your designs.

You can also make a quick check using Firefox. Load the page that has the CSS you want to check and choose Tools → JavaScript Console. Click the errors button and you'll see listed any CSS code that Firefox doesn't understand.

Tip: If you have a page with an internal style sheet, but want to use an external style sheet, then just cut all of the code between the <style> tags (without the tags themselves). Then create a new text file, and paste the CSS into the file. Save the file with a .css extension–*global.css,* for example–and link it to your page, using one of the techniques described next.

Once you create an external style sheet, you must connect it to the Web page you wish to format. You can attach a style sheet to a Web page using HTML's <link> tag or CSS's own @import directive—a command that basically does the same thing as the link tag. All current Web browsers treat these two techniques the same, and both let you attach style sheets to a Web page, so choosing one is mostly a matter of preference. (For the one exception, see the box below.)

Note: The @import directive can do one thing the <link> tag can't: attach external style sheets to an external style sheet. This advanced technique is discussed on page 388.

Too Old to @Import

You can link external style sheets to Web pages using either an HTML <link> tag or the CSS @import directive. The only time it makes a difference is when your visitors use certain older browsers—notably Netscape Navigator 4.

This very old browser usually mangles CSS, even to the point of rendering Web pages unreadable.

Navigator 4 also doesn't understand the @import directive and ignores any style sheets linked this way—a fact that you can use to your advantage. If you always use the @import method, then Navigator 4 doesn't try to display the page using those CSS styles. Your Web pages don't look as good for those visitors, but at least they're readable.

Linking a Style Sheet Using HTML

One method of adding an external style sheet to a Web page is to use the HTML <link> tag. You write the tag slightly differently depending on whether you're using HTML or XHTML. For example, here's HTML:

```
<link rel="stylesheet" type="text/css" href="css/global.css">
```

Here's XHTML:

```
<link rel="stylesheet" type="text/css" href="css/global.css" />
```

The only difference is how you end the tag. The link tag's an empty element, since it has *only* an opening tag and no matching, closing </link> tag. In XHTML, you need to add a closing slash (like this: />) to terminate the tag; HTML doesn't require the extra slash.

Otherwise, the link tag's the same in HTML and XHTML and requires three attributes:

- **rel** indicates the type of link—in this case, a link to a style sheet.

- **type** lets the browser know what kind of data to expect—a text file, containing CSS.

- **href** points to the location of the external CSS file on the site. The value of this property is an URL, and works the same as the *src* attribute you use when adding an image to a page, or the *href* attribute of a link pointing to another page.

Tip: You can attach multiple style sheets to a Web page by adding multiple <link> tags, each pointing to a different style sheet file. This technique's a great way to organize your CSS styles, as you can see in Chapter 14 (page 388).

Linking a Style Sheet Using CSS

CSS includes a built-in way to add external style sheets—the @import directive. You add the directive inside of an HTML <style> tag, like so:

```
<style type="text/css">
@import url(css/global.css);
</style>
```

Unlike HTML's <link> tag, @import is part of the CSS language and has some definite un-HTML-like qualities:

- To make the connection to the external CSS file, you use *url* instead of *href*, and enclose the path in parentheses. So in this example, *css/global.css* is the path to the external CSS file. Quotes around the URL are optional, so *url(css/global.css)* and *url("css/global.css")* both work.

Note: Not only does quoting the path of an URL in CSS add a couple of extra characters to the file, Internet Explorer 5 for the Mac has trouble understanding URLs with quotes.

• As with the <link> tag, you can include multiple external style sheets using more than one @import:

```
<style type="text/css">
@import url(css/global.css);
@import url(css/forms.css);
</style>
```

• You can add regular CSS styles after the @import directives if, for example, you want to create a rule that applies just to that one page, but take advantage of the same design rules used throughout the site to format the rest of the page.

Note: You'll learn how rules interact and how you can create a rule that overrides other rules on page 89. You can even create an external CSS file that contains only @import directives linking to *other* external style sheets; a technique often used to help organize your styles (see page 388).

Here's an example:

```
<style type="text/css">
@import url(css/global.css);
@import url(css/forms.css);
p { color:red; }
</style>
```

Technically, you should place all the @import lines *before* any CSS rules, as shown here, but it's okay if you forget. Web browsers are supposed to ignore any style sheets you import after a CSS rule, but all current Web browsers ignore that restriction.

Tutorial: Creating Your First Styles

The rest of this chapter takes you through the basic steps for adding inline styles, writing CSS rules, and creating internal and external style sheets. As you work through this book, you'll help design a fictitious Web site called CosmoFarmer.com, creating various aspects of its design, and eventually styling entire pages of the site. To get started, you need to download the tutorial files located on the book's companion Web site at *www.sawmac.com/css/*. Click the tutorial link and download the Zip archive containing the files (detailed instructions for unzipping the files are on the Web site as well). Each chapter's files are in a separate folder, named *chapter_2, chapter_3,* and so on.

Next, you need to launch your favorite Web page editing software, whether it's a simple text editor like Notepad or TextEdit, or a visually oriented program like Dreamweaver or Microsoft Expression Web Designer (for information on selecting an editor, see page 7).

CSS: The Missing Manual

WORKAROUND WORKSHOP

Don't Get Caught in the Cache

A browser's cache is a great speed-boost for Web surfers. Whenever the cache downloads and stores a frequently used file—like an external CSS file or an image—it saves precious moments traveling the relatively sluggish highways of the Internet. Instead of redownloading the next time it needs the same file, the browser can go straight to the new stuff—like a yet-to-be-viewed page or graphic.

But what's good for your visitors isn't always good for you. Because the Web browser caches and recalls downloaded external CSS files, you can often get tripped up as you work on a site design. Say you're working on a page that uses an external style sheet, and you preview the page in a browser. Something doesn't look quite right, so you return to your Web editor and change the external CSS file. When you return to the Web browser and reload the page, the change you just made doesn't appear! You've just been caught by the cache. When you reload a Web page, browsers don't always reload the external style sheet, so you may not be seeing the latest and greatest version of your styles.

You have two ways around this snafu: turn off the cache or force the browser to reload everything.

In most browsers you can *force reload* a page (which also reloads all linked files) by pressing the Ctrl (⌘) key and pressing the browser's Reload button; Ctrl+F5 also works on Windows for Internet Explorer; and Ctrl+Shift+R (⌘-Shift-R) is Firefox's keyboard shortcut.

You can also completely turn off the cache. In Internet Explorer, choose Tools → Internet Options → General tab; in the Temporary Internet Files section, click Settings. Make sure the "Check for newer versions of stored pages" option's set to "Every visit to the page." Click OK twice to close the Internet Options window. In Firefox, choose Tools → Options (on Windows), or Firefox → Preferences (Mac) to open Firefox's Preferences window; click the Privacy button, then the Cache tab, and then set the cache disk space to 0.

For Safari on the Mac, download the free Safari Enhancer at *www.versiontracker.com/dyn/moreinfo/macosx/17776*.

Turning off the cache can drastically slow your regular Web surfing activity, so make sure you turn it back on once you're done editing your CSS files.

Note: If you use Dreamweaver, then check out Appendix B to learn how to use that program to create styles and style sheets. Dreamweaver, along with many other HTML-editing programs, also lets you work on the raw HTML code by switching to Code View: Give that a shot for this tutorial.

Creating an Inline Style

When you type a CSS rule (just like the ones described on page 27) directly into a page's HTML, you're creating an *inline* style. Inline styles offer none of the time- and bandwidth-saving benefits of style sheets, so the pros hardly ever use them. Still, in a pinch, if you absolutely must change the styling on a single element on a single page, then you may want to resort to an inline style. And if you do, you at least want the style to work properly. The important thing is to carefully place the style within the tag you want to format. Here's an example that shows you exactly how to do it:

1. **In your Web page editing program, open the file *chapter_2 → basic.html*.**

    This simple-but-elegant XHTML file contains a couple of different headings, a paragraph, an unordered list, and a copyright notice inside an <address> tag. You'll start by creating an inline style for the <h1> tag.

---

2. **Click inside the opening <h1> tag and type** *style="color: red;"*.

The tag should look like this:

```
<h1 style="color: red;">
```

The style attribute is HTML, not CSS so you use the equals sign after it and enclose all of the CSS code inside quotes. Only the stuff inside the quotes is CSS. In this case, you've added a property named color—which affects the color of text—and you've set that property to red (page 102 talks more about coloring text). The colon separates the property name from the property value that you want. Next you'll check the results in a Web browser.

3. **Open the** *basic.html* **page in a Web browser.**

For example, choose File → Open File, depending on your browser. Many HTML editors also include a "Preview in Browser" function, which, with a simple keyboard shortcut, or menu option, opens the page in a Web browser. It's worth checking your program's manual to see if it includes this timesaving feature.

When you view the page in a browser, the headline is now red. Inline styles can include more than one CSS property. You'll add another property next.

4. **Return to your HTML editor, click after the semicolon following the word "red" and type** *font-size: 4em;*.

The semicolon separates two different property settings. The <h1> tag should look like this:

```
<h1 style="color: red;font-size: 4em;">
```

5. **Preview the page in a Web browser. For example, click your browser window's Reload button (but make sure you've saved the XHTML file first.).**

The headline's now massive in size. And, you've had a taste of how labor-intensive inline styles are. Making all the <h1> headings on a page look like this one could take days of typing and add acres of HTML code.

6. **Return to your page editor and delete the entire style property, which returns the heading tag back to its normal <h1>.**

Next, you'll create a style sheet within a Web page.

Creating an Internal Style Sheet

A better approach than inline styles is using a style sheet that contains multiple CSS rules to control multiple elements of a page. In this section, you'll create a style that affects all top-level headings in one swoop. This single rule automatically formats every <h1> tag on the page.

1. **With the file *basic.html* open in your text editor, click directly after the closing </title> tag. Then hit Return and type *<style type="text/css">*.**

   The HTML should now look like the following (the stuff you've added is in bold):

   ```
   <title>Basic Web Page</title>
   <style type="text/css">
   </head>
   ```

   The opening <style> tag marks the beginning of the style sheet; you'll follow this tag with a CSS selector that marks the beginning of your first style.

2. **Press the Enter or Return key, and type *h1 {*.**

   The h1 indicates the tag to which the Web browser should apply the upcoming style.

   The weird bracket thingy after the h1 is called an opening brace, and it marks the beginning of the CSS properties for this style. In other words, it says, "the fun stuff comes right after me."

3. **Press Enter (Return) to create a new line, hit the Tab key, and type *color :red;*.**

   You've typed the same style property as the inline version—*color*—and set it to *red*. As explained back on page 29, the final semicolon marks the end of the property declaration.

Note: Technically, you don't have to put the style property on its own line, but it's a good idea. With one property per line, it's a lot easier to quickly scan a style sheet and see all the properties for each style. Also, the tab's another helpful visual organizing technique (you can also insert a few spaces instead). The indentation makes it easy to discern all of your rules at a glance, since the selectors (like h1 here) line up along the left edge, with the properties spaced a bit out of the way.

---

4. **Press Enter (Return) again and add four additional properties, like so:**

   ```
   font-size: 2em;
   font-family: Arial, sans-serif;
   margin: 0;
   border-bottom: 2px dashed black;
   ```

   Each of these properties adds a different visual effect to the headline. The first two assign a size and font to the text, the third removes space from the around the headline, and the last property adds a line underneath the headline. Part Two covers all these properties in detail.

   Your work on this style is complete, so next you'll indicate its end.

5. **Press Enter (Return) and type a single closing brace on the last line: *}*.**

   As the partner of the opening brace you typed in step 2, this brace's job is to tell the Web browser "here ends this particular CSS rule." All you need to wrap up the style sheet is a closing tag.

6. **Press Enter (Return) and type** </*style*>.

The closing </style> tag marks the end of the style sheet. Congratulations—you've just created an internal style sheet. The code in your page should now look like so:

```
<title>Basic Web Page</title>
<style type="text/css">
h1 {
    color: red;
    font-size: 2em;
    font-family: Arial, sans-serif;
    margin: 0;
    border-bottom: 2px dashed black;
}
</style>
</head>
```

7. **Preview the page in a Web browser.**

You can preview the page by opening it in a Web browser as described in step 3 on page 36, or, if the page is still open in a browser window, then just click the Reload button. In either case, the page should now look like Figure 2-3.

Next you'll add another style.

Note: Always remember to add the closing </style> tag at the end of an internal style sheet. When you don't, a Web browser displays the CSS style code followed by a completely unformatted Web page—or no Web page at all.

---

8. **Back in your text editing program, click after the closing brace of the h1 style you just created, press Return, and then add the following rule:**

```
p {
    color: #003366;
    font-size: .9em;
    line-height: 150%;
    margin-top: 0;
}
```

This rule formats every paragraph on the page. Don't worry too much right now about what each of these CSS properties is doing. Later chapters cover these properties in depth.

9. **Preview the page in a browser.**

The page is starting to shape up. You can see what stylistic direction the page is headed in. To finish the page, add rules to format the Heading 2, unordered list, and copyright notice.

CSS: The Missing Manual

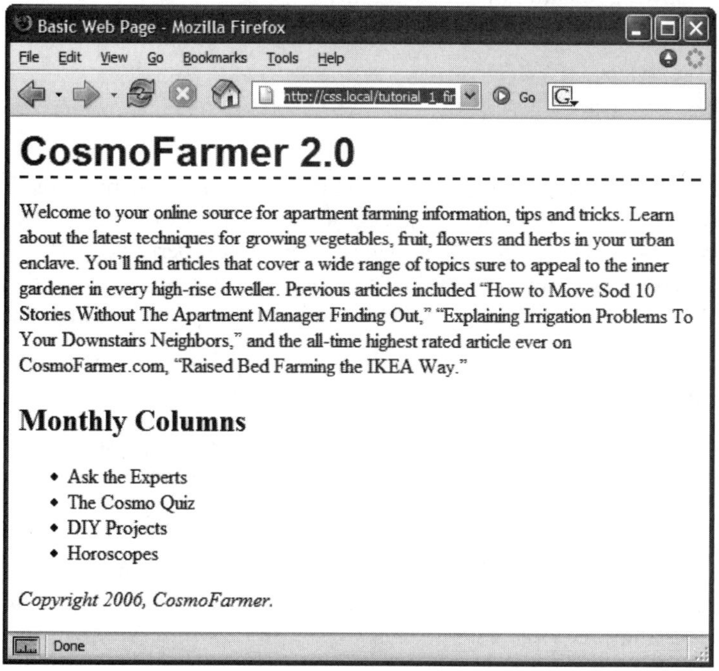

Figure 2-3:
CSS easily formats text in creative ways, letting you change fonts, text colors, font sizes, and even adding decorative borders and underlines.

The process you've just worked through is CSS in a nutshell: Start with an HTML page, add a style sheet, and create CSS rules to make the page look great. In the next part of this tutorial, you'll see how to work more efficiently using external style sheets.

Creating an External Style Sheet

Since it groups all of your styles at the top of the page, an internal style sheet's a lot easier to create and maintain than the inline style you created a few pages ago. Also, an internal style sheet lets you format any number of instances of a tag on a page, like the <h1> tag by typing one simple rule. But an external style sheet's even better—it can store all of the styles for an *entire Web site*. Editing one style in the external style sheet updates the whole site. In this section, you'll take the styles you created in the previous section and put them in an external style sheet.

1. **In your text editing program, create a new file and save it as** *global.css* **in the same folder as the Web page you've been working on.**

   External style sheet files end with the extension .css. The file name *global.css* indicates that the styles contained in the file apply throughout the site. (But you can use any file name you like, as long as it ends with the .css extension.)

   Start by adding a new style to the style sheet.

2. Type the following rule into the *global.css* file:

```
body {
    background-image: url(images/bg.jpg);
    background-repeat: repeat-x;
}
```

This rule applies to the body tag—the tag that holds all the content visible in a Web browser window—and adds a background image to the page. Unlike a similar property in HTML, the CSS background-image property can display the graphic in many different ways—in this case, tiled horizontally across the top of the page. You can read more about background image properties on page 172.

Instead of recreating the work you did earlier, just copy the styles you created in the previous section and paste them into this style sheet.

3. **Open the *basic.html* page that you've been working on and copy all of the text *inside* the <style> tags. (Don't copy the <style> tags themselves.)**

Copy the style information the same way you'd copy any text. For example, choose Edit → Copy or press Ctrl-C (⌘-C).

4. **In the empty *global.css* file, paste the style information by selecting Edit → Paste, or pressing Ctrl-V (⌘-V).**

An external style sheet never contains any HTML—that's why you didn't copy the <style> tags.

5. **Save and close *global.css*.**

Now you just need to clean up your old file and link the new style sheet to it.

6. **Return to the *basic.html* file in your text editor and delete the <style> tags *and* all of the CSS rules you typed in earlier.**

You no longer need these styles, since they're in the external style sheet you're about to attach.

7. **In the space where the styles used to be (between the closing </title> tag and the opening <body> tag) type the following:**

```
<link href="global.css" rel="stylesheet" type="text/css" />
```

The <link> tag is one way to attach a style sheet to a page; another option is the CSS @import directive, as discussed on page 33. The link tag specifies the location of the external style sheet. (You can read up on the two other attributes—*rel* and *type*—on page 33.)

Note: In this example, the style sheet file's in the same folder as the Web page. If it were in a different folder from the page, then you'd use a *document-* or root-*relative* path to indicate where the file is. The routine's the same as when you link to any Web page. (For a brief primer on document- and root-relative links visit: *www.communitymx.com/content/article.cfm?cid=230AD*.)

---

8. **Save the file and preview it in a Web browser.**

   It should look the same as in step 9 on page 38, with the one addition of a groovy graphic running along the top edge of the page (thanks to the CSS you added in step 2). The CSS rules in this external style sheet are the same as the ones from the internal style sheet; they're just located in a different place. To demonstrate how useful it can be to keep your styles in their own external file, you'll attach the style sheet to another Web page.

Note: If the Web page doesn't have any formatting (for example, the CosmoFarmer heading isn't red), then you've probably mistyped the code from step 6, or saved the *global.css* file in a folder other than the one where the *basic.html* file is. In this case, just move the *global.css* into the same folder.

---

9. **Open the file *chapter_2 → linked_page.html.***

   This lead story from CosmoFarmer.com contains some of the same HTML tags—h1, h2, p, and so on—as the other Web page you've been working on.

10. **Click after the closing </title> tag and press Enter (Return).**

    You'll now link to the style sheet.

11. **Type the same <link> tag you did in step 6 above.**

    The Web page code should look like this (the code you just typed appears in bold):

    ```
    <title>Explaining Irrigation Problems To Your Downstairs Neighbors</title>
    <link href="global.css" rel="stylesheet" type="text/css" />
    </head>
    ```

12. **Save the page and preview it in a Web browser.**

    Ta-da! Just one line of code added to the Web page is enough to instantly transform its appearance. To demonstrate how easy it is to update an external style sheet, you'll do so by editing one style and adding another.

13. **Open the *global.css* file and add the CSS declaration *margin-left: 25px;* at the end of the p style.**

    The code should look like this (the bold text is what you've just added):

    ```
    p {
        color: #003366;
        font-size: .9em;
        line-height: 150%;
        margin-top: 0;
        margin-left: 25px;
    }
    ```

    Last but not least, create a new rule for the h2 tag.

14. Click at the end of the p style's closing }, press Enter (Return), and add the following rule:

```
h2 {
    color: #FFFFCC;
    margin-bottom: 0;
    padding: 5px 0px 3px 25px;
    background-color: #999999;
}
```

Most of these CSS properties you've encountered already. You'll learn about padding and backgrounds in Chapter 7.

15. Save the file *global.css* and preview both the *basic.html* and *linked_page.html* files in a Web browser. Figure 2-4 shows the completed *linked_page.html* file.

Notice that the appearance of both pages changes, based on the simple edits you made to the CSS file. Close your eyes and imagine that your Web site has a thousand pages. Aaaahhhhhhh, the power.

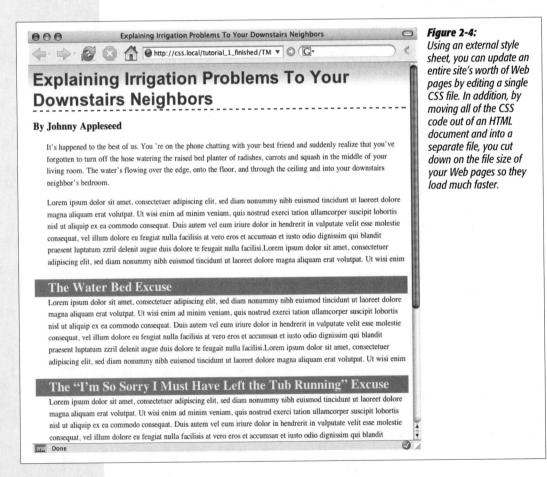

Figure 2-4:
Using an external style sheet, you can update an entire site's worth of Web pages by editing a single CSS file. In addition, by moving all of the CSS code out of an HTML document and into a separate file, you cut down on the file size of your Web pages so they load much faster.

Selector Basics: Identifying What to Style

Every CSS style has two basic parts: a selector and a declaration block. (And if that's news to you, go back and read the previous chapter.) The declaration block carries the formatting properties—text color, font size, and so on—but that's just the pretty stuff. The magic of CSS lies in those first few characters at the beginning of every rule—the selector. By telling CSS *what* you want it to format (see Figure 3-1), the selector gives you full control of your page's appearance. If you're into sweeping generalizations, then you can use a selector that applies to many elements on a page at once. But if you're a little more detail oriented (OK, a *lot* more), other selectors let you single out one specific item or a collection of similar items. CSS selectors give you a lot of power: This chapter shows you how to use them.

```
h1 {
    font-family: Arial, sans-serif;
    color: #CCCCFF;
}
```

Figure 3-1:
The first part of a style, the selector, indicates the element or elements of a page to format. In this case, h1 stands for "every heading 1 or <h1> tag on this page."

Note: If you'd rather get some hands-on experience before studying the ins and outs of CSS selectors, then jump to the tutorial on page 61.

Tag Selectors: Page-Wide Styling

Tag selectors—sometimes called *type* selectors—are extremely efficient styling tools, since they apply to every occurrence of an HTML tag on a Web page. With them, you can make sweeping design changes to a page with very little effort. For example, when you want to format every paragraph of text on a page using the same font, color, and size, you merely create a style using *p* (as in the <p> tag) as the selector. In essence, a tag selector redefines how a browser displays a particular tag.

Prior to CSS, in order to format text, you had to wrap that text in a <font> tag. To add the same look to every paragraph on a page, you often had to use the <font> tag multiple times. This process was a lot of work, and required a lot of HTML, making pages slower to download and more time-consuming to update. With tag selectors you don't actually have to do anything to the HTML—just create the CSS rule, and let the browser do the rest.

Tag selectors are easy to spot in a CSS rule, since they bear the exact same name as the tag they style—*p, h1, table, img,* and so on. For example, in Figure 3-2, the *h2* selector (top) applies some font styling to all <h2> tags on a Web page (bottom).

```
h2 {
    font-family:"Century Gothic", "Gill Sans", sans-serif;
    color:#000000;
    margin-bottom:0;
}
```

Figure 3-2:
A tag selector affects every instance of the tag on the page. This page has three <h2> tags (indicated by the black labels at the left edge of the browser window). A single CSS style with a selector of h2 controls the presentation of every <h2> tag on the page.

Note: As Figure 3-2 makes clear, tag selectors don't get the less than (<) and greater than (>) symbols that surround HTML tags. So when you're writing a rule for the *<p>* tag, for example, just type the tag's name—*p*.

CSS: THE MISSING MANUAL

Tag selectors have their downsides, however. What if you want *some* paragraphs to look different from other paragraphs? A simple tag selector won't do, since it doesn't provide enough information for a Web browser to identify the difference between the <p> tags you want to highlight in purple, bold, and large type from the <p> tags you want to leave with normal, black text. Fortunately, CSS provides just such a tool—*class selectors*, described next.

Class Selectors: Pinpoint Control

When you don't want *every* instance of a paragraph or heading tag to get the same styling, CSS lets you create a *class* selector with a name of your choosing, and then selectively apply it to certain bits of HTML on your page. For example, you can create a class style named *.copyright* and then apply it only to a paragraph containing copyright information, without affecting any other paragraphs.

Class selectors also let you pinpoint an exact element on a page, regardless of its tag. Say you want to format a word or two inside of a paragraph, for example. In this case, you don't want the entire <p> tag affected, just a single phrase inside it, so you can use a class selector to indicate just those words. You can even use a class selector to apply the same formatting to multiple elements that have different HTML tags. For example, you can give one paragraph and one second-level heading the same styling—perhaps a color and a font that you've selected to highlight special information, as shown in Figure 3-3. Unlike tag selectors which limit you to the existing HTML tags on the page, you can create as many class selectors as you like and put them anywhere you want.

Note: When you want to apply a class selector to just a few words contained inside another tag (like the middle paragraph in Figure 3-3), you need a little help from the <span> tag (page 18). See the box on page 47 for more detail.

You've probably noticed the period that starts every class selector's name—such as *.copyright* and *.special*. It's one of a few rules to keep in mind when naming a class:

- All class selector names must begin with a period. That's how Web browsers spot a class selector in the style sheet.

- CSS permits only letters, numbers, hyphens, and underscores in class names.

- After the period, the name must always start with a *letter*. For example, *.9lives* isn't a valid class name, but *.crazy8* is. You can have classes named *.copy-right* and *.banner_image,* but not *.-bad* or *._as_bad.*

- Class names are case sensitive. For example, CSS considers *.SIDEBAR* and *.sidebar* two different classes.

```
.special {
    color:#FF0000;
    font-family:"Monotype Corsiva";
}
```

Figure 3-3:
Class selectors let you make highly targeted design changes. For example, you can stylize one instance of an <h2> heading ("Wet Sod is Heavy Sod"). The class selector .special tells the browser to apply the style to just that single <h2> tag. Once you've created a class selector, you can use it on other tags, like the top paragraph on this page.

class="special"

Apart from the name, you create class styles exactly like tag styles. After the class name, simply slap on a declaration block containing all of the styling you desire:

```
.special {
color:#FF0000;
font-family:"Monotype Corsiva";
}
```

Because tag styles apply across the board to all tags on a Web page, you merely have to define them in the head of the page: the HTML tags that make them work are already in place. The extra freedom you get with class styles, though, comes with a little more work. Using class selectors is a two-step process. After you create a class rule, you must then indicate *where* you want to apply that formatting. To do so, you add a class attribute to the HTML tag you wish to style.

Say you create a class *.special* that you'll use to highlight particular page elements. To add this style to a paragraph, add a class attribute to the <p> tag, like so:

```
<p class="special">
```

Note: In the HTML, as part of the class attribute, you *don't* put a period before the class name; the period's only required for the class selector name in a style sheet.

When a Web browser encounters this tag, it knows to apply the formatting rules contained in the .*special* style to the paragraph. You can also apply class formatting to only part of a paragraph or heading by adding a <span> tag as described in the box below.

Once you create a class style, you can apply it to just about any tag on the page. Although they give you almost limitless formatting possibilities, classes aren't always the right tool when using CSS for laying out a page. Enter the ID selector, which lets you designate a formatting rule for one specific use on a page, as described next.

GEM IN THE ROUGH

Divs and Spans

Chapter 1 introduced you to <div> and <span>, two generic HTML tags that you can bend to your CSS wishes. When there's no HTML tag that exactly delineates where you want to put a class or ID style you've created, use a <div> or <span> to fill in the gaps.

The div tag identifies a logical *division* of the page like a banner, navigation bar, sidebar, or footer. You can also use it to surround any element that takes up a chunk of the page, including headings, bulleted lists, or paragraphs. (Programmer types call these *block-level* elements because they form a complete "block" of content, with line breaks before and after them.) The <div> tag works just like a paragraph tag: type the opening <div>, add some text, a photo, or some other content inside it, and then end it with the closing </div>.

The div tag has the unique ability to contain *several* block-level elements, making it a great way to group tags that are logically related such as the logo and navigation bar in a page's banner, or a series of news stories that compose a sidebar. Once grouped in this way, you can apply specific formatting to just the tags inside the particular div, or move the entire div-tagged chunk of content into a particular area, such as the right side of the browser window (CSS can help you control the visual layout of your pages in this manner as described in Part 3 of this book).

For example, say you added a photo to a Web page; the photo also has a caption that accompanies it. You could wrap a <div> tag (with a class applied to it) around the photo and the caption to group both elements together:

```
<div class="photo">
<img src="holidays.jpg"
 alt="Penguins getting frisky"/>
<p>Mom, dad and me on our yearly trip
 to Antarctica.</p>
</div>
```

Depending on what you put in the declaration block, the .*photo* class can add a decorative border, background color, and so on, to both photo and caption. Part 3 of this book shows you even more powerful ways to use <div> tags—including nested divs.

A <span> tag, on the other hand, lets you apply a class or ID style to just *part* of a tag. You can place <span> tags around individual words and phrases (often called *inline* elements) within paragraphs to format them independently. Here, a class called .*companyName* styles the inline elements "CosmoFarmer.com," "Disney," and "ESPN":

```
<p>Welcome to <span class="companyName">
CosmoFarmer.com</span>, the parent
company of such well-known corporations
as <span class="companyName">Disney
</span> and <span class="companyName">
ESPN</span>...well, not really.</p>
```

ID Selectors: Specific Page Elements

CSS reserves the ID selector for *identifying* a unique part of a page like a banner, navigation bar, or the main content area. Just like a class selector, you create an ID by giving it a name in CSS and then you apply it by adding the ID to your page's HTML code. So what's the difference? As explained in the box on page 49, ID selectors have some specific uses in JavaScript-based or very lengthy Web pages. Otherwise, compelling reasons to use IDs over classes are few.

When deciding whether to use a class or an ID, follow these rules of thumb:

- To use a style several times on a page, you **must use classes**. For example, when you have more than one photo on your page, use a class selector to apply styling—like a border—to each of them.

- Use IDs to identify sections that occur only once per page. CSS-based layouts often rely on ID selectors to identify the unique parts of a Web page, like a sidebar or footer. Part 3 shows you how to use this technique.

- Consider using an ID selector to sidestep style conflicts, since Web browsers give ID selectors priority over class selectors. For example, when a browser encounters two styles that apply to the same tag but specify different background colors—the ID's background color wins. (See page 96 for more on this topic.)

Note: Although you should apply only a single ID to a single HTML tag, a browser won't blow up or set off alarm bells if you apply the same ID to two or more tags on the same page. In fact, most browsers will apply the CSS from an ID style correctly in this case. However, your HTML won't validate (see page 22) and your Web designer friends may stop talking to you.

Should you decide to use an ID selector, creating one is easy. Just as a period indicates the name of a class selector, a pound or hash symbol identifies an ID style. Otherwise, follow the exact same naming rules used for classes (page 45). This example provides background color and sizing:

```
#banner {
 background: #CC0000;
 height: 300px;
 width: 720px;
}
```

Applying IDs in HTML is similar to applying classes, but uses a different attribute named, logically enough, *id*. For example, to indicate that the last paragraph of a page is that page's one and only copyright notice, you can create an ID style named *#copyright* and add it to that paragraph's tag:

```
<p id="copyright">
```

Note: As with class styles, you use the # symbol only when naming the style in the style sheet. You leave the # off when using the ID's name as part of an HTML tag: <div id="banner">.

Proper IDs

ID selectors have a few powers that class selectors lack. These benefits actually have nothing to do with CSS, so you may never need an ID. But if you're curious:

- JavaScript programming utilizes ID selectors to locate and manipulate parts of a page. For example, programmers often apply an ID to a form element like a text box for collecting a visitor's name. The ID lets JavaScript access that form element and work its magic—like making sure the field isn't empty when the visitor clicks Submit.

- IDs also let you link to a specific part of a page, making long Web pages quicker to navigate. If you have an alphabetic glossary of terms, then you can use an ID selector to create links to the letters of the alphabet. When your visitors click "R", they jump immediately to all the "R" words on the page. First, create an ID for each letter of the alphabet (*#R*). When you create the link in HTML, add the pound symbol and the ID name to the end of the URL followed by the ID name—*index.html#R*. This link points directly to an element with the ID of *#R* on the page *index. html.* (When used this way, the ID behaves just like a named anchor—<a name="section1">Section 1</ a>—in HTML.)

Styling Tags Within Tags

Choosing whether to style your page with tag selectors or class selectors is a tradeoff. Tag selectors are fast and easy, but they make every occurrence of a tag look the same, which is fine—if you want every <h1> on your page to look exactly like all the rest. Class and ID selectors give you the flexibility to style individual page elements independently, but creating a new CSS style just to change one heading's font takes a heck of a lot more work—and HTML code. What you need is a way to combine the ease of tag selectors with the precision of classes and IDs. CSS has just the thing—*descendent selectors.*

You use descendent selectors to format a whole bunch of tags in a similar manner (just like tag selectors), but only when they're in a particular part of a Web page. It's like saying, "Hey you <a> tags in the navigation bar, listen up. I've got some formatting for you. All you other <a> tags, just move along; there's nothing to see here."

Descendent selectors let you format a tag based on its relationship to other tags. To understand how it works, you need to delve a little bit more deeply into HTML. On the bright side, the concepts underlying descendent selectors help you understand several other selector types, too, as discussed later in this chapter.

Note: Descendent selectors were called *contextual selectors* in CSS 1.

The HTML Family Tree

The HTML that forms any Web page is akin to a family tree, where the HTML tags represent various family members. The first HTML tag you use on a page—the <html> tag—is like the grandpappy of all other tags. The <html> tag surrounds the <head> tag and the <body> tag, which makes <html> the *ancestor* of both. Similarly, a tag inside of another tag is a *descendent*. The <title> tag in the following example is the <head> tag's descendent:

```
<html>
 <head>
  <title>A Simple Document</title>
 </head>
 <body>
  <h1>Header</h1>
  <p>A paragraph of <strong>important</strong>text.</p>
 </body>
</html>
```

You can turn the above HTML code into a diagram, like Figure 3-4, showing the relationships between the page's tags. First there's the <html> tag; it's divided into two sections represented by the <head> and <body> tags. Those two tags contain other tags that in turn may contain other tags. By seeing which tags appear inside which other tags, you can diagram any Web page.

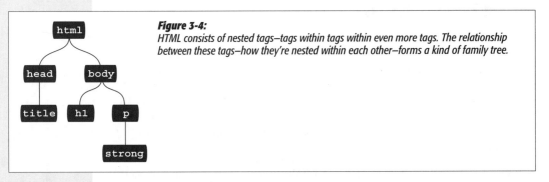

Figure 3-4:
HTML consists of nested tags–tags within tags within even more tags. The relationship between these tags–how they're nested within each other–forms a kind of family tree.

Tree diagrams help you figure out how CSS sees the relationship of one element on a page to another. Many of the selectors in this chapter, including descendent selectors, rely on these relationships. The most important relationships are:

- **Ancestor.** As explained at the beginning of this chapter, an HTML tag that wraps around another tag is its ancestor. In Figure 3-4, the <html> tag is an ancestor of all other tags, while the <body> tag is an ancestor for all of the tags inside of *it*—the <h1>, <p>, and <strong> tags.

- **Descendent.** A tag inside one or more tags is a descendent. In Figure 3-4, the <body> tag is a descendent of the <html> tag, while the <title> tag is a descendent of *both* the <head> and <html> tags.

- **Parent**. A parent tag is the *closest* ancestor of another tag. In Figure 3-4, a parent is the first tag directly connected to and above another tag. Thus, the <html> tag is the parent of the <head> and <body> tags, but of no other tags. And, in this diagram, the <p> tag is the parent of the <strong> tag.

- **Child**. A tag that's directly enclosed by another tag is a child. In Figure 3-4, both the <h1> and <p> tags are children of the <body> tag, but the <strong> tag isn't—since that tag is directly wrapped inside the <p> tag.

- **Sibling**. Tags that are children of the same tag are called *siblings,* just like brothers and sisters. In an HTML diagram, sibling tags are next to each other and connected to the same parent. In Figure 3-4, the <head> and <body> tags are siblings, as are the <h1> and <p> tags.

Thankfully, that's where CSS 2.1 draws the line with this family metaphor, so you don't have to worry about aunts, uncles, or cousins. (Though rumor has it CSS 10 *will* include in-laws.)

Building Descendent Selectors

Descendent selectors let you take advantage of the HTML family tree by formatting tags differently when they appear inside certain other tags or styles. For example, say you have an <h1> tag on your Web page, and you want to emphasize a word within that heading with the <strong> tag. The trouble is, most browsers display both heading tags and the <strong> tag in bold, so anyone viewing the page can't see any difference between the emphasized word and the other words in the headline. Creating a tag selector to change the <strong> tag's color and make it stand out from the headline isn't much of a solution: you end up changing the color of *every* <strong> tag on the page, like it or not. A descendent selector lets you do what you really want—change the color of the <strong> tag *only when* it appears inside of an <h1> tag.

The solution to the <h1> and <strong> dilemma looks like this:

```
h1 strong { color: red; }
```

Here *any* <strong> tag inside an h1 is red, but other instances of the <strong> tag on the page, aren't affected.

Descendent selectors style elements that are nested inside other elements, following the exact same pattern of ancestors and descendents as the tags in the HTML family tree.

You create a descendent selector by tacking together selectors according to the part of the family tree you want to format, with the most senior ancestor on the left, and the actual tag you're targeting on the far right. For example, in Figure 3-5 notice the three links (the <a> tag) inside of bulleted list items, and another link inside of a paragraph. To format the bulleted links differently than the other links on the page, you can create the following descendent selector:

```
li a { font-family: Arial; }
```

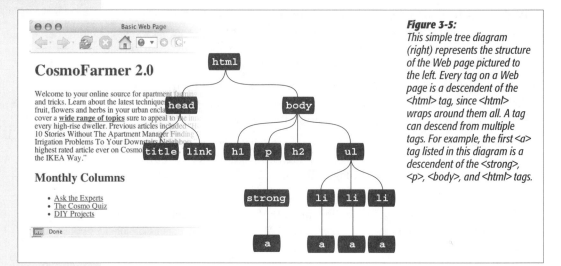

Figure 3-5:
This simple tree diagram (right) represents the structure of the Web page pictured to the left. Every tag on a Web page is a descendent of the <html> tag, since <html> wraps around them all. A tag can descend from multiple tags. For example, the first <a> tag listed in this diagram is a descendent of the <strong>, <p>, <body>, and <html> tags.

This rule says, "Format all links (*a*) that appear inside a list item (*li*) by using the Arial font." A descendent selector can contain more than just two elements. The following are all valid selectors for the <a> tags inside of the bulleted lists in Figure 3-5:

```
ul li a
body li a
html li a
html body ul li a
```

Note: One reason you would tack on additional descendent selectors is if you've written several different rules that simultaneously format a tag. Formatting instructions from a long-winded descendent selector can override simple class or tag styles. More on that in the next chapter.

These four selectors—all of which do the same thing—demonstrate that you don't have to describe the entire lineage of the tag you want to format. For instance, in the second example—*body li a*—*ul* isn't needed. This selector works as long as there's an <a> tag that's a descendent (somewhere up the line) of an <li> tag (which is also a descendent of the <body> tag). This selector can just as easily apply to an <a> that's inside of an <em> tag, that's inside of a <strong> tag, that's inside an <li> tag, and so on.

You're not limited to just tag selectors, either. You can build complex descendent selectors combining different types of selectors. For example, suppose you want your links to appear in yellow only when they're in introductory paragraphs (which you've designated with a class style named *intro*). The following selector does the trick:

```
p.intro a { color: yellow; }
```

Quick translation: Apply this style to every link (*a*) that's a descendent of a paragraph (*p*) that has the *intro* class applied to it. Note that there's no space between *p* and *.intro*, which tells CSS that the *intro* class applies specifically to the <p> tag.

If you add a space, you get a different effect:

```
p .intro a { color: yellow; }
```

This seemingly slight variation selects an <a> tag inside of any tag styled with the *.intro* class, that's itself a descendent of a <p> tag.

Leaving off the ancestor tag name (in this case the *p*) provides a more flexible style:

```
.intro a {color: yellow; }
```

This selector indicates any <a> tag inside of *any other* tag—<div>, <h1>, <table>, and so on—with the *.intro* class applied to it.

Descendent selectors are a very powerful weapon in your CSS arsenal. You can find many more powerful ways to use them in Chapter 14.

Styling Groups of Tags

Sometimes you need a quick way to apply the same formatting to several different elements. For example, maybe you'd like all the headers on a page to share the same color and font. Creating a separate style for each header—*h1, h2, h3, h4* and so on—is way too much work, and if you later want to change the color of all of the headers, then you have six different styles to update. A better approach is to use a *group* selector. Group selectors let you apply a style to multiple selectors at the same time.

Constructing Group Selectors

To work with selectors as a group, simply create a list of selectors separated by commas. So to style all of the heading tags with the same color, you can create the following rule:

```
h1, h2, h3, h4, h5, h6 { color: #F1CD33; }
```

This example consists of only tag selectors, but you can use any valid selector (or combination of selector types) in a group selector. For example, here's a selector that applies the same font color to the <h1> tag, the <p> tag, any tag styled with the *.copyright* class, *and* the tag with the *#banner* ID.

```
h1, p, .copyright, #banner { color: #F1CD33; }
```

Note: If you want a bunch of page elements to share *some* but not all of the same formatting properties, then you can create a group selector with the shared formatting options, and individual rules, with unique formatting, for each individual element. The ability to use multiple styles to format a single element is a powerful CSS feature. See Chapter 5 for details.

The Universal Selector (Asterisk)

You can think of a group selector as shorthand for applying the same style properties to several different page elements. CSS also gives you a sort of über group selector—the *universal* selector. An asterisk * is universal selector shorthand for selecting *every single* tag.

For example, say you want all the tags on your page to appear in bold type. Your group selector might look something like the following:

```
a, p, img, h1, h2, h3, h4, h5 ...yadda yadda... { font-weight: bold; }
```

The asterisk, however, is a much shorter way to tell CSS to select *all* HTML tags on the page:

```
* { font-weight: bold; }
```

You can even use the universal selector as part of a descendent selector, so you can apply a style to all of the tags that descend from a particular page element. For example, *#banner* * selects every tag inside the page element to which you've applied the *#banner* ID.

Since the universal selector doesn't specify any particular type of tag, it's hard to predict its effect on an entire Web site's worth of pages all composed of a variety of different HTML tags. To format many different page elements, Web page gurus rely on *inheritance*—a CSS trait discussed in depth in the next chapter.

Pseudo-Classes and Pseudo-Elements

Sometimes you need to select parts of a Web page that don't have tags per se, but are nonetheless easy to identify, like the first line of a paragraph, or a link as you move your mouse over it. CSS gives you a handful of selectors for these doohickeys—*pseudo-classes* and *pseudo-elements*.

Styles for Links

Four pseudo-classes let you format links in four different states based on how a visitor has interacted with that link. They identify when a link's in one of the following four states:

- **a:link** selects any link that your guest hasn't visited yet, while the mouse isn't hovering over or clicking it. This style is your regular, unused Web link.

- **a:visited** is a link that your visitor has clicked before, according to the Web browser's history. You can style this type of link differently than a regular link to tell your visitor, "Hey, you've been there already!"

- **a:hover** lets you change the look of a link as your visitor passes the mouse over it. The rollover effects you can create aren't just for fun—they can provide useful visual feedback for buttons on a navigation bar.

You can also use the *:hover* pseudo-class on elements other than links. For example, you can use it to highlight text in a <p> or <div> when your guests mouse over it.

Note: In Internet Explorer 6 and earlier, *:hover* works only on links. For a JavaScript workaround, see the box on page 57.

• **a:active** lets you determine how a link looks *as* your visitor clicks. In other words, it covers the brief nanosecond when someone's pressing the mouse button, before releasing it.

Chapter 9 shows you how to design links using these selectors to help your visitors click their way around your site.

Tip: You can live a long, healthy, productive life without reading about the selectors in the next few sections. Many Web designers never use them. The selectors you've learned so far–tag, class, ID, descendent, group, and so on–let you build absolutely beautiful, functional, and easily maintained Web sites. If you're ready for the fun stuff–designing Web pages–then skip to the tutorial on page 61. You can always finish reading this discussion some cold, rainy night by the fire.

GEM IN THE ROUGH

Styling Paragraph Parts

The typographic features that make books and magazines look cool, elegant, and polished didn't exist in the early Web era. (After all, when did scientists ever worry about looking cool?) CSS provides two pseudo-elements–*:first-letter* and *:first-line*–that give your Web pages the design finesse that print has enjoyed for centuries.

The *:first-letter* pseudo-element lets you create a *drop cap*– an initial letter that jumps out from the rest of the paragraph with bigger or bolder font formatting, as at the beginning of a book chapter.

Styling the *:first-line* of a paragraph in a different color keeps your reader's eye moving and makes text appear appealing and fresh. (If you're intrigued, Chapter 6 is all about formatting text.)

More Pseudo-Classes and -Elements

The CSS guidelines define several powerful pseudo-class and element selectors beside the ones covered so far. Unfortunately, the most popular browser around— Internet Explorer 6 for Windows—doesn't recognize them. So most Web surfers can't appreciate any design elements you create with these selectors (at least until they upgrade to IE 7 or switch to Mozilla Firefox—or trade in their PCs for Macs). Meanwhile, you can work around this problem using JavaScript, as described in the box on page 57.

:before

The *:before* pseudo-element does something no other selector can: It lets you add content preceding a given element. For example, say you wanted to put "HOT TIP!" before certain paragraphs to make them stand out, like the boxes in this book that say "UP TO SPEED" and "POWER USERS' CLINIC." Instead of typing that text in your page's HTML, you can let the *:before* selector do it for you. This approach not only saves on code, but if you decide to change the message from "HOT TIP!" to, say, "Things to know," then you can change every page on your site with one quick change to your style sheet. (The downside is that this special message is invisible to browsers that don't understand CSS or don't understand the *:before* selector.)

First, create a class (.*tip*, say) and apply it to the paragraphs that you want to precede with the message, like so: *<p class="tip">*. Then, add your message text to the style sheet:

```
p.tip:before {content: "HOT TIP!" }
```

Whenever a browser encounters the *.tip* class in a <p> tag, it dutifully inserts the text "HOT TIP!" just before the paragraph.

The technical term for text you add with this selector is *generated content,* since Web browsers create (generate) it on the fly. In the page's HTML source code, this material doesn't exist. Whether you realize it or not, browsers generate their own content all the time, like the bullets in bulleted lists and numbers in ordered lists. If you want, you can even use the *:before* selector to define how a browser displays its bullets and numbers for lists.

Despite its potential, Internet Explorer 6 and earlier versions ignore the *:before* selector offhand. Even up-to-date programs like Safari and Firefox don't apply generated content consistently. (See the *content* property listed in Appendix A on page 429 for more information and a list of resources on this topic.)

:after

Exactly like the *:before* selector, the *:after* pseudo-element adds generated content—but after the element, not before. You can use this selector, for example, to add closing quotation marks (") after quoted material.

:first-child

Going back to the HTML family tree analogy for a moment, recall what a child tag is: any tag directly enclosed by another tag. (In Figure 3-5, <h1>, <p>, <h2>, and <ul> are all children of the <body> tag.) The *:first-child* pseudo-element lets you select and format just the *first* of however many children an element may have.

Getting Internet Explorer 6 Up to Speed

If you're a Web designer, you've probably got the latest version of Firefox, Opera, or Safari on your computer. Unfortunately, most of the world doesn't. The vast majority of Web surfers use Internet Explorer 6 on Windows—and IE 5.5 has a respectable number of holdouts as well. The fact is, most people resist upgrading their software—if they even know how to do it. Even with the release of IE 7, IE 6 will probably stick around for quite some time.

So, when you're designing a mainstream Web site (not one for hardcore netizens), you should still factor Internet Explorer 6 into your designs. But that doesn't mean giving up all the cool selectors discussed on these pages, such as *:before*, *:after*, and *:hover*. Believe it or not, with a little help from JavaScript and several pioneering and stubborn programmers before you, you can write scripts that teach IE how to handle these types of selectors.

For example, CSSHOVER teaches Internet Explorer 6 for Windows what to do with the *:focus* (below) and *:hover* selectors (when applied to elements other than links). You can read about and download this quick, simple script at *www.xs4all.nl/~peterned/csshover.html*. This cool bit of JavaScript simplifies the creation of CSS-based drop-down navigation menus like the ones you can read about at *www.seoconsultants.com/css/menus/tutorial/*.

An even more ambitious project, from JavaScript expert Dean Edwards, lets Internet Explorer 5 and 6 for Windows take advantage of all CSS 2 selectors as well as many space age selectors from the not-yet-finalized CSS 3 standard. Edwards' set of scripts—named IE7—lets you use selectors like *:before*, *:after*, *:first-child*, and the advanced selectors discussed on page 58. You can learn more about this amazing project at *http://dean.edwards.name/IE7/overview/*.

A <ul> tag, for example, which creates a bulleted list, can have many list items as children. (In Figure 3-5, the <ul> tag has three <li> children.) To format just the first list item (in boldface), you can write this rule:

```
li:first-child { font-weight: bold; }
```

Because the *:first-child* selector includes only the name of the child element, never the parent, this style formats any <li> tag that's the first child of *any* other tag, not just <ul>. List items always fall within lists, so you know the selector *li:first-child* affects all lists on the page—unordered or ordered. With other tags, however, the *:first-child* selector gets a little tricky. For example, in Figure 3-5, the selector *p:first-child* would have no effect at all, since the <p> tag is a child of the <body> tag, but it isn't the *first* child—the <h1> tag is.

Since the HTML parent-child relations can change each time you edit a Web page, it's hard to predict how the *:first-child* selector will behave as you develop your Web site. Also, this selector doesn't work at all in Internet Explorer 6 or earlier versions—another reason to avoid it unless absolutely necessary.

:focus

The *:focus* pseudo-class works much like the *:hover* pseudo-class. While *:hover* applies when a visitor mouses over a link, *:focus* applies when the visitor does something to indicate her attention to a Web page element—usually by clicking or tabbing into it. In programmery lingo, when a visitor clicks in a text box on a Web form, she puts the *focus* on that text box. That click's a Web designer's only clue as to where the visitor's focusing her attention.

The *:focus* selector is mostly useful for giving your visitor feedback, like changing the background color of a text box to indicate where he's about to type. (Single-line text fields, password fields, and multi-line <textarea> boxes are common targets for the *:focus* selector.) This style, for example, adds a light yellow color to any text box a visitor clicks or tabs into:

```
input:focus { background-color: #FFFFCC; }
```

The *:focus* selector applies only while the element's in focus. When a visitor tabs into another text field or clicks anywhere else on the page, she takes the focus—and the CSS properties—away from the text box.

Tip: Learning how to write selectors can sometimes feel like learning hieroglyphics. To translate a selector into straightforward language, visit the Selectoracle at *http://gallery.theopalgroup.com/selectoracle/*. This great resource lets you type in a selector and spits out a clear description of which page elements on a page the style affects.

Advanced Selectors

The CSS 2 guidelines provide a few more powerful selectors that give you even finer control over Web page styling. Like some of the selectors you've seen previously, the selectors in this section don't work in Windows Internet Explorer 6 and earlier. (But you can try the JavaScript workaround in the box on page 57.)

Child Selectors

Similar to the descendent selectors described earlier in this chapter, CSS lets you format the children of another tag with a *child* selector. The child selector uses an additional symbol—an angle bracket (>) to indicate the relationship between the two elements. For example, the selector *body > h1* selects any <h1> tag that's a child of the <body> tag.

Unlike a descendent selector, which applies to *all* descendents of a tag (children, grandchildren, and so on), the child selector lets you specify which child of which parent you mean. For example, in Figure 3-6, there are two <h2> tags. Using a plain old descendent selector—*body h2*—selects both <h2> tags. Even though both <h2> tags are inside of the <body> tag, though, only the second one is a child of the <body> tag. The first <h2> is directly inside of a <div> tag, so its parent is <div>. Since the two <h2> tags have different parents, you can use a child selector to get at them individually. To select only the second <h2> tag, your child selector looks like this: *body > h2*. If you want the first <h2> tag, then you must use this child selector instead: *div > h2*.

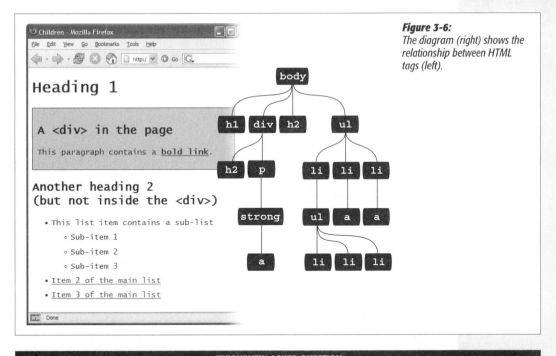

Figure 3-6:
The diagram (right) shows the relationship between HTML tags (left).

FREQUENTLY ASKED QUESTION

Making Lists Look Great

When would I ever use a child selector? Just from reading this chapter, I already know enough selectors to get at just about any page element, so why learn another?

There's one design challenge where child selectors can't be beat—and it comes up in more Web sites than you think. Any time you have an unordered list with one or more unordered lists nested inside (as in Figure 3-6), you can use child selectors to visually organize these categories and subcategories of information. You can format the first level of list items one way, and the second level of list items another way. Content presented in this manner looks neat, professional, and readable (and your visitors will love you for it).

First, create a class style for the outermost nested level in your list and call it, say, *.mainList*. For this top level, you might use a sans-serif font, a little larger than your other text, perhaps in bold or a different color. Subsequent categories can be smaller, in a serif font like Times for easiest reading.

When you have a lot of text, styling each subcategory level a bit differently helps visually orient your visitors in the material.

Apply the *.mainList* class style to the first <ul> tag: *<ul class="mainList">*. Then use a child selector (*ul.mainList > li*) to select just the first set of list items, and add your desired text styling for the first subcategory. This styling applies only to the <li> tags that are children of the <ul> tag with the *.mainList* style applied to it. The child <li> tags of any subsequent nested <ul> tags are unaffected, so you can style them independently with the proper child selectors. For example, to style the <li> tags of the first nested list, use this selector *ul.mainList > li > ul > li*. (A descendent selector like *ul li*, by contrast, selects the list items of all unordered lists on the page—nested ones and all.)

Adjacent Siblings

Parent-child relationships aren't the only ones in the HTML family tree. Some-times you need to select a tag based not on its parent tag, but on its surrounding siblings—the tags that share a common parent. A tag that appears immediately after another tag in HTML is called an *adjacent sibling*. In Figure 3-6, the <div> tag is the adjacent sibling of the <h1> tag, the <p> tag is the adjacent sibling of the <h2> tag, and so on.

Using an adjacent sibling selector, you can, for example, give the first paragraph after each heading different formatting from the paragraphs that follow. Suppose you want to remove the margin that appears above that <p> tag so that it sits right below the heading without any gap. Or perhaps you want to give the paragraph a distinct color and font size, like a little introductory statement.

The adjacent sibling selector uses a plus sign (+) to join one element to the next. So to select every paragraph following each <h2> tag, use this selector: *h2 + p*. The last element in the selector (*p*, in this case) is what gets the formatting, but only when it's next to its brother <h2>.

Attribute Selectors

CSS provides a way to format a tag based on any attributes it has. For example, say you want to place borders around the images on your page—but only around the important photos. You don't want to include your logo, buttons, and other little doodads that also have an <img> tag. Fortunately, you realize that you've given all the photos descriptions using the *title* attribute, which means you can use an *attribute selector* to identify just the important images.

Tip: The HTML *title* attribute's a great way to add tooltips (pop-up messages) to links and images on a page. It's also one way to inform search engines about the useful information on a Web page. Learn more about it at *http://webdesign.about.com/od/htmltags/a/aa101005.htm*.

With attribute selectors, you can single out tags that have a particular property. For example, here's how to select all <img> tags with a title attribute:

```
img[title]
```

The first part of the selector is the name of the tag (*img*) while the attribute's name goes in brackets: *[title]*.

CSS doesn't limit attribute selectors to tag names: You can combine them with classes, too. For example, *.photo[title]* selects every element with the *.photo* class style and an HTML title attribute.

To get more specific, you can select elements that not only share a particular attribute, but also have an exact value set for that attribute. For example, when you want to highlight links that point to a particular URL, create an eye-catching attribute selector, like so:

```
a[href="http://www.cosmofarmer.com"]{ color:red; font-weight:bold; }
```

Adding a value to an attribute selector's very useful when working with forms. Many form elements have the same tag, even if they look and act differently. The checkbox, text box, Submit button, and other form fields all share the <input> tag. The type attribute's value is what gives the field its form and function. For example, *<input type="text">* creates a text box, and *<input type="checkbox">* creates a checkbox.

To select just text boxes in a form, for example, use this selector:

```
input[type="text"]
```

Note: The CSS 3 guidelines promise even more variations on the attribute selector.

Tutorial: Selector Sampler

In the rest of this chapter, you'll create a variety of selector types and see how each affects a Web page. This tutorial starts with the basic selector types and then moves on to more advanced styles.

To get started, you need to download the tutorial files located on this book's companion Web site at *www.sawmac.com/css/*. Click the tutorial link and download the files. All of the files are enclosed in a ZIP archive, so you'll need to unzip them first. (Detailed instructions for unzipping the files are on the Web site.) The files for this tutorial are contained inside the folder named *chapter_03*.

INDIGNANTLY ASKED QUESTION

Keeping It Internal

Hey, what's up with the internal style sheet in this tutorial? Chapter 2 recommends using external style sheets for a bunch of reasons.

Think you're pretty smart, eh? Yes, external style sheets usually make for faster, more efficient Web sites, for all the reasons mentioned in *Chapter 2*. However, internal style sheets make your life easier when you're designing a single page at a time, as in this tutorial. You get to work in just one Web page file instead of flipping back and forth between the external style sheet file and the Web page.

Furthermore, you can preview your results without constantly refreshing your browser's cache; flip back to the box on page 35 for more on that quirkiness.

Many hotshot Web designers like to begin their designs with an internal style sheet, since it's faster and it avoids any problems with all that cache nonsense. Here's their secret: Once they've perfected their design, they simply copy the code from the internal style sheet, paste it into an external style sheet, and then link the style sheet to their site's pages as described on page 33.

---

1. **Open *selector_basics.html* in your favorite text editor.**

   This page is made of very basic HTML tags. The most exciting thing about it is the graphic banner (see Figure 3-7). But you'll liven things up in this tutorial. You'll start by adding an internal style sheet to this file.

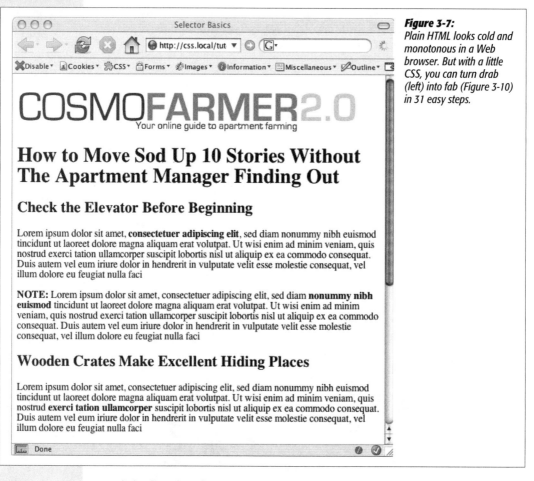

Figure 3-7:
Plain HTML looks cold and monotonous in a Web browser. But with a little CSS, you can turn drab (left) into fab (Figure 3-10) in 31 easy steps.

2. **Click directly after the closing </title> tag, hit Return and type <style type="text/css">.**

This is the opening style tag, which lets a Web browser know that the information that follows is Cascading Style Sheet instructions. The HTML should now look like this (the stuff you added is in bold):

```
<title>Selector Basics</title>
<style type="text/css">
</head>
```

Type selectors—such as the tag selector you're about to create—are the most basic type of selector. (If you completed the tutorial in the last chapter, you've already created a few.)

3. **Press Enter (Return), and then type p {**

To create a tag selector, simply use the name of the HTML tag you wish to format. This style applies to all paragraphs of text within <p> tags.

4. **Hit Return again and add the following four CSS properties to supply the style's formatting—color, size, font, and left indent:**

```
color: #5f9794;
font-family: "Century Gothic", "Gill Sans", Arial, sans-serif;
font-size: 1em;
margin-left: 50px;
```

Press Enter (Return) to place each CSS property on its own line. It's also a good idea to visually organize your CSS code by indenting each property with the Tab key.

Note: These property names and their values may look unfamiliar. For now, just type them as is. You'll learn what 1em and 50px mean, along with all the ins and outs of text formatting properties, in Chapter 6.

---

5. **Complete this style by pressing Enter (Return) and then typing a closing bracket (}), which marks the end of the style. Your completed style should look like this:**

```
p {
color:#5f9794;
font-family: "Century Gothic", "Gill Sans", Arial, sans-serif;
font-size: 1em;
margin-left:50px;
}
```

Finally, you'll add the closing <style> tag to complete the style sheet.

6. **Hit Return to create a new, blank line and type </style>.**

Your style sheet's complete. Time for a look-see.

7. **Open the page in a Web browser to preview your work.**

Unless you tinker with the preference settings, most browsers display black text in a standard serif font like Times. If your CSS style works properly, then you should see seven indented paragraphs in a sans-serif font in an attractive dark teal color (see Figure 3-8).

Creating a Group Selector

Sometimes several different elements on a page share the same look. For instance, you may want all your headings to have the same font and color for a consistent style. Instead of creating separate styles and duplicating the same property settings for each tag—<h1>, <h2>, and so on—you can group the tags together into a single selector.

1. **Return to your text editor and the *selector_basics.html* file.**

You'll add a new style below the <p> tag style you just created.

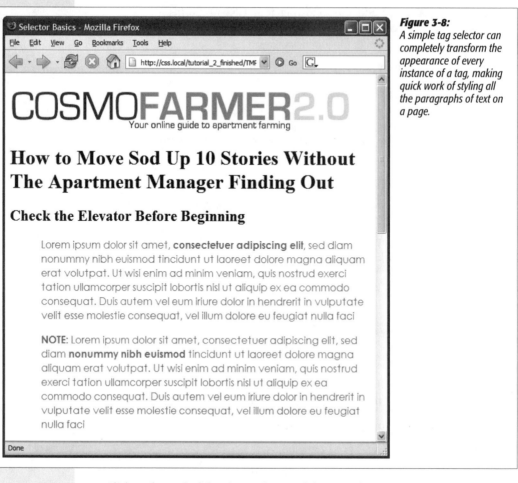

Figure 3-8:
*A simple tag selector can
completely transform the
appearance of every
instance of a tag, making
quick work of styling all
the paragraphs of text on
a page.*

2. **Click at the end of the closing brace of the tag selector, press Enter (Return) to start a new line, and then type** *h1, h2, h3 {.*

   As explained earlier in this chapter, a group selector is simply a list of selectors separated by commas. This rule applies the same formatting, which you'll add next, to all <h1>, <h2>, and <h3> tags on the page.

3. **Hit Return, and then add two CSS properties:**

   ```
   color: #102536;
   font-family: Georgia, Times, serif;
   ```

   You're adding some basic text formatting options, just as you did in the previous steps.

4. **Finally, hit Enter (Return), and then type the closing brace to complete this style. It should look like this:**

   ```
   h1, h2, h3 {
     color:#102536;
   ```

```
        font-family: Georgia, Times, serif;
    }
```

5. **Save the file, and preview it in a Web browser.**

The <h1> heading near the top of the page and the <h2> headings introducing each of the three sections all have the same font and font color.

Creating and Applying a Class Selector

Tag selectors are quick and efficient, but they're a bit indiscriminate in how they style a page. What if you want to style a single <p> tag differently than all the other <p> tags on a page? A class selector is the answer.

1. **Return to your text editor and the *selector_basics.html* file.**

Add a new style below the group selector style you just created.

2. **Click at the end of the closing brace of the *h1, h2, h3* selector, press Enter (Return), and then type *.note {*.**

This style's name, *note*, indicates its purpose: to highlight paragraphs that contain extra bits of information for your site's visitors. Once you create a class style, you can apply it wherever these notes appear—like the second paragraph, in this case.

3. **Hit Return, and then add the following list of properties to the style:**

```
        font-size: .85em;
        color: #294e56;
        margin: 0 100px;
        padding: 10px;
        border: 1px solid #73afb7;
        background-color: #fbef99;
```

4. **Finally, complete the style by pressing Return and typing the closing brace. The completed class style should look like this:**

```
    .note {
      font-size: .85em;
      color:#294e56;
      margin: 0 100px;
      padding: 10px;
      border: 1px solid #73afb7;
      background-color: #fbef99;
    }
```

If you preview the page now, you see no changes. Unlike tag selectors, class selectors don't have any affect on a Web page until you apply the style in the HTML code.

5. In the page's HTML, locate the <p> tag that begins with the word "Note:" inside <strong> tags.

To apply a class style to a tag, simply add a *class* attribute, followed by the class selector's name—in this case, the *.note* style you just created.

6. Click just after the "p" in the <p> tag, and then type a space followed by *class="note"*. The HTML should now look like this (what you just typed is in bold):

```
<p class="note"><strong>NOTE:</strong> Lorem ipsum dolor
```

Be sure *not* to type *class=".note"*. In CSS, the period's necessary to indicate a class style name; in HTML, it's verboten.

Note: Despite the name, there's no reason you can't add this class to other tags as well, not just the <p> tag. If you happen to want to apply this formatting to an <h2> tag, for example, then your HTML would look like this: <h2 class="note">.

---

7. Save and preview the Web page in a browser.

The note paragraph is nicely highlighted on the page (see Figure 3-9).

Figure 3-9:
You can make detailed formatting changes with class selectors. A class style gives this one paragraph different formatting from all other paragraphs on the page, making it stand out as a distinctive note.

Note: If your page doesn't look like Figure 3-9, then you may have mistyped the name of a property or its value. Double-check your code with the steps on page 65. Also, make sure to end each declaration—property:value combination—with a semicolon and conclude the style with a closing brace at the very end. When your style's not working correctly, missing semicolons and closing braces are frequent culprits.

Creating and Applying an ID Selector

You can apply class selectors to multiple elements on a page. For example, you can use the *note* class you made in the previous exercise to create any number of notes on a page. ID selectors look and act just like classes, but you can apply an ID only *once* per page. Web designers frequently use ID selectors to indicate unique sections of a page, as explained on page 47.

In this exercise, you'll create a style that sets a specific width for a Web page's content, and centers it in the middle of the browser window. Once you create the ID selector, apply it to the page using a <div> tag.

1. **Return to your text editor and the *selector_basics.html* file.**

   Add a new style below the *.note* class style you created before.

2. **Click after the previous style's closing bracket (}), hit Return or Enter to create a new line, and then type *#wrapper {***

   ID selectors always begin with the pound symbol (#). The style's name indicates its role on the page: Use it to wrap all of the other content on the page, as though you're boxing it up. That way, the set width and other formatting apply to the entire package.

3. **Hit Return again, and then type:**

   ```
   width:680px;
   margin: 0 auto;
   padding: 0 20px;
   border-left: 1px solid #666666;
   border-right: 1px solid #666666;
   ```

   These properties provide a width for the content, set the margins so the content floats in the center of the Web browser, and add a little space between the page content and left and right border lines.

4. **Finish the style by typing the closing brace. The whole thing should look like this:**

   ```
   #wrapper {
   width:680px;
   margin: 0 auto;
   padding: 0 20px;
   border-left: 1px solid #666666;
   border-right: 1px solid #666666;
   }
   ```

Just as with a class, this style doesn't *do* anything until you apply it to the page. So you'll add a <div> tag to the page's HTML, delineating where you want the ID style to apply.

5. **Find the page's opening <body> tag. Click after the tag's closing >, and then hit Enter.**

   You'll place the opening <div> tag here, before the contents of the page.

6. **Type <div id="wrapper"> .**

   The <div> appears between the <body> and <h1> tags, like so:

   ```
   <body>
   <div id="wrapper">
   <h1><img src="images/logo.gif" alt="CosmoFarmer 2.0" width="553"
    height="70" />
   ```

   Next, you'll close the <div> tag to indicate the end of the wrapper.

7. **Scroll down the page until you find the last paragraph on the page—the one containing the copyright notice. Click after the closing </p> tag, hit Return, and then type </div>.**

   The closing </div> is sandwiched between that last paragraph and the closing </body> tag:

   ```
   <p>Copyright 2006, <a href="http://www.cosmofarmer.com/">
    CosmoFarmer.com </a></p>
   </div>
   </body>
   ```

8. **Save the page, and preview it in a browser.**

   Everything on the page, the CosmoFarmer logo and all of the text, now have a set width and float in the center of the browser window (see Figure 3-10). Even if you resize the browser window (try it!), the content remains centered.

Note: Internet Explorer 5 for Windows, won't center the content on the page as described in step 8. It requires a little more work to accomplish that. You won't find specific instructions on how to do that here, but you'll find a detailed explanation of how to center a page in IE 5 starting on page 314.

Creating a Descendent Selector

On the *selectors_basics.html* page, you see a couple of words inside the <h2> tags that require special emphasis. The page's HTML uses the <strong> tag to indicate these special words, but since browsers automatically make headings *and* <strong> tags bold, you can't see any difference when you preview the page in a Web browser. How can you make those words stand out from the rest of the heading—without messing up all the other <strong> tags on the page?

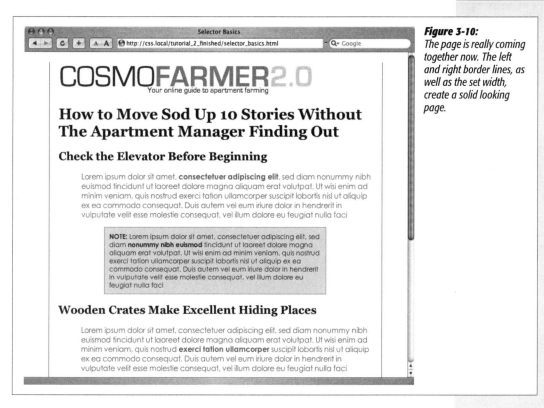

Figure 3-10:
The page is really coming together now. The left and right border lines, as well as the set width, create a solid looking page.

As you saw earlier in this chapter, CSS provides a simple solution for targeting just the <strong> tags that appear inside those headings—descendent selectors—and now's your chance to see one in action.

1. **Return to your text editor and the *selector_basics.html* file. Create a new empty line for the descendent selector style.**

    If you just completed the previous steps, click after the closing brace of the *#wrapper* style, and then hit Enter (Return).

2. **Type *h2 strong {***

    The last tag in the selector—*strong*—is the element you ultimately want to format. In this case, the style formats the <strong> tag only when it's *inside* an <h2> tag. It has no effect on <strong> tags inside paragraphs, lists, or <h1> tags, for example.

3. **Hit Enter (Return), type *color: red;*, and then hit Enter (Return) again to create another blank line. Finish the style by typing the closing brace character.**

    The finished style should look like this:

```
h2 strong {
  color: red;
}
```

4. **Save the page and preview it in a Web browser.**

The word "Before" should appear red in the first <h2> heading, as should the words "Excellent" and "Heavy" in the other two headings.

Descendent selectors are among the most powerful CSS tools. Professional Web designers use them extensively to target particular tags without littering the HTML with CSS classes. You can learn a lot more about descendent selectors in Chapter 14.

Note: You can see a completed version of the page you've just created in the *chapter_03_finished* folder.

Saving Time with Inheritance

Children inherit traits from their parents—eye color, height, male-pattern baldness, and so on. Sometimes, we inherit traits from more distant ancestors like grandparents or great-grandparents. As you saw in the previous chapter, the metaphor of family-relations is part of the structure of HTML as well. And just like humans, HTML tags can inherit CSS properties from their ancestors.

What Is Inheritance?

In a nutshell, inheritance is the process by which CSS properties applied to one tag are passed on to nested tags. For example, a <p> tag is always nested inside of the <body> tag, so properties applied to the <body> tag get inherited by the <p> tag. Say you created a CSS tag style (page 43) for the <body> tag that sets the *color* property to a dark red. Tags that are descendents of the <body> tag—that is, the ones inside the <body> tag—will inherit that color property. That means that any text in those tags—<h1>, <h2>, <p>, whatever—will appear in that same dark red color.

Inheritance works through multiple generations as well. If a tag like the <em> or <strong> tag appears inside of a <p> tag, then the <em> and the <strong> tags also inherit properties from any style applied to the <body> tag.

Note: As discussed in Chapter 3, any tag inside of another tag is a *descendent* of that tag. So a <p> tag inside the <body> tag is a descendent of the <body>, while the <body> tag is an *ancestor* of the <p> tag. *Descendents* (think kids) inherit properties from ancestors (think parents and grandparents).

Although this sounds a bit confusing, inheritance is a *really* big time-saver. Imagine if no properties were passed onto nested tags and you had a paragraph that contained other tags like the <em> tag to emphasize text or the <a> tag to add a link. If you created a style that made the paragraph purple, 24px tall, using the Arial font, it would be weird if all the text inside the <em> tag reverted to its regular, "browser-boring" style (see Figure 4-1). You'd then have to create another style to format the <em> tag to match the appearance of the <p> tag. What a drag.

Inheritance doesn't just apply to tag styles. It works with any type of style; so when you apply a class style (see page 45) to a tag, any tags inside that tag inherit properties from the styled tag. Same holds true for ID styles, descendent selectors, and the other types of styles discussed in Chapter 3.

How Inheritance Streamlines Style Sheets

You can use inheritance to your advantage to streamline your style sheets. Say you want all the text on a page to use the same font. Instead of creating styles for each tag, simply create a tag style for the <body> tag. (Or create a class style and apply it to the <body> tag.) In the style, specify the font you wish to use, and all of the tags on the page inherit the font: body { font-family: Arial, Helvetica, sans-serif; }. Fast and easy.

You can also use inheritance to apply style properties to a *section* of a page. For example, like many Web designers, you may use the <div> tag (page 47) to define an area of a page like a banner, sidebar, or footer. By applying a style to a <div> tag, you can specify particular CSS properties for all of the tags inside just that section of the page. If you want all the text in a sidebar to be the same color, you'd create a style setting the color property, and then apply it to the <div>. Any <p>, <h1>, or other tags inside the <div> inherit the same font color.

Tip: You'll find lots more uses for the <div> tag when laying out a page using CSS in Part 3.

The Limits of Inheritance

Inheritance isn't all-powerful. Many CSS properties don't pass down to descendent tags at all. For example, the border property (which lets you draw a box around an element) isn't inherited, and with good reason. If it were, then every tag inside an element with the border property would also have a border around it. For example, if you added a border to the <body> tag, then every bulleted list would also have a box around it, and each bulleted item in the list would also have a border (Figure 4-2).

Tip: There's a complete list of CSS properties in Appendix A, including details on which ones get inherited.

Figure 4-1:

Inheritance lets tags copy properties from the tags that surround them.

Top: The paragraph tag is set with a specific font-face, size, and color. The tags inside each paragraph inherit those properties so they look like the rest of the paragraph.

Bottom: If inheritance didn't exist, the same page would look like this figure. Notice how the strong, em, and a tags inside the paragraph retain the font-face, size, and color defined by the browser. To make them look like the rest of the paragraph, you'd have to create additional styles—a big waste of time.

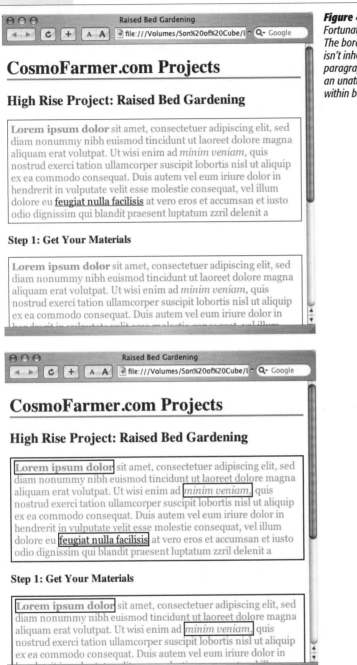

Figure 4-2:
Fortunately, not all properties are inherited. The border applied to the paragraphs at top isn't inherited by the tags inside those paragraphs. If they were, you'd end up with an unattractive mess of boxes within boxes within boxes (bottom).

Here are examples of times when inheritance doesn't strictly apply:

- As a general rule, properties that affect the placement of elements on the page, or the margins, background colors, and borders of elements aren't inherited.

- Web browsers use their own inherent styles to format various tags: headings are big and bold, links are blue, and so on. When you define a font-size for the text on a page and apply it to the <body> tag, headings still appear larger than paragraphs, and <h1> tags are still larger than <h2> tags. It's the same when you apply a font color to the <body>; the links on the page still appear in good old-fashioned, Web-browser blue.

- When styles conflict, the more specific style wins out. In other words, when you've specifically applied CSS properties to an element—like specifying the font-size for an unordered list—and those properties conflict with any inherited properties—like a font-size set for the <body> tag—the browser uses the font size applied to the <ul> tag.

Note: These types of conflicts between styles are very common, and the rules for how a browser deals with them are called the *cascade*. You'll learn about that in the next chapter.

Tutorial: Inheritance

In this three-part tutorial, you'll see how inheritance works. First, you'll create a simple tag selector and watch it pass its characteristics on to nested tags. Then, you'll create a class style that uses inheritance to alter the formatting of an entire page. Finally, you'll see where CSS makes some welcome exceptions to the inheritance rule.

To get started, you need to download the tutorial files located on this book's companion Web site at *www.sawmac.com/css/*. Click the tutorial link and download the files. All of the files are enclosed in a ZIP archive, so you'll need to unzip them first. (Detailed instructions for unzipping the files are on the Web site.) The files for this tutorial are contained in the folder named *chapter_04*.

A Basic Example: One Level of Inheritance

To see how inheritance works, start by adding a single tag style and see how it affects the tags nested inside. The next two parts of this tutorial will build upon your work here, so save the file when you're done.

1. **Open the file *inheritance.html* in your favorite text editor.**

   Now add an internal style sheet to this file.

Note: In general, it's better to use external style sheets for a Web site, for reasons discussed in Chapter 2 (page 30). But sometimes it's easier to start your CSS-based design in an internal style sheet, as in this example, and turn it into an external style sheet later.

---

2. **Click directly after the closing </title> tag. Hit Enter (Return), and then type** *<style type="text/css">*.

This opening style tag lets a Web browser know that CSS instructions are to follow.

You need to create a style that applies to all <p> tags.

3. **Press Enter (Return) and type** *p {*.

You've started creating a tag selector that applies to all <p> tags on the page.

4. **Press Enter (Return) again, and then add one CSS property to create the style:** *color: #5f9794;*

As you've seen in the previous tutorials, the color property sets the color of text.

5. **Complete the style by pressing Enter (Return), and then typing a closing bracket to mark the end of the style. At this point your completed style should look like this:**

```
p {
    color: #5f9794;
}
```

Finally, add the closing <style> tag to complete the style sheet.

6. **Hit Enter (Return) to create a new, blank line, and then type** *</style>*.

Your style sheet is complete.

7. **Open the page in a Web browser to preview your work.**

The color of the page's seven paragraphs has changed from black to teal (see Figure 4-3).

But notice how this <p> tag style affects *other* tags: Tags *inside* of the <p> tag also change color. For example, the text inside the <em> and <strong> tags changes to teal while maintaining its italic and bold formatting. This kind of behavior makes a lot of sense. After all, when you set the color of text in a paragraph, you expect *all* the text in the paragraph—regardless of any other tags inside that paragraph—to be the same color.

Without inheritance, creating style sheets would be very labor intensive. If the <em> and <strong> tags didn't inherit the color property from the <p> tag selector, then you'd have to create additional styles—perhaps descendent selectors like *p em* and *p strong*—to correctly format the text.

Using Inheritance to Restyle an Entire Page

Inheritance works with class styles as well—any tag with any kind of style applied to it passes CSS properties to its descendents. With that in mind, you can use inheritance to make quick, sweeping changes to an entire page.

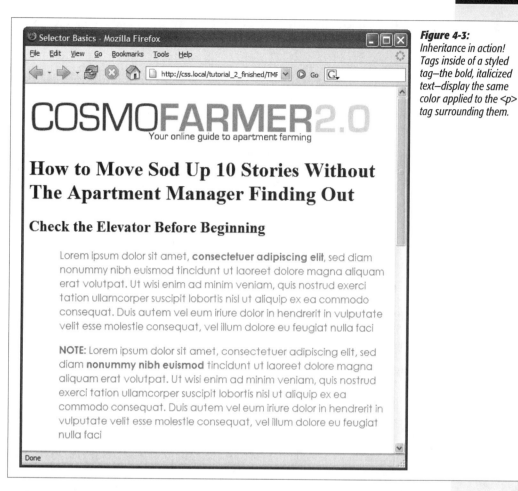

Figure 4-3:
Inheritance in action! Tags inside of a styled tag—the bold, italicized text—display the same color applied to the <p> tag surrounding them.

1. Return to your text editor and the *inheritance.html* file.

   You'll add a new style below the <p> tag style you created.

2. Click at the end of the closing brace of the *p* selector. Press Return to create a new line, and then type *.pageStyle {*.

   You're about to create a new class style that you'll apply to the body tag.

3. Hit Enter (Return) again, and then add the following list of properties to the style:

   ```
   font-family: Arial, Helvetica, sans-serif;
   font-size: 1em;
   color: #fdd041;
   ```

4. **Finally complete the style by pressing Enter (Return) and typing the closing brace. The whole thing should look like this:**

```
.pageStyle {
    font-family: Arial, Helvetica, sans-serif;
    font-size: 1em;
    color: #fdd041;
}
```

This completed class style sets a font, font-size, and color for the body tag. But thanks to inheritance, all tags inside of the body tag (which are also all the tags visible inside a browser window) use the same font.

5. **Find the opening <body> tag (just a couple lines below the style you just created), and then type** *class="pageStyle"*.

The tag should now look like this: *<body class="pageStyle">*. It applies the class to the body tag.

6. **Save and preview the Web page in a browser.**

As you can see in Figure 4-4, your class style has created a seamless, consistent appearance throughout all text in the body of the page. Both headings and paragraphs inside the <body> tag have taken on the new font styling.

The page as a whole looks great, but now look more closely: The color change affected only the headings and the font-size change affected only the paragraphs. How did CSS know that you didn't want your headings to be the same 1em size as the body text? And why didn't the nested <p> tags inherit your new color styling from the <body> tag?

You're seeing the "Cascading" aspect of Cascading Style Sheets in action. In this example, your <p> tags have two color styles in conflict—the <p> tag style you created on page 76 and the <body> class style you created here. When styles collide, the browser has to pick one. As discussed on page 86, the browser uses the more specific styling—the color you assigned explicitly for <p> tag. You'll learn much more about the rules of the cascade in the next chapter.

Inheritance Inaction

Inheritance doesn't always apply and that isn't necessarily a bad thing. For some properties, inheritance would have a negative effect on a page's appearance. You'll see another example of inheritance *inaction* in the final section of this tutorial. Margin styles don't get inherited by descendent tags—and you wouldn't want them to, as you'll see in this example.

1. **Enter (Return) to your text editor and the** *inheritance.html* **file.**

You'll expand on the p tag style you just created.

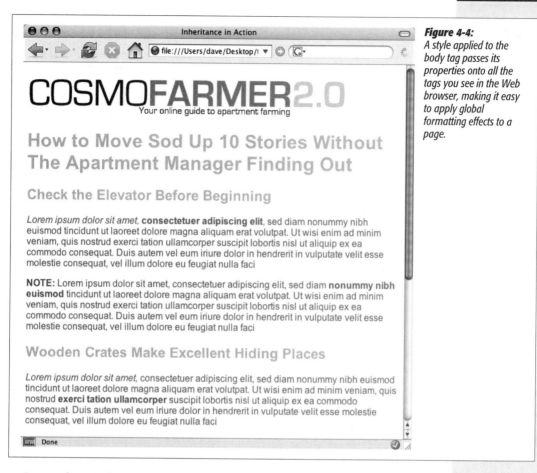

Figure 4-4:
A style applied to the body tag passes its properties onto all the tags you see in the Web browser, making it easy to apply global formatting effects to a page.

2. Locate the *p* style, click at the end of the color property (*color :#5f9794;*), and then press Enter (Return) to create a new line.

   You'll indent the paragraphs on the page by adding a left margin.

3. Type *margin-left: 50px;*. The style should now look like this:

```
p {
    color: #5f9794;
    margin-left: 50px;
}
```

   The margin-left property indents the paragraph 50px from the left.

4. **Save the file and preview it in a Web browser.**

   Notice that all of the <p> tags are indented 50px from the left edge of the browser window, but that tags *inside* the <p> tag (for example, the <em> tag) don't have any additional indentation (see Figure 4-5). This behavior makes sense: It would look weird if there was an additional 50px of space to the left of each <em> and each <strong> tag inside of a paragraph!

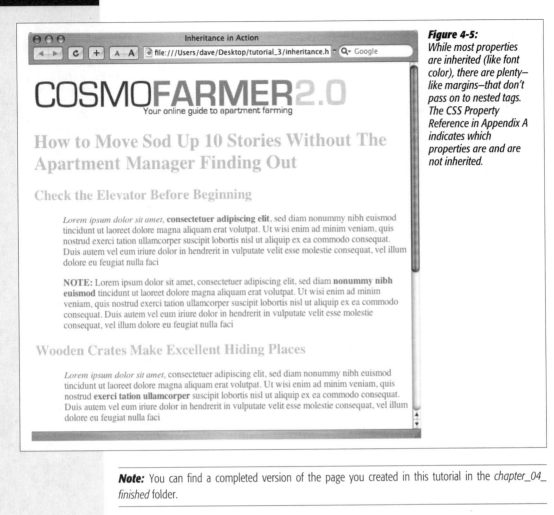

Figure 4-5:
While most properties are inherited (like font color), there are plenty—like margins—that don't pass on to nested tags. The CSS Property Reference in Appendix A indicates which properties are and are not inherited.

Note: You can find a completed version of the page you created in this tutorial in the *chapter_04_ finished* folder.

Managing Multiple Styles: The Cascade

As you create increasingly complex style sheets, you'll sometimes wonder why a particular element on a page looks the way it does. CSS's inheritance feature, as discussed in the previous chapter, creates the possibility that any tag on a page is potentially affected by any of the tags surrounding it. For example, the <body> tag can pass properties on to a paragraph and a paragraph may pass its own formatting instructions on to a link within the paragraph. In other words, that link can inherit CSS properties from *both* the <body> and the <p> tag—essentially creating a kind of Frankenstyle that combines parts of two different CSS styles.

Then there are times when styles collide—the same CSS property is defined in multiple styles, all applying to a particular element on the page (for example, a <p> tag style in an external style sheet and another <p> tag style in an internal style sheet). When that happens, you can see some pretty weird stuff, like text that appears bright blue, even though you specifically applied a class style with the text color set to red. Fortunately, there's actually a system at work: a basic CSS mechanism known as the *cascade*, which governs how styles interact, and which styles get precedence when there's a conflict.

Note: This chapter deals with issues that arise when you build complex style sheets that rely on inheritance and more sophisticated types of selectors like descendent selectors (page 49). The rules are all pretty logical, but they're about as fun to master as the tax code. If that's got your spirits sagging, consider skipping the details and instead do the tutorial on page 91 to get a taste of what the cascade is and why it matters. Or jump right to the next chapter which explores fun and visually exciting ways to format text. You can always return to this chapter later after you've mastered the basics of CSS.

How Styles Cascade

The *cascade* is a set of rules for determining which style properties get applied to an element. It specifies how a Web browser should handle multiple styles that apply to the same tag, and what to do when CSS properties conflict. Style conflicts happen in two cases: through inheritance when the same property is inherited from multiple ancestors, and when one or more styles apply to the same element (maybe a <p> tag style in an external style sheet and another <p> tag style in an internal style sheet).

Inherited Styles Accumulate

As you read in the last chapter, CSS inheritance ensures that related elements—like all the words inside a paragraph, even those inside a link or another tag—share similar formatting. It spares you from creating specific styles for each tag on a page. But since one tag can inherit properties from *any* ancestor tag—a link for example, inheriting the same font as its parent <p> tag—determining why a particular tag is formatted one way can be a bit tricky. Imagine a font applied to the <body> tag, a font size applied to a <p> tag, and a font color applied to an <a> tag. Any <a> tag inside of a paragraph, would inherit the font from the body and the size from the paragraph. In other words, the inherited styles combine to form a hybrid style.

The page shown in Figure 5-1 has three styles: one for the <body>, one for the <p> tag, and one for the <strong> tag. The CSS looks like this:

```
body { font-family: Verdana, Arial, Helvetica, sans-serif; }
p { color: #999999; }
strong { font-size: 24px; }
```

The <strong> tag is nested inside a paragraph, which is inside the <body> tag. That <strong> tag inherits from both of its ancestors, so it inherits the font-family property from the body and the color property from its parent paragraph. In addition, the <strong> tag has a bit of CSS applied directly to it—a 24px font-size. The final appearance of the tag is a combination of all three styles. In other words, the <strong> tag appears exactly as if you'd created a style like this:

```
strong {
    font-family: Verdana, Arial, Helvetica, sans-serif;
    color: #999999;
    font-size: 24px;
}
```

Nearest Ancestor Wins

In the previous example, various inherited and applied tags smoothly combined to create an overall formatting package. But what happens when inherited CSS properties conflict? Think about a page where you've set the font-color for both the body and paragraph tags. Now imagine that within one paragraph, there's a

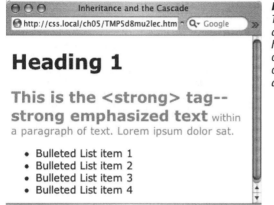

Figure 5-1:
Thanks to inheritance, it's possible for multiple styles to affect the appearance of one tag. Here the <strong> tag has a specific color, font-family, and font size, even though only a single property is applied directly to that tag. The other two formatting options were inherited from the tag's ancestors: the <body> and the <p> tags.

<strong> tag. Which color gets applied to text inside the <strong> tag? The color inherited from the body or the paragraph? Ladies and gentleman, we have a winner: the paragraph. That's because the Web browser obeys the style that's closest to the tag in question.

In this example, any properties inherited from the <body> tag are rather generic. They apply to all tags. A style applied to a <p> tag, on the other hand, is much more narrowly defined. Its properties apply only to <p> tags and the tags inside them.

In a nutshell, if a tag doesn't have a specific style applied to it, then in the case of any conflicts from inherited properties, the nearest ancestor wins (see Figure 5-2, number 1).

Here's one more example, just to make sure the concept sinks in. If a CSS style defining the color of text were applied to a <table> tag, and another style defining a *different* text color were applied to a <td> tag inside that table, then tags inside that table cell (<td>) such as a paragraph, headline, or unordered list would use the color from the <td> style, since it's the closest ancestor.

The Directly Applied Style Wins

Taking the "nearest ancestor" rule to its logical conclusion, there's one style that always becomes king of the CSS family tree—any style applied directly to a given tag. Suppose a font-color's set for the body, paragraph, *and* strong tags. The paragraph style is more specific than the body style, but the style applied to the <strong> tag is more specific than either one. It formats the <strong> tags and only the <strong> tags, overriding any conflicting properties inherited from the other tags (see Figure 5-2, number 2). In other words, properties from a style specifically applied to a tag beat out any inherited properties.

This rule explains why some inherited properties don't "appear" to inherit. A link inside a paragraph whose text is red still appears browser-link-blue. That's because

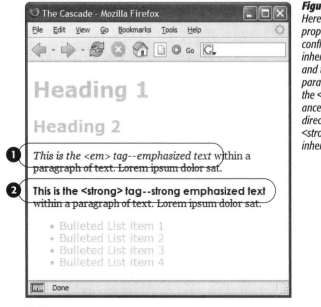

Figure 5-2:
Here's how Web browsers figure out which properties to display when inherited properties conflict: The <em> tag in the first paragraph (1) inherits the font-family from both the <body> tag and the paragraph. But since the body and paragraph have different fonts applied to them, the <em> tag uses the font specified for its closest ancestor—the <p> tag. When a style applies directly to a tag— the font-family is specified for the <strong> tag (2)—browsers ignore conflicting inherited properties.

browsers have their own predefined style for the <a> tag, so an inherited text color won't apply.

Tip: You can learn how to overcome preset tag styles, and change link colors to your heart's content. See page 212 for the solution.

One Tag, Many Styles

Inheritance is one way that a tag can be affected by multiple styles. But it's also possible to have multiple styles apply *directly* to a given tag. For example, say you have an external style sheet with a <p> tag style and attach it to a page that has an internal style sheet that *also* includes a <p> tag style. And just to make things really interesting, one of the <p> tags on the page has a class style applied to it. So for that one tag, three different styles directly format it. Which style—or *styles*—should the browser obey?

The answer: It depends. Based on the types of styles and where they come from, a browser may apply one or more of them at once. Here are a few situations in which multiple styles can apply to the same tag:

- **The tag has both a tag selector and a class style applied to it.** For example, a tag style for the <h2> tag, a class style named *.leadHeadline* and this HTML: <h2 class="leadHeadline">Your Future Revealed!</h2>. Both styles apply to this <h2> tag.

CSS: The Missing Manual

Note: Hold onto your hat if you're worried about what happens when these multiple styles conflict; details to follow.

- **The same style name appears more than once in the style sheet.** There could be a group selector (page 53) like *.leadHeadline, .secondaryHeadline, .newsHeadline* and the class style *.leadHeadline* in the same style sheet. (See the Note on page 53 for reasons why you'd want to do this.) Both of these rules define how any element with a class of *leadHeadline* looks.

- **A tag has both a class and an ID style applied to it.** Maybe it's an ID named *#banner*, a class named *.news*, and this HTML: <div id="banner" class="news">. Properties from both the *banner* and *news* styles apply to this <div> tag.

- **There's more than one style sheet containing the *same* style name attached to a page.** The same-named styles can arrive via @import, link, or an internal style sheet.

- **There are complex selectors targeting the same tag.** This situation's common when you use descendent selectors (page 49). For example, say you have a div tag in a page (like this: *<div id="mainContent">*) and inside the div is a paragraph with a class applied to it: *<p class="byline">*. The following selectors apply to this paragraph:

—#mainContent p

—#mainContent p.byline

—p.byline

—.byline

If more than one style applies to a particular element, then a Web browser combines the properties of all those styles, *as long as they don't conflict.* An example will make this concept clearer. Imagine you have a paragraph that lists the name of the Web page's author, including a link to his email address. The HTML might look like this:

```
<p class="byline">Written by <a href="mailto:jean@cosmofarmer.com">Jean
Graine de Pomme</a></p>
```

Meanwhile, the page's style sheet has three styles that format the link:

```
a { color: #6378df; }
p a { font-weight: bold }
.byline a { text-decoration: none; }
```

The first style turns all <a> tags powder blue; the second style makes all <a> tags that appear inside a <p> tag bold; and the third style removes the underline from any links that appear inside an element with the *byline* class applied to it.

All three styles apply to that very popular <a> tag, but since none of the properties are the same, there are no conflicts between the rules. The situation is similar to the inheritance example above (page 82): the styles combine to make one über-style containing all three properties, so this particular link appears powder blue, bold, *and* underline-free.

Note: Your head will really start to ache when you realize that this particular link's formatting can also be affected by inherited properties. For example, it would inherit any font-family that's applied to the paragraph. A few tools can help sort out what's going on in the cascade. (See the box on page 88.)

Specificity: Which Style Wins

The previous example is pretty straightforward. But what if the three styles listed on page 85 each had a *different* font specified for the *font-family* property? Which of the three fonts would a Web browser pay attention to?

As you know if you've been reading carefully so far, the cascade provides a set of rules that helps a Web browser sort out any property conflicts; namely, *properties from the most specific style win*. But as with the styles listed on page 85, sometimes it's not clear which style is most specific. Thankfully, CSS provides a formula for determining a style's *specificity* that's based on a value assigned to the style's selector—a tag selector, class selector, ID selector, and so on. Here's how the system works:

- A tag selector is worth **1 point**.

- A class selector is worth **10 points**.

- An ID selector is worth **100 points**.

- An inline style (page 35) is worth **1000 points**.

The bigger the number, the greater the specificity. So say you create the following three styles:

- a tag style for the <img> tag (specificity = 1)

- a class style named *.highlight* (specificity = 10)

- an ID style named *#logo* (specificity = 100)

Then, say your Web page has this HTML: *<img id="logo" class="highlight" src="logo.gif" />*. If you define the same property—such as the border property—in all three styles, then the value from the ID style (*#logo*) always wins out.

Note: A pseudo-element (like *:first-child* for example) is treated like a tag selector and is worth 1 point. A pseudo-class (*:link*, for example) is treated like a class and is worth 10 points. (See page 54 for the deal on these pseudo-things.)

Since descendent selectors are composed of several selectors—*#content p*, or *h2 strong*, for example—the math gets a bit more complicated. The specificity of a descendent selector is the total value of all of the selectors listed (see Figure 5-3).

selector	id	class	tag	total
p	0	0	1	1
.byline	0	1	0	10
p.byline	0	1	1	11
#banner	1	0	0	100
#banner p	1	0	1	101
#banner .byline	1	1	0	110
a:link	0	1	1	11
p:first-line	0	0	2	2
h2 strong	0	0	2	2
#wrapper #content .byline a:hover	2	2	1	221

Figure 5-3:
When more than one style applies to a tag, a Web browser must determine which style should "win out" in case style properties conflicts. In CSS, a style's importance is known as specificity and is determined by the type of selectors used when creating the style. Each type of selector has a different value, and when multiple selector types appear in one style— for example the descendent selector #banner p—the values of all the selectors used are added up.

Note: Inherited properties don't have any specificity. So even if a tag inherits properties from a style with a large specificity—like #banner—those properties will always be overridden by a style that directly applies to the tag.

The Tiebreaker: Last Style Wins

It's possible for two styles with conflicting properties to have the same specificity. ("Oh brother, when will it end?" Soon, comrade, soon. The tutorial's coming up.) A specificity tie can occur when you have the same selector defined in two locations. You may have a <p> tag selector defined in an internal style sheet and an external style sheet. Or two different styles may simply have equal specificity values. In case of a tie, the style appearing last in the style sheet wins.

Here's a tricky example using the following HTML:

```
<p class="byline">Written by <a class="email" href="mailto:jean@cosmofarmer.
com">Jean Graine de Pomme</a></p>
```

In the style sheet for the page containing the above paragraph and link, you have two styles:

```
p a.email { color: blue; }
p.byline a { color: red; }
```

Both styles have a specificity of 12 (10 for a class name and 2 for two tag selectors) and both apply to the <a> tag. The two styles are tied. Which color does the browser use to color the link in the above paragraph? Answer: Red, since it's the second (and last) style in the sheet.

FREQUENTLY ASKED QUESTION

Get a Little Help

My head hurts from all of this. Isn't there some tool I can use to help me figure out how the cascade's affecting my Web page?

Trying to figure out all the ins and outs of inherited properties and conflicting styles confuses many folks at first. Furthermore, doing the math to figure out a style's specificity isn't even your average Web designer's idea of fun, especially when there are large style sheets with lots of descendent selectors.

Fortunately, you have a few tools that can figure the cascade out for you. Dreamweaver 8 (*www.adobe.com*) includes a helpful CSS panel. A glance at it tells you which styles apply to any selected element and the end result of the cascade. In other words, you get an element's ultimate list of applied properties—its "Frankenstyle". A less expensive alternative is the dedicated CSS editor Style Master (*www.westciv.com/style_master/*). With Style Master, you can select an element from a Web page and see which styles apply to it, including the properties of each style.

Then there's the free Firefox extension, View Formatted Source (*https://addons.mozilla.org/extensions/moreinfo. php?application=firefox&id=697*). It lets you view which styles apply to a particular element (though it doesn't show you any of the inherited styles).

Mac fans may want to check out XyleScope (*www. culturedcode.com*). XyleScope lets you look at any page on the Web (or your hard drive) and determine, among other things, which properties (from inherited or directly applied styles) apply to a given selection on the page. Finally, a free choice for Mac folk is Apple's Web browser, Safari. A Web Inspector feature provides a wealth of information about a Web page, its CSS, and the effect of the cascade on the page's tags. It isn't available in the currently shipping versions of Safari, but the adventurous can download a "nightly build" (meaning a work-in-progress) of Safari to test this feature now: *http://webkit.opendarwin.org/blog/ ?p=41*.

Now suppose that the style sheet looked like this instead:

```
p.byline a { color: red; }
p a.email { color: blue; }
```

In this case, the link would be *blue*. Since *p a.email* appears after *p.byline a* in the style sheet, its properties win out.

What happens if you've got conflicting rules in an external and an internal style sheet? In that case, the placement of your style sheets (within your HTML file) becomes very important. If you first add an internal style sheet using the <style> tag (page 30) and *then* attach an external style sheet farther down in the HTML using the <link> tag (page 33), then the style from the external style sheet wins. (In effect, it's the same principle at work that you just finished reading about: *The style appearing last in the style sheet wins.*) The bottom line: Be consistent in how you place external style sheets. It's best to list any external style sheets first, and then include any internal styles.

Tip: Any external style sheets attached with the @import rule have to appear before internal styles within a <style> tag. See page 30 for more information on external and internal style sheets.

Overruling Specificity

CSS provides a way of overruling specificity entirely. You can use this trick when you absolutely, positively want to make sure that a particular property can't be overridden by a more specific style. Simply insert *!important* after any property to shield it from specificity-based overrides.

For example, consider the two following styles:

```
#nav a { color: red; }
a { color: teal !important; }
```

Normally, a link inside an element with the ID of #nav would be colored red since the *#nav a* style is much more specific than the *a* tag style.

However, including *!important* after a property value means that specific property always wins. So in the above example, all links on the page–including those inside an element with the #nav id–are teal.

Note that you apply *!important* to an individual property, not an entire style. Finally, when two styles both have *!important* applied to the same property, the more specific style's *!important* rule wins.

Internet Explorer 6 and earlier sometimes has trouble with *!important* rules, and occasionally completely ignores them.

Controlling the Cascade

As you can see, the more CSS styles you create, the greater the potential for formatting snafus. For example, you may create a class style specifying a particular font and font-size, but when you apply the style to a paragraph, nothing happens! This kind of problem is usually related to the cascade. Even though you may think that directly applying a class to a tag should apply the class's formatting properties, it may not if there's a style with greater specificity.

You have a couple of options for dealing with this kind of problem. First, you can use *!important* (as described in the box above) to make sure a property *always* applies. The *!important* approach is a bit heavy handed, though, since it's hard to predict that you'll never, ever, want to overrule an *!important* property someday. Read on for two other cascade-tweaking solutions.

Changing the Specificity

The top picture in Figure 5-4 is an example of a specific tag style losing out in the cascade game. Fortunately, most of the time, you can easily change the specificity of one of the conflicting styles and save *!important* for real emergencies. In Figure 5-4 (top), two styles format the first paragraph. The class style—*.intro*— isn't as specific as the *#sidebar p* style, so *.intro*'s properties don't get applied to the paragraph. To increase the specificity of the class, add the ID name to the style: *#sidebar .intro*.

Selective Overriding

You can also fine-tune your design by *selectively* overriding styles on certain pages. Say you've created an external style sheet named *global.css* that you've attached to each page in your site. This file contains the general look and feel for your site—

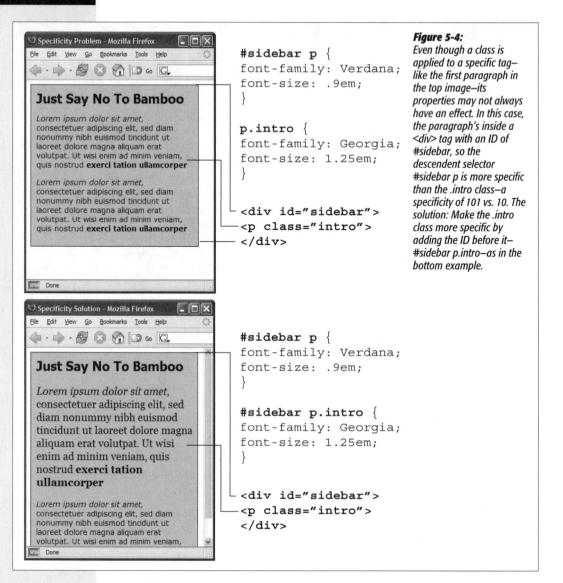

Figure 5-4:
Even though a class is applied to a specific tag— like the first paragraph in the top image—its properties may not always have an effect. In this case, the paragraph's inside a <div> tag with an ID of #sidebar, so the descendent selector #sidebar p is more specific than the .intro class—a specificity of 101 vs. 10. The solution: Make the .intro class more specific by adding the ID before it— #sidebar p.intro—as in the bottom example.

the font and color of <h1> tags, how form elements should look, and so on. But maybe on your home page, you want the <h1> tag to look slightly different than the rest of the site—bolder and bigger, perhaps. Or the paragraph text should be smaller on the home page so you can wedge in more information. In other words, you still want to use *most* of the styles from the *global.css* file, but you simply want to override a few properties for some of the tags (<h1>, <p>, and so on).

One approach is to simply create an internal style sheet listing the styles that you want to override. Maybe the *global.css* file has the following rule:

```
h1 {
    font-family: Arial, Helvetica, sans-serif;
```

```
    font-size: 24px;
    color: #000;
}
```

You want the <h1> tag on the home page to be bigger and red. So just add the following style in an internal style sheet on the home page:

```
h1 {
    font-size: 36px;
    color: red;
}
```

In this case, the <h1> tag on the home page would use the font Arial (from the external style sheet) but would be red and 36 pixels tall (from the internal style).

Tip: Make sure you attach the external style sheet *before* the internal style sheet in the <head> section of the HTML. This ensures that the styles from the internal style sheet win out in cases where the specificity of two styles are the same, as explained on page 87.

Another approach would be to create one more external style sheet—*home.css* for example—that you attach to the home page in addition to the *global.css* style sheet. The *home.css* file would contain the style names and properties that you want to overrule from the *global.css* file. For this to work, you need to make sure the *home. css* file appears *after* the *global.css* file in the HTML, like so:

```
<link rel="stylesheet" type="text/css" href="css/global.css">
<link rel="stylesheet" type="text/css" href="css/home.css">
```

Or, if you're using the @import method:

```
<style type="text/css">
@import url(css/global.css);
@import url(css/home.css);
</style>
```

Tip: Another way to fine-tune designs on a page-by-page basis is to use different ID names for the <body> tag of different types of pages—for example #review, #story, #home—and then create descendent selectors to change the way tags on these types of pages look. This technique's discussed on page 243.

Tutorial: The Cascade in Action

In this tutorial, you'll see how styles interact and how they can sometimes conflict to create unexpected results. First, you'll create two styles and see how some properties are inherited and how others are overruled by the cascade. Then you'll see how inheritance affects tags on a page, and how a browser resolves any CSS conflicts. Finally, you'll learn how to troubleshoot problems created by the cascade.

To get started, you need to download the tutorial files located on this book's companion Web site at *www.sawmac.com/css/*. Click the tutorial link and download the files. All of the files are enclosed in a ZIP archive, so you'll need to unzip them first. (Go to the Web site for detailed instructions on unzipping the files.) The files for this tutorial are contained inside the folder named *chapter_05*.

Creating a Hybrid Style

In this example, you'll create two styles. One style formats all the paragraphs of the page; and another, more specific style, reformats two paragraphs in a particular spot on the page.

1. **Using your favorite text or Web page editor, open the file *cascade.html* located in the *chapter_05* folder.**

   You'll start by creating an internal style sheet. (See pages 308 and 61 for more on internal and external style sheets and when to use which.)

2. **Click directly after the closing </title> tag. Press Enter (Return), and then type *<style type="text/css">*.**

   It's a good idea to write *both* the opening and closing style tags *before* you start adding styles. This will help you avoid the sometimes common problem of forgetting to add the closing style tag—a mistake that leads to all sorts of weird display problems in Web browsers.

3. **Press Enter (Return) twice, and then type *</style>*.**

   Now you'll add a basic tag style to format the paragraphs of text on the page.

4. **Place your cursor in the empty line between the opening and closing style tags. Type the following style:**

   ```
   p {
       font-family: Arial, Helvetica, sans-serif;
       font-size: .9em;
       line-height: 175%;
       color: #73AFB7;
   }
   ```

   The CSS line-height property sets the *leading* or space between lines of text. (See page 112 for more on this property.)

5. **Preview the page in a Web browser.**

   All of the paragraphs should be formatted using Arial, and a light blue color. There should also be a greater-than-usual amount of space between each line in a paragraph. That's the line-height property in action.

   Next, you'll create a style for the paragraphs that appear inside a special area of the page—a <div> tag with an ID of *note*. (The <div> is already part of the HTML of this page.)

6. **Return to your Web page editor, click directly after the end of the new <p> tag style, and press Enter (Return) to create an empty line. Add the following style:**

```
#note p {
    line-height: normal;
    color: #993366;
}
```

You've just created a descendent selector (page 49) that formats all <p> tags that appear *inside* of a tag with an ID of *note* applied to it. In other words, only the paragraphs that are inside the <div> on this page are affected by these instructions.

Notice that this style has two properties—line-height and color—that conflict with the instructions provided in the *p* style you created earlier. To see how a browser deals with this conflict, you'll preview the page.

7. **Preview the page once again in a Web browser.**

You'll notice that the two paragraphs that appear below the headline "Just Say No To Bamboo" are purple, and that the paragraphs are less spaced out than other paragraphs on the page. Their line-height's also smaller than the other paragraphs.

Because the *#note p* style is more *specific*, its properties are more important than the simple *p* style. So in the case where there's a conflict—the line-height and color—the *#note p* properties win out.

However, since *#note p* doesn't assign values to the font-family or font-size properties, those properties in the *p* tag style *are* applied to the two paragraphs. According to the rules of the cascade, properties from multiple styles—the *p* and *#note p* styles—combine to create a hybrid style.

Combining Cascading and Inheritance

CSS properties can accumulate or add-up due to inheritance as well. In other words, as a tag inherits properties from surrounding tags (its ancestors), those properties mix (and perhaps conflict) with styles purposely applied to the tag. You'll create a style that will be inherited by all the tags on the page, and you'll see how, in the case of conflicts, some properties from that style are ignored.

1. **Return to your Web page editor and the *cascade.html* file.**

You'll now add a new tag style for the <body> tag.

2. **Add the following style to the internal style sheet below the *#note p* style you just added:**

```
body {
    color: #000066;
    letter-spacing: 1px;
}
```

This sets an overall text color for the page, and adds one pixel of space between each letter, spreading the letters out a little on the page. Both these properties are inherited, so any tags inside the <body> tag will display these properties.

3. **Preview the page in a Web browser to see the effect (see Figure 5-5).**

Notice that the letters that appear in the headlines and paragraphs are spaced apart a small amount, creating an airy quality to the text. That's the effect of all of the tags inheriting the letter-spacing property.

However, the color property, although inherited by the paragraph tags, isn't applied to them because it conflicts with more specific rules—the color properties set in the *p* and *#note p* styles.

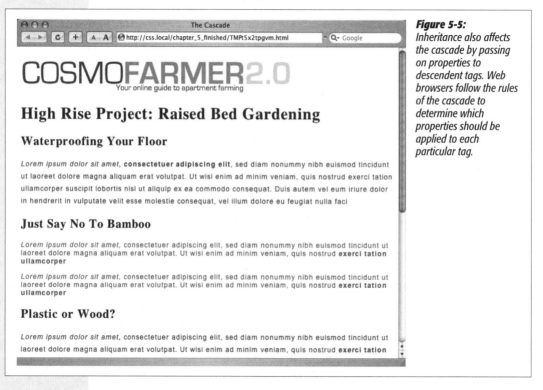

Figure 5-5:
Inheritance also affects the cascade by passing on properties to descendent tags. Web browsers follow the rules of the cascade to determine which properties should be applied to each particular tag.

As you can see, understanding exactly why a tag is formatted the way it is requires understanding of the cascade and inheritance, as well as a little bit of detective work to trace the origin of each property that a Web browser applies to a tag on the page. For example, the paragraphs inside the <div> tag are formatted using properties from three different styles (see Figure 5-6).

Overcoming Conflicts

Because of how CSS properties sometimes conflict when several styles apply to the same tag, you'll sometimes find your pages don't look exactly as you planned.

body *tag style*	~~color:#000066;~~ `letter-spacing: 1px;`

p
tag style
	`font-family:Arial, Helvetica, sans-serif;`
	`font-size: .9em;`
	~~line-height:175%;~~
	~~color: #73AFB7;~~

#sidebar p *descendent* *selector*	`line-height:normal;` `color: #993366;`

Figure 5-6:
Due to inheritance and the cascade, a single tag on a page can get its properties from multiple CSS styles, creating a hybrid style. The final appearance of the two paragraphs below the headline beginning "Just Say No" (see Figure 5-5) comes from properties of three styles listed in this diagram from least to most specific (top to bottom). The crossed-out properties are overridden by more specific styles.

When that happens you'll need to do a little work to find out why, and rejigger your CSS selectors to make sure the Cascade is working to produce the results you want.

1. **Return to your Web page editor and the *cascade.html* file.**

   You'll now create a new style that you'll use to highlight the introductory paragraph of the *#note* section.

2. **Add the following style to the internal style sheet below the body tag style you created on page 93:**

   ```
   .intro {
       font-weight: bold;
       color: #FF0000;
   }
   ```

   Next, you'll apply this class style to a tag.

3. **Locate the <p> tag that appears directly below *<h2>Just Say No To Bamboo</h2>*, and then add the following class attribute:**

   ```
   <p class="intro">
   ```

4. **Preview the page in a Web browser.**

   You'll notice that the paragraph turns bold, but the text color remains the same as the other paragraph inside the <div>.

   What gives? Following the rules of the cascade, *.intro* is a basic class selector, while the *#note p* is a descendent selector composed of both an ID and a tag name. These add up to create a more specific style, so its style properties overrule any conflict between it and the *.intro* style.

   In order to make the *.intro* style work, you'll need to give it a little juice by making its selector more powerful.

5. Return to the *cascade.html* file in your Web page editor and change the name of the style from *.intro* to *#note p.intro*.

Now you have a descendent selector composed of an ID, a tag, and a class. This style's more specific than *#note p* and its properties override those in any less specific style.

6. Preview the page in a Web browser.

Voila! The paragraph changes to bright red. If you didn't have a clear understanding of the cascade, you'd be scratching your head wondering why the color property didn't work.

In this and the previous four chapters, you've covered the basics of CSS. Now, in Part 2, it's time to take that knowledge and apply it to real design challenges, making Web pages look great.

Part Two:
Applied CSS

2

Formatting Text

Most Web sites still rely on words to get their messages across. Sure, people like to look at photos, movie clips, and Flash animations, but it's the reading material that keeps 'em coming back. People are hungry for news, gossip, how-to articles, recipes, FAQs, jokes, information lists, and other written content. With CSS, you can—and *should*—make your headlines and body text grab a visitor's attention as compellingly as any photo.

CSS offers a powerful array of text-formatting options, which let you assign fonts, color, sizes, line-spacing and many other properties that can add visual impact to headlines, bulleted lists, and regular old paragraphs of text (see Figure 6-1). This chapter reveals all, and then finishes up with a tutorial where you can practice assembling CSS text styles and put them to work on an actual Web page.

Formatting Text

The first thing you can do to make text on your Web site look more exciting is to apply different fonts to headlines, paragraphs, and other written elements on your pages. To apply a font to a CSS style, you use the *font-family* property:

```
font-family: Arial;
```

Note: In real life, when you put a CSS property into action, you must, of course, include all the other necessities of a complete style declaration block and style sheet, as described in Chapter 2: *p { font-family: Arial; }*, for example. When you see examples like font-family: Arial;, remember that's just the property in isolation, distilled down for your book-reading benefit.

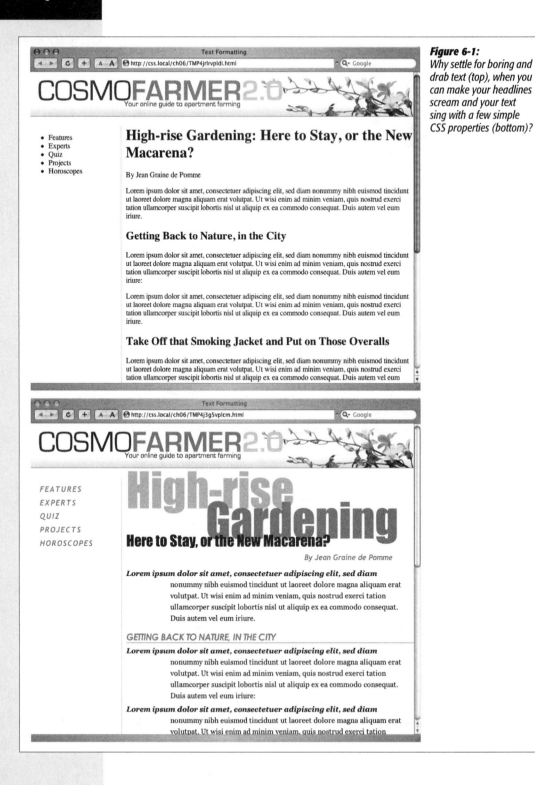

Figure 6-1:
Why settle for boring and drab text (top), when you can make your headlines scream and your text sing with a few simple CSS properties (bottom)?

Know Your Font Types

You can find literally tens of thousands of different fonts to express your every thought: from bookish, staid, and classical type faces to rounded, cartoonish squiggles. But almost all fonts fall into one of two categories: *serif* and *sans-serif*. Serif fonts are best for long passages of text, as it's widely believed that the serifs–those tiny "hands" and "feet" at the end of a letter's main strokes–gently lead the eye from letter to letter, making text easier to read. Examples of serif fonts are Times, Times New Roman, Georgia, and the font in the main body paragraphs of this book.

Sans-serif fonts, on the other hand, are often used for headlines, thanks to their clean and simple appearance. Examples of sans-serif fonts include Arial, Helvetica, Verdana, and Formata, which you're reading now. Some people believe that you should use *only* sans-serif fonts on Web pages because they think the delicate decorative strokes of serif fonts don't display well on the coarse resolution of a computer screen. In the end, your aesthetic judgment is your best guide. Pick the types of fonts you think look best.

Choosing a Font

Choose a font that makes your text eye-catching (especially if it's a headline) and readable (especially if it's main body text), as discussed in the box above. Unfortunately, you can't use just any font you want. Well, actually you *can* use any font you want, but it won't show up on a viewer's computer unless she's installed the same font on her system. So that handcrafted font you purchased from the small font boutique in Nome, Alaska, won't do you any good on the Web—unless each person viewing your site has also bought and installed that font. Otherwise, your visitors' Web browsers will show your text in a default font, which is usually some version of Times for body text, and Arial or Helvetica for headlines.

Tip: For one cutting edge method of using any font you'd like for headline text, there's a Flash-driven technique known as sIFR. Find out about it at *http://wiki.novemberborn.net/sifr*.

One solution's to specify the font you'd *like* to use, as well as a couple of back-up choices. If your viewer's computer has your first-choice font, then that's what she'll see. But when the first font isn't installed, the browser looks down the list until it finds a font that is. The idea is to specify a list of similar-looking fonts that are common to a variety of operating systems, like so:

```
font-family: Arial, Helvetica, sans-serif;
```

In this example, a Web browser first looks to see if the Arial font's installed; if it is, then that font's used; if not, the browser next looks for Helvetica, and if that isn't installed, then it finally settles for a generic font—sans-serif. (For more information on common Mac and PC fonts, see Figure 6-2.) When you list a generic font type (like sans-serif or serif), the viewer's browser gets to choose the actual font. But at least you can define its basic character. Here are some commonly used combinations, including a generic font type at the end of each list:

• Arial, Helvetica, sans-serif

• "Times New Roman", Times, serif

- "Courier New", Courier, monospace

- Georgia, "Times New Roman", Times, serif

- Verdana, Arial, Helvetica, sans-serif

- Geneva, Arial, Helvetica, sans-serif

- Tahoma, "Lucida Grande", Arial, sans-serif

- "Lucida Console", Monaco, monospace

- "Marker Felt", "Comic Sans MS", fantasy

- "Century Gothic", "Gill Sans", Arial, sans-serif

Note: When a font name's more than a single word, it must be enclosed by quotes like this: "Times New Roman".

Adding Color to Text

Black and white's great for *Casablanca* and Woody Allen films, but when it comes to text, a nice skyline blue looks much sharper and classier than drab black. Coloring your text with CSS is easy. In fact, you've used the *color* property in a few tutorials already. You have several different ways to define the exact color you want, but they all follow the same basic structure. You type *color:* followed by a color value:

```
color: #3E8988;
```

In this example, the color value is a hexadecimal number indicating a muted shade of teal (more in a moment on what hexadecimal is).

Every graphics program from Fireworks to Photoshop to GIMP lets you select a color using hexadecimal or RGB values. Also, the color pickers built into Windows and Macs let you use a color wheel or palette to select the perfect color and translate it into a hexadecimal or RGB value.

Tip: If your color design sense needs some help, you can find lots of attractive, coordinated collections of colors at *www.colorschemer.com/schemes/*.

Hexadecimal color notation

The most common color system used by Web designers is hexadecimal notation. A color value—like *#6600FF*—actually contains 3 hexadecimal numbers—in this example 66, 00, FF—each of which specify an amount of red, green, and blue, respectively. As in the RGB color system described next, the final color value is a blend of the amounts of red, green, and blue specified by these numbers.

Tip: You can shorten the hexadecimal numbers to just three characters if each set contains the same two numbers. For example, shorten #6600FF to #60F, or #FFFFFF to #FFF.

Internet Explorer 6/Windows XP Pro	Firefox 1.5/Mac OS X
Arial	Arial
Arial Black	**Arial Black**
Arial Narrow	Arial Narrow
Comic Sans MS	Comic Sans MS
	Courier
Courier New	Courier New
Century Gothic	Century Gothic
	Geneva
Georgia	Georgia
	Gill Sans
Helvetica	Helvetica
	Lucida Grande
Lucida Console	
	Marker Felt
	Monaco
Tahoma	Tahoma
Times	Times
Times New Roman	Times New Roman
Trebuchet MS	Trebuchet MS
Verdana	Verdana
✕ ⓘ ⚓ ⚔ ✦ (Webdings)	✕ ⓘ ⚓ ⚔ ✦ (Webdings)
sans-serif	sans-serif
serif	serif
monospace	monospace
FANTASY	fantasy

Figure 6-2:
While Mac and Windows used to come with very different sets of preinstalled fonts, there's been some convergence in the past few years. These days, you can count on the average Mac or PC to have the following fonts: Arial, Arial Black, Arial Narrow, Comic Sans MS, Courier New, Georgia, Times New Roman, Trebuchet MS, Verdana, and Webdings. If your audience includes Linux fans, then all bets are off, though Helvetica, Times, and Courier are safe bets. For a concise listing of fonts common to the two operating systems, check out www.ampsoft.net/webdesign-l/WindowsMacFonts.html.

RGB

You can also use the RGB—red, green, blue—method familiar in computer graphics programs. The color value consists of three numbers representing either percentages (0–100 percent) or numbers between 0–255 for each hue (red, green and blue). So when you want to set the text color to white (perhaps to set it off from an ominous dark page background), you can use this:

```
color: rgb(100%,100%,100%);
```

or

```
color: rgb(255,255,255);
```

Tip: If all these numbers and digits have your head spinning, then you can always fall back on the classic HTML color keywords. (Just don't expect your site to win any awards for originality.) There are 17 colors—aqua, black, blue, fuchsia, gray, green, lime, maroon, navy, olive, orange, purple, red, silver, teal, white, and yellow. In CSS, you add them to your style like so: *color: fuchsia;.*

Changing Font Size

Varying the size of text on a Web page is a great way to create visual interest and direct your visitors' attention to important areas of a page. Headlines in large type sizes capture your attention, while copyright notices displayed in small type subtly recede from prominence.

The *font-size* property sets text size. It's always followed by a unit of measurement, like so:

```
font-size: 1em;
```

The value and unit you specify for the font size (in this example, 1em) determine the size of the text. CSS offers a dizzying selection of sizing units: keywords, ems, exs, pixels, percentages, picas, points, even inches, centimeters and millimeters.

Units of measurement commonly used with printed materials—picas, points, inches, and so on—don't work well on Web pages because you can't predict how they'll look from one monitor to the next. But you may have occasion to use points when creating style sheets for printer-friendly pages, as described in Chapter 13 (page 365). Only a few of the measurement units—pixels, keywords, ems, and percentages—make sense when you're sizing text for a computer monitor. The rest of this section explains how they work.

Using Pixels

Varying Pixel values are the easiest to understand, since they're completely independent from any browser settings. When you specify, for example, a 36-pixel font size for an <h1> tag, the Web browser displays text that's 36 pixels tall, period. Web designers cherish pixel values because they provide consistent text sizes across different types of computers and browsers. (Well, not *all* Web designers. See the box on page 105 for one limitation of pixel sizing.)

To set a pixel value for the font-size property, type a number followed by the abbreviation *px*:

```
font-size: 36px;
```

Note: Don't include a space between the number and the unit type. For example, *36px* is correct, but *36 px* isn't.

The Problem with Pixels

It sounds like pixel values give me complete control over text size. Why bother using any other kind of text-sizing value?

Unfortunately, in Internet Explorer 6 (and earlier) for Windows, there's one serious limitation to pixel text sizes: The *viewer* gets no control over text size. Some people—especially those with limited eyesight—use IE's View → Text Size command to pump up text to a size that's easier to read. However, IE *won't* resize any text that's sized with a pixel value. IE adheres to what the designer wants, with no concern for the person behind the wheel of the browser.

Whether or not to use pixel values is something of a holy war in Web design circles. Many Web developers believe pixel-sized text creates an *accessibility issue*. That is, it potentially limits access to your site for people with disabilities.

Internet Explorer 7, like most other Web browsers currently available, *does* let you resize pixel-sized text. As IE 7 becomes more popular, you'll be able to use pixel values without worrying about the limitations of IE 6.

Meanwhile, the best you can do is consider your audience. If you're creating a site that's aimed at older folks or destined for use in schools, then use one of the resizable text options like keywords, ems, or percentages. Anywhere you're likely to find a combination of older computers and people with special needs, make accessibility more of a priority.

Using Keywords, Percentages, and Ems

Three ways of sizing text with CSS—keywords, percentages, and ems—work by either adding to or subtracting from the text size already on the viewer's browser screen. In other words, if you don't specify a size for text using CSS, a Web browser falls back on its pre-programmed settings. In most browsers, text inside a non-header tag's displayed 16 pixels tall—that's called the *base text size*.

Web surfers can adjust their browsers by pumping up or dropping down that base size. In Internet Explorer, for example, you can choose View → Text Size and select an option such as Larger or Smaller to adjust the text size on the screen; in Firefox, it's View → Text Size → Increase (or Decrease); and in Safari the menu options are View → Make Text Smaller and View → Make Text Bigger.

When you resize text with CSS, the browser takes the base text size (whether it's the original 16 pixels or some other size the viewer ordered) and adjusts it up or down according to your keyword, em, or percentage value.

Keywords

CSS provides seven keywords which let you assign a size that's relative to the base text size: *xx-small*, *x-small*, *small*, *medium*, *large*, *x-large*, and *xx-large*. The CSS looks like this:

```
font-size: large;
```

The medium option's the same as the browser's base font size. Each of the other options decreases or increases the size by a factor of 1.2. For example, say the base text size is 16 pixels. Setting the font size to *large* makes the text 19 pixels, while a setting of small sets it to 13 pixels. If your visitor adjusts the text size, *large* simply multiplies that size by 1.2, whatever it may be. Some eagle-eyed nerdlington could choose View → Text Size → Smaller to really cram a lot of fine print on the screen. Your *large* setting boosts his 13-point text to a healthy 16—not exactly large, but still bigger than any base-sized text on the same page.

Keywords are pretty limited: You have only seven choices. When you want more control over the size of your text, turn to one of the other font-sizing options discussed next.

Note: Due to a bug in Internet Explorer 5 for Windows, using these keywords results in text that displays one size smaller than in other browsers. For example, *small* comes out as *x-small* in IE 5. (To defeat this bug, check out the section called "Setting the font size" on this Web page: *http://simon.incutio.com/archive/2003/05/20/defeatingIE5*.)

Percentages

Like keywords, percentage values adjust text in relationship to the font size defined by the browser, but they give you much finer control than just *large, x-large,* and so on. Every browser has a pre-programmed base text size, which in most browsers is 16 pixels. You can adjust this base size in your browser through the browser's Options (or Preferences) or via the View menu (see page 105). Whatever setting's been chosen, the base text size for a particular browser's equivalent to 100 percent. In other words, for most browsers, setting the CSS percentage to 100 percent is the same as setting it to 16 pixels.

Say you want to make a particular headline appear 2 times the size of average text on a page. You simply set the font size to 200 percent, like so:

```
font-size: 200%;
```

Or, when you want the text to be slightly smaller than the default size, use a value like 90% to shrink the font size down a bit.

The above examples are pretty straightforward, but here's where it gets a little tricky: Font size is an inherited property (see Chapter 4), meaning that any tags inside of a tag that has a font size specified inherit that font size. So the exact size of 100 percent can change if a tag inherits a font-size value.

For example, at the lower-left of Figure 6-3, there's a <div> tag that has its font size set to 200 percent. That's two times the browser's base text size, or 32 pixels. All tags inside that <div> inherit that text size and use it as the basis for calculating their text sizes. In other words, for tags inside that <div>, 100 percent is 32 pixels. So the <h1> tag inside the <div> that has a font size of 100 percent displays at two times the base-text size for the page, or 32 pixels.

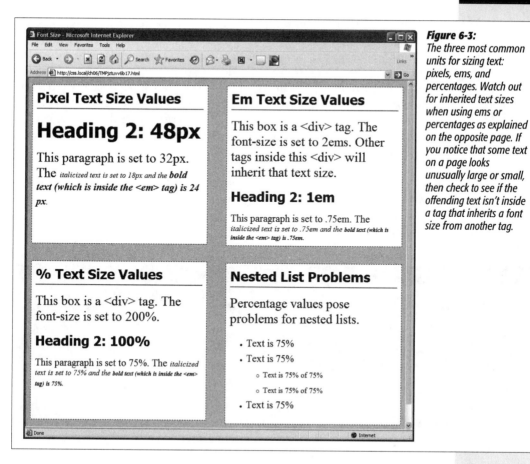

Figure 6-3:
The three most common units for sizing text: pixels, ems, and percentages. Watch out for inherited text sizes when using ems or percentages as explained on the opposite page. If you notice that some text on a page looks unusually large or small, then check to see if the offending text isn't inside a tag that inherits a font size from another tag.

Ems

Once you understand percentages, you know everything you need to understand ems. The two work exactly the same way, but many Web designers use ems because of its roots in typography.

The word *em* comes from the world of printed (as in paper) typography, where it refers to the size of a capital letter M for a particular font. As it's worked its way into the Web world, an em in CSS no longer means the same thing as in typography. Think of it as referring to the base text size. That is, a value of 1em means the same thing as a value of 100 percent as described in the previous section. You can even say it the opposite way: A percentage value is just an em multiplied by 100: .5em is 50 percent, .75em is 75 percent, 3em is 300 percent and so on.

For example, this CSS does the exact same thing as *font-size: 200%;* (opposite page).

```
font-size: 2em;
```

Note: As with pixel values, there's no space between the number and the word *em*. Also, even if you specify more than one em, you never add an *s* to the end: *2.5em*, never *2.5ems*.

When it comes to inheritance, ems also work just like percentage values. See the upper right of Figure 6-3 for an example. The bottom paragraph's set to .75em, which, since the <p> tag inherits the 2em (32 pixel) setting from the <div> tag, works out to .75 × 32, or 24 pixels. Inside the <p> tag are two other tags that also have a font-size setting of .75em. The innermost tag, a <strong> tag is set to .75em or, in essence, 75 percent of its *inherited* size. There's a lot of math to this one: 32 pixels (inherited from the <div> tag) × .75 (inherited from the <p> tag) × .75 (inherited from the <em> tag) × .75 (the <strong> tag's own font size). The result of this brainteaser is a text size of roughly 14 pixels.

Note: Internet Explorer 6 and earlier sometimes has problems displaying text when only em units are used. You have two ways around this: Either stick with percentage values, or set the font size for the body of the page to a percentage and then use em units to size other text. For some mysterious reason, this trick seems to fix the bugs in IE.

WORKAROUND WORKSHOP

Untangling the Nest

Inherited font-size values can cause problems for nested lists. (See the bottom-right square of Figure 6-3.) If you create a style like *ul { font-size: 75% }*, then a nested list, which is a <ul> tag inside of another <ul> tag, is set to 75 percent of 75 percent—making the text in the nested list smaller than the rest of the list.

To get around this conundrum, create an additional descendent selector style (page 49) like this: *ul ul {font-size: 100%}*. This style sets any ul tag inside of a ul to 100 percent; in other words, 100 percent of the surrounding ul tag's font size. In this example, it keeps any nested lists to 75 percent.

Tip: You can make type stand out on a page in many different ways. Making certain words larger than others, or making some text darker, lighter, or brighter visually sets them apart from the surrounding text. Contrast is one of the most important principles to good graphic design; it can help highlight important messages, guide a reader's eye around a page, and generally make understanding a page easier. For a quick overview of typographic contrast, check out this page: *www.creativepro.com/story/feature/19877.html.*

Formatting Words and Letters

Although you'll spend a lot of time fine-tuning the color, size, and fonts of the text on your Web pages, CSS also lets you apply other common text formatting properties (like bold and italics) as well as some less common ones (like small caps and letter spacing).

Tip: CSS lets you combine multiple text properties, but don't get carried away. Too much busy formatting makes your page harder to read. Worst of all, your hard work loses its impact.

Italicizing and Bolding

Web browsers display type inside the <em> and <i> tags in *italicized* type, and text inside the <strong>, <b>, <th> (table header), and header tags (<h1>, and so on) in **bold** type. But you can control these settings yourself—either turn off bold for a headline, or italicize text that normally isn't—using the *font-style* and *font-weight* properties.

To italicize text, add this to a style:

```
font-style: italic;
```

Alternatively, you can make sure text *isn't* italicized, like so:

```
font-style: normal;
```

Note: The font-style property actually has a third option–*oblique*–which works identically to *italic*.

The font-weight property lets you make text bold or not. In fact, according to the rules of CSS, you can actually specify nine numeric values (100-900) to choose subtle gradations of boldness (from super-extra-heavy [900] to ultra-nearly-invisible-light [100]). Of course, the fonts you use must have 9 different weights for these values to have any visible effect for your Web site's visitors. And since there aren't any fonts that work this way with Web browsers yet, you have far fewer options for this property to worry about. So, for now, to make text bold:

```
font-weight: bold;
```

And to make text un-bold:

```
font-weight: normal;
```

Tip: Since headlines are already displayed as bold type, you may want to find another way of highlighting a word or words that are strongly emphasized or bolded inside a headline. Here's one way:

```
h1 strong { color: #3399FF; }
```

This descendent selector changes the color of any <strong> tags (usually displayed as bold) that appear inside a <h1> tag.

Capitalizing

Capitalizing text is pretty easy—just hit the caps lock key and start typing, right? But what if you want to capitalize every heading on a page, and the text you've copied and pasted from a Word document is lowercase? Rather than retyping the headline, turn to the CSS *text-transform* property. With it, you can make text all uppercase, all lowercase, or even capitalize the first letter of each word (for titles and headlines). Here's an example:

```
text-transform: uppercase;
```

For the other two options, just use *lowercase;* or *capitalize;*.

Because this property is inherited, a tag that's nested inside a tag with *text-transform* applied to it gets the same uppercase, lowercase, or capitalized value. To tell CSS *not* to change the case of text, use the *none* value:

```
text-transform: none;
```

Small caps

For more typographic sophistication, you can also turn to the *font-variant* property, which lets you set type as small-caps. In small cap style, lowercase letters appear as slightly downsized capital letters, like so: POMP AND CIRCUMSTANCE. While difficult to read for long stretches of text, small caps lend your page an old-world, bookish gravitas when used on headlines and captions. To create small-cap text:

```
font-variant: small-caps;
```

Decorating

CSS also provides the *text-decoration* property to add various enhancements to text. With it, you can add lines over, under, or through the text (see Figure 6-4), or for real giggles you can make the text blink like a No Vacancy sign. Use the text-decoration property by adding one or more of the following keywords: *underline, overline, line-through,* or *blink.* For example, to underline text:

```
text-decoration: underline;
```

You can also combine multiple keywords for multiple effects. Here's how to add a line over and under some text:

```
text-decoration: underline overline;
```

But just because you *can* add these not-so-decorative decorations to text, doesn't mean you should. For one thing, anyone who's used the Web for any length of time instinctively associates any underlined text with a link and tries to click it. So it's not a good idea to underline words that aren't part of a link. And the *blink* property is like a neon sign crying "Amateur! Amateur! Amateur!"

Tip: You can get a similar effect to underlining and overlining by adding a border to the bottom or top of an element (see page 141). The big advantage of borders is that you can control their placement, size, and color to create a more attractive design that doesn't look like a link.

The *overline* option simply draws a line above text, while *line-through* draws a line right through the center of text. Some designers use this strike-through effect to indicate an edit on a page where text has been removed from the original manuscript. Coupled with the *a:visited* selector, you can also create a cool effect where previously visited links are crossed out like a shopping list.

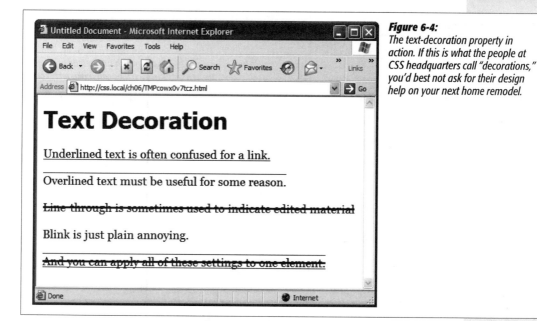

Figure 6-4:
The text-decoration property in action. If this is what the people at CSS headquarters call "decorations," you'd best not ask for their design help on your next home remodel.

Finally, you can turn off all decorations by using the *none* keyword like this:

```
text-decoration: none;
```

Why do you need a text-decoration property that removes decorations? The most common example is removing the line that appears under a link. (See page 212.)

Letter and Word Spacing

Another way to make text stand out from the crowd is to adjust the space that appears between letters or words (see Figure 6-5). Reducing the space between letters using the CSS *letter-spacing* property can tighten up headlines making them seem even bolder and heavier while fitting more letters on a single line. Conversely, increasing the space can give headlines a calmer, more majestic quality. To reduce the space between letters, you use a negative value like this:

```
letter-spacing: -1px;
```

A positive value adds space between letters:

```
letter-spacing: 10px;
```

Likewise, you can open up space (or remove space) between words using the *word-spacing* property. This property makes the space wider (or narrower) without actually affecting the words themselves:

```
word-spacing: 2px;
```

With either of these properties, you can use any type of measurement you'd use for text sizing—pixels, ems, percentages—with either positive or negative values.

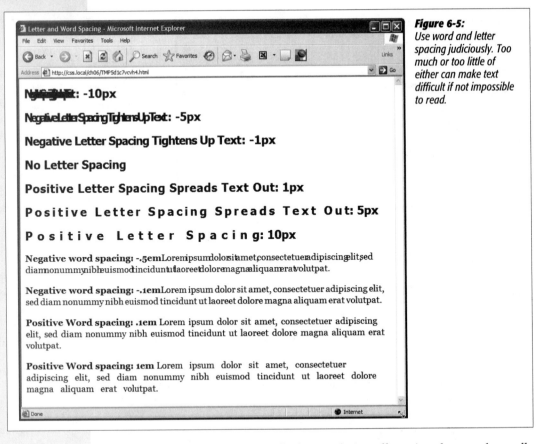

Figure 6-5:
Use word and letter spacing judiciously. Too much or too little of either can make text difficult if not impossible to read.

Unless you're going for some really far-out design effect—in other words, totally unreadable text—keep your values small. Too high a negative value, and letters and words overlap. To keep the message of your site clear and legible, use both letter and word spacing with care.

Formatting Entire Paragraphs

Rather than individual words, some CSS properties apply to chunks of text. You can use the properties in this section on complete paragraphs, headlines, and so on.

Adjusting the Space Between Lines

In addition to changing the space between words and letters, CSS lets you adjust the space between lines of text using the *line-height* property. The bigger the line height, the more space that appears between each line of text (see Figure 6-6).

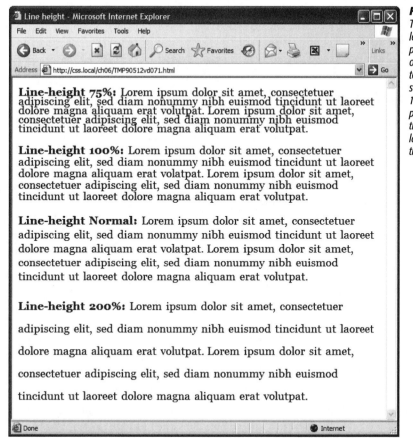

Figure 6-6:
*The line-height property
lets you spread a
paragraph's lines apart
or bring them closer
together. The normal
setting is equivalent to
120 percent, so a smaller
percentage tightens up
the lines (top), while a
larger percentage pushes
them apart (bottom).*

Line spacing by pixel, em, or percentage

Just as with the font-size property, you can use pixels, ems, or percentages to set
the size of line height:

```
line-height: 150%;
```

In general, percentages or ems are better than pixels, because they change according to, and along with, the text's font-size property. If you set the line height to 10
pixels, and then later adjust the font size to something much larger (like 36 pixels), because the line height remains at 10 pixels, then your lines overlap. However, using a percentage (150 percent, say) means the line-height spacing adjusts
proportionally whenever you change the font-size value.

The normal line-height setting for a browser is 120 percent. So, when you want to
tighten up the line spacing, use a value less than 120 percent. To spread lines apart,
use a value greater than 120 percent.

Note: To determine the amount of space that appears between lines of text, a Web browser subtracts the font size from the line height. The result—called *leading*—is the amount of space between lines in a paragraph. Say the font size is 12 pixels, and the line height (set to 150 percent) works out to 18 pixels. 18 minus 12 equals 6 pixels, so the browser adds 6 pixels of space between each line.

Line spacing by number

CSS offers one other measurement method specific to line height, which is simply a number. You write it like this:

```
line-height: 1.5;
```

There's no unit (like em or px) after this value. The browser multiplies this number by the font size to determine the line height. So if the text is 1em and the line-height value's 1.5, then the calculated line height is 1.5em. In most cases, the effect's no different from specifying a value of 1.5em or 150 percent. But sometimes this multiplication factor comes in handy, especially since nested tags inherit the line-height value of their parents.

For example, say you set the line-height property of the <body> tag to 150 percent. All tags inside the page would inherit that value. However, it's not the percentage that's inherited; it's the *calculated* line-height. So, say the font size for the page is set to 10 pixels; 150 percent of 10 is 15 pixels. Every tag would inherit a line-height of 15 pixels, not 150 percent. So if you happened to have a paragraph with large, 36 pixel text, then its line-height—15 pixels—would be much smaller than the text, making the lines squish together in a hard-to-read mess.

In this example, instead of using a line-height of 150 percent applied to the <body> tag, you could have all tags share the same basic proportional line-height by setting the line-height to 1.5. Every tag, instead of inheriting a precise pixel value for line height, simply multiplies its font size by 1.5. So in the above example of a paragraph with 36 pixel text, the line-height would be 1.5 × 36 or 54 pixels.

Aligning Text

One of the quickest ways to change the look of a Web page is with paragraph alignment. Using the *text-align* property, you can center a paragraph on a page, align the text along its left or right edge, or justify both left and right edges (like the paragraphs in this book). Normally, text on a page is left aligned, but you may want to center headlines to give them a formal look. Languages that read from right to left, like Hebrew and Arabic, require right-alignment. To change the alignment of text, use any of the following keywords—*left*, *right*, *justify*, *center*:

```
text-align: center;
```

Justified text looks great on a printed page—mainly because the fine resolution possible with printing allows for small adjustments in spacing. This fine spacing prevents large, unsightly gaps or rivers of white space flowing through the paragraphs. Web pages are limited to much coarser spacing because of the generally

A Shorthand Method for Text Formatting

Writing one text property after another gets tiring, especially when you want to use several different text properties at once. Fortunately, CSS offers a shorthand property called *font*, which lets you combine the following properties into a single line: font-style (page 109), font-variant (page 110), font-weight (page 109), font-size (page 109), line-height (page 112) and font-family (page 101). For example, the declaration *font: italic bold small-caps 18px/150% Arial, Helvetica, sans-serif;* creates bold, italicized type in small caps, using 18px Arial (or Helvetica or sans-serif) with a line height of 150 percent. Keep these rules in mind:

- You don't have to include every one of these properties, but you *must* include the font size and font family: *font: 1.5em Georgia, Times, serif;*.

- Use a single space between each property value. You use a comma only to separate fonts in a list like this: *Arial, Helvetica, sans-serif*.

- When specifying the line height, add a slash after the font size followed by the line-height value, like this: *1.5em/150% or 24px/37px*.

- The last two properties must be font-size (or *font-size/line-height*) followed by font-family, in that order. All the other properties may be written in any order. For example both *font: italic bold small-caps 1.5em Arial;* and *font: bold small-caps italic 1.5em Arial;* are the same.

Finally, omitting a value from the list is the same as setting that value to normal. Say you created a <p> tag style that formatted all paragraphs in bold, italics, and small caps with a line height of 2000 percent (not that you'd actually *do* that). If you then created a class style named, say, *.specialParagraph* with the following font declaration *font: 1.5em Arial;* and applied it to one paragraph on the page, then that paragraph would *not* inherit the italics, bold, small caps, or line-height. Omitting those four values in the *.specialParagraph* style is the same as writing this: *font: normal normal normal 1.5em/normal Arial;*.

low-resolution of monitors. So when you use the *justify* option, the space between words can vary significantly from line to line, making the text harder to read. When you want to use the *justify* option on your Web pages, test it thoroughly to make sure the text is attractive and readable.

Indenting the First Line and Removing Margins

In many books, the first line of each paragraph is indented. This first-line indent marks the beginning of a paragraph when there are no spaces separating paragraphs. On the Web, however, paragraphs don't have indents but are instead separated by a bit of space—like the paragraphs in this book.

If you have a hankering to make your Web pages look less like other Web pages and more like a handsomely printed book, take advantage of the CSS *text-indent* and *margin* properties. With them, you can add a first-line indent and remove (or increase) the margins that appear at the beginning and ends of paragraphs.

First-line indents

You can use pixel and em values to set the first-line indent like this:

```
text-indent: 25px;
```

or

```
text-indent: 5em;
```

A pixel value's an absolute measurement—a precise number of pixels—while an em value specifies the number of letters (based on the current font size) you want to indent.

Tip: You can use negative text-indent values to create what's called a *hanging indent* where the first line starts further to the left than the other lines in the paragraph. (Think of it as "hanging" off the left edge.)

You can also use a percentage value, but with the *text-indent* property, percentages take on a different meaning than you've seen before. In this case, percentages aren't related to the font size; they're related to the width of the element containing the paragraph. For example, if the text-indent is set to 50 percent, and a paragraph spans the entire width of the Web browser window, then the first-line of the paragraph starts half the way across the screen. If you resize the window, both the width of the paragraph and its indent change. (You'll learn more about percentages and how they work with the width of elements on page 146.)

Controlling margins between paragraphs

Many designers hate the space that every browser throws in between paragraphs. Before CSS, there was nothing you could do about it. Fortunately, you can now tap into the *margin-top* and *margin-bottom* properties to remove (or, if you wish, expand) that gap. To totally eliminate a top and bottom margin, write this:

```
margin-top: 0;
margin-bottom: 0;
```

To eliminate the gaps between *all* paragraphs on a page, create a style like this:

```
p {
    margin-top: 0;
    margin-bottom: 0;
}
```

As with text-indent, you can use pixel or em values to set the value of the margins. You can also use percentages, but as with text-indent, the percentage is related to the *width* of the paragraph's containing element. Because it's confusing to calculate the space above and below a paragraph based on its width, it's easier to stick with either em or pixel values.

Tip: Because not all browsers treat the top and bottom margin of headlines and paragraphs consistently, it's often a good idea to simply *zero out* (that is, eliminate) all margins at the beginning of a style sheet. To see how this works, turn to page 390.

For a special effect, you can assign a *negative* value to a top or bottom margin. For example a -10px top margin moves the paragraph up 10 pixels, perhaps even visually overlapping the page element above it. (See the main headline in Figure 6-1 for an example.)

Formatting the First Letter or First Line of a Paragraph

CSS also provides a way of formatting just a part of a paragraph using the *:first-letter* and *:first-line* pseudo-elements. Technically, these aren't CSS properties, but types of selectors (page 54) that determine what part of a paragraph CSS properties should apply to. With the *:first-letter* pseudo-element, you can create an initial capital letter to simulate the look of a hand-lettered manuscript. To make the first letter of each paragraph bold and red you could write this style:

```
p:first-letter {
    font-weight: bold;
    color: red;
}
```

To be more selective and format just the first letter of a particular paragraph, you can apply a class style to the paragraph—*.intro*, for example—and create a style with a name like this: *.intro:first-letter*.

The *:first-line* pseudo element formats the initial line of a paragraph (see Figure 6-7). You can apply this to any block of text like a heading (*h2:first-line*) or paragraph (*p:first-line*). As with *:first-letter,* you can apply a class to just one paragraph and format only the first line of that paragraph. Say you wanted to capitalize every letter in the first line of the first paragraph of a page. Apply a class to the HTML of the first paragraph—*<p class="intro">*—and then create a style like this:

```
.intro:first-line { text-transform: uppercase; }
```

Styling Lists

The <ul> and <ol> tags create bulleted and numbered lists, like lists of related items or numbered steps. But you don't always want to settle for the way Web browsers automatically format those lists. You may want to swap in a more attractive bullet, use letters instead of numbers, or even completely eliminate the bullets or numbers.

Types of Lists

Most Web browsers display unordered lists (<ul> tags) using round bullets, and numbered lists (<ol> tags) using...well...numbers. With CSS, you can choose from among three types of bullets—*disc* (a solid round bullet), *circle* (a hollow round bullet), or *square* (a solid square). There are also six different numbering

Figure 6-7:
The :first-letter pseudo element formats the first letter of the styled element, like the "initial caps" to the left.

The :first-line selector, on the other hand, styles the first line of a paragraph. Even if your guest resizes the window (bottom), the browser still styles every word that appears on a paragraph's first line.

schemes—*decimal, decimal-leading-zero, upper-alpha, lower-alpha, upper-roman,* or *lower-roman* (see Figure 6-8). You select all these options using the *list-style-type* property, like so:

```
list-style-type: square;
```

or

```
list-style-type: upper-alpha;
```

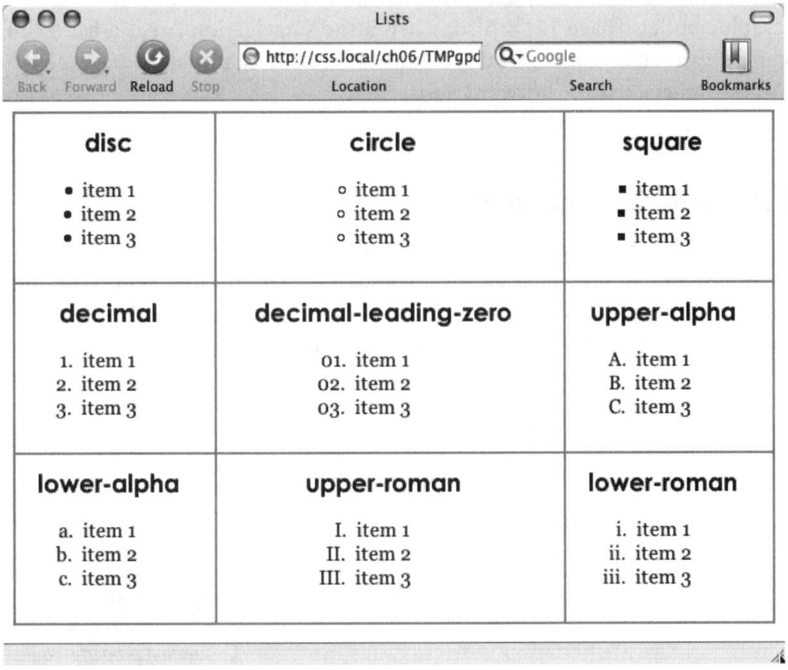

Figure 6-8:
Many Web browsers display the decimal and decimal-leading-zero options identically. Firefox and other Mozilla-based browsers like Camino (pictured here) correctly display the decimal-leading-zero setting by adding a 0 before single digit-numbers—01, for example.

Tip: If you feel like rushing a fraternity or sorority, you can also replace numbers with Greek letters—α, β, γ—using the *lower-greek* option.

Most of the time, you use this property on a style that's formatting an <ol> or <ul> tag. Typical examples include an *ol* or *ul* tag style—*ul { list-style-type: square; }*—or a class you're applying to one of those tags. However, you can also apply the property to an individual list item (<li> tag) as well. You can even apply different types of bullet styles to items within the same list. For example, you can create a style for a <ul> tag that sets the bullets to *square*, but then create a class named *.circle* that changes the bullet type to *circle*, like this:

```
.circle { list-style-type: circle; }
```

You can then apply the class to every other item in the list to create an alternating pattern of square and circular bullets:

```
<ul>
<li>Item 1</li>
<li class="circle">Item 2</li>
<li>Item 3</li>
<li class="circle">Item 4</li>
</ul>
```

At times you'll want to completely hide bullets, like when you'd rather use your own graphic bullets (page 121). Also, when a site's navigation bar is a list of links, you can use an <ul> list, but hide its bullets (see the example on page 218). To turn off the bullets, use the keyword *none*:

```
list-style-type: none;
```

Positioning Bullets and Numbers

Web browsers usually display bullets or numbers hanging to the left of the list item's text (Figure 6-9, left). With CSS, you can control the position of the bullet (somewhat) using the *list-style-position* property. You can either have the bullet appear *outside* of the text (the way browsers normally display bullets) or *inside* the text block itself (Figure 6-9, right):

```
list-style-position: outside;
```

or

```
list-style-position: inside;
```

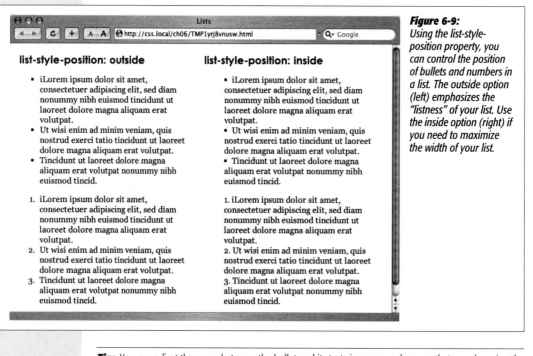

Figure 6-9:
Using the list-style-position property, you can control the position of bullets and numbers in a list. The outside option (left) emphasizes the "listness" of your list. Use the inside option (right) if you need to maximize the width of your list.

Tip: You can adjust the space between the bullet and its text—increase or decrease that gap—by using the *padding-left* property (see page 135). To use it, you create a style that applies to the <li> tags. This technique works only if you set the list-style-position property to the *outside* option (or don't use list-style-position at all).

In addition, if you don't like how Web browsers indent a list from the left edge, then you can remove that space by setting both the margin-left and padding-left properties to 0 for the list. To remove the indent from all lists, you could create this group selector:

```
ul, ol {
    padding-left: 0;
    margin-left: 0;
}
```

Or, you could create a class style with those properties and apply it to a particular <ul> or <ol> tag. The reason you need to set both the padding and margin properties is because some browsers use padding (Firefox, Mozilla, Safari) and some use margin (Internet Explorer) to control the indent. (You'll learn more about the margin and padding properties in the next chapter.)

Browsers normally display one bulleted item directly above another, but you can add space between list items using the margin-top or margin-bottom properties on the particular list items. These properties work for spacing list items exactly as for spacing paragraphs, as explained on page 116. You just need to make sure that the style applies to the <li> tags by creating a class style and applying it individually to each <li> tag. Or, better yet, create an <li> tag style or descendent selector. The style should *not* apply to the <ul> or <ol> tag. Adding margins to the top or bottom of those tags simply increases the space between the list and the paragraphs above or below it—not the space between each item in the list.

Graphic Bullets

If you're not happy with squares and circles for your bullets, create your own. Using an image-editing program like Photoshop or Fireworks, you can quickly create colorful and interesting bullets. Clip art collections and most symbol fonts (like Webdings) provide great inspiration.

Tip: You can also find many examples of bullets on the Web. Go to *www.stylegala.com/features/bulletmadness/* to find over 200 free bullet icons.

The CSS *list-style-image* property lets you specify a path to a graphic on your site, much as you'd specify a file when adding an image to a page using the *src* attribute of the HTML <img> tag. You use the property like this:

```
list-style-image: url(images/bullet.gif);
```

The term *url* and the parentheses are required. The part inside the parentheses—*images/bullet.gif* in this example—is the path to the graphic. Notice that, unlike HTML, you don't use quotation marks around the path.

FREQUENTLY ASKED QUESTION

Customizing List Bullets and Numbers

I'd like the numbers in my numbered lists to be bold and red instead of boring old black. How do I customize bullets and numbers?

CSS gives you a few ways to customize the markers that appear before list items. For bullets, you can use your own graphics as described on page 121. You have two other techniques available: one that's labor intensive, but works on most browsers, and one that's super geeky, cutting-edge, and doesn't work on Internet Explorer 6 for Windows or earlier.

First, the labor-intensive way. Say you want the numbers in an ordered list to be red and bold, but the text to be plain, unbolded black. Create a style that applies to the list—like a class style you apply to the <ol> or <li> tags—with a text color of red, and the font weight set to bold. At this point, everything in the list—text included—is red and bold.

Next, create a class style—*.regularList*, for example—that sets the font color to black and font weight to normal (that is, not bold). Then (and this is the tedious part), wrap a <span> tag around the text in each list item and apply the class style to it. For example: *<li><span class="regularList">Item 1</span></li>*. Now the bullets are bold and red and the text is black and normal. Unfortunately, you have to add that <span> to *every* list item!

The cool, "I'm so CSS-savvy," way is to use what's called *generated content.* Basically, generated content's just stuff that isn't actually typed on the page, but is added by the Web browser when it displays the page. A good example is bullets themselves. You don't type bullet characters when you create a list; the browser adds them for you. With CSS, you can have a browser add content and even style that content, before each <li> tag. For an introduction to generated content, visit *www.richinstyle.com/guides/generated2.html.* The official (read: technical and confusing description) is at *www.w3.org/TR/REC-CSS2/generate.html.*

Note: When specifying a graphic in an *external* style sheet, the path to the image is relative to the style sheet file, not the Web page. You'll learn more about how this works on page 172, as you start to use images with CSS.

While the list-style-image property lets you use a graphic for a bullet, it doesn't provide any control over its placement. The bullet may appear too far above or below the line, requiring you to tweak the bullet graphic until you get it just right. A better approach—one you'll learn in Chapter 8—is to use the *background-image* property. That property lets you very accurately place a graphic for your bulleted lists.

Tip: As with the *font* property (see the box on page 115), there's a shorthand method of specifying list properties. The *list-style* property can include a value for each of the other list properties—list-style-image, list-style-position, and list-style-type. For example, *ul { list-style: circle inside; }* would format unordered lists with the hollow circle bullet on the inside position. When you include both a style type and style image—*list-style: circle url(images/bullet.gif) inside;*—Web browsers use the style type circle in this example—if the graphic can't be found.

Tutorial: Text Formatting in Action

In this tutorial, you'll gussy up headlines, lists, and paragraphs of text using CSS's powerful formatting options.

To get started, you need to download the tutorial files located on this book's companion Web site at *www.sawmac.com/css/*. Click the tutorial link and download the files. All of the files are enclosed in a ZIP archive, so you'll need to unzip them first. (Go to the Web site for detailed instructions on unzipping the files.) The files for this tutorial are contained inside the folder named *chapter_06*.

Setting Up the Page

1. Launch your Web browser and open the file *chapter_6 → text.html* (see Figure 6-10).

   As usual, you'll be working on a Web page from CosmoFarmer.com. In this case, there's already an external style sheet attached to the page, adding some design and layout touches. It's a glimpse of some of the things you'll be learning in future chapters. For now, concentrate on improving the look of the text on this page.

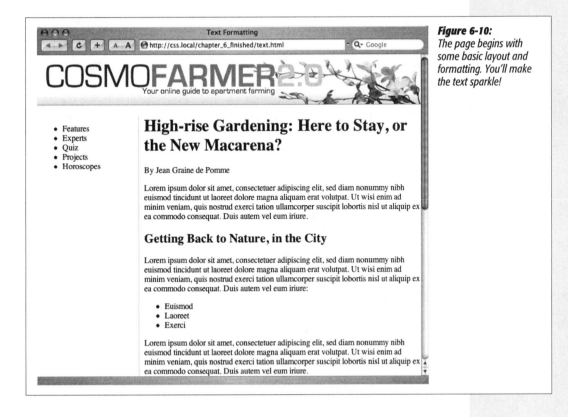

Figure 6-10:
The page begins with some basic layout and formatting. You'll make the text sparkle!

2. **Open the file *text.html* in your favorite text editor.**

   Start by adding an internal style sheet to this file. (Yes, external style sheets are better, but it's perfectly OK to start your design with an internal sheet. See the box on page 61.)

3. **In the <head> of the Web page, click directly after the <link> tag (used to attach the external style sheet). Hit Enter (Return), and then type *<style type="text/css">*.**

   Now that you've created the opening style tag, create a style that defines some general properties for all text on the page.

4. **Press the Enter (Return) key and type *body {***

   This is a basic tag selector that applies to the <body> tag. As discussed in Chapter 4, other tags inherit the properties of this tag. You can set up some basic text characteristics like font, color, and font size for later tags to use as their starting point.

5. **Press Enter (Return) again, and then add the following three properties:**

   ```
   color: #102536;
   font-family: Tahoma, "Lucida Grande", Arial, sans-serif;
   font-size: 62.5%;
   ```

   These three instructions set the color of the text to a dark blue, the font to Tahoma (or one of 3 others depending on which font is installed—see page 101), and sets the font size to 62.5 percent.

   Note: Why set the page's base font to 62.5 percent? It just so happens that 62.5 percent times 16 pixels (the normal size of text in most Web browsers) equals 10 pixels. With 10 pixels as a starting point, it's easy to compute what other text sizes will look like on the screen. For example, 1.5em would be 1.5 x 10 or 15 pixels. 2em is 20 pixels, and so on—easy multiples of ten. For more on this interesting discovery and more font-sizing strategies, visit *http://clagnut.com/blog/348/*.

   ---

6. **Complete this style by pressing Enter (Return), and typing a closing bracket to mark the end of the style.**

   At this point, your completed style should look like this:

   ```
   body {
       color: #102536;
       font-family: Tahoma, "Lucida Grande", Arial, sans-serif;
       font-size: 62.5%;
   }
   ```

   Finally, add the closing <style> tag to complete the style sheet.

7. **Hit Enter (Return) to create a new, blank line, and then type *</style>*.**

   Your style sheet is complete.

8. Save the page, and open it in a Web browser to preview your work.

   The text on the page changes color and font.

You'll also notice that the headings aren't, proportionally, as small as the other text on the page. (The cascade you read about last chapter rears its ugly head.) Yes, the <h1> and <h2> tags inherit the 62.5 percent font size set in the <body> tag style. However, every browser includes its own style sheet with specific font-size settings for heading tags, which overrule the size specified in the body. You'll fix this problem next.

Formatting the Headings and Paragraphs

Now that the basic text formatting is done, it's time to refine the presentation of the headlines and paragraphs.

1. **Return to your text editor and the** *text.html* **file. Click at the end of the closing brace of the body tag selector, press Enter (Return) to create a new line, and then type** *h1 {*.

   This style formats all <h1> tags on the page.

2. **Hit Enter (Return), and then type these two CSS properties:**

   ```
   font-size: 2.4em;
   color: #14556B;
   ```

   You've just changed the color of the <h1> tags and set their size to 2.4em, which for most browsers (unless the visitor has tweaked his browser's font settings) is 24 pixels tall.

3. **Finally, complete this style by hitting Enter (Return) and typing the closing brace.**

   The completed style should look like this:

   ```
   h1 {
       font-size: 2.4em;
       color: #14556B;
   }
   ```

4. **Save the file, and preview it in a Web browser.**

   Next, spruce up the appearance of the other headings and paragraphs.

5. **Return to your text editor and the** *text.html* **file. Click after the closing brace of the** *h1* **tag style and add the following two styles:**

   ```
   h2 {
       font-size: 1.5em;
       color: #993;
   }
   p {
   ```

```
      font-size: 1.2em;
      text-indent: 2em;
      line-height: 150%;
}
```

The *p* style introduces the text-indent property, which indents the first line of a paragraph, and the line-height property, which sets the spacing between lines. A percentage of 150 percent adds a little more space between lines in a paragraph than you'd normally see in a Web browser. This extra breathing room gives the text a lighter, airier quality and makes the sentences a little easier to read (but only if you speak Latin).

6. **Save the page, and open it in a Web browser to preview your work.**

    The page is coming together nicely, but the space between paragraphs and between the headings and the paragraphs is too distracting. You'll tighten it up a bit next.

7. **Return to your text editor and the *text.html* file. Locate the *h2* tag style you created earlier, and add the margin-bottom property.**

    The style now looks like this:

```
h2 {
    font-size: 1.5em;
    color: #993;
    margin-bottom: 5px;
}
```

    This addition (in bold) reduces the gap between the bottom of every <h2> tag and the next element on the page to 5 pixels. It also provides a consistent value, since the amount of space added below <h2> tags varies from browser to browser. Next, you control the paragraphs.

8. **Edit the <p> tag style by adding the following two properties to the end of the style:**

```
      margin-top: 0;
      margin-bottom: 5px;
```

    The margin-top property controls the space above the paragraphs. In this case, you've completely eliminated the space above each paragraph. To add a little space between each paragraph, use the margin-bottom property.

9. **Save the page, and open it in a Web browser to preview your work.**

    At this point, the page should look like Figure 6-11.

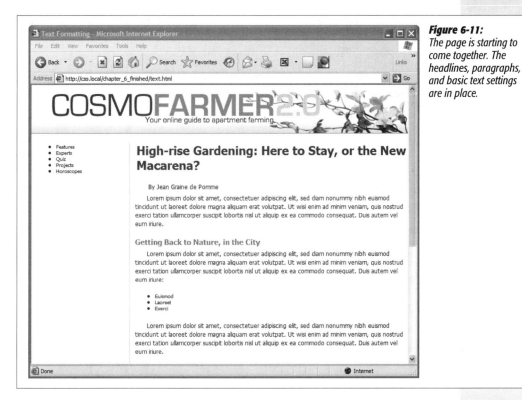

Figure 6-11:
The page is starting to come together. The headlines, paragraphs, and basic text settings are in place.

Formatting Lists

Notice that the page you're working on has two lists: a bulleted list of the different sections of the site in the left sidebar, and a bulleted list of three items in the main body copy. Use descendent selectors (see page 49) to target and format each list differently.

1. **Return to your text editor and the *text.html* file. Click at the end of the closing brace of the <p> tag selector, press Enter (Return) to create a new line, and then type *#content ul {*.**

   The main content of the page is contained in a <div> tag with an ID selector named *content*. You're now creating a rule that you want to apply only to bulleted lists (<ul> tags) that appear *inside* the main content area. You can achieve this with the descendent selector *#content ul*, which simply instructs the Web browser to apply this style to any <ul> tag that appears inside a page element with an ID of *content*. In other words, bulleted lists that appear elsewhere—like the one in the left-hand sidebar—won't be affected by this style.

2. **Press Enter (Return), and then type:**

   ```
   font-size: 1.2em;
   list-style-type: square;
   ```

This sets the font size for the text inside the bulleted list to 1.2em. The second line sets the bullet style to *square*—displaying a square bullet icon instead of the usual round bullet found in most Web browsers.

3. **Press Enter (Return) and then type the closing brace to complete the style. The finished rule should look like this:**

```
#content ul {
    font-size: 1.2em;
    list-style-type: square;
}
```

Finally, add a little bit of space between each bulleted item using the <li> (list item) tag's *bottom-margin* property.

4. **Press Enter (Return), and then add the following style:**

```
#content li {
    margin-bottom: 5px;
}
```

Again, you're using a descendent selector to target just the <li> tags that appear inside the main content area of the page. Next, work on the list in the sidebar.

5. **Press Enter (Return) to create a new blank line, and then add the following style:**

```
#mainNav ul {
    font-size: 1.2em;
    list-style-type: none;
}
```

Here, you're using a descendent selector to target lists that appear inside the sidebar (a <div> tag with the ID of *mainNav*). The list-style-type property not only lets you change a bullet from a circle to a square, but can also completely eliminate any bullet.

6. **Save the page, and open it in a Web browser to preview your work.**

If you look closely, you'll notice that the list in the sidebar is indented quite a bit on the left. Web browsers normally indent lists, so you have to add a couple of CSS properties to eliminate that extra space.

7. **Return to your text editor and the *text.html* page. Add a line below the list-style-type property you just added, and then type:**

```
margin-left: 0;
padding-left: 0;
```

Due to a difference in the way browsers display lists, you need to set the margin and padding properties to 0. (See page 121 for details.)

Lastly, center the text, and turn it all into uppercase letters.

8. Add the last two properties highlighted below. The finished style should look like this:

```
#mainNav ul {
    font-size: 1.2em;
    list-style-type: none;
    margin-left: 0;
    padding-left: 0;
    text-transform: uppercase;
    text-align: center;
}
```

Finally, to finish up, add a bit of space between each item in the sidebar.

9. Add this style *below* the *#mainNav ul* style you just created:

```
#mainNav li {
    margin-bottom: 10px;
}
```

10. Save the page and preview it in a Web browser.

The page should now look like Figure 6-12.

Figure 6-12:
CSS lets you control the formatting of bulleted lists, even letting you remove the bullets entirely (left). By using descendent selectors, you can format lists differently depending on where they appear in the page (for example the left sidebar, or main content area on this page).

Adding the Finishing Touches

For the last bit of design, pull out all the stops and incorporate several text formatting properties to alter the look of the author's byline.

1. **Return to your text editor and the *text.html* file.**

   First, you'll mark up one of the paragraphs with a class, so you can create a specific style for the authors' credits.

2. **Locate the paragraph tag with the byline—*<p>By Jean Graine de Pomme </p>*. Add a class attribute to the <p> tag:**

   ```
   <p class="byline">By Jean Graine de Pomme </p>
   ```

   Now you can create a class style to target that particular paragraph.

3. **Click at the end of the closing brace of the *#mainNav li* tag selector you just added, press Return to create a new line, and then type *.byline {* .**

   This is the beginning part of a class style. It just needs a few properties and a closing brace.

4. **Add the following three properties and the closing brace to create the class style by typing the following:**

   ```
   color: #73afb7;
   font-size: 1.5em;
   margin-bottom: 10px;
   }
   ```

   By now, you should feel comfortable with these properties, which set the size and color of the paragraph, as well as adjust the space below it. Next, make the text stand out in bold.

5. **Add a new line below the margin-bottom property of the .byline style, and then type:**

   ```
   font-weight: bold;
   ```

   Now format the style in small caps and spread out the letters a little to give the byline a formal and regal look that makes it stand out from the page.

6. **Add another line after the font-weight property you just added and add two more properties:**

   ```
   letter-spacing: 1px;
   font-variant: small-caps;
   ```

   If you preview the page now, you'll notice that the byline's indented the same amount as the other paragraphs. Due to the cascade, the byline (which is a <p> tag) gets that formatting from the <p> tag style's text-indent property. To get rid of that indent, you need to override the setting in the class style.

7. Add a text-indent property to the .byline style and set its value to 0. The final style should look like this:

```
.byline {
    color: #73afb7;
    font-size: 1.5em;
    margin-bottom: 10px;
    font-weight: bold;
    letter-spacing: 1px;
    font-variant: small-caps;
    text-indent: 0;
}
```

Time to test your hard work.

8. **Save the file and preview it in a Web browser.**

It should look like Figure 6-13. You can compare your work to the finished *text. html* page located in the *chapter_06_finished* folder.

Congratulations! You've explored many of the text-formatting properties offered by CSS, and turned ho-hum HTML into an attractive, attention-getting design. In the next chapter, you'll explore graphics, borders, margins, and other powerful design options offered by CSS.

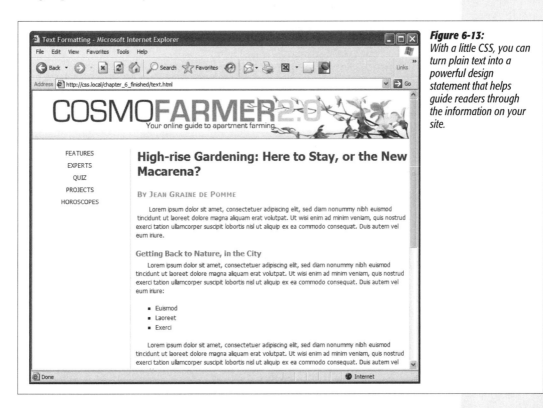

Figure 6-13:
With a little CSS, you can turn plain text into a powerful design statement that helps guide readers through the information on your site.

Margins, Padding, and Borders

Every HTML tag is surrounded by a world of properties that affect how the tag appears in a Web browser. Some properties—like borders and background colors—are immediately obvious to the naked eye. Others, though, are invisible—like padding and margin. They provide a bit of empty space on one or more sides of a tag. By understanding how these properties work, you can create attractive columns, decorative sidebars, and control the space around them (what designers call *white space*) so your pages look less cluttered, lighter, and more professional.

Taken together, the CSS properties discussed in this chapter make up one of the most important concepts in CSS—the *box model*.

Understanding the Box Model

You probably think of letters, words, and sentences when you think of a paragraph or headline. You also probably think of a photo, logo, or other picture when you think of the <img> tag. But a Web browser treats these (and all other) tags as little *boxes*. To a browser, any tag's a box with something inside it—text, an image, or even other tags containing other things, as illustrated in Figure 7-1.

Surrounding the content are different properties that make up the box:

- *Padding* is the space between the content and the content's border. Padding is what separates a photo from the border that frames the photo.

- *Border* is the line that's drawn around each edge of the box. You can have a border around all four sides, on just a single side, or any combination of sides.

- *Background-color* fills the space inside the border, including the padding area.

- *Margin* is what separates one tag from another. The space that commonly appears between the tops and bottoms of paragraphs of text on a Web page, for example, is the margin.

For a given tag, you can use any or all of these properties in combination. You can set just a margin for a tag, or add a border, margins, *and* padding. Or you can have a border and margin but no padding, and so on. If you don't adjust any of these properties, then you'll end up with the browser's default settings, which you may or may not like. For example, while browsers usually don't apply either padding or borders to any tags on a page, some tags like headings and paragraphs have a pre-set top and bottom margin. (Throughout this chapter you'll learn about these default settings as well as how to override them.)

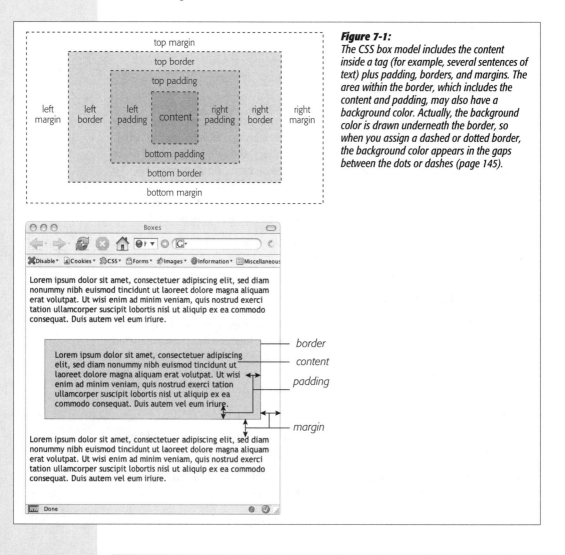

Figure 7-1:
The CSS box model includes the content inside a tag (for example, several sentences of text) plus padding, borders, and margins. The area within the border, which includes the content and padding, may also have a background color. Actually, the background color is drawn underneath the border, so when you assign a dashed or dotted border, the background color appears in the gaps between the dots or dashes (page 145).

Control Space with Margins and Padding

Both margins and padding add space around content. You use these properties to separate one element from another—for example, to add space between a left-hand navigation menu and the main page content on the right—or to inject some white space between content and a border. You may want to move the border away from the edge of a photo (see Figure 7-2).

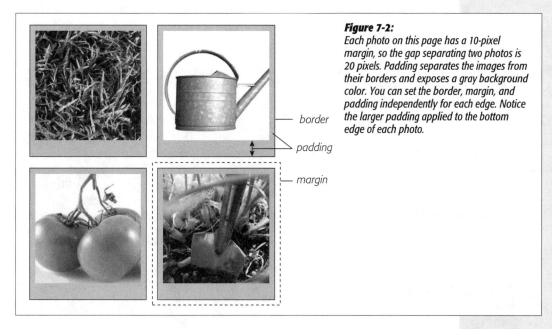

Figure 7-2:
Each photo on this page has a 10-pixel margin, so the gap separating two photos is 20 pixels. Padding separates the images from their borders and exposes a gray background color. You can set the border, margin, and padding independently for each edge. Notice the larger padding applied to the bottom edge of each photo.

border

padding

margin

Padding and margin function similarly and unless you apply a border or background color, you can't really tell whether the space between two tags is caused by padding or by a margin. But if you have a border around an element or a background behind it, then the visual difference between the two properties is significant. Padding adds space between the content and the border and keeps the content from appearing cramped inside the box, while margins add white space (often called a *gutter*) between elements giving the overall look of the page a lighter appearance.

You can control each side of the margin or padding for an element independently. Four properties control margin edges: *margin-top, margin-right, margin-bottom,* and *margin-left*. Similarly, four properties control padding: *padding-top, padding-right, padding-bottom,* and *padding-left*. You can use any valid CSS measurement to define the size of a margin or padding, like so:

```
margin-right: 20px;
padding-top: 3em;
margin-left: 10%;
```

*Marg: XX.XX XX XX
Top Right Bottom Left*

Pixels and ems are commonly used and act just as they do with text (see page 104). A 20-pixel margin adds 20 pixels of space, and 3ems of padding adds space equal to 3 times the font size of the styled element. You can also use percentage values, but they're tricky. (See the box below for the details.)

Tip: To remove all the space for a margin or padding, use 0 (*margin-top: 0* or *padding-bottom: 0,* for example). To remove space around all four edges of the browser window—to let a banner or logo or other page element butt right up to the edge without a gap—give the body tag a margin of 0, and a padding of 0: *margin: 0; padding 0;.* The margin property works for most browsers, except Opera. Opera requires that padding be set to 0 instead.

Margins, Padding, and Percentages

When you use percentages, Web browsers calculate the amount of space based on the *width of the containing element.* On a simple Web page, the containing element is the body of the page, and it fills the browser window. In this case, the percentage value's based on the width of the browser window at any given time. Say the window is 760 pixels wide. In that case, a 10 percent left margin adds 76 pixels of space to the left edge of the styled element. But if you resize the browser window, then that value changes. Narrowing the browser window to 600 pixels changes the margin to 60 pixels (10 percent of 600).

However, the containing element isn't always the width of the browser window. As you'll see in later chapters, when you create more sophisticated layouts, you can introduce new elements that help organize your page.

You may want to add a <div> tag to a page in order to group related content into a sidebar area. (You'll see an example of this in the tutorial on page 163.) That sidebar might have a specified width of 300 pixels. Tags inside the sidebar consider the <div> tag their containing element. So a tag in the sidebar with a right margin of 10 percent will have 30 pixels of empty space to its right.

To make matters more confusing, top and bottom percentage values are calculated based on the width of the containing element, not its height. So a 20 percent top margin is 20 percent of the width of the styled tag's container.

Margin and Padding Shorthand

You'll frequently want to set all four sides of a style's margin or padding. But typing out all four properties (margin-right, margin-left, and so on) for each style gets tedious. Fear not: you can use the shortcut properties named *margin* and *padding* to set all four properties quickly:

```
margin: 0 10px 10px 20px;
padding: 10px 5px 5px 10px;
```

Tip: If the value used in a CSS property is 0, then you don't need to add a unit of measurement. For example, just type *margin: 0;* instead of *margin: 0px;.*

The order in which you specify the four values is important. It must be *top*, *right*, *bottom*, and *left*. If you get it wrong, you'll be in trouble. In fact, the easiest way to keep the order straight is to remember to stay out of TRouBLe—top, right, bottom, and left.

If you want to use the same value for all four sides, it's even easier—just use a single value. If you want to remove margins from all <h1> tags, you can write this style:

```
h1 { margin: 0; }
```

Similarly, use shorthand to add the same amount of space between some content and its border:

```
padding: 10px;
```

Tip: When you're using the same value for both top and bottom and another value for both left and right, you can use two values. *margin: 0 2em;* sets the top *and* bottom margins to 0 and the left *and* right margins to 2ems.

Colliding Margins

When it comes to CSS, two plus two doesn't always equal four. You could run into some bizarre math when the bottom margin of one element touches the top margin of another. Instead of adding the two margins together, a Web browser applies the larger of the two margins (Figure 7-3, top). Say the bottom margin of an unordered list is set to 30 pixels and the top margin of a paragraph following the list is 20 pixels. Instead of adding the two values to create 50 pixels of space between the list and the paragraph, a Web browser uses the *largest* margin—in this case 30 pixels. If you don't want this to happen, then use top or bottom padding instead (Figure 7-3, bottom).

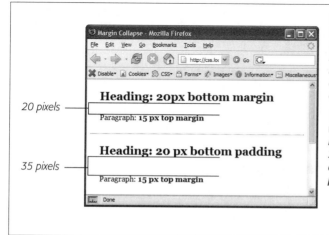

Figure 7-3:
When two vertical margins meet, the smaller one collapses. Although the top headline has a bottom margin of 20 pixels and the paragraph has a top margin of 15 pixels, a Web browser adds only 20 pixels of space between the two elements.

To get the full 35 pixels' worth of space that you want, use padding instead of margins, as shown in the bottom headline. Here, the heading has 20 pixels of bottom padding. Those 20 pixels get added to the 15-pixel top margin of the paragraph to form a 35-pixel gap.

Things get even weirder when one element's *inside* another element. This situation can lead to some head-scratching behavior. For example, say you add a "warning" box to a page (like a <div> tag to hold a warning message inside it). You add a 20 pixel top and bottom margin to separate the warning box from the heading above it and the paragraph of text below it. So far so good.

But say you insert a heading inside the warning box, and to put a little room between it and the top and bottom of the div, you set the heading's margin to 10 pixels. You may think you're adding 10 pixels of space between the heading and the top and bottom of the div, but you'd be wrong (Figure 7-4, left). Instead, the margin appears *above* the div. In this case, it doesn't matter how large a margin you apply to the headline—the margin still appears *above* the div.

Note: In the lingo of CSS, this phenomenon's known as "collapsing margins," meaning two margins actually become one.

You have two ways around this problem: Either add a small amount of padding around the <div> tag or add a border to it. Since border and padding sit *between* the two margins, the margins no longer touch, and the headline has a little breathing room (Figure 7-4, right).

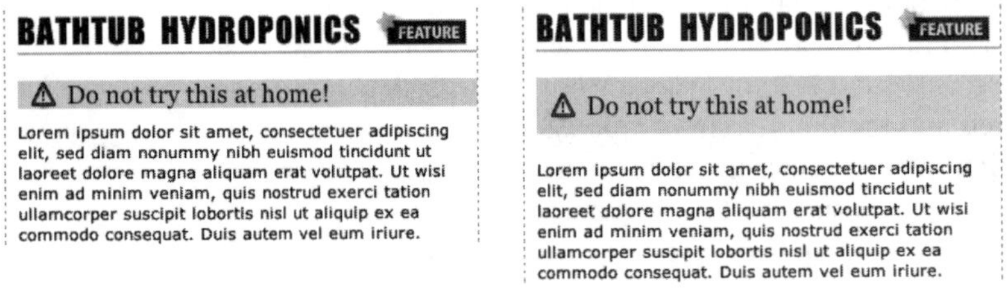

Figure 7-4:
Holy shrinking margins Batman!

Left: Whenever vertical margins touch, even when one element is inside another element, the margins collapse.

Right: To solve this dilemma, add a little padding or a border around the containing element (the <div>, in this case).

Note: Horizontal (left and right) margins and margins between floating elements (page 152) don't collapse in this way. Absolutely and relatively positioned elements—which you'll learn about in Chapter 12—don't collapse either.

Removing Space with Negative Margins

Most measurements in CSS have to be a positive value—after all what would text that's *negative 20 pixels* tall (or short) look like? Padding also has to be a positive value. But CSS allows for many creative techniques using negative margins. Instead of adding space between a tag and elements around it, a negative margin *removes*

CSS: The Missing Manual

space. So you can have a paragraph of text overlap a headline, poke out of its containing element (a sidebar or other layout <div>), or even disappear off an edge of the browser window. And, hey, you can even do something useful with negative margins.

Even when you set the margins between two headlines to 0, there's still a little space between the text of the headlines (thanks to the text's line-height as described on page 112 in the last chapter). That's usually a good thing, since it's hard to read sentences that bunch together and touch. But, used in moderation, tightening the space between two headlines can produce some interesting effects. The second headline of Figure 7-5 (the one that begins "Raise Tuna") has a top margin of -10px applied to it. This moves the headline up 10 pixels so it slightly overlaps the space occupied by the headline above it. Also, the left and right borders of the "Extra! Extra!" headline actually touch the letters of the larger headline.

You can also use a negative margin to simulate negative padding. In the third headline of Figure 7-5, the one that begins with "The Extraordinary Technique," a line appears directly under the text. This line is actually the *top* border for the paragraph that follows. (You'll learn how to add borders on page 141.) But because that paragraph has a negative top margin, the border moves up and under the headline. Notice how the descending tail for the letter Q in the headline actually hangs *below* the border. Since padding—the space between content (like that letter Q) and a border—can't be negative, you can't move a bottom border up over text or any other content. But you get the same effect by applying a border to the following element and using a negative margin to move it up.

Figure 7-5:
In this example, to make the last paragraph's top border look like it's actually the bottom border for the headline above it, add a little padding to the paragraph. Around 5 pixels of top padding moves the paragraph down from the border, while 4ems of left padding indents the paragraph's text, still allowing the top border to extend to the left edge.

Tip: You can actually use a negative top margin on the paragraph, or a negative bottom margin on the headline. Both have the same effect of moving the paragraph up close to the headline.

Displaying Inline and Block-Level Boxes

Although Web browsers treat every tag as a kind of box, not all boxes are alike. CSS has two different types of boxes—*block boxes* and *inline boxes*—that correspond to the two types of tags—inline and block-level tags. A *block-level* tag creates a break before and after it. The <p> tag, for example, creates a block that's separated from tags above and below. Headlines, <div> tags, tables and lists are other examples of block-level tags.

Inline tags don't create a break before or after them. They appear on the same line as content and tags beside them. The <strong> tag is an inline tag. A word formatted with this tag happily sits next to other text—even text wrapped in other inline tags like <em>. In fact, it would look pretty weird if you emphasized a single word in the middle of a paragraph with the <strong> tag and that word suddenly appeared on its own line by itself. Other inline tags are <img> for adding images, <a> for creating links, and the various tags used to create form fields.

In most cases, CSS works the same for inline boxes and block boxes. You can style the font, color, and background and add borders to both types of boxes. However, when it comes to margins and padding, browsers treat inline boxes differently. While you can add space to the left or right of an inline element using either left or right padding or left or right margins, you can't increase the height of the inline element with top or bottom padding or margins. In the top paragraph in Figure 7-6, the inline element is styled with borders, a background color, and 20 pixels of margin on all four sides. But the browser only adds space to the left and right sides of the inline element.

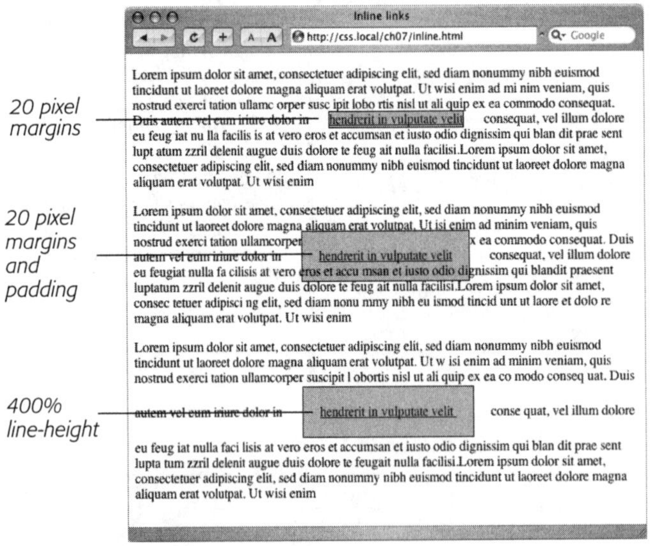

Figure 7-6:
Adding top or bottom margins and padding doesn't make an inline element any taller, so you can run into some weird formatting. In the middle paragraph, the background and borders of a link overlap the text above and below. The background appears on top of the line before the styled inline text, but underneath the line following it because the browser treats each line as if it's stacked on top of the previous line. Normally, that isn't a problem since lines of text don't usually overlap. To create space above and below an inline element, add the line-height property to the inline element. (The exact amount depends on how large the margin and padding are. In this case, a 400 percent line height expands the line enough so the background and border don't overlap any text.)

Note: One exception to the rule that inline elements don't get taller when padding or margin are added is the <img> tag (even though it's an inline tag). Web browsers correctly expand the height of the image's box to accommodate any padding and margins you add.

At times, you may wish an inline element behaved more like a block-level element and vice versa. Bulleted lists present each item as its own block—each list item's stacked above the next. But what if you want to change that behavior so the list items appear side by side, all on a single line (as in a navigation bar, as you'll see on page 222 in Chapter 9)? Or you may want to treat an inline element like a block-level element. Maybe you want an image embedded in a paragraph to be on its own line, with space above and below.

Fortunately, CSS includes a property that lets you do just that—the *display* property. With it, you can make a block-level element act like an inline element:

    display: inline;

Or you can make an inline element like an image or link behave like a block-level element:

    display: block;

Note: The *display* property has a myriad of possible options, most of which aren't supported in today's browsers. However, one value, *none*, is supported by most browsers and has many uses. It does one simple thing–completely hides the styled element so it doesn't appear in a Web browser. With a dab of Java-Script programming, you can make an element hidden in this way instantly become visible, simply by changing its display back to either *inline* or *block*. You can even make an element with a display of *none* suddenly appear using CSS.

Adding Borders

A border is simply a line that runs around an element. As shown back in Figure 7-1, it sits between any padding and margins you set. A border around every edge can frame an image or mark the boundaries of a banner or other page element. But borders don't necessarily have to create a full box around your content. While you can add a border to all four edges, you can just as easily add a border to just the bottom or any combination of sides. This flexibility lets you add design elements that don't necessarily feel like a border. For example, add a border to the left of an element, make it around 1em thick, and it looks like a square bullet. A single border under a paragraph can function just like the <hr> (horizontal rule) by providing a visual separator between sections of a page.

You control three different properties of each border: *color*, *width*, and *style*. The color can be a hexadecimal number, a keyword or an RGB value, just like with text (see page 102). A border's width is the thickness of the line used to draw the border. You can use any CSS measurement type (except percentages) or the keywords

---

thin, medium, and *thick.* The most common and easily understood method is simply pixels.

Finally, the style controls the type of line drawn. There are many different styles, and some look very different from browser to browser, as you can see in Figure 7-7. You specify the style with a keyword. For example *solid* draws a solid line and *dashed* creates a line made up of dashes. CSS offers these styles: *solid, dotted, dashed, double, groove, ridge, inset, outset, none,* and *hidden.*

Tip: *None* and *hidden* work the same way: they remove the border entirely. The *none* value's useful for turning off a single border. (See the example on page 144.)

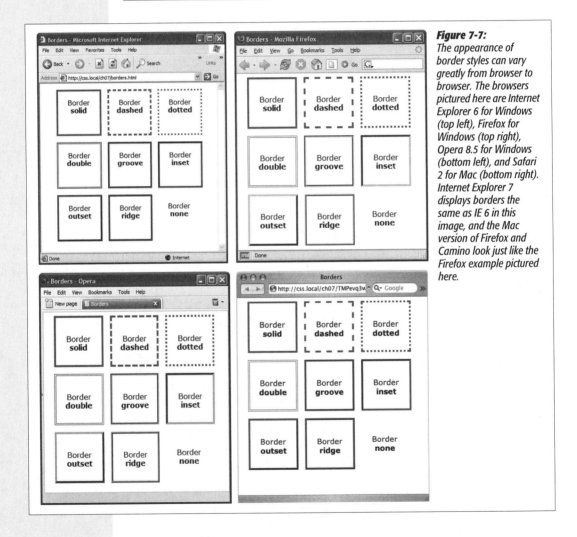

Figure 7-7:
The appearance of border styles can vary greatly from browser to browser. The browsers pictured here are Internet Explorer 6 for Windows (top left), Firefox for Windows (top right), Opera 8.5 for Windows (bottom left), and Safari 2 for Mac (bottom right). Internet Explorer 7 displays borders the same as IE 6 in this image, and the Mac version of Firefox and Camino look just like the Firefox example pictured here.

Note: In Windows' Internet Explorer version 6 and earlier, a 1 pixel dotted border looks just like a 1 pixel dashed border.

Border Property Shorthand

If you've ever seen a list of the different border properties available in CSS, you may think borders are really complex. After all, there are 20 different border properties, which you'll meet in the following sections, plus a couple that apply to tables. But all these properties are merely variations on a theme that provide different ways of controlling the same three properties—color, width, and style—for each of the four borders. The most basic and straightforward property is *border*, which simply adds four borders:

```
border: 4px solid #F00;
```

The above style creates a solid, red, 4-pixel border. You can use this property to create a basic frame around a picture, navigation bar, or other item that you want to appear as a self-contained box.

Note: The order in which you write the properties doesn't matter. *border: 4px solid #F00;* works as well as *border: #F00 solid 4px;*.

Formatting Individual Borders

You can control each border individually using the appropriate property: *border-top*, *border-bottom*, *border-left*, or *border-right*. These properties work just like the regular border property, but they control just one side. The following property declaration adds a 2-pixel, red, dashed line below the style:

```
border-bottom: 2px dashed red;
```

You can combine the *border* property with one of the edge-specific properties like border-left to define the basic box for the entire style, but customize a single border. Say you want the top, left, and right sides of a paragraph to have the same type of border but you want the bottom border to look slightly different. You can write four lines of CSS, like this:

```
border-top: 2px solid black;
border-left: 2px solid black;
border-right: 2px solid black;
border-bottom: 4px dashed #333;
```

Or, you can achieve the same effect as the previous four lines of CSS with just two lines:

```
border: 2px solid black;
border-bottom: 4px dashed #333;
```

The first line of code defines the basic look of all four borders, and the second line redefines just the look of the bottom border. Not only is it easier to write two lines of CSS instead of four but it also makes changing the style easier. If you want to change the color of the top, left, and right borders to red, then you only have to edit a single line, instead of three:

```
border: 2px solid red;
```

When you use this shortcut method—defining the basic look of all four borders using the border property and then overriding the look of a single border with one of the edge-specific properties like border-left—it's crucial that you write the code in a specific order. The more general, global border setting must come first, and the edge-specific setting second, like so:

```
border: 2px solid black;
border-bottom: 4px dashed #333;
```

Because the border-bottom property appears second, it overrides the setting of the border property. If the border-bottom line came before the border property, then it would be cancelled out by the border property, and all four borders would be identical. The last property listed can overrule any related properties listed above it. This is an example of the CSS Cascade that you read about in Chapter 5.

You can also use this shortcut method to turn off the display of a single border with the *none* keyword. Say you want to put a border around three sides of a style (top, left, and bottom) but no border on the last side (right). Just two lines of code get you the look you're after:

```
border: 2px inset #FFCC33;
border-right: none;
```

The ability to subtly tweak the different sides of each border is the reason there are so many different border properties. The remaining 15 properties let you define individual colors, styles, and widths for the border and for each border side. For example, you could rewrite *border: 2px double #FFCC33;* like this:

```
border-width: 2px;
border-style: double;
border-color: #FFCC33;
```

Since you're using three lines of code instead of one, you'll probably want to avoid this method. However, each border edge has its own set of three properties, which are helpful for overriding just one border property for a single border edge. The right border has these three properties: *border-right-width*, *border-right-style*, and *border-right-color*. The left, top, and bottom borders have similarly named properties—*border-left-width*, *border-left-style*, and so on.

Imagine that you want to have a two-pixel, dashed border around the four edges of a style, but you want each border to be a different color. (Perhaps you're doing a Web site for kids.) Here's a quick way to do that:

```
border: 2px dashed green;
border-left-color: blue;
border-right-color: yellow;
border-bottom-color: red;
```

This set of rules creates a two-pixel dashed border around all four edges, while making the top edge green (from the first property declaration), the left edge blue, the right edge yellow, and the bottom edge red.

You can change the width of just a single border like this: *border-right-width: 4px;*. One nice thing about this approach is that if you later decide the border should be solid, you need to edit only the generic border property by changing *dashed* to *solid*.

Tip: You usually add padding whenever you use borders. Padding provides space between the border and any content, such as text, images, or other tags. Without padding, borderlines usually sit too close to the content.

Coloring the Background

It's a cinch to add a background to an entire page, an individual headline, or any other page element. Use the background-color property followed by any of the valid color choices described on page 102. If you want, add a shockingly bright green to the background of a page with this line of code:

```
body { background-color: #6DDA3F; }
```

Alternatively, you can create a class style named, say, *.review* with the background-color property defined, and then apply the class to the body tag in the HTML, like so: *<body class="review">*.

Note: You can also place an image in the background of a page and control that image's placement in many different ways. You'll explore that in the next chapter.

Background colors come in handy for creating many different visual effects. You can create a bold-looking headline by setting its background to a dark color and its text to a light color. (You'll see an example of this "reverse type" effect in the tutorial on page 162.) Background colors are also a great way to set off part of a page like a navigation bar, banner, or sidebar.

Tip: When you use background colors and borders, keep the following in mind: If the border style is either dotted or dashed (see Figure 7-7), the background color shows in the empty spaces between the dots or dashes. In other words, Web browsers actually paint the background color *under* the borderline.

Determining Height and Width

Two other CSS properties that form part of the CSS box model are useful for assigning dimensions to an object, such as a table, column, banner, or sidebar. The *height* and *width* properties assign a height and width to the content area of a style. You'll use these properties often when building the kinds of CSS layouts described in Part III of this book, but they're also useful for more basic design chores like assigning the width of a table, creating a simple sidebar, or creating a gallery of thumbnail images (like the one described in the steps on page 183).

Adding these properties to a style is very easy. Just type the property followed by any of the CSS measurement systems you've already encountered. For example:

```
width: 300px;
width: 30%;
height: 20em;
```

Pixels are, well, pixels. They're simple to understand and easy to use. They also create an exact width or height that doesn't change. An *em* is the same as the text size for the styled element. Say you set the text size to 24px; an em for that style is 24px, so if you set the width to 2em, then it would be 2x24 or 48 pixels. If you don't set a text size in the style, the em is based on the inherited text size (see page 107).

For the width property, percentage values are based on the percentage of the width of the style's containing element. If you set the width of a headline to 75 percent and that headline isn't inside any other elements with a set width, then the headline will be 75 percent of the width of the browser window. If the visitor adjusts the size of his browser, then the width of the headline will change. However, if the headline's contained inside a <div> (maybe to create a column), that's 200 pixels wide, so the width of that headline will be 150 pixels. Percentage values for the height property work similarly, but are based on the containing element's height, instead of width.

GEM IN THE ROUGH

Minimum and Maximum

CSS also supports a few other properties related to height and width: *min-height*, *min-width*, *max-height*, and *max-width*. These properties let you set a minimum width or height—meaning the element must be *at least* that width or height—or a maximum width or height. The element can't be wider or taller than a set amount.

These properties are useful in the flexible layouts described on page 280, since they let you keep your design within a reasonable space for either very small monitors or very large monitors. Unfortunately, Internet Explorer 6 and earlier doesn't understand these properties. *C'est la guerre.* You can read more about these properties on page 289.

Calculating a Box's Actual Width and Height

While the width and height properties seem pretty straightforward, there are a few nuances that often throw people for a loop. First of all, there's a difference between the value you set for a style's width and height and the amount of space that a Web browser actually uses to display the style's box. The width and height properties set the width and height of the *content area* of the style—the place where the text, images, or other nested tags sit. (See Figure 7-1 for a refresher on where the content area sits within the overall box model.) The actual width—that is, the amount of screen real estate given by the Web browser—is the total of the widths of the margins, borders, padding, and width properties, as illustrated in Figure 7-8.

Say you've set the following properties:

```
margin: 10px;
border-width: 5px;
padding: 15px;
width: 100px;
```

When the width property is set, you always know how much room is allocated just for your content—the words and images that fill the space—regardless of any other properties you may set. You don't need to do any math, because the value of the width property is the room for your content (in the above example, 100 pixels). Of course, you *do* have to perform a little math when you're trying to figure out exactly how much space an element will take up on a Web page. In the above example, the width that a Web browser allocates for the style's box is 160 pixels: 20 pixels for the left and right margins, 10 pixels for the left and right borders, 30 pixels for the left and right padding, and 100 pixels for the width. (And versions of Internet Explorer for Windows older than version 6 get the whole thing wrong—see page 150—forcing you to do a little extra work for those browsers.)

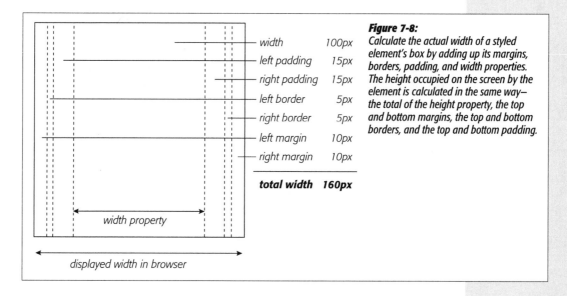

width	100px
left padding	15px
right padding	15px
left border	5px
right border	5px
left margin	10px
right margin	10px
total width	**160px**

width property

displayed width in browser

Figure 7-8:
Calculate the actual width of a styled element's box by adding up its margins, borders, padding, and width properties. The height occupied on the screen by the element is calculated in the same way— the total of the height property, the top and bottom margins, the top and bottom borders, and the top and bottom padding.

Be careful when you specify heights for page elements. Unless you're sure of the exact dimensions of the content of a tag, it's hard to know exactly how tall a box will be. Say you created a style for a pull quote to highlight an interesting comment from an article and you set the pull quote box to a width of 100px and a height of 100px. When you add too much text to the pull quote, the box will grow taller than 100 pixels and you'll run into some weird problems (see Figure 7-9). Even if the text fits within the 100-pixel height, a visitor to your site may increase the font size in her browser, making the text larger than the height you specified.

Controlling the Tap with the Overflow Property

When the content inside a styled tag's larger than the style's defined width and height, some weird things happen. As shown in Figure 7-9, IE 6 and earlier just let the box expand to fit the larger content, while other browsers let the content spill out of the box (past the borders and often over other content).

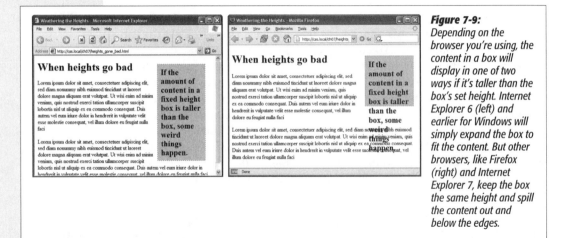

Figure 7-9:
Depending on the browser you're using, the content in a box will display in one of two ways if it's taller than the box's set height. Internet Explorer 6 (left) and earlier for Windows will simply expand the box to fit the content. But other browsers, like Firefox (right) and Internet Explorer 7, keep the box the same height and spill the content out and below the edges.

Fortunately, you can control what a browser should do in this situation with the *overflow* property. Overflow accepts four keywords that control how content that overflows the edges of a box should be displayed:

- *visible.* This option is what browsers do normally. It's the same as not setting the property at all (Figure 7-10, top).

- *scroll.* Lets you add scroll bars (Figure 7-10, middle). It creates a kind of mini-browser window in your page and looks similar to old-school HTML frames, or the HTML <iframe> tag. You can use *scroll* to provide a lot of content in a small amount of space. Unfortunately, scroll bars *always* appear when you use this option, even if the content fits within the box.

Figure 7-10:
The overflow property gives you three basic ways to deal with text that doesn't fit inside a box. Visible displays the content anyway (top); scroll and auto add scroll bars (middle); and hidden just doesn't show anything that doesn't fit (bottom).

- *auto.* To make scroll bars optional, use the *auto* option. It does the same thing as scroll, but adds scroll bars only when needed.

- *hidden.* Hides any content that extends outside the box (Figure 7-10, bottom). This option's a bit dangerous, since it can make some content disappear from the page. But it comes in handy for solving some IE browser bugs (see page 302).

Fixing IE 5's Broken Box Model

Here's a bit of bad news: Versions 5.5 and earlier of Internet Explorer for Windows doesn't always calculate width and height correctly. Unlike other browsers, it doesn't set the actual area taken up by an element to the total value of the margins, border, padding, and width (or height) property. Instead, IE 5.5—and IE 6 in quirks mode (page 24)—only uses the margin and width. It includes padding and borders as *part of the width property value*, making the content area smaller than in most browsers, as illustrated in Figure 7-11.

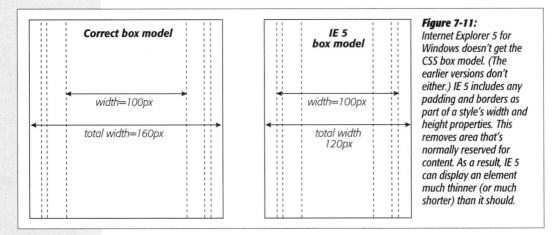

Figure 7-11:
Internet Explorer 5 for Windows doesn't get the CSS box model. (The earlier versions don't either.) IE 5 includes any padding and borders as part of a style's width and height properties. This removes area that's normally reserved for content. As a result, IE 5 can display an element much thinner (or much shorter) than it should.

Here's how IE 5 would handle the box in Figure 7-8. All current browsers set aside 160 pixels for the width of the box. The total width of that same styled element would be 10 + 10 (left and right margins) + 100 (width property) for a grand total of *120 pixels*. But in Windows IE 5, that sidebar would look 40 pixels thinner than in other browsers. In fact, the actual width dedicated to the content is equal to 100 (the width property) – 30 (left and right padding) – 10 (left and right border). The text in a sidebar with these settings would be crammed into 60 pixels, instead of the appropriate 100 pixels. The same's true for the height property. IE 5 treats the height value as the total of the content, top and bottom padding, and top and bottom border. So boxes also appear shorter in IE 5 than in other browsers.

You have many different ways around this problem. Here are a few of the most common:

- **Don't apply padding or borders to the style containing the width or height property.** The problem crops up only when padding or borders are set, so avoiding these properties prevents the problem entirely. But if you want to add a decorative border, you can't very well avoid the *border* property.

- **Use two tags—one to set the width/height and another, nested tag, to set padding and borders.** Say you want to have a 100 pixel wide pull quote style, but you also want it to have borders and padding (and, of course, you want it to work in IE 5). You can create the following HTML for the pull quote:

```
<div class="pullquote">
<div class="inner_pullquote">
This is the content of the pull quote.
</div>
</div>
```

Then, in your style sheet, add the following two styles:

```
.pullquote { width: 100px; }
.inner_pullquote {
    padding: 10px;
    background-color: #333;
    border: 1px dotted red;
}
```

The first style sets the width for the first <div> tag—the parent tag that surrounds the other parts of the pull quote. Since it has only a width specified, all browsers (including IE 5) will display the box at 100 pixels wide. The second, inner <div> has the padding and border set, but no width, so once again there's no IE 5 problem. This solution lets you use borders and padding and works in all browsers, but it requires extra HTML coding and an extraneous <div> tag just to support one dying browser.

- **Send IE 5 a different width/height value.** Many Web developers prefer this elegant solution, although it requires a little math. The basic idea is to give IE 5.5 and earlier a special width value that's equal to the width value you set for other browsers, plus the combined value of the padding and borders. You have many different ways to specify a CSS property and value to just one browser, like the advanced method discussed in Chapter 14 (page 399). A simple method is the *star html hack* (see the box on page 152).

Take the example in Figure 7-8. The width value in this case is 100 pixels: There are 15 pixels worth of left padding and 15 pixels of right padding, as well as 10 pixels of total border width (both left and right borders). Adding those together you get 140 pixels. Now say you've created a class style for this page called *.pullquote*. This style has all of the basic settings you want: margins, padding, borders, width, and so on. All you need to do is feed IE 5.5 and earlier a different width. So below the .pullquote style, add the following:

```
* html .pullquote {
    width: 140px;
    w\idth: 100px;
}
```

This style must come after the original .pullquote style, since it overrides the width property for that style. Essentially, this new style's invisible to every browser except IE 6 and earlier. (IE 7 ignores it as well.) The first property sets the width to 140px (the correct value for IE 5), but since IE 6 gets this new value *and* handles the box model correctly, you have to reset the width to 100 pixels in order for IE 6 to display the style correctly. That's where that second, weirdo property—*w\idth*—comes in. It's actually valid CSS, but it's understood only by IE 6—IE 5.5 throws its hands up in disgust and ignores it. Thus, *w\idth* resets the width property to 100 pixels for IE 6 and everyone's happy (except for the poor Web designers who have to learn these crazy workarounds).

- **Ignore IE 5 entirely.** This last option may sound a little discriminatory, but it's worth checking out your Web server's log file to see if you even have any visitors coming to your site with IE 5.5 or earlier. Although this antiquated browser still has a few dedicated fans, their numbers are dwindling. And if your site targets a more tech-savvy crowd, then you may not even need to bother designing with IE 5 in mind. (Lucky you.)

BROWSER BUG

Special Rules for IE 6 and Earlier

Dealing with the surprisingly inconsistent ways different browsers display pages is the bane of every Web designer. What looks great in Internet Explorer may fall completely apart in Firefox, or vice versa. Throughout this book you'll find tips on browser management and ways to overcome the worst browser bugs. Not surprisingly, Internet Explorer 6, which is over half a decade old, is plagued by many display problems. Internet Explorer 5 has even more. For example, both IE 5 and 6 have trouble displaying float-based layouts, as you'll see in Chapter 11 (page 302). And IE 5 doesn't always calculate the width of a box correctly (page 150).

To overcome these bugs, you frequently have to send properties and values to IE that are different than the ones used by other browsers. To that end, there's an easy way to create CSS styles that apply only to IE 6 and earlier–the *star html hack*. In this method, you begin the style with the following: ** html*. If you want to have an *h1* tag style that applies only to IE 6 and earlier, then name the style ** html h1*. All other browsers see the style as a descendent selector that doesn't make any sense, so they promptly ignore it.

You'll frequently use the star html hack to override some setting from a style that other (better) browsers display properly but IE gets wrong. In that case, apply the ** html* hack *after* the correct style. Say you create a class style named *.sidebar* that creates an attractive sidebar box for news and site navigation links. Due to a weird bug in IE, the sidebar may appear three pixels off to the left or right (see page 304). To counteract this snafu, you can add this IE-only special fix after the regular .sidebar style:

```
* html .sidebar { margin-left: -3px }
```

You'll see the ** html* hack in a couple of places in this book (like this chapter's tutorial on page 167). You'll learn other techniques for managing Internet Explorer in Chapter 14 (page 399).

Internet Explorer 7 *doesn't* understand the ** html* hack, so it'll ignore these types of styles. Fortunately, IE 7 has fixed many of the bugs that plagued earlier versions of the browser so the fixes supplied by ** html* styles aren't usually needed for that browser.

Wrap Content with Floating Elements

HTML normally flows from the top of the browser window down to the bottom, one headline, paragraph, or block-level element on top of another. This word processor–like display is visually boring (Figure 7-12, top), but with CSS, you're far from stuck with it. You'll learn lots of new methods for arranging items on a Web page in Part 3, but you can spice up your pages plenty with one little CSS property—*float.*

The float property moves an element to either the left or right. In the process, content below the floated element moves up and wraps around the float (Figure 7-12, bottom). Floating elements are ideal for moving supplemental information out of the way of the main text of a page. Images can move to either edge, letting text wrap elegantly around them. Similarly, you can shuttle a sidebar of related information and links off to one side.

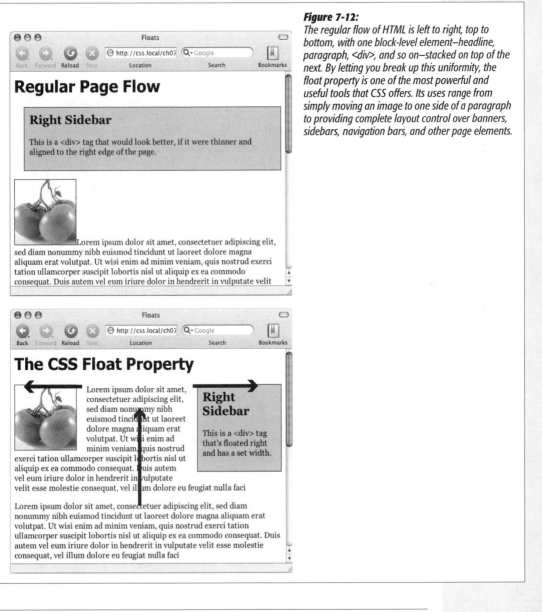

Figure 7-12:
The regular flow of HTML is left to right, top to bottom, with one block-level element—headline, paragraph, <div>, and so on—stacked on top of the next. By letting you break up this uniformity, the float property is one of the most powerful and useful tools that CSS offers. Its uses range from simply moving an image to one side of a paragraph to providing complete layout control over banners, sidebars, navigation bars, and other page elements.

While you can use floats in some complex (and confusing) ways, as you'll see in Chapter 11, the basic property is very simple. It takes one of three keywords, *left*, *right*, or *none*, like so:

```
float: left;
```

- *left.* Slides the styled element to the left, while content below wraps around the right side of the element.

- *right.* Slides the element to the right.

- *none.* Turns off the float and returns the object to its normal position.

Note: Floating an image is similar to setting the <img> tag's align attribute to either *left* or *right*. That little bit of HTML is deprecated (page 3), so use the CSS float property instead.

Floated elements move to the left or right edge of the browser window, or of their *containing element,* if there is one. You may have a box on the page that's 300 pixels wide and is itself floated to the right edge of the browser window. Inside that box, you've got an image that floats to the left. That image slides to the left edge of that 300 pixel-wide box—not the left edge of the browser window.

You can even use the float property with an inline element (see page 140) such as the <img> tag. In fact, floating a photo to the left or right using CSS is a very common use of the float property. A Web browser treats a floated inline element just like a block-level element, so you don't run into the problems with padding and margin that normally trouble inline elements (see page 140).

You can also float a block-level element like a headline or paragraph. A common technique's to float a <div> tag containing other HTML tags and page content to create a kind of containing box. In this way, you can create sidebars, pull quotes, and other self-contained page elements. (You'll see an example of this in this chapter's tutorial.) When you float block-level elements, it's a good idea to set the width property as well. This way, you can control how much horizontal space the block takes up and how much space is available for the content below it to move up and wrap around the block.

Note: The *source order*—the order in which you write your HTML—has a big impact on the display of floated elements. The HTML for the floated tag must appear *before* the HTML of any content that wraps around the floated element. Say you've created a Web page composed of an <h1> tag, followed by a <p> tag. Toward the end of that <p> tag, you've also inserted a photo using the <img> tag. If you float that photo to the right, say, then the <h1> tag and most of the content inside that <p> tag will still appear above the photo; only content that follows the <img> tag will wrap around the left side of the image.

Backgrounds, Borders, and Floats

To the consternation of many Web designers, backgrounds and borders don't float the same way as other page elements. Say you float an element—a sidebar for example—to the right. The content below the sidebar moves up and wraps around it, just as it should. But if that content has a background or border set on it, then that background or border actually appears *underneath* the floated sidebar (Figure 7-13, left). In essence, a Web browser wraps the text around the float, but not the border or background. Believe it or not, this is absolutely kosher, and how (according to the rules) it's supposed to work. Of course, you may not want to follow these rules; you might want to have the border or background stop when it reaches the floated element (Figure 7-13, right). With a little CSS magic, you can do it.

First, you need to add one rule to the style that has background or borders running underneath the float. Once you locate the style, add this line: *overflow: hidden;*. The overflow property (discussed in more detail on page 148) makes any background or border that extends underneath the float disappear.

Another approach is to add a borderline around the floated element; when you make the borderline thick enough and match its color to the background color of the page, the border looks just like empty space—even though it's covering and hiding the background color and borderlines that are extending below it.

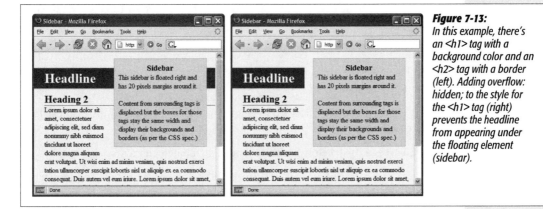

Figure 7-13:
In this example, there's an <h1> tag with a background color and an <h2> tag with a border (left). Adding overflow: hidden; to the style for the <h1> tag (right) prevents the headline from appearing under the floating element (sidebar).

Stopping the Float

Sometimes you need a way to tell a tag to ignore a floated element. You may have a copyright notice that should always appear at the bottom of the browser window. If you have a particularly tall sidebar that's floated to the left side of the page, the copyright notice might actually be drawn up the page and wrap around the float. Instead of appearing at the bottom of the page, the copyright is sitting up the page next to the sidebar. You want the copyright notice part of your page to refuse to wrap around the floated element and instead drop below it.

Other problems occur when you have several floated items close together. If the floated items aren't very wide, they float up and next to each other, and if they're of varying heights they can get into an unattractive logjam (see Figure 7-14, top). In this case, the floated elements *shouldn't* float next to each other. CSS provides the *clear* property for just these types of problems.

When overflow: hidden Fails

The *overflow: hidden* property prevents backgrounds and borders from awkwardly running under floating elements (Figure 7-13). But nothing's ever that simple in the world of Web browsers. While this one line of code works for Internet Explorer 7, Firefox, Camino, and Safari, it doesn't work reliably in Opera (at least version 8.5), and Internet Explorer 5 and 6 for Windows just ignore it.

Alas there's no apparent fix for Opera, but there's something you can do for IE 5 and 6. For those browsers, you need to add one additional rule: *zoom: 1;*.

This is a Microsoft-only property that lets you enlarge an element on a page. In this case, though, it's just a weird way to force IE 5 and 6 to stop a border or background from extending underneath the floated element. (For more detail on why this zoom thing works, see "Got Layout?" on page 307.)

You may want to put the IE-specific zoom rule in an IE-only style (see the box on page 152). You can even put it in a completely separate IE-only external style sheet (page 399).

You'll also find an example of this problem and its solution in the tutorial starting on page 167.

The *clear* property instructs an element to *not wrap around a floated* item. By clearing an element, you essentially force it to drop down below the floated item. Also, you can control which type of float (left or right) is cleared or force a style to simply ignore both types of floats.

The *clear* property accepts the following options:

- *left*. The style will drop below elements that are floated left but will still wrap around right-floated objects.

- *right*. Forces a drop below right-floated objects but still wraps around left-floated objects.

- *both*. Forces a drop below both left- and right-floated elements.

- *none*. Turns off clearing altogether. In other words, it makes an item wrap around both left- and right-floated objects, which is how Web browsers normally work.

In the case of a copyright notice that must appear at the bottom of the page, you'd want it to clear both left- and right-floated objects—it should always be below other content and should never wrap to the left or right of any other item. Here's a class style that would do just that:

```
.copyright {
    clear: both;
}
```

Figure 7-14 shows how the *clear* property can prevent floated items of varying heights from clumping together. All three photos in that figure have a right float applied to them. In the top figure, the photo of the tomatoes (1) is the first image on the page and appears at the far right edge. The second image (2) obeys the float set on the first image and wraps up to the left of it. The last photo (3) isn't wide enough to sit next to the second photo (2) but still tries to wrap around both (1) and (2). It gets stuck in the process.

Using *clear: right;* on the images prevents the photos from sitting next to each other (Figure 7-14, bottom). The clear applied to the second photo prevents it from wrapping up next to the first image, while the last image's right clear property forces it to appear below the second image.

Figure 7-14:

Top: Sometimes you don't want an element to wrap around a floated object.

Bottom: Applying the clear property (in this case clear: right;) to each image prevents them from sitting next to each other. The clear applied to photo (2) prevents it from wrapping up next to image (1). Applying clear: right to photo (3) forces it to appear below photo (2).

Tip: This business of left floats, right floats, and how to clear them sounds complicated—and it is. This section gives you a basic introduction. You'll see the subject again in Chapter 11 and eventually learn how to use floats in more sophisticated ways.

Tutorial: Margins, Backgrounds, and Borders

In this tutorial, you'll explore elements of the CSS box model, adjust the spacing around objects on a page, add colorful borders to items on a page, and control the size and flow of page elements.

To get started, you need to download the tutorial files located on this book's companion Web site at *www.sawmac.com/css/*. Click the tutorial link and download the files. (All of the files are enclosed in a ZIP archive. See detailed instructions for unzipping the files on the Web site.) The files for this tutorial are contained inside the *chapter_07* folder.

Controlling Page Margins

As usual, you'll be working on a Web page from CosmoFarmer.com. You'll start by controlling the margin around the edges of the Web page.

Tip: For a sneak preview of the final result, check out Figure 7-18.

1. **Launch a Web browser and open the file *chapter_07 → sidebar.html*.**

   In this case, there's already an external style sheet attached to the page that adds some basic text formatting, as you can see in Figure 7-15.

2. **In your favorite text editor, open *chapter_07 → sidebar.html*.**

   Start by adding an internal style sheet to this file.

3. **Click directly after the closing </link> tag (used to attach the external style sheet), hit Enter (Return), and then type *<style type="text/css">*.**

   You've just created the opening style tag. Next, you'll create a style that sets the margin around the edges of the page and adds a color to the background.

4. **Press the Enter (Return) key, and then type the following style:**

   ```
   body {
       margin-top: 15px;
       margin-left: 0;
       margin-right: 0;
       padding: 0;
       background-color: #f8faf1;
   }
   ```

   This style makes the page's background a light gray-green. The margin settings indent the page content 15 pixels from the top of the window but remove all

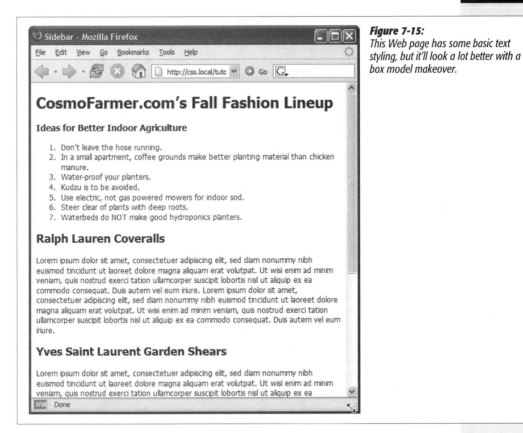

Figure 7-15:
*This Web page has some basic text
styling, but it'll look a lot better with a
box model makeover.*

space from the left and right edges. In other words, content butts right up against the left and right edges of the browser window. You could have done the same thing with the margin shorthand property (page 136) like this: *margin: 15px 0 0 0;*.

Note: The padding property (*padding: 0;*) in this style accommodates the Opera browser, which uses *padding* instead of *margin* to define the space around the edges of the browser window.

Finally you'll add the closing <style> tag to complete the style sheet.

5. **Hit Enter (Return) to create a new, blank line, and then type </style>.**

   Your style sheet's complete and you're ready to check the page.

6. **Save the file and preview the page in a Web browser.**

   The top line of text is placed a little way down from the top of the browser window, while the left edge of each headline and paragraph touches the left side of the browser window. The type looks cramped on the left side like that, but you'll fix it later in this tutorial.

Next, adjust the spacing around the headlines and paragraphs.

Adjusting the Space Around Tags

Web browsers automatically insert a bit of space above and below headlines, paragraphs, lists, forms, and other block-level HTML elements. The exact amount varies from browser to browser, so you get more predictable results by setting this value yourself, as described in the following steps.

1. Return to your text editor and the *sidebar.html* file. Click at the end of the closing brace of the body tag selector, press Enter (Return) to create a new line, and then add these two styles:

   ```
   h1 {
       margin: 0;
   }
   h2 {
       margin-top: 10px;
       margin-bottom: 0;
   }
   ```

   The first style removes all margins from all <h1> tags, and the second removes the bottom margin from all <h2> tags and sets their top margins to 10 pixels. If you preview the page now, you'll see that it actually doesn't look any different. But you can detect a gap above the <h1> tag at the top of the page, as well as space above and below each <h2> tag. That's because there are still margins above and below the paragraph tags and the <h3> tag ("Ideas for Better Indoor Agriculture").

Note: The gap between the <h2> and <p> tags didn't change at all because the bottom margin of the <h2> tag and the top margin of the <p> tag were already collapsed. (See page 137 to learn more about the mystery of *collapsing margins.*)

Next, remove the space between the tops of the paragraphs and the bottoms of the <h2> tag.

2. Click at the end of the closing brace of the *h2* tag selector, press Enter (Return) to create a new line, and then add this style:

   ```
   p {
       margin-top: 0;
       margin-bottom: 10px;
   }
   ```

3. Save the file and preview the page in a Web browser.

   The gap between the headline and the paragraphs below has gone away, but there's still a 10-pixel space between each paragraph thanks to the *margin-bottom* setting (Figure 7-16).

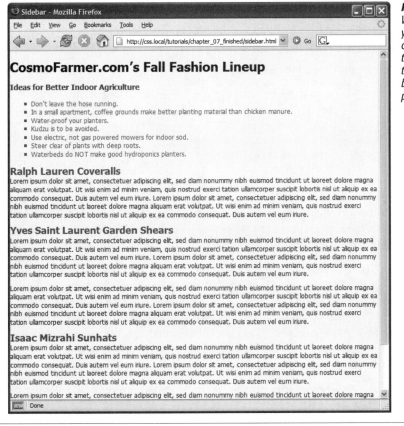

Figure 7-16:
With just a few short styles, you can add background colors, control margins throughout the page, and tighten up the space between headlines and paragraphs.

Emphasizing Text with Backgrounds and Borders

Backgrounds can colorize a page or highlight a sidebar, but you can use them for plenty of other purposes—like making headlines stand out. Borders, too, are more versatile than they get credit for. Sure, they're fine for framing images, adding lines around tables, and drawing boxes on a Web page, but a single border can draw attention to headlines, separate paragraphs of text, and replace the gray, clunky-looking HTML <hr> tag. In this section, you'll use backgrounds and borders to emphasize the page headings.

1. Return to your text editor and the *sidebar.html* file.

   It's time to edit the *h1* style you already created.

2. Add two properties to the *h1* style, so that it looks like this:

```
h1 {
    margin: 0;
    border-top: solid 2px #fbef99;
    border-bottom: solid 2px #fbef99;
}
```

These two properties add a yellow line above and below the headline. If you preview the page now, you'll see the two lines are too close to the text. There could also stand to be a little more breathing room between the left edge of the page and the text in the headline. You'll make those two adjustments next.

3. **Add some padding to the *h1* style:**

```
h1 {
    margin: 0;
    border-top: solid 2px #fbef99;
    border-bottom: solid 2px #fbef99;
    padding: 5px 0 5px 25px;
}
```

Padding indents the text of the headline from its borders. This shorthand method of specifying the padding properties (page 136) indents the text 5 pixels from the top line, 0 from the right edge, and 5 pixels from the bottom line while indenting the left edge 25 pixels.

If you preview the page, you'll see that the two lines extend the full length of the browser window, touching both the left and right edges, while the headline text is nicely indented. Now you can see the reason for setting the left and right margins of the body to 0—it allows the heading's border lines to extend across the browser window without gaps on the left or right side. In a moment, you'll also indent the *h2* and *p* tags, but first add a bit more punch to that opening headline by adding a background color.

4. **Add two more properties to the *h1* style—a background color and a text color—like so:**

```
h1 {
    margin: 0;
    border-top: 2px solid #FBEF99;
    border-bottom: 2px solid #FBEF99;
    padding: 5px 0 5px 25px;
    background-color: #294e56;
    color: #fff;
}
```

With this adjustment, the white headline text jumps out from a dark stripe across the page. Next, add a bottom underline to each <h2> tag.

5. **Edit the *h2* style by adding a margin and bottom border, as follows:**

```
h2 {
    margin-top: 10px;
    margin-bottom: 0px;
    margin-left: 25px;
    border-bottom: 1px solid #5f9794;
}
```

The left margin indents the headline, moving it away from the left edge of the browser window and aligning it with the text in the <h1> tag. You need to make the same change to the paragraph tags, in order to line them up as well.

6. **Add a 25px left margin to the *p* style:**

```
p {
    margin-top: 0;
    margin-bottom: 10px;
    margin-left: 25px;
}
```

This step indents the paragraphs to match the indent of the other headlines. You can also rewrite these three margin settings using the margin shortcut property: *margin: 0 0 10px 25px;*.

7. **Save the file and preview the page in a Web browser.**

The page should look like Figure 7-17. The bulleted list of items doesn't look very good yet. This sidebar element needs to look like a real sidebar—placed in its own box and moved to the side of the page. You'll do that in the next section.

Building a Sidebar

Sidebars are common elements in most types of print publications like magazines, books, and newspapers. They compartmentalize and highlight small chunks of information like a resource list, contact information, or a related anecdote. But to be effective, sidebars shouldn't interrupt the flow of the main story. They should, like the name says, sit unobtrusively off to one side, which you can easily make happen with CSS.

1. **Return to your text editor and the *sidebar.html* file.**

First, you must isolate the region of the page that makes up the sidebar. The <div> tag (page 47) is the perfect tool. You can enclose any amount of HTML into its own self-contained chunk by wrapping it in a <div> tag.

2. **Click *before* the opening <h3> tag (the one with the "Ideas for Better Indoor Agriculture" headline). Then type *<div class="sidebar">*, and press Enter (Return).**

This CSS marks the beginning of the sidebar and applies a class to it. You'll create the *.sidebar* class style in the next step, but first you need to indicate the end of the sidebar by closing the <div>.

3. **Click after the closing </ul> tag. (This indicates the end of a bulleted list.) Press Enter (Return), and then type *</div>*.**

You've just wrapped a headline and bulleted list inside a <div> tag. Next, you'll create a style for it.

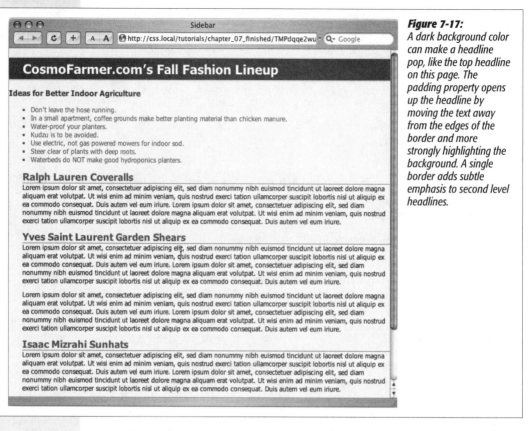

4. In the page's style sheet, add the following style below the <p> style you created earlier:

```css
.sidebar {
    width: 200px;
    float: right;
    margin: 10px;
}
```

This style sets the width of the content area (where the text appears) to 200 pixels, floats it to the right side of the browser window, and adds 10 pixels of space around the box.

If you preview the page in a browser, you'll see that the basic shape and placement of the sidebar's set, but there's one problem: The <h2> tags appear *underneath* the box. Even though the floated sidebar moves the text of the headlines out of the way, floats don't displace border or backgrounds. Those just appear right under the floated sidebar (see page 154). You can easily adjust for this bit of CSS frailty by editing the <h2> tag style you created earlier.

Note: If your site's audience includes a lot of Opera fans (the Web browser, not the musical extrava-
ganza), then skip step 5 and just live with the border extending underneath the floated sidebar. This fix is
more like a break for that browser.

5. **Locate the h2 style and add the *overflow* property, like so:**

   ```
   h2 {
       margin-top: 10px;
       margin-bottom: 0px;
       margin-left: 25px;
       border-bottom: 1px solid #5F9794;
       overflow: hidden;
   }
   ```

   Setting the overflow property to *hidden* hides the borders that pass beyond the
   headline text and under the floating element. (Unfortunately, Internet Explorer
   6 and 5 don't get it and still display the borders underneath the sidebar. But
   you'll fix that in the next section.)

   In the meantime, make the sidebar stand out by adding a border and background color.

6. **Add the following two properties to the .sidebar style:**

   ```
   border: solid 1px #fdd041;
   border-top-width: 5px;
   ```

   The first property, *border*, is a shorthand method of setting the style, width, and
   color of all four borders. In this, case, it creates a 1-pixel, solid yellow line around
   the sidebar. The second property, *border-top-width*, overrides the 1-pixel width
   set by the border property, creating a thicker top border for some visual interest.

   Finally, you'll add a little padding to indent the text from the inside edges of the
   box, as well as a background color.

7. **Add two more properties to the sidebar style, like so:**

   ```
   .sidebar {
       width: 200px;
       float: right;
       margin: 10px;
       border: solid 1px #fdd041;
       border-top-width: 5px;
       padding: 10px;
       background-color: #fbef99;
   }
   ```

   The background-color property adds a light yellow color to the sidebar and
   covers the borders of the <h2> tags. To finish up the sidebar, you'll create a few
   descendent selectors to control the formatting for the tags inside the sidebar.

First, you'll address the <h3> tag, which in some browsers (notably Firefox) has unnecessary space above it.

8. **Add this style to your style sheet:**

```
.sidebar h3 {
    margin: 0;
    text-align: center;
}
```

This descendent selector style affects only <h3> tags that appear *inside* a tag that has the .sidebar class applied to it. It centers the text and eliminates any margins around the headline. Because Web browsers indent lists, you'll notice that the bulleted list in the narrow sidebar looks weird with such a large left indent.

9. **Add one more style to the style sheet:**

```
.sidebar ul {
    padding: 0;
    margin: 10px 0 0 0;
}
```

Because some browsers use the left padding property and others use the left margin property to indent lists, you need to make sure both are set to 0 in order to reliably eliminate a left margin from lists. In this case, we've added 10 pixels of top margin space above the list to separate it a bit from the headline above.

If you preview the page now, you'll notice one big error. The bullets appear either outside of the sidebar box, or not at all (in the case of Internet Explorer). Simply adding a little indent to the list items brings the bullets back into view.

10. **Add the following style to indent each bulleted item:**

```
.sidebar li {
    margin-left: 1.5em;
}
```

This style adds enough space to the left of each list item, moving the bullets back into view. Now it's time to preview your handiwork.

11. **Save the file and preview the Web page in a browser.**

The page should look like Figure 7-18.

Unfortunately, the page doesn't look like Figure 7-18 in Internet Explorer 6 or 5 for Windows. A couple of bugs in those browser versions affect the page's appearance for the worse. Read on for the fixes.

Fixing the Browser Bugs

While the *sidebar.html* file looks just fine in Internet Explorer 7, earlier versions of that browser don't display the page correctly. If you have access to either of these browsers, check it out. You'll see the problems.

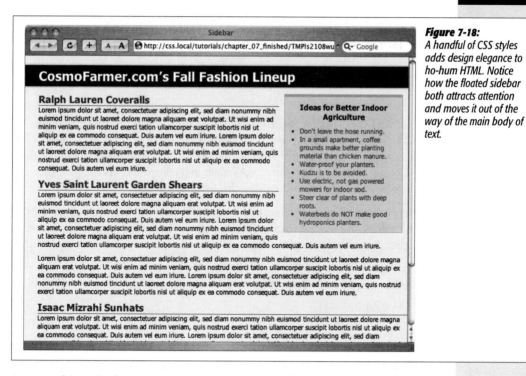

Figure 7-18:
*A handful of CSS styles
adds design elegance to
ho-hum HTML. Notice
how the floated sidebar
both attracts attention
and moves it out of the
way of the main body of
text.*

For one thing, the border under the two <h2> headlines travels underneath the sidebar. In step 5 on page 165, you used the *overflow* property to fix this problem in most browsers, but you need something else to get IE 5 and 6 straightened out. In addition, the margin around the sidebar is noticeably larger on the right. And in IE 5, the sidebar's much smaller than in other browsers.

Tip: If you don't have access to check for yourself, just trust that problems are there and use this section to learn how to fix them for the sake of your visitors who are stuck with IE 5 or 6.

The first bug, the overextended borders, affects both IE 5 and 6. You'll tackle this one first:

1. **Return to your text editor and the *sidebar.html* file.**

   You first need to create a style that *only* Internet Explorer 6 and earlier can read.

2. **Add this new style to the end of the *sidebar.html* page's style sheet:**

   ```
   * html h2 {

   }
   ```

The * *html* part of the style is in fact an incorrect CSS selector. However, IE 6 and earlier consider it legitimate, so by adding *h2* to create a descendent selector, Internet Explorer 6 and earlier treats this as a valid style for formatting any <h2> tag. (See page 152 for more on this technique.)

So far, you've just got an empty style. Time to add some properties.

3. **Add the following property to the new style:**

```
* html h2 {
    zoom: 1;
}
```

Zoom isn't an official CSS property. It's a Microsoft-only property meant to enlarge an element on a page. That's not why you're using it here, though. In this case, the zoom property prevents the border from extending under the float in IE 5 and 6. *It fixes the border bug—albeit* in a completely arcane way. (See the box on page 307 for more details on this browser voodoo.)

Next problem: The double-margin bug that's causing that extra space on the right side of the sidebar. Since this bug affects both IE 5 and 6, you'll create another * *html* style for the sidebar. (Remember, * *html* hides the rest of this selector—*.sidebar*—from all browsers except IE 6 for Windows and earlier.)

4. **Add this style to your style sheet:**

```
* html .sidebar {
    display: inline;
}
```

This use of the *display* property is another nonsensical bit of CSS. But it does the job: It tricks IE into removing the extra right-hand margin. (See page 302 for a full explanation.)

Two down, one to go. Internet Explorer 5 on Windows incorrectly calculates the width of the sidebar, so it looks thinner than in other browsers. Blame it on the old *IE 5 box model bug* (see page 150).

5. **To fatten up the skinny sidebar, add this property to the * *html .sidebar* style:**

```
width: 222px;
```

Why 222 pixels? The .sidebar style you created in step 4 on page 164 has a width of 200 pixels. All other browsers dedicate 200 pixels to the content only—the headline and bulleted list. IE 5, on the other hand, includes the widths of the borders and padding as part of this 200 pixels, making the actual area dedicated to the content much smaller in that browser. For IE 5 to provide the same room as other browsers for the headline and bulleted list, you need to give a width value equal to *the combined width of the content, borders, and padding*. So, 200 pixels (the width value for the content) plus 2 pixels (the width of the left and right borders), plus 20 pixels (the widths of the left and right padding) equals 222 pixels.

At this point, you've successfully tricked IE 5 to display the sidebar at the same width as all other browsers. But you're not off the hook yet. Because IE 6 also gets this width sent to it, you must tell IE 6 to reset the width property *back* to 200 pixels.

6. **Add one final property to this style so that it looks like this:**

```
* html .sidebar {
    display: inline;
    width: 222px;
    w\idth: 200px;
}
```

No, that backslash isn't a typo, nor is it teenage text-messaging slang for "your jeans are too tight." The backslash in the property name *w\idth* is just another example of strange-but-true browser trickery. IE 5 ignores the misspelled property, while IE 6 understands that it's the width property and that you're setting its value back to 200px. (See page 151 for all the gruesome details.)

7. **Save the file and preview the page in Internet Explorer 5 or 6 on Windows.**

The page should now look like Figure 7-18 in those browsers as well. Dealing with these browser bugs is an unfortunate reality for every Web developer. You'll learn solutions (also known as *hacks*) to particular bugs throughout this book. Also, in Chapter 14, you'll learn even more strategies for dealing with hacks used to fix Internet Explorer browser bugs.

Going Further

To try out your newfound skills, try this exercise on your own: Create a class style for formatting the copyright notice that appears at the bottom of the *sidebar.html* page (called, say, *.copyright*). In this style, add a border above the copyright notice, change its text color, shrink its font size, and change the type to uppercase. (Hint: Use the *text-transform* property discussed on page 109.) After you've created the style, apply it to the paragraph with the copyright notice.

The solution's in the *sidebar_finished.html* file inside the *ch07_finished* folder.

Adding Graphics to Web Pages

No matter how much you gussy up your text or fiddle with borders and margins, nothing affects the appearance of your site more than the images you add to it. And once again, CSS gives you more image control than HTML ever dreamed of. You can work with graphics in CSS on two fronts: the <img> tag and the *background-image* property (which you can attach to any number of tags).

This chapter delves into some of the creative ways you can deploy images with CSS. The best way to learn how to use graphics in CSS is to see them in action, so this chapter has two—count 'em, two—tutorials. By creating a photo gallery Web page and using images for overall page styling, you'll be an image-slinging pro in no time.

CSS and the <img> Tag

The venerable <img> tag has been the workhorse of photo-heavy Web sites since the beginning of the World Wide Web. Even sites without photos use it to add logos, navigation buttons, and illustrations. While CSS doesn't have any properties specifically aimed at formatting images, you can take advantage of the CSS properties you've already learned to enhance your site's graphics. For example, the *border* property's a quick and simple way to frame an image or unify the look of a gallery of photos. Here's a rundown of the CSS properties most commonly used with images:

- **Borders.** Use one of the many border properties (page 141) to frame an image. You'll see an example of this in the tutorial on page 184. Since each border side can be a different color, style, and width, you've got lots of creative options here.

- **Padding.** The padding property (page 135) adds space between a border and an image. By putting a little breathing room between a photo and its frame, padding simulates the fiberboard *mat* that's used in traditional picture frames to surround and offset the image. And by setting a background color (page 145), you can even change the color of the "mat."

- **Float.** Floating an image moves it to either the left or right edge of the page, or—if the image is contained in another layout element such as a sidebar—the image's containing element (page 136). Text and other page elements then wrap around the image. You can even float multiple images to create a flexible, multi-row image gallery. You'll see an example of this in the tutorial on page 188.

- **Margins.** To add space between an image and other page content, use the *margin* property (page 135). When you float an image, the text that wraps around it is usually uncomfortably close to the image. Adding a left margin (for right-floated images) or right margin (for left-floated images) adds space between text and the graphic.

In most cases, you won't create a style for the <img> tag itself. Formatting this tag's too broad a brush, since it formats *all* images on your page—even those with very different functions such as the logo, navigation buttons, photos, and even graphic ads. You wouldn't, after all, want the same black frame around all of those images. Instead, you should use a class style, such as *.galleryImage*, or *.logo* to apply the style selectively.

Another approach is to use a descendent selector (page 49) to target images grouped together in one section of a page. If you have a gallery of photos, you can place all of the photos inside a <div> tag with an ID name of *gallery*, and then create a style for just the images inside that <div>, like this: *#gallery img*.

Background Images

The background-image property is the key to making visually stunning Web sites. Learn how to use it and its cousin properties, and you can make your site stand head and shoulders above the rest. For an example of the power of background images, check out *www.csszengarden.com* (Figure 8-1). The HTML for both the pages shown here is exactly the same; the visual differences are accomplished by using different background images. How's that for CSS power?

If you've built a few Web sites, you've probably used an image for the background of a page—perhaps a small graphic that repeats in the background of the browser window creating a (hopefully) subtle pattern. That time-honored HTML method used the <body> tag's *background* attribute. But CSS does the same job better.

Note: In the next few pages, you'll meet three background image properties by learning the individual CSS code for each one. Later in the chapter you'll learn a shorthand method that'll save you a lot of typing.

Figure 8-1:
CSSzengarden.com showcases the power of Cascading Style Sheets by demonstrating how you can transform a single HTML file into two utterly different looking pages with the help of CSS. The real secret to making each of the wonderful designs look unique is the extensive use of background images. (In fact, when you look at these pages' HTML code, you'll see there isn't a single <img> tag in it.)

The background-image property adds a graphic to the background of an element. To put an image in the background of a Web page, you can create a style for the <body> tag:

```
body { background-image: url(images/bg.gif); }
```

The property takes one value: the keyword *url*, followed by a path to the graphic file enclosed in parentheses. You can use an absolute URL like this—*url(http://www.cosmofarmer.com/image/bg.gif)*—or a document- or root-relative path like these:

```
url(../images/bg.gif) /* document-relative */
url(/images/bg.gif) /* root-relative */
```

As explained in the box on page 175, document-relative paths provide directions in relation to the style sheet file, *not* the HTML page you're styling. These will be one and the same, of course, if you're using an internal style sheet, but you need to keep this point in mind if you're using an *external* style sheet. Say you've got a folder named *styles* (containing the site's style sheets) and a folder named *images* (holding the site's images). Both these folders are located in the site's main folder along with the home page (Figure 8-2). When a visitor views the home page, the external style sheet's also loaded (step 1 in Figure 8-2). Now, say the external style sheet includes a style for the <body> tag with the background image property set to use the graphic file *bg.gif* in the images folder. The document-relative path would lead from the style sheet to the graphic (step 2 in Figure 8-2). In other words, the style would look like this:

```
body { background-image: url(../images/bg.gif);
```

This path breaks down like this: ../ means "go up one level" (that is, up to the folder containing the *styles* folder); *images/* means "go to the images folder"; and *bg.gif* specifies that file.

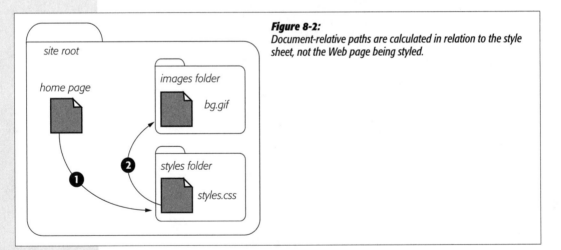

Figure 8-2:
Document-relative paths are calculated in relation to the style sheet, not the Web page being styled.

In the examples so far, the path isn't enclosed in quotes as in HTML but quotes are fine, too. In CSS, all three of the following code lines are kosher:

```
background-image: url(images/bg.gif);
background-image: url("images/bg.gif");
background-image: url('images/bg.gif');
```

CSS: The Missing Manual

Note: Internet Explorer 5 for Mac doesn't recognize URLs that are specified inside of *single* quotes like this: *url('images/bg.gif')*.

URL Types

In CSS, you need to specify an *URL* when you add a background image or attach an external style sheet using the @import method (page 33). An URL or *Uniform Resource Locator* is a path to a file located on the Web. There are three types of paths: *absolute path*, *root-relative path*, and *document-relative path*. All three simply indicate where a Web browser can find a particular file (like another Web page, a graphic, or an external style sheet).

An absolute path is like a postal address—it contains all the information needed for a Web browser located anywhere in the world to find the file. An absolute path includes http://, the hostname, and the folder and name of the file. For example: *http://www.cosmofarmer.com/images/bluegrass.jpg*.

A *root-relative* path indicates where a file's located relative to a site's top-level folder—the site's root folder. A root-relative path doesn't include http:// or the domain name. It begins with a / (slash) indicating the root folder of the site (the folder the home page is in). For example */images/ bluegrass.jpg* indicates that the file *bluegrass.jpg* is located inside a folder named *images*, which is itself located in the site's top-level folder. An easy way to create a root-relative path is to take an absolute path and strip off the http:// and the host name.

A *document-relative* path specifies the path from the current document to the file. When it comes to a style sheet, this means *the path from the style sheet to the specified file*, not the path from the current Web page to the file.

Here are some tips on which type to use:

• If you're pointing to a file that's not on the same server as the style sheet, you *must* use an absolute path. It's the only type that can point to another Web site.

• Root-relative paths are good for images stored on your own site. Since they always start at the root folder, you can move the style sheet around without affecting the path from the root to the image on the site. However, they're difficult to use when first building your designs: you can't preview root-relative paths unless you're viewing your Web pages through a Web server—either your Web server out on the Internet, or a Web server you've set up on your own computer for testing purposes. In other words, if you're just opening a Web page off your computer using the browser's File → Open command, then you won't see any images placed using root-relative paths.

• Document-relative paths are the best when you're designing on your own computer without the aid of a Web server. You can create your CSS files and then review them in a Web browser simply by opening a Web page stored on your hard drive. These pages will work fine when you move them to your actual, living, breathing Web site on the Internet, but you'll have to re-write the URLs to the images if you move the style sheet to another location on the server.

Controlling Repetition

One problem with the old HTML *background* attribute is that the graphic always tiles, filling up the entire background of a Web page. (Not only that, it's being phased out from current HTML standards.) Fortunately, CSS gives you far greater control. Using the *background-repeat* property you can specify how (or if at all) an image tiles:

```
background-repeat: no-repeat;
```

The property accepts four values: *repeat*, *no-repeat*, *repeat-x*, and *repeat-y*:

- *repeat* is the normal setting for background images that you want to display
  from left to right and top to bottom until the entire space is filled with a graphic
  (Figure 8-3).

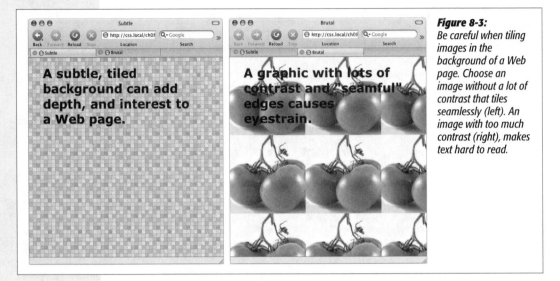

Figure 8-3:
*Be careful when tiling
images in the
background of a Web
page. Choose an
image without a lot of
contrast that tiles
seamlessly (left). An
image with too much
contrast (right), makes
text hard to read.*

- *no-repeat* displays the image a single time, without tiling or repetition. It's a
  very common option, and you'll frequently use it when placing images into the
  background of tags other than the body. You can use it to place a logo in the
  upper corner of a page or for using custom graphics for bullets in lists, to name
  a couple. (You'll see the bullet example in action in the tutorial on page 201.) In
  another example, you'll use it at the top of a <div> tag to create a rounded edge
  at the top of a box (page 203).

- *repeat-x* repeats an image horizontally along the x-axis (the horizontal width of
  the page, if your geometry's rusty). It's perfect for adding a graphical banner to
  the top of a Web page (Figure 8-4, left) or a decorative border along the top or
  bottom of a headline. (See page 200 in the tutorial for an example of this effect.)

- *repeat-y* repeats an image vertically along the y-axis (the vertical length of the
  page). You can use this setting to add a graphic sidebar to a page (Figure 8-4,
  right) or to add a repeating drop shadow to either side of a page element (like a
  sidebar).

Positioning a Background Image

Placing and tiling a background image is just half the fun. With the *background-
position* property, CSS lets you control the exact placement of an image in a
number of ways. You can specify both the horizontal and vertical starting points
for a graphic in three ways—keywords, exact values, and percentages.

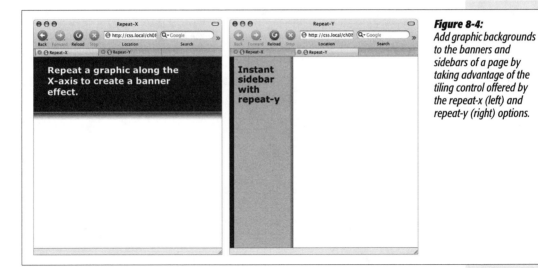

Figure 8-4:
*Add graphic backgrounds
to the banners and
sidebars of a page by
taking advantage of the
tiling control offered by
the repeat-x (left) and
repeat-y (right) options.*

Keywords

You get two sets of keywords to work with. One controls the three horizontal positions—*left*, *center*, *right*—and the other controls the three vertical positions—*top*, *center*, *bottom* (Figure 8-5). Suppose you want to place a graphic directly in the middle of a Web page. You can create a style like this:

```
body {
    background-image: url(bg_page.jpg);
    background-repeat: no-repeat;
    background-position: center center;
}
```

To move that graphic to the top-right corner, just change the background position to this:

```
background-position: right top;
```

Note: If you've decided to tile an image (by setting background-repeat to one of the values listed in the previous section), then the background-position property controls the *starting* point of the first tile. So, for example, if you use the *repeat* option, you'll still see the entire background filled by the image. It's just that the position of the *first* tile changes based on which background-position setting you used.

Keywords are really useful when you want to create vertical or horizontal banners. If you wanted a graphic that's centered on a page and tiled downwards in order to create a backdrop for content (Figure 8-6, left), then you'd create a style like this:

```
body {
    background-image: url(background.jpg);
    background-repeat: repeat-y;
    background-position: center top;
}
```

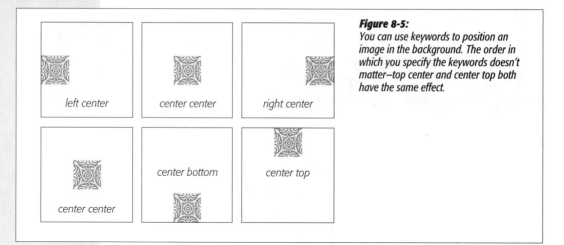

Figure 8-5:
You can use keywords to position an image in the background. The order in which you specify the keywords doesn't matter—top center and center top both have the same effect.

Likewise, using the *bottom, center,* or *top* keywords you can position a horizontally repeating image using repeat-x (page 175) in a particular place on the page (or within a styled element). Use the technique shown on the right side of Figure 8-6, to position a line under headlines in the tutorial on page 200.

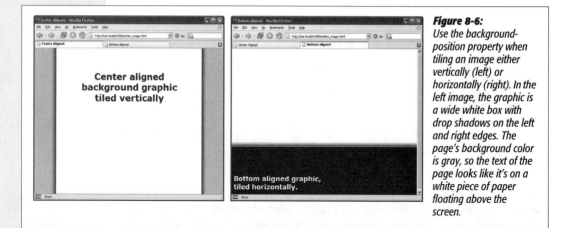

Figure 8-6:
Use the background-position property when tiling an image either vertically (left) or horizontally (right). In the left image, the graphic is a wide white box with drop shadows on the left and right edges. The page's background color is gray, so the text of the page looks like it's on a white piece of paper floating above the screen.

BROWSER BUG

Bottoming Out in Firefox

When displaying an image in the background of a Web page, Firefox doesn't always vertically position the image in the way you'd expect. For example, if you set the vertical position to *bottom,* the image doesn't always appear at the bottom of the browser window. This happens when the content on a page is shorter than the browser window is tall.

If the Web page has only a couple of paragraphs of text and it's displayed on a really large monitor, Firefox treats the "bottom" as the bottom of the last paragraph, not the bottom of the browser window. If you run into this annoyance, then just add this style to your style sheet: *html { height: 100%; }*.

Precise Values

You can also position background images using pixel values or ems. You use two values: one to indicate the distance between the image's left edge and the container's left edge, and another to specify the distance between the image's top edge and the style's top edge. (Put another way, the first value controls the horizontal position, the second value controls the vertical position.)

Say you want custom bullets for a list. If you add a background image to the <li> tag, the bullets often don't line up exactly (see Figure 8-7, top). So you can just nudge the bullets into place using the background-position property (Figure 8-7, bottom). If the list would look better with, say, the bullets five pixels farther to the right and eight pixels farther down, then add this declaration to the style defining the background image:

```
background-position:5px 8px;
```

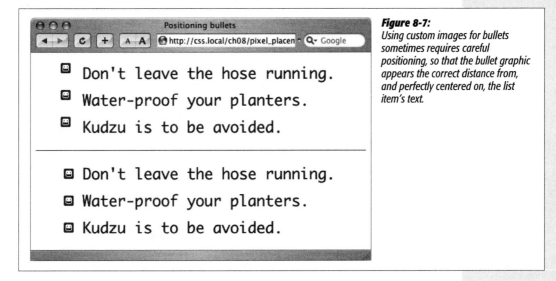

Figure 8-7:
Using custom images for bullets sometimes requires careful positioning, so that the bullet graphic appears the correct distance from, and perfectly centered on, the list item's text.

You can't specify distances from the *bottom* or *right* using pixel or em measurements, so if you want to make sure an image is placed in the exact bottom right corner of the page or a styled element, then use keywords (*bottom right*) or percentages, as discussed next. However, you can use negative values to move an image off the right edge or above the top edge, hiding that portion of the image from view. You may want to use negative values to crop out part of a picture. Or, if the background image has lots of extra white space at the top or left edge, you can use negative values to eliminate that extra space.

Percentage Values

Finally, you can use percentage values to position a background image. Using percentages in this manner is tricky, and if you can achieve the effect you're after with the keyword or precise values discussed previously, then use them. But you have to use percentages to position an element in a spot that's proportional to the width of an element. For example, if you want to place a graphic three-quarters of the way across a headline, and you don't know the width of the element.

Note: Percentage values are also useful for a little trick often used with float-based layouts to give left and right sidebars background colors or graphics that span the entire height of a Web page (see the Note on page 299).

As with pixel or em values, you supply two percentages: one to indicate the horizontal position and the second to indicate the vertical position. What the percentage is measuring is a little tricky. In a nutshell, a percentage value aligns the specified percentage of the image with the same percentage of the styled element. What?

The best way to understand how percentage values work is to look at a few examples. To position an image in the middle of a page (like the one shown in the center of Figure 8-8) you'd write this:

```
background-position:50% 50%;
```

This declaration places the point on the image that's 50 percent from its left edge directly on top of the point that's 50 percent from the left edge of the page (or whatever element you've styled with the background image). The declaration also aligns the point on the image that's 50 percent from its top with the point that's 50 percent from the top edge of the page or styled element. In other words, the center of the image is aligned with the center of the element. This means that, when using percentages, the exact point on the image that's being aligned can be a moving target. (That's because your styled element's positioning percentages can change if your visitors resize their browsers.)

As with pixel and em values, you can specify negative percentage values, though the results can be hard to predict. You can also mix and match pixel/em values with percentage values. For example, to place an image that's 5 pixels from the element's left edge, but placed in the middle of the element's height, you could use this:

```
background-position: 5px 50%;
```

Due to poor browser support, don't mix and match percentages or pixels/ems with keywords: *top 50px*, for example. Some browsers can handle this combination, but some can't.

Note: Although background images can raise the visual quality of your Web pages, they usually don't show up if your visitor prints the page. Most browsers *can* print out the backgrounds, but it usually requires extra work on your visitor's part. If you plan to have your visitors print pages from your site, then you may want to keep using the <img> tag to insert mission-critical images like your site logo, or a map to your store.

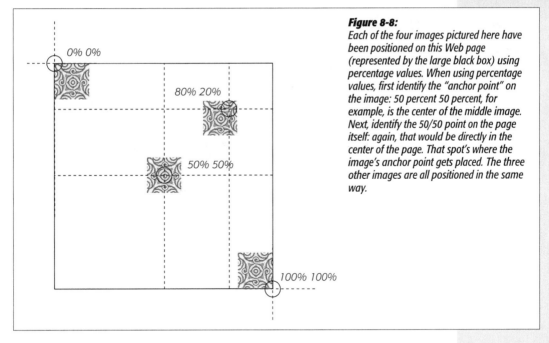

Figure 8-8:
Each of the four images pictured here have been positioned on this Web page (represented by the large black box) using percentage values. When using percentage values, first identify the "anchor point" on the image: 50 percent 50 percent, for example, is the center of the middle image. Next, identify the 50/50 point on the page itself: again, that would be directly in the center of the page. That spot's where the image's anchor point gets placed. The three other images are all positioned in the same way.

Fixing an Image in Place

Normally, if there's a background image on a Web page and the visitor has to scroll down to see more of the page, the background image scrolls as well. As a result, any pattern in the background of the page appears to move along with the text. Furthermore, when you have a non-repeating image in the background, it can potentially scroll off the top of the page out of view. If you've placed the site's logo or a watermark graphic in the background of the page, then you may *not* want it to disappear when visitors scroll.

The CSS solution to such dilemmas is the *background-attachment* property. It has two options—*scroll* and *fixed*. Scroll is the normal Web browser behavior; that is, it scrolls the background image along with the text and other page content. Fixed, however, keeps the image in place in the background (see Figure 8-9). So if you want to place your company's logo in the upper left corner of the Web page, and keep it there even if the viewer scrolls, then you can create a style like this:

```
body {
    background-image: url(images/logo.gif);
    background-repeat: no-repeat;
    background-attachment: fixed;
}
```

The *fixed* option's also very nice when using a repeating, tiled background. When you have to scroll, the page's text disappears off the top, but the background doesn't move: the page content appears to float gracefully above the background.

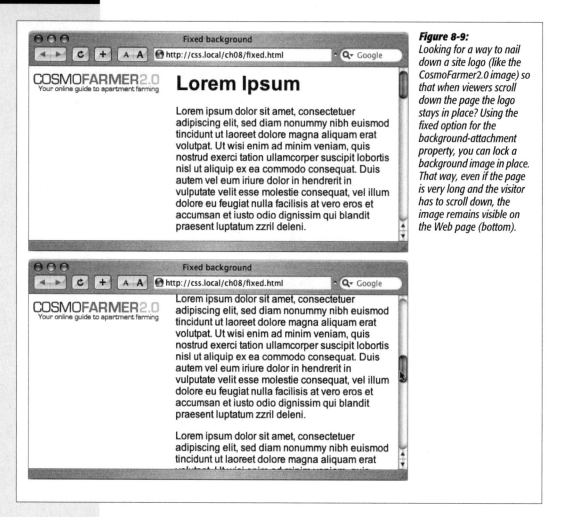

Figure 8-9:
*Looking for a way to nail
down a site logo (like the
CosmoFarmer2.0 image) so
that when viewers scroll
down the page the logo
stays in place? Using the
fixed option for the
background-attachment
property, you can lock a
background image in place.
That way, even if the page
is very long and the visitor
has to scroll down, the
image remains visible on
the Web page (bottom).*

Note: CSS lets you "fix" the background image for a style applied to any element, not just the <body> tag. However, the Windows versions of Internet Explorer 6 and earlier only understand the *background-attachment* property when used with a style applied to the <body> tag.

Using Background Property Shorthand

As you can see from the examples above, to really take control of background images you need to harness the power of several different background properties. But typing out *background-image, background-attachment,* and so on again and again can really take its toll on your hands. But there's an easier way—the *background* shorthand property.

You can actually bundle all the background properties (including the *background-color* property you learned about last chapter) into a single line of streamlined CSS.

Finding Free Imagery

*I'm not an artist. I can't draw, can't paint, don't even own
a digital camera. Where can I find artwork for my site?*

Thank goodness for the Web. It's the one-stop shop for creative geniuses who couldn't paint themselves into a corner
if they tried. There are plenty of pay-to-download sites for
stock photos and illustrations, but there are also quite a few
completely free options. For photos, check out Morgue File
(*www.morguefile.com*), which despite the grisly name has
many wonderful photos supplied free of charge by people
who love to take pictures. The Creative Commons site provides options as well: *http://creativecommons.org/image/*.
Open Photo (*http://openphoto.net/gallery/browse.html*)
also supplies images based on Creative Commons licenses.
(Although they don't cost money, not all photos on these
sites can be used in commercial projects. Make sure you
read the fine print for any photo you wish to use.)

If you're looking for bullets to add to lists, icons to super-
charge your navigation bar, or patterns to fill the screen,
there are plenty of sites to choose from. Bullet Madness
(*www.stylegala.com/features/bulletmadness/*) offers 200
bullets including variations on the common arrow, circle and
square as well as more detailed bullets representing software icons, iPods, folders, and more. Some Random Dude
(no, really; that's the name of the Web site) offers a set of
121 icons free of charge: *www.somerandomdude.net/srd-
projects/sanscons*. And if you're looking for interesting tiling
patterns, check out the patterns on these sites:

- Kaliber10000 (*www.k10k.net/pixelpatterns/*)

- Pattern4u (*www.kollermedia.at/pattern4u/*)

- Squidfingers (*http://squidfingers.com/patterns/*)

Simply type *background* followed by the values for *background-color, background-
image, background-attachment,* and *background-position.* The following style sets
the background to white, and adds a non-repeating fixed background image smack
dab in the middle of the page:

```
body { background: #FFF url(bullseye.gif) scroll center center no-repeat; }
```

You don't need to specify all of the property values either. You can use one or any
combination of them. For example: *background: yellow* is the equivalent of
background-color: yellow. Any property value you leave out simply reverts to its
normal behavior, so say you specified only an image:

```
background: url(image/bullseye.gif)
```

That's the equivalent of this:

```
background: url(image/bullseye.gif) fixed left top repeat;
```

Because the background property is so much faster to type, and it achieves all the
same ends as its long-winded siblings, use it liberally when adding background
images (and colors) to your styles.

Tutorial: Creating a Photo Gallery

A photo gallery's a perfect example of an eye-catching Web page. This tutorial
brings together a variety of image styling techniques. You'll format images with
frames and captions, create a photo gallery that's flexible enough to look great in a

variety of window sizes, and use background images to create professional-looking drop shadows.

To get started, you need to download the tutorial files located on this book's companion Web site at *www.sawmac.com/css/*. Click the tutorial link and download the files. All of the files are enclosed in a ZIP archive, so you need to unzip them first. (There are detailed instructions on the Web site.) The files for this tutorial are in the *chapter_08* folder.

Framing an Image

1. Launch a Web browser and open the file *chapter_08 → image_ex → image.html*.

   As usual, you'll be working on a Web page from CosmoFarmer.com (Figure 8-10). In this case, there's already an external style sheet attached to the page, adding some basic text formatting.

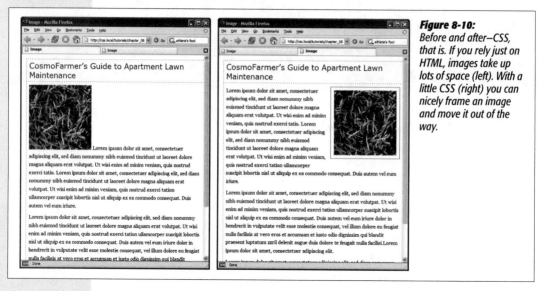

Figure 8-10:
Before and after—CSS, that is. If you rely just on HTML, images take up lots of space (left). With a little CSS (right) you can nicely frame an image and move it out of the way.

2. Open the file *image.html* in your favorite text editor.

   Start by adding an internal style sheet and an empty class style.

Note: The same caveat that you've read in previous tutorials about creating internal style sheets applies here. (See the box on page 61.) In the final tutorial in this chapter, you'll go through the process of converting an internal style sheet into an external style sheet.

---

3. Click directly after the <link> tag (used to attach the external style sheet), hit Return, and then type the following:

   ```
   <style type="text/css">
   img.figure {
   ```

```
    }
    </style>
```

This CSS adds a new internal style sheet just above the closing </head> tag. The selector *img.figure* targets any <img> tag with the *figure* class applied to it. You'll use this to selectively format only the images you want.

4. **Add float and margin properties to the style you just created, like so:**

```
    float: right;
    margin-left: 10px;
    margin-bottom: 10px;
```

The right float moves the image to the right side of the page, letting the text move up and wrap around the photo's left edge. The left and bottom margins give the photo a little breathing room and move it away from the text. Next, you'll add a border and some padding to make the image look more like a real snapshot.

5. **Add border and padding, so that the finished style looks like this:**

```
    img.figure {
        float: right;
        margin-left: 10px;
        margin-bottom: 10px;
        border: 1px solid #666;
        padding: 10px;
    }
```

If you preview the page right now, you won't see a change, since the class style has no effect until you've added the class to a tag.

6. **Locate the <img> tag and add *class="figure"* so that the tag looks like this:**

```
    <img src="../images/grass.jpg" alt="Apartment Grass" width="200" height="200"
    class="figure" />
```

Now that image takes on all of the formatting properties you defined for the *.figure* class style.

7. **Preview the page in a Web browser. It should look like the right image in Figure 8-10.**

You can find the completed version of this exercise, *image_finished.html* in the *chapter_08_finishe → image_ex* folder.

A picture may be worth a thousand words, but sometimes you still need a few words to explain a picture. So in the next part of this tutorial, you'll add a caption below the photo.

Note: Internet Explorer 5 for Windows doesn't display the padding between the photo and its border. D'oh!

Adding a Caption

You'll frequently want to add a caption to an image or photo to provide more information about the subject, where the photo was taken, and so on. Instead of just floating the image, as you did in the previous exercise, you want the caption text to float as well. The best way to float both is to wrap the image and the text in a container—a <div> tag—that's floated as a single unit. This method keeps the photo and its related text together. If you decide later that you want to change their layout—perhaps float them to the left—no problem: You simply change the formatting for the entire container.

1. **In a text editor, open the file *chapter_08 → caption_ex → caption.html* folder.**

   Begin by adding a little HTML to create the container.

2. **Locate the <img> tag in the code, and add *<div class="figure">* before that tag.**

   This marks the beginning of the container. Now close the <div> to indicate the end of the container.

3. **Find the closing </p> tag of the paragraph directly after the image and type *</div>*. The code should now look like this:**

   ```
   <div class="figure">
   <img src="../images/grass.jpg" alt="Creeping Bentgrass" width="200"
   height="200"/>
   <p>Figure 1: Creeping Bentgrass is best suited for outdoor use and should be
   avoided by the indoor farmer.</p>
   </div>
   ```

   In previous tutorials you created a new, internal style sheet. In this exercise, you'll edit the existing external style sheet (*styles.css*) that's linked to this Web page.

4. **Open the file *chapter_08 → caption_ex → styles.css*.**

   Because this is an external style sheet, you'll notice there's no <style> tag. That tag's necessary only for internal style sheets.

5. **Scroll to the bottom of the file and add the following style to the end:**

   ```
   .figure img {
       border: 1px solid #666;
       padding: 10px;
   }
   ```

   This descendent selector (page 49) affects any <img> tag *inside* any other tag with the *figure* class applied to it—in this case, the <div> you just added. Since you're using a descendent selector here (and in step 7), you don't need to add a class to the <img> tag. As a result, you save a little typing, cut down on HTML code, and make the page load faster for your site's visitors.

Next, you'll format the <div> so that it floats the photo and caption text to the right edge of the page.

6. **Add this style to the *styles.css* file:**

```
div.figure {
    float: right;
    width: 222px;
    margin: 15px 10px 5px 10px;
}
```

You've already used the *float: right* property in this tutorial, and the margin adds a little white space around all four edges of the <div>. But what's the width for, you ask? Although the photo has a set width (200 pixels; see step 3) the caption paragraph doesn't. When you don't set a width, the paragraph makes the <div> expand wider than the photo. In this case, you want the caption to be just as wide as the photo and its frame.

The 222 pixels comes from a little math used to calculate the entire area taken up by the photo on the page: while the photo is only 200 pixels wide, the 10 pixels of left and right padding as well as the image's 1-pixel left border and 1-pixel right border, make the entire width of the photo equal to 222 pixels, from border to border. Next, spruce up the look of the caption text.

7. **Add the following style to the *styles.css* style sheet:**

```
.figure p {
    font: bold 1em/normal Verdana, Arial, Helvetica, sans-serif;
    color: #333;
    text-align: center;
}
```

This style uses some of the properties you learned about in Chapter 6 to create a center-aligned, bold, and gray caption using the Verdana font. Fortunately, the font shorthand property (see page 115) in the first line lets you roll four different properties into a single style declaration.

Again, you're taking advantage of a descendent selector (*.figure p*) to target just the caption paragraph. To make the caption stand out even more, add a background color and border.

8. **Add three properties to the *.figure p* style, like so:**

```
.figure p {
    font: bold 1em/normal Verdana, Arial, Helvetica, sans-serif;
    color: #333;
    text-align: center;
    background-color: #e6f3ff;
    border: 1px dashed #666;
    padding: 5px;
}
```

The purpose of the *background-color, border,* and *padding* properties should be clear—to create a colored box around the caption. Now it's time to preview your work.

9. **Save both the *caption.html* and *styles.css* files and preview the *caption.html* file in a Web browser.**

(Now you see one reason why it's easier to develop a design using an internal style sheet—you need to work in and save only one file instead of two.)

The page looks great: The photo and caption float to the right, and the caption stands out boldly. There's one small problem, though: If you look at the left and right edges of the paragraph, you'll notice they're indented slightly and aren't as wide as the photo. Here's an example of one of the many head-scratching situations you'll find as you work with CSS.

In this case, you've run into a problem with the cascade. The caption text is inside a <p> tag, and, as it happens, there's a tag style for the <p> tag in the *styles.css* file. When you look at that style, you see it sets margins—10 pixels on the top and bottom and 8 pixels on the left and right. You want to override those margins, and you can do so by adding new margins to a more specific style. (See page 86 for a discussion of *specificity* and the cascade.) Fortunately, you already have a more specific style—*.figure p*—so you need only add margins to that style to override the margins from the more generic *p* style.

10. **Add a margin property to the *.figure p* style, like so:**

```
.figure p {
    font: bold 1em/normal Verdana, Arial, Helvetica, sans-serif;
    color: #333;
    text-align: center;
    background-color: #e6f3ff;
    border: 1px dashed #666;
    padding: 5px;
    margin: 10px 0 0 0;
}
```

This removes margins on all sides of the caption except the top, which adds 10 pixels of space between the caption and the photo above.

11. **Save the *caption.html* and *styles.css* files. Preview *caption.html* file in a Web browser.**

The page should now look like Figure 8-11. (You can find a completed version of this page in the *chapter_08_finished → caption_ex* folder.)

Building a Photo Gallery

Folks used to rely on the HTML <table> tag to create rows and columns for holding the pictures in a photo gallery. But you can achieve the same effect with a little CSS and far less HTML.

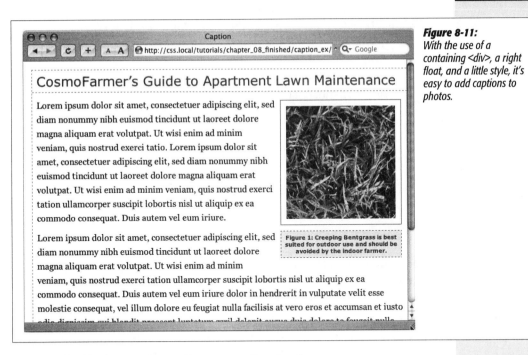

Figure 8-11:
*With the use of a
containing <div>, a right
float, and a little style, it's
easy to add captions to
photos.*

1. **Open the file** *chapter_08 → gallery_ex → gallery.html.*

   First, a quick review of the HTML used to construct the photo gallery. The page
   contains nine photos and photo captions. Each photo and caption is contained
   in a <div> with a class named *figure* applied to it. This <div> functions just like
   the similar <div> used in the previous exercise for adding a caption. The photo
   itself is contained in another <div> with a class of *photo*:

   ```
   <div class="figure">
       <div class="photo">
       <img src="../images/dandelion.jpg" alt="Dandelion" width="200"
   height="200" />
       </div>
       <p>Figure 6: The dandelion: scourge of the apartment farmer. </p>
   </div>
   ```

Note: That second <div> will come in handy for the next exercise, when you learn to add drop shadows
to the photos.

2. **Locate the <link> tag near the top of the file, place your cursor *after* that tag,
   and then press Enter (Return) to create a new blank line.**

   The <link> tag attaches an external style sheet containing some basic formatting.

3. **Add an internal style sheet. Then add two new styles, as follows:**

```
<style type="text/css">
.photo img {
    border: 1px solid #666;
    background-color: #FFF;
    padding: 4px;
}

.figure p {
    font: 1.1em/normal Arial, Helvetica, sans-serif;
    text-align: center;
    margin: 10px 0 0 0;
}
</style>
```

These two styles add a border to each image in the gallery, and set the font, alignment, and margins of the captions. They use descendent selectors to target just the images and paragraphs inside the gallery.

All of the images and captions are themselves wrapped in one <div> with an ID of *gallery*, since enclosing the group of photos in another <div> provides even more formatting options. You could set a specific width for the gallery or add a border around it. But that enclosing <div> also provides another way to target the photos and paragraphs using descendent selectors. For example, *#gallery img* and *#gallery p* are also valid descendent selectors in this case. The main difference between the two approaches is the specificity of the styles (see page 86). Because *#gallery img* is more specific than *.photo img*, its formatting options override the *.photo img* style.

Next, place the photos side by side.

Note: When you insert the internal style sheet, make sure to place it in the page's head section, between the link tag and the closing </head> tag.

---

4. **Add the following style to the internal style sheet you just created:**

```
.figure {
    float: left;
    width: 210px;
    margin: 0 10px 10px 10px;
}
```

This style floats each photo/caption pair to the left. In effect, it places the photos side-by-side until there's no more room in the row. The browser then drops the next photos down a row, until all of the photos are displayed one row on top of the next. The width is the *total* width of the photo plus padding and borders. In this example, it's 200 pixels for the photo, 8 pixels for left and right padding, and 2 pixels for left and right borders.

CSS: The Missing Manual

Tip: In this fictitious photo gallery, each picture's the same width. In the real world, you may have pictures of varying sizes. See the box below for a trick that lets you arrange rows of pictures of different widths. Using different height images won't work (as you'll see in step 5). When you've got images with differing heights, stick with HTML tables.

When One Width Doesn't Fit All

It's a breeze to set up a photo gallery—like the CosmoFarmer one—when the photos are conveniently all the same width. But what if you have photos of differing widths? One solution's to create a style for each different width and apply the style to the <div> with the *figure* class. (That's tons of work, so it would pay to do some photo editing work to standardize your photos to just a handful of different widths first.)

You can take advantage of CSS's ability to apply two classes to one tag like this: *<div class="figure w300">*. This <div> tag has both the *figure* and *w300* class styles applied to it.

Then create a class style, for example *.w300*, and set the width to the width of the image (in this case, 300) plus 10 to cover the padding and borders: *.w300 { width: 310 }*. For this trick to work, you must either remove the width setting on the *.figure* style or add the *.w300* style *after* the *.figure* style in the style sheet. Here's why: The two width definitions conflict (one's 210 the other's 300), so the browser has to break the tie using the cascade (see Chapter 5). Since *.figure* and *.w300* have the same specificity, the one that's defined last in the style sheet wins.

---

5. **Save the file and preview the *gallery.html* page in a Web browser. It should look like the left image in Figure 8-12.**

    Adjust the width of your browser window to make it thinner and wider and watch how the images reflow into the space. Aha—something's not quite right. The second row of images has two empty spaces where photos should be. This problem occurs because the caption for the second image on the first line is taller than the other captions on the line. Images that jump down to another row bump into that caption and can't get by it. (You can read more about this *float* property snafu on page 157.) Fortunately, there's a simple fix to this dilemma.

6. **Return to your text editor and the *gallery.html* file. Locate the *.figure p* style and add a height to it. The finished style should look like this:**

    ```
    .figure p {
        font: 1.1em/normal Arial, Helvetica, sans-serif;
        text-align: center;
        margin: 10px 0 0 0;
        height: 5em;
    }
    ```

    Adding this property sets a uniform height for each caption. In this case, it's tall enough to support the lines of caption text. (If you needed more text, you'd just increase the height.)

Note: You don't need the height property if you're sure each floated element is the same height. This could happen if you don't have captions and all of the photos are the same height, or each caption has the same number of lines of text.

---

7. **Save the file and preview the page in a Web browser. See the right side of Figure 8-12.**

   If you resize the browser window, the gallery reformats itself. With a wider window you can fit four or even five images on a row, but if you make it smaller you'll see only one or two images per row.

   The gallery looks good, but if you're using Internet Explorer you may have noticed another problem. If you resize the browser window, the dashed border on the left edge of the page disappears. There's a fix for this crazy bug, too.

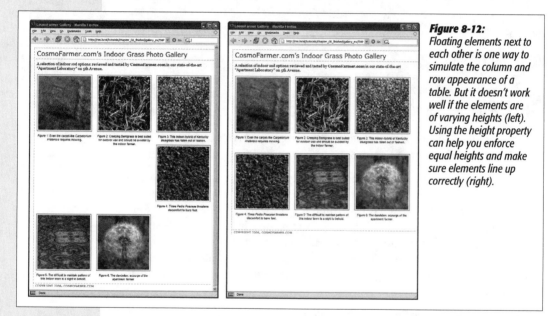

Figure 8-12:
Floating elements next to each other is one way to simulate the column and row appearance of a table. But it doesn't work well if the elements are of varying heights (left). Using the height property can help you enforce equal heights and make sure elements line up correctly (right).

8. **At the end of the internal style sheet (after all other styles), add the following:**

```
/* IE 5/6 border erase bug */
* html #gallery {
    width: 100%;
}
```

   As always, when adding styles to an internal style sheet, be sure to put the CSS code in *between* the opening <style> tag and its matching closing </style> tag.

   This style uses the * *html* hack (see page 152) to target just IE 6 and earlier and apply a property that miraculously fixes the problem. The first line of code—/* *IE 5/6 border erase bug* */—is a CSS comment. It's just a note that lets you know the purpose of the following style.

Tip: The end of a style sheet is a good place to group any styles like this one that fix browser bugs. This way, you can quickly identify and remove these weird styles when the buggy browser finally falls into disuse. Another good idea is to put browser hacks like this into their own external style sheet, as discussed on page 399.

9. **Save the file.**

You'll improve on the gallery's look in the next exercise.

Adding Drop Shadows

Your gallery looks good, but you can make it even more impressive. Adding drop shadows under each photo lends the page an illusion of depth and a realistic 3-D quality. But before you fire up Photoshop, you'll be glad to know there's no need to add individual drop shadows. Instead, you can make CSS automatically add a shadow to any image you want.

First you need a drop shadow graphic—just an image with fuzzy right and bottom black edges. There's one in the *chapter_08 → gallery_ex* folder, but you can make your own in Photoshop, Fireworks, or any other image editing program that has a blur or drop shadow filter. (In Fireworks, for example, you'd create a white box and apply the drop shadow filter to it. Then save the file in GIF format.)

1. **In a text editor, open the *gallery.html* file you completed in the previous exercise.**

   First, add a background image to the <div> tag that surrounds each image.

2. **Add this style to the gallery page's style sheet:**

   ```
   .photo {
       background: url(drop_shadow.gif) right bottom no-repeat;
   }
   ```

   This *.photo* style adds a background image—*drop_shadow.gif*—to the lower-right corner of the photo <div>. The *no-repeat* value means the graphic won't tile.

   If you preview the page now, you won't see much. That's because the drop shadow appears in the background. On top is the photo itself, which you styled in step 3 on page 190 to have a white background, a black border, and four pixels of padding. What you need is a way to reveal that background image.

   One clever technique pioneered by Richard Rutter (*www.clagnut.com*) is to move the image up and to the left a little—essentially moving it outside of its containing <div> tag. CSS provides a mechanism known as *positioning* that lets you control the exact placement of an element. You'll learn more about positioning in Chapter 12, but for now you need to add only three properties to the *.photo img* style you created in step 3 on page 190 to reveal the drop shadow.

Note: Negative margins are another way to achieve the drop shadow shift. For details, see *http://1976design.com/blog/archive/2003/11/14/shadows/*.

3. **Locate the** *.photo img* **style, and add three positioning properties like so:**

```
.photo img {
    border: 1px solid #666;
    background-color: #FFF;
    padding: 4px;
    position: relative;
    top: -5px;
    left:-5px;
}
```

In a nutshell, these three properties simply move the photo up and to the left five pixels, exposing the underlying drop shadow graphic of the <div>. In fact, the very reason for using a <div> here is to provide an element to hold a background image.

4. **Save the file and preview the page. It should look like Figure 8-13.**

Each image has its own drop-shadow, and you didn't even have to open Photoshop!

Note: The graphic you used here is around 375x375 pixels, so it accommodates images only up to that size. You can use this same technique for larger images, but you'll need to create your own drop shadow.

Of course, you're not completely done—unless you don't care about supporting Internet Explorer 5. That browser doesn't place the shadow correctly.

5. **To fix the display problem in IE 5, add one last style to the end of the internal style sheet:**

```
/* IE 5 placement bug */
* html #gallery img {
    width: 100%;
}
```

You can use this drop-shadow method on any graphic, not just those inside a gallery. The key is surrounding the <img> tag with a container <div>, applying a drop shadow graphic to that <div> and offsetting the <img> tag with negative top and left placement. Use this same effect to add a drop shadow to any box element, such as a sidebar or pull-quote.

You can find a completed version of this tutorial in the *chapter_08_finished →
gallery_ex* folder.

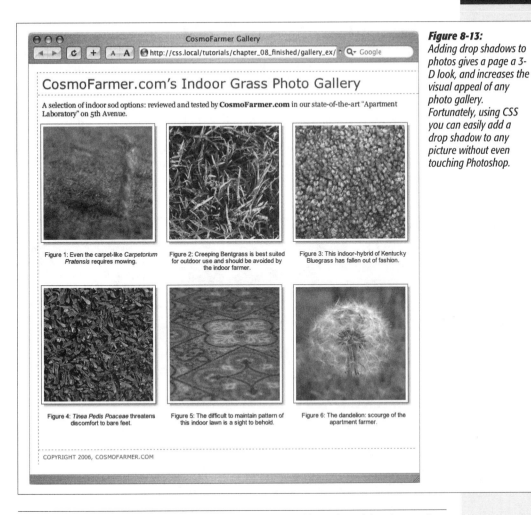

Figure 8-13:
*Adding drop shadows to
photos gives a page a 3-
D look, and increases the
visual appeal of any
photo gallery.
Fortunately, using CSS
you can easily add a
drop shadow to any
picture without even
touching Photoshop.*

Note: You may have noticed that the drop shadows you just created have abrupt left and top endings.
They don't fade like actual drop shadows. To learn how to create more sophisticated drop shadows, check
out *www.alistapart.com/articles/cssdrop2/* and *www.ploughdeep.com/onionskin/*.

Tutorial: Using Background Images

The CSS *background-image* property is the secret weapon of modern Web design.
It can turn a ho-hum text-heavy Web page into a dazzling swirl of imagery. Since
you can use it to add an image to the background of any HTML tag, the designs
you can create are limited only by your imagination. The drop shadow example in
the previous tutorial is just one example of creative background image use. Other
common background image frills include applying a page background and adding
custom bullets to unordered lists. You'll explore some of these common tasks in
this tutorial.

Adding an Image to the Page Background

Whether it's an intricate pattern, a logo, or a full-screen photograph, images appear in the background of many a Web page. In fact, adding an image to the background of a page is probably the most common application of the background-image property.

1.   **In your text editor, open the file** *chapter_08 → bg_ex → sidebar.html.*

This page is similar to the one you created in the last chapter's tutorial. It has a floated sidebar and uses background colors to highlight portions of the page (Figure 8-14, top).

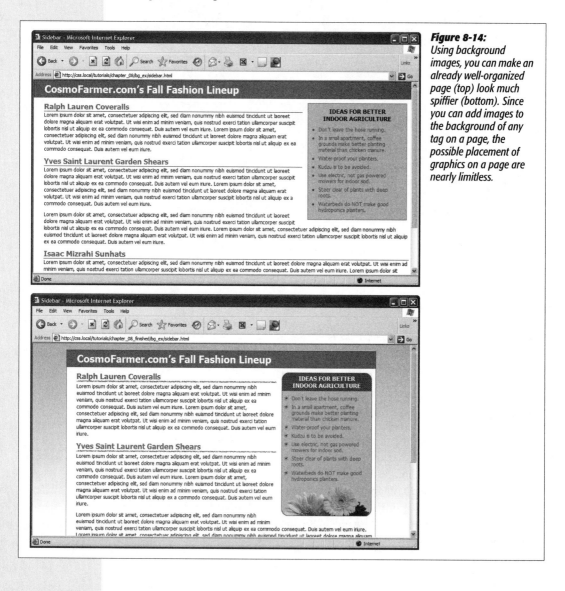

Figure 8-14:
Using background images, you can make an already well-organized page (top) look much spiffier (bottom). Since you can add images to the background of any tag on a page, the possible placement of graphics on a page are nearly limitless.

To start, you'll add a <div> tag to create a container for the page's content. For a change of pace from the previous exercises, where the content on the page always fit the browser window's width, you'll create a design that's a set width and is centered in the middle of the browser window.

2. **Locate the opening *<body>* tag and, directly *below* it, add the following tag:**

   ```
   <body>
   <div id="wrapper">
   ```

   This opening <div> tag marks the beginning of the container. You need to add a closing </div> tag next.

3. **Near the bottom of the file, locate the closing </body> tag. Add this </div> tag directly *above* it:**

   ```
   </div>
   </body>
   ```

   You've wrapped all of the page's content in a single container. Now you'll add a style defining a width for the container and centering it in the browser window. This file already has an internal style sheet that provides some basic formatting. You'll add this new style to that style sheet.

4. **Insert the following style between the *body* and *h1* tag styles:**

   ```
   #wrapper {
       width: 760px;
       margin: 15px auto 0 auto;
       text-align: left;
   }
   ```

   This ID style defines how the <div> you just inserted should look. The 760-pixel width means the entire width should fit inside monitors that have a resolution of at least 800x600 pixels (a safe bet for the vast majority of monitors out there today). The *margin* property uses the keyword *auto* for both the left and right margins, which tells a Web browser to split the difference between either side of the container, effectively centering the container inside the browser window. So, if the browser window of the visitor viewing this page is 900 pixels wide, then there'll be 70 pixels of space on both the left and right sides (900-760=140; 140 divided by the two sides equals 70 pixels on either side).

   The last style declaration—*text-align: left*—simply aligns all text to the left edge. Left-alignment is how text usually appears, but in this case, you're using the declaration to help solve a problem in IE 5 for Windows. (More on that in step 6.)

   First, you'll add an image to the page's background.

5. **Locate the *body* tag style. (It's the first one in the internal style sheet.) Add the following three lines of CSS to it:**

```
background-image: url(images/page_bg.jpg);
background-repeat: repeat-x;
background-position: left top;
```

The first line of code points to the image—*page_bg.jpg*—you want to display on the page. This graphic's a gradient that starts as a vibrant green at the top and fades to white at the bottom. The graphic isn't as tall as the page content, so without further instructions, it would tile over and over across and down the page. At a certain point down the page, that vibrant green would reappear and fade once again downward to white. To prevent this unsightly snafu, you've set the background-repeat property so that the image tiles from left to right in order to fit any width of browser window, but doesn't tile *down* the page. The last line positions the image to start at the top left edge of the page.

Note: Using background property shorthand (page 182), you can condense the three lines of code from step 5 (and the background-color property already defined in the body style) into a single line of CSS: *background: white url(images/page_bg.jpg) left top repeat-x.*

Finally, complete this style by fixing an IE 5 for Windows bug. That browser doesn't understand the auto margins you set in step 4, so it won't center the container <div>. You need to add one more property to the style for IE 5's benefit.

6. **Edit the *body* style by adding the *text-align* CSS property. The completed style should look like this:**

```
body {
    font-family: Tahoma, "Lucida Grande", Arial, sans-serif;
    font-size: 62.5%;
    margin: 0;
    padding: 0;
    background-color: white;
    background-image: url(images/page_bg.jpg);
    background-repeat: repeat-x;
    background-position: center top;
    text-align: center;
}
```

Note: Centering the text on the page using the text-align property forces Internet Explorer 5 to center the container <div>. (IE 6 and 7 don't need this extra help since those browsers understand the *auto* value used for the left and right margins in step 4.) However, all of the text *inside* the <div> is aligned in the center as well. Fortunately, you fixed that problem in step 4 when you set the *text-align* to *left*, restoring normal alignment to the text inside the <div>.

7. **Save the file and preview it in a Web browser.**

   The background graphic's bright green gradient drips down the page. Unfortunately, the graphic is also in the text's background, making some parts difficult to read. You'll take care of that by adding a background color and graphic to the <div> tag.

8. **Return to your text editor and the *sidebar.html* file. Edit the *#wrapper* style like so:**

```
#wrapper {
    width: 760px;
    margin: 15px auto 0 auto;
    background: #FFF url(images/wrapper_bg.gif) center top no-repeat;
    text-align: left;
}
```

   This *background* property shorthand sets the background of the <div> to white, adds an image named *wrapper_bg.gif* to the background, centers that graphic at the top of the <div>, and sets it to display only once (no repeating).

   If you preview the page now, you'll see the area where the text sits is white. You'll also notice reddish lines on either side of the <div> that fade at the bottom. The effect's subtle, but noticeable (Figure 8-15).

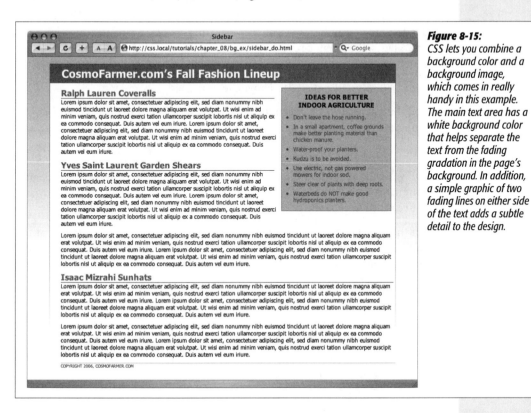

Figure 8-15:
CSS lets you combine a background color and a background image, which comes in really handy in this example. The main text area has a white background color that helps separate the text from the fading gradation in the page's background. In addition, a simple graphic of two fading lines on either side of the text adds a subtle detail to the design.

Replacing Borders with Graphics

The *border* property (page 141) is a useful tool in your design arsenal, but the limited number of border styles CSS offers can get boring. A hand-drawn line with the texture of charcoal on rough paper would catch your visitors' attention better than a plain, straight one. You can skip the border property and add any kind of line you want as a background image—easy as pie. In this tutorial, you'll replace the underline below each <h2> tag with a custom graphic that looks like a hand-drawn line.

1. **Return to your text editor and the *sidebar.html* file. Locate the *h2* tag style, remove the *border-bottom* property, and then add two background properties, so that the style looks like this:**

   ```
   h2 {
       font-size: 1.8em;
       color: #7BA505;
       margin: 10px 5px 0 25px;
       overflow: hidden;
       background-image: url(images/underline.gif);
       background-repeat: repeat-x;
   }
   ```

   The *background-image* property specifies which graphic to use in the background of every <h2> tag on the page, while the *repeat-x* value makes sure that the graphic online tiles horizontally. In other words, no matter how long the <h2> tag is, the graphic repeats, giving the illusion of one solid line.

   If you preview the file now, you'll see that the underline doesn't exactly line up. In fact, it isn't *under* at all. It's above the headlines!

2. **Add the following style declaration to the *h2* style below the *background-repeat* property:**

   ```
   background-position: left bottom;
   ```

   You've changed the graphic's starting location so it appears at the left edge and bottom of the <h2> tags. If you preview the page now, though, you may not notice much improvement. The underline runs *into* the headline text.

   But there's an easy fix. Since the bottom value used here puts the graphic at the bottom of the block created by the <h2> tag, you need only to increase the overall height of the block to move the line down a bit. You'll do this with a little bottom *padding*.

3. **Edit the *h2* style one last time, so that it looks like this:**

   ```
   h2 {
       font-size: 1.8em;
       color: #7BA505;
       margin: 10px 5px 0 25px;
       overflow: hidden;
   ```

```
        background-image: url(images/underline.gif);
        background-repeat: repeat-x;
        background-position: left bottom;
        padding-bottom: 7px;
    }
```

Padding, as you'll recall from page 135, is the space between the border and the content. It also increases the overall height of the box—in this case by adding seven pixels of bottom padding. Now, the line graphic is placed at the bottom of the *h2* block, but in the empty space created by the bottom padding.

4. **Save the file and preview the page in a Web browser.**

Each <h2> tag has the hand-drawn underline. Next you'll tackle the sidebar box, making it look a little less boxy and jazzing up the bulleted lists.

Using Graphics for Bulleted Lists

The average bullet used for unordered lists is a black dot—not very inspiring. But you can use the background-image property to replace those drab bullets with any image you want. The first step's to hide the bullets that normally appear beside list items.

1. **Return to your text editor and the *sidebar.html* page. Locate the *.sidebar li* style near the end of the internal style sheet.**

This descendent selector targets any <li> tag that appears inside another tag with a class of *sidebar*.

2. **Replace the two CSS properties in the *.sidebar li* style with *list-style: none;* the style should now look like this:**

```
    .sidebar li {
        list-style: none;
    }
```

This removes the bullet. Now add the graphic.

Note: You can just as well apply *list-style: none;* to a style affecting the <ul> or <ol> tags to remove bullets from *each* list item.

---

3. **Add the following two properties to the *.sidebar li* style:**

```
    background-image: url(images/flower_bullet.gif);
    background-repeat: no-repeat;
```

You've seen these two properties before. They add an image to the background and turn off repeating so that the graphic appears only once.

If you preview the page, you'll see that the bullets currently overlap the list text and the list items are a little jammed together (Figure 8-16, left). A little padding and margin will fix this.

4. Add two more properties to the *.sidebar li* style:

```
padding-left: 18px;
margin-bottom: 6px;
```

The left padding adds empty space, effectively moving the text out of the way in order to display the new bullet icon. The bottom margin adds just a bit of breathing room between each list item (Figure 8-16, middle).

There's just one final flaw. The bullet image is a tad too high on the line, causing the tip of the icon to stick out too far above the text. But you can easily fix that with the *background-position* property.

5. Finish this style by adding *background-position: 0px 2px;* The completed style should look like this:

```
.sidebar li {
    list-style: none;
    background-image: url(images/flower_bullet.gif);
    background-repeat: no-repeat;
    background-position: 0px 2px;
    padding-left: 18px;
    margin-bottom: 6px;
}
```

This last style declaration positions the bullet icon to the far left, two pixels from the top of the list item. It moves the icon down just a smidgen, enough to make the bullet look perfect.

Note: As discussed on page 122, this kind of exact positioning is precisely why you should use the *background* property instead of the *list-style-image* property for adding graphic bullets to your lists.

---

6. Save the file and preview the page in your browser.

The list should now have fanciful flower icons instead of dreary black circles (Figure 8-16, right).

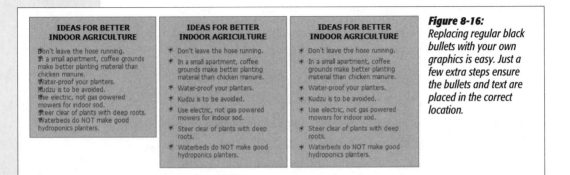

Figure 8-16:
Replacing regular black bullets with your own graphics is easy. Just a few extra steps ensure the bullets and text are placed in the correct location.

Adding Rounded Corners to the Sidebar

At this point, the sidebar, like much of the page, is rather boxy. To add visual variety, soften the sidebar's appearance with some rounded corners.

In a nutshell, you'll first add a background image with rounded corners to the bottom of the sidebar. Then, for the rounded corners at the top of the box, you'll add a background image to the first tag in the sidebar (the <h3> tag).

1. **Return to your text editor and the *sidebar.html* file that you've been working on.**

    The graphic you'll place in the bottom of the sidebar has a decorative photo and two rounded lower corners.

2. **Locate the *.sidebar* style in the file's internal style sheet. Replace the background-color declaration—*background-color: #CBF622;*—with this:**

    ```
    background: #CBF622 url(images/bg_bottom.gif) center bottom no-repeat;
    ```

    This shorthand property includes the same background color you just replaced plus instructions for adding a graphic to the center and bottom of the sidebar.

    Preview the page now, and you'll see the graphic, but a few things aren't quite right, as shown at left in Figure 8-17. There's space on both the left and right side of the image, so it doesn't look like it's actually the bottom of the sidebar—it just looks like a photo *inside* the sidebar. Also, you can't read all of the text since some of it overlaps the image. Finally, the border around the sidebar appears outside of the graphic, making the sidebar appear to still have a square bottom. You'll tackle these problems one by one.

3. **In the *.sidebar* style, remove the following property declaration: *padding: 10px;***

    The graphic is 220 pixels wide, and the width of the sidebar is also set to 220 pixels. However, the 10 pixels of padding adds 10 pixels of space around the sidebar, and 20 pixels (left and right) to the overall width of the sidebar. Removing the padding property makes the sidebar shrink down to the width of the graphic.

Note: The rounded corners technique used here is for a fixed-width box. That means if you change the width of the sidebar, you'll need to recreate the graphics at the same width to match. For a few techniques that let you create rounded corners with more flexibility—and require more CSS and HTML code—visit these pages:

www.vertexwerks.com/tests/sidebox/

www.sperling.com/examples/box/

www.456bereastreet.com/lab/teaser/flexible/

To add some room at the bottom of the sidebar, so that the picture doesn't interfere with the text, turn to the *padding-bottom* property.

4. **Add the style declaration *padding-bottom: 75px;* to the *.sidebar* style.**

   Padding is the space between the borders of an element and the content. By adding 75 pixels of bottom padding, you ensure that there's plenty of room for the background image, so that text can never overlap it.

   There's one final problem to fix: The border around the sidebar appears around the background graphic (Figure 8-17, middle). Simply removing the border does the trick.

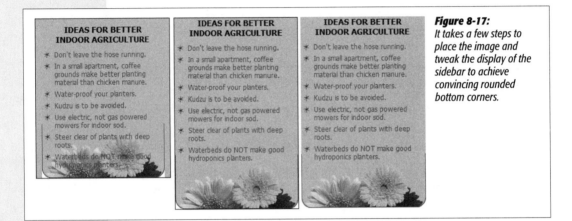

Figure 8-17:
It takes a few steps to place the image and tweak the display of the sidebar to achieve convincing rounded bottom corners.

5. **Remove the border property from *.sidebar*, so that the final version of the style looks like this:**

```
.sidebar {
    width: 220px;
    float: right;
    margin: 10px;
    background: #CBF622 url(images/bg_bottom.gif) center bottom no-repeat;
    padding-bottom: 75px;
}
```

6. **Save the file and preview it in a Web browser.**

   The sidebar should look like Figure 8-17, right. Notice that even though you eliminated the border, there's still a borderline around the bottom, curved corners, and sides of the base of the sidebar. That line isn't created with CSS; it's just a line drawn directly on the graphic. You'll next insert a graphic to make the top of the sidebar box rounded as well.

   It would be really cool if you could add a background image to the top of the sidebar and a different background image to the bottom of the sidebar. This way you'd have rounded corners on both the top and bottom, but the sidebar itself could expand to fit whatever content was added to it.

Unfortunately, CSS 2.1 lets you add only one background image per style, so you must find something else to "hook" the second background image on, like a tag somewhere in the sidebar. In this case, since the image adds rounded corners to the top of the sidebar box, you can apply the style to the first tag inside the sidebar. You'll use a descendent selector to do that.

Note: Future versions of CSS will allow multiple background images for a single style. So far, only one browser—Safari—recognizes them.

---

7. **Locate the** *.sidebar h3* **style in the external style sheet. (It's directly below the** *.sidebar* **style you just modified.) Then add the following line of code to the style:**

   ```
   background: url(images/top_bg.gif) center top no-repeat;
   ```

   By now, this kind of shortcut style should look familiar. It adds a graphic to the top and center of the style. In this case, it'll appear in the background of the <h3> tag inside the sidebar. At this point, the rounded corners are in place, and the box is, well, a little less boxy. You'll just add a few final touches to the headline by making the text white so it stands out from the newly added graphic and adding a little padding above and below the headline so it isn't so cramped.

8. **Add two additional properties to the** *.sidebar h3* **style so that it looks like this:**

   ```
   .sidebar h3 {
       font-size: 1.4em;
       margin: 0;
       text-align: center;
       text-transform: uppercase;
       background: url(images/top_bg.gif) center top no-repeat;
       color: #FFF;
       padding: 5px;
   }
   ```

   If you preview the page now, the sidebar looks finished…almost. Look closely at the left and right edges and you'll notice that while there's an outline around the bottom graphic, that line doesn't appear on either side of the sidebar where the bulleted list appears (Figure 8-18, left).

   One solution would be to simply make the bottom graphic a solid background color without an outline, but that wouldn't be much fun. Instead, you'll add left and right borders to the bulleted list. The lines from the border overlap the outline on the graphic, giving the appearance of one unified line running around the entire sidebar.

9. **Find the** *.sidebar ul* **style. Then add two border declarations so the final style looks like this:**

   ```
   .sidebar ul {
       color: #666;
   ```

```
        font-size: 1.2em;
        margin: 0;
        padding: 10px 5px 0 5px;
        border-left: 1px solid #E73A10;
        border-right: 1px solid #E73A10;
    }
```

Now the unordered list has two borders on either side. Because there's no padding on the sidebar itself, those borders extend to the very edges, making them appear to actually be bordering the sidebar (Figure 8-18, right).

10. **Save the file and preview the page in a Web browser.**

The final page makes use of background images in ways that may not feel immediately like images at all—to create the curved sidebar corners and complete its borders. Creative use of background images adds depth to your Web page designs, and makes your Web site look richer and more professional.

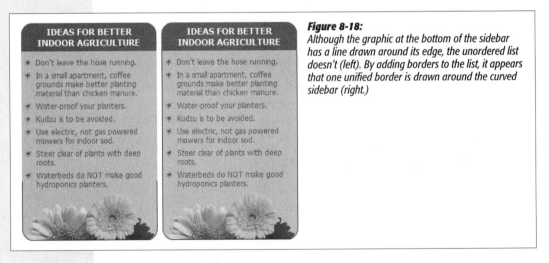

Figure 8-18:
Although the graphic at the bottom of the sidebar has a line drawn around its edge, the unordered list doesn't (left). By adding borders to the list, it appears that one unified border is drawn around the curved sidebar (right.)

Creating an External Style Sheet

There's one final task to perform. It's one that you'll probably do time and time again in your CSS career. After you've finalized your design using an internal style sheet, it's time to take those styles and place them in an external style sheet for use by all of the pages of your site.

1. **In your text editor, create a new file. Save it as** *styles.css* **in the same folder as the** *sidebar.html* **file.**

This document is your external style sheet. You'll copy the styles you embedded in the *sidebar.html* file and paste them into this file.

2. **Return to the *sidebar.html* file, and select all of the code between the opening \<style\> and closing \</style\> tags.**

   Don't select the style tags themselves. Those are HTML code, and an external style sheet must contain *only* CSS code.

3. **Cut the code from the file by choosing Edit → Cut.**

   You're removing the code from this page, since you'll link to the external style sheet in a moment.

4. **Return to the empty *styles.css* file, and paste the code by choosing Edit → Paste. Save the file.**

   Now all of the CSS code is in its own file. You can link any page in your site to this file and your pages can share the same formatting instructions.

   Now you just need to attach the style sheet to the HTML page.

5. **Return to the *sidebar.html* file. Make sure the \<style\> tags are still in place, and then add one line of code between these tags:**

   ```
   <style type="text/css">
   @import url(styles.css);
   </style>
   ```

Note: The other way to attach an external style sheet is with a link tag (page 33). To use this tag, first remove the opening and closing \<style\> tags from the Web page, and then add *\<link rel="stylesheet" type="text/css" href="styles.css" /\>*

---

6. **Save both files and preview the *sidebar.html* file in a Web browser.**

   The page should look the same as before you completed these last six steps (right image in Figure 8-14). The only difference is behind the scenes: Instead of a single file you now have two files: one for the CSS and another for the HTML. (You can find a completed version in the *chapter_08_finished → bg_ex* folder.)

Note: If the page doesn't look right, then make sure you saved the *styles.css* file in the same folder as the *sidebar.html* file. If you didn't, you'll need to modify the *url(styles.css)* in step 5 above to reflect the correct path to the style sheet. If you stored *styles.css* in a folder named *styles* that's *inside* the *bg_ex* folder, for example, then you'd change it to *url(styles/styles.css)*.

Sprucing Up Your Site's Navigation

It's safe to say that without links there'd be no Web. The ability to be on one page, then click something onscreen and suddenly see a page on a computer half a world away is what makes the Web so useful. Links are also how your visitors navigate their way around your Web site. That's why Web designers agonize over making their links look good and work properly.

In this chapter, you'll learn how to style links to make them stand out from other text. You can also make your links provide visual cues so your site's visitors can see where they are—and where they've been. You'll learn how to use CSS to create onscreen buttons and navigation bars just like the pros use. And in the tutorial section, you'll get some hands-on experience creating a full set of navigation features that work in all browsers.

Selecting Which Links to Style

As always in CSS, you have to select something before you can style it. For links, you need to tell CSS not only *what* you want to style, but *when*. Web browsers keep track of how a visitor interacts with links, and then displays that link differently depending on the link's status, or *state*. When you use a CSS link selector, you can target a specific link state as well.

Understanding Link States

Most browsers recognize four basic link states: an unvisited link, a link that's been visited already (meaning the URL is stored in the browser's history), a link that the visitor's mouse is poised over, and a link that's being clicked. As described in

Chapter 3 (page 54), CSS gives you four pseudo-class selectors to accompany these states—*:link, :visited, :hover,* and *:active.* Using them, you can apply different formatting to each state, so there's no doubt in your visitor's mind whether he's been there or done that.

Note: Firefox and Safari also recognize a pseudo-class called *:focus.* Links get *:focus* when mouse-averse visitors use the keyboard to tab to them. This pseudo-class is also fun to use with form text fields, as you'll see on page 272.

Suppose you want to change the text color for an unvisited link from boring browser blue to vivid orange. Add this style:

```
a:link { color: #F60; }
```

Once someone's clicked that link, its state changes to *visited,* and its color to the purple used by most browsers. To change that color to deep red, use this style:

```
a:visited { color: #900; }
```

Tip: When you want to style both unvisited and visited links the same, use the group selector *a:link, a: visited.* You can also use the generic *a* style, but if you have any named anchors that link to other parts of the same Web page (such as *<a name="resources">Other Resources</a>*), the *a* selector styles them, too.

The *:hover* pseudo-class offers many creative possibilities. (You'll learn quite a few later in this chapter.) It lets you completely alter the look of a link when a visitor moves her mouse over it. If you've used cumbersome JavaScript to make graphic buttons change when a mouse hovers over them, you'll love being able to create the same effect with CSS alone (page 216). But to start with a simple example, this style changes the color of a link as a mouse passes over it:

```
a:hover { color: #F33; }
```

And finally, for those obsessive compulsive designers who leave no design stone unturned, you can even change the look of a link for the few milliseconds when a visitor is actually clicking it. Here's how:

```
a:active {color: #B2F511; }
```

In most cases, you'll include at least *:link, :visited:,* and *:hover* styles in your style sheets for maximum design control. But in order for that to work, you must specify the links in a particular order: *link, visited, hover,* and *active.* Use this easy mnemonic to remember it: LoVe/HAte. So here's the proper way to add all four link styles:

```
a:link { color: #F60; }
a:visited { color: #900; }
a:hover { color: #F33; }
a:active {color: #B2F511; }
```

If you change the order, the hover and active states won't work. For example, if you put *a:hover* before *a:link* and *a:visited,* then the color change won't take effect when hovering.

Note: Why does the order matter? That would be thanks to our friend the cascade (see Chapter 5). All those styles have the same specificity, so the order in which they appear in the code determines the style that wins out. Since a link can be both *unvisited* and *hovered over*, if the *a:link* style comes last in the code, then it wins and the color from *a:hover* never gets applied.

Targeting Particular Links

The styles in the previous section are basic *a* tag styles. They target certain link states, but they style *all* links on a page. What if you want to style some links one way and some links another way? A simple solution is to apply a class to particular link tags. Say you have a bunch of links within the body of an article, some of which point to other stories on your Web site and others that point outside to other sites. You may want to identify external links in some way so visitors can tell they're about to leave your site. In this case, you can apply a class to these external links, like this:

```
<a href="http://www.hydroponicsonline.com" class="external">Visit this great
resource</a>
```

To style this link in its own way, you'd create styles like this:

```
a.external:link { color: #F60; }
a.external:visited { color: #900; }
a.external:hover { color: #F33; }
a.external:active {color: #B2F511; }
```

Leaving off the *a,* and only specifying the class, works too:

```
.external:link { color: #F60; }
.external:visited { color: #900; }
.external:hover { color: #F33; }
.external:active {color: #B2F511; }
```

Now only those links with a class of 'external' will get this formatting.

Note: These examples change only the links' color, but that's just to make it simple for demonstration purposes. You can use *any* CSS property to format links. As you'll see on the next page, you have lots of creative ways to style links.

Grouping links with descendent selectors

If a bunch of links appear together in one area of a page, you can also save time by using *descendent selectors.* As discussed on page 49, a descendent selector lets you target a tag that appears within another tag. Say you have five links that lead to the main sections of your site. They represent your main navigation bar, and so you want to give them a distinctive look. Just wrap those links in a <div> tag and apply a class or ID to it like this: *<div id="mainNav">*. Now you have an easy way to identify and format just those links:

```
#mainNav a:link { color: #F60; }
#mainNav a:visited { color: #900; }
#mainNav a:hover { color: #F33; }
#mainNav a:active {color: #B2F511; }
```

Using descendent selectors, it's easy to style links differently for different areas of a Web page. (See page 394 in Chapter 14 for a thorough discussion of the power of descendent selectors.)

Styling Links

Now that you know how to create a selector that targets links, how should you style them? Any way you want! There aren't any CSS properties intended just for links. You have full access to all CSS properties, so you're limited only by your imagination. Just make sure your links look like links. Not that they need to be blue and underlined, but links must look different from non-link text so visitors know they can click them.

If you make a link look like a button—adding a border, including a background, and making it change color when moused over—most people will understand they can click it. Likewise, links that appear in long passages of text should look clearly distinct. You can make links stand out by bolding the text, keeping the traditional underline, coloring the background, or adding a hover style. You can even add a graphic (like an arrow) that provides a clear visual cue that clicking the text takes you somewhere else.

Tip: Unless you set an <img> tag's border attribute to 0, Web browsers usually add a 1-pixel border around linked images. To prevent this from happening, add this basic style to your style sheets: *a img { border: none;}*.

Underlining Links

Since the beginning of the Web, vibrant blue, underlined text has signaled, "Click here to go there." But that underline and color are often the first two things a designer wants to change. Underlines are such a common way to mark a link that they're boring. (See #1 in Figure 9-1.) Fortunately, you can do several things to eliminate or improve on the standard underline, while still ensuring that your links are identifiable:

- **Remove the underline entirely**. To eliminate the regular underline, use the *text-decoration* property and the *none* value:

```
a:link {text-decoration: none;}
```

Of course, removing the underline completely can confuse your visitors. Unless you provide other visual cues, your links look exactly the same as all the other text (#2 in Figure 9-1). So if you go this route, then make sure you highlight the links in some other way, like making link text bold (#3 in Figure 9-1), coloring the background, adding an informative graphic (page 216), or making the link look like a button (page 214.)

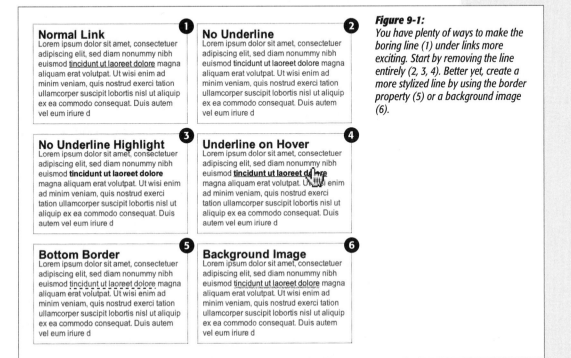

Figure 9-1:
You have plenty of ways to make the boring line (1) under links more exciting. Start by removing the line entirely (2, 3, 4). Better yet, create a more stylized line by using the border property (5) or a background image (6).

- **Underline when mousing over.** Some designers remove underlines for all links, highlight them in some other way, and then add the underlines back when the visitor moves his mouse over the link, as shown in #4 in Figure 9-1. To do so, simply remove the underline for links, and then reintroduce it using the *:hover* pseudo-class:

```
a:link, a:visited {
    text-decoration: none;
    background-color: #F00;
}
a:hover {
    background-color: transparent;
    text-decoration: underline;
}
```

• **Use a bottom border.** You can't control the color, width, or style of a regular link underline. It's always a solid, 1-pixel line, in the same color as the link text. For greater variety, use the *border-bottom* property instead, like #5 in Figure 9-1. Hiding the normal underline and adding a dashed-line border looks like this:

```
a {
    text-decoration: none;
     border-bottom: dashed 2px #9F3;
}
```

You can alter the style, width, and color of the border as described on page 141. To put more space between the text and the border, use the *padding* property.

• **Use a background image.** You can customize the look of links even further by using a graphical line. For example, #6 in Figure 9-1 uses a graphic that looks like a hand-drawn line. There's a similar technique for underlining headlines in Chapter 8's tutorial (page 200). Start by creating an underline graphic using a program like Fireworks or Photoshop, which have brush tools that simulate the look of a crayon, felt-tip marker, or whatever. Next, create a style for the link that removes the normal underline and adds a background image. Make sure the graphic repeats horizontally and is positioned at the bottom of the link. You may also need to add a little bottom padding to position the line. Here's an example:

```
a {
    text-decoration: none;
    background: url(images/underline.gif) repeat-x left bottom;
    padding-bottom: 5px;
}
```

It's best to use this technique for short, one- to three-word links, since if the link runs longer than a single line, then Windows Internet Explorer (including IE 7 as of this writing) adds the graphic only to the bottom of the *last* line. Or, you can find a workaround to this problem at: *http://home.tiscali.nl/ developerscorner/imaging/fun-links.html.*

Creating a Button

You can also make links look like the buttons in the dialog boxes and toolbars you see in computer programs. Buttons look great in navigation bars, but you can also use them for any small (one- or two-word) links on your pages. Your main allies in this task are the *border, background-color,* and *padding* properties. With them, it's easy to create a wide range of boxy-looking buttons (see Figure 9-2).

Say you added a class to a link that you'd like to style as a button: *<a link="stale. html" class="button">Free Donuts Here!</a>.* To add a basic black outline around this link (like the top-left image in Figure 9-2), you'd create this style:

```
a.button {
    border: solid 1px #000;
}
```

You can get fancier by adding a background color as well, like so:

```
a.button {
    border: solid 1px #000;
    background-color: #333;
}
```

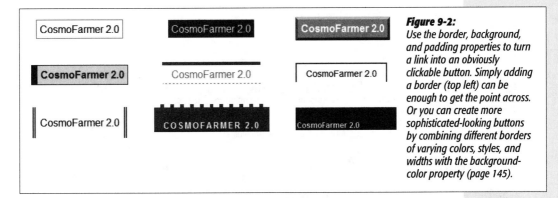

Figure 9-2:
Use the border, background, and padding properties to turn a link into an obviously clickable button. Simply adding a border (top left) can be enough to get the point across. Or you can create more sophisticated-looking buttons by combining different borders of varying colors, styles, and widths with the background-color property (page 145).

Mind you, all four borders don't need to be the same width, type, or color. You don't even have to have four borders. One common design technique is to add a beveled look to a button using four different border colors, as shown at top-right in Figure 9-2. Creating the beveled look isn't difficult, but you need to remember what makes something look three-dimensional—the light source. Imagine a light shining on one of the four sides; that side is the lightest, while the side opposite is the darkest (since the raised button's blocking the light and putting that side into a "shadow"). The other 2 sides should have shades in between the "lit" and "shadow" borders. Here's the CSS you use to create the beveled design in the top right corner of Figure 9-2:

```
a.button {
    background: #B1B1B1;
    color: #FFF;
    font-weight: bold;
    border-width: 4px;
    border-style: solid;
    border-top-color: #DFDFDF;
    border-right-color: #666;
    border-bottom-color: #333;
    border-left-color: #858585;
}
```

Keep in mind that you can (and probably should) create a :hover state for your buttons as well. That way, your buttons can react when a visitor moves her mouse over the link, providing useful visual feedback. In the case of a beveled button, reversing the various colors—make a dark background lighter, a light border darker, and so on—is very effective.

Using Graphics

Adding graphics to links is one of the easiest and most visually exciting ways to spruce up your site's navigation. There are any number of possible techniques and designs, but none of the good ones involve an HTML <img> tag. Instead, you can easily add attractive and informative imagery to any link using the CSS *background-image* property. You can see several examples in Figure 9-3. (You'll also learn more advanced techniques for using images to create graphical buttons and rollovers starting on page 235.)

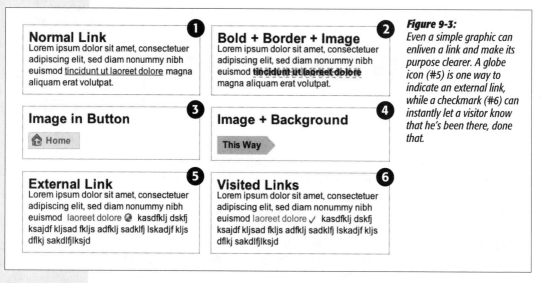

Figure 9-3:
Even a simple graphic can enliven a link and make its purpose clearer. A globe icon (#5) is one way to indicate an external link, while a checkmark (#6) can instantly let a visitor know that he's been there, done that.

If you need a refresher on *background-image* and related properties, flip back to page 172. Meanwhile, here are a few things to keep in mind when you use images with links:

- **Don't forget *no-repeat*.** Normally a background graphic tiles repeatedly in the background. With many graphics, that effect looks awful for links (see #2 Figure 9-3). Unless you're using a subtle pattern like a gradient fill, remember to set the repeat option to stop the tiling like this: *background-repeat: no-repeat;*.

- **Control placement with *background-position*.** To place an image accurately in the background, use the *background-position* property (page 176). When you want to place an image on the far right edge of a link but centered vertically on the line, use this CSS: *background-position: right center.*

For more accurate placement, use a specific value such as pixels or ems. These units of measurement make it easy to scoot a graphic a couple of pixels away from the left edge of the link. By combining these units with a percentage value, you can easily center a graphic vertically within a link, but place it an exact amount away from the left edge: *background-position: 10px 50%;*.

Note: In positioning background images, the first value is the horizontal placement (left to right); the second's vertical placement (top to bottom).

Unfortunately, there's no way to exactly place an image from the right or bottom edges. So if you want to move an image in from the right edge a bit, then you have two options: First, in your image editing program, you can add empty space to the right edge of the graphic. The amount of empty space you add should be equivalent to how much you want to indent that graphic from the right. Once you've created the graphic, use the *background-position* property to place the graphic on the right edge of the element; for example, *background-position: right top;*. Or you can use percentage values: *background-position: 90% 75%;* places the point that lies 90 percent from the left edge of the image on top of the point 90 percent from the left edge of the styled element. As you can imagine, this method doesn't provide complete accuracy so you'll need to experiment a little. (See page 179 for more on how percentage positioning works.)

- **Padding gives you room.** If you're using an image or icon to mark a link (like examples 3, 5, and 6 in Figure 9-3), then make sure to add padding on the side the image is on to move the link text out of the way. For instance, the third example in Figure 9-3 has 30 pixels of left padding to prevent the word "Home" from overlapping the picture of the house, while a little right padding makes room for the globe and checkmark in examples 5 and 6.

Note: Since the <a> tag is an inline element, adding top and bottom padding (or, for that matter, top and bottom margins) has no effect. See page 140 for the reason why. You can, however, turn a link into a "block level" element so that it can accept top and bottom padding and margins. You'll see this technique later in this chapter.

- **Use the pseudo-classes.** Don't forget the *:hover* and *:visited* pseudo-classes. They can add great dynamic effects and provide helpful feedback about your links. You can swap in a *different* background graphic for any of these pseudo-classes, so you could, for example, have a dim lightbulb graphic in the background of a normal link, but change that graphic to a lit bulb when the mouse travels over it. Or don't use a graphic for the background of unvisited links, but once they're visited add a checkmark graphic to clearly identify their used status (example 6 in Figure 9-3).

Should you decide to use a graphic for a link's *:hover* state, remember that browsers don't download the graphic until your visitor's mouse actually hovers over the link, so there'll be a noticeable delay before the graphic appears. Once the graphic's downloaded, however, the delay goes away. See page 229 for a technique to prevent this awkward problem.

Note: For an in-depth discussion on styling visited links, visit this page: *http://www.collylogic.com/?/comments/ticked_off_links_reloaded/*.

Building Navigation Bars

Every site needs good navigation features to guide visitors to the information they're after—and help them find their way back. Most sites are organized in sections, such as Products, Contact Info, Corporate Blog, and so on. This structure lets visitors know what information to expect and where they can find it. Much of the time, you find links to a site's principal sections in a *navigation bar*. CSS makes it easy to create a great looking navigation bar, rollover effects and all.

Using Unordered Lists

At heart, a navigation bar's nothing more than a bunch of links. More specifically, it's actually a *list* of the different sections of a site. Back in Chapter 1 you learned HTML's mission is to provide meaningful structure to your content. Accordingly, you should always use a tag that's appropriate to the meaning of that content. For a list of items, that's the <ul> or unordered list tag—the same one you use to create bulleted lists. It doesn't matter whether you want your list to have *no* bullets or to stretch horizontally across the top of the page: You can do all that by styling the <ul> tag with CSS. Figure 9-4 shows an example.

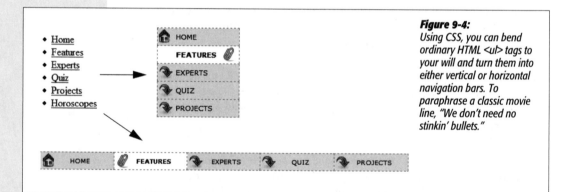

Figure 9-4:
Using CSS, you can bend ordinary HTML <ul> tags to your will and turn them into either vertical or horizontal navigation bars. To paraphrase a classic movie line, "We don't need no stinkin' bullets."

The HTML for a nav bar is straightforward. There's a single link inside each individual list item. Also, you need a way to style just that unordered list. (You don't want *actual* lists of items to look like navigation bars.) Applying a class or id to the <ul> tag is a good approach:

```
<ul class="nav">
<li><a href="index.html">Home</a></li>
<li><a href="news.html">News</a></li>
<li><a href="reviews.html">Reviews</a></li>
</ul>
```

The CSS varies a bit depending on whether you want a horizontal of vertical navigation bar. In either case, you need to do two things:

- **Remove the bullets.** Unless the navigation bar is supposed to look like a bulleted list, remove the bullets by setting the *list-style-type* property to none:

  ```
  ul.nav { list-style-type: none; }
  ```

- **Eliminate padding and margins.** Since browsers indent list items from the left, you need to remove this added space as well. Some browsers do the indenting using *padding* and others use *margin*, so you need to set both to 0:

  ```
  ul.nav {
      list-style-type: none;
      padding-left: 0;
      margin-left: 0;
  }
  ```

These two steps essentially make each list item look like any plain old block-level element, such as a paragraph or headline (except that a browser doesn't insert margins between list items). At this point, you can begin styling the links. If you want a vertical navigation bar, read on; for horizontal nav bars, see page 222.

Vertical Navigation Bars

A vertical navigation bar is just a bunch of links stacked one on top of the next. Removing the bullets and left margin and padding (as explained in the previous section) gets you most of the way there, but you need to know a few additional tricks to get things looking right:

1. **Display the link as a block.**

   Since the <a> tag is an inline element, it's only as wide as the content inside it. Buttons with different length link text (like Home and Our Products) are different widths. The staggered appearance of different width buttons stacked on top of each other doesn't look good, as you can see in #1 in Figure 9-5. In addition, top and bottom padding and margins have no effect on inline elements. To get around these limitations, style the link as a block element:

   ```
   ul.nav a { display: block; }
   ```

   The block value not only makes each button the same width, it also makes the entire area of the link clickable. That way, when your visitors click areas where there's no link text (like the padding around the link), they still trigger the link. (Internet Explorer 6 and earlier has problems with this technique, so look for the fix on page 246.)

2. **Constrain the width of the buttons.**

   Making links block level elements also means they're as wide as the tag they're nested in. So when they're just sitting in a page, those links stretch the width of the browser window (see #2 in Figure 9-5). You have several ways to make them

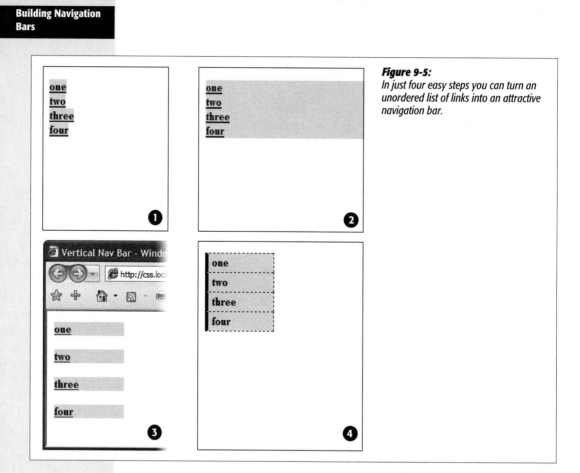

Figure 9-5:
In just four easy steps you can turn an unordered list of links into an attractive navigation bar.

a little narrower. First you can just set the width of the <a> tag. If you want each button to be 8 ems wide, for example, then add that to the *width* property:

```
ul.nav a {
    display: block;
    width: 8em;
}
```

Setting a width for any of the tags that wrap around those links—such as the <li> or <ul> tags—also works.

If the button text occupies only one line, you can also center the text vertically so there's equal space above and below the link text. Just add a height to the link *and* set its *line-height* property to the same value: *a { height: 1.25em; line-height: 1.25em; }*.

Note: You may not need to set an explicit width if the nav bar's located inside a page layout element that itself has a width. As you'll read in Part 3, it's easy to create a sidebar that hugs the left (or right) edge of a page. The sidebar has a set width, so plopping the unordered list nav bar inside it automatically constrains the width of the buttons.

Unfortunately, when you don't set an explicit width for the <a> tag, IE has a couple of problems with these links. First, every version (including 7, as of this writing), displays large gaps between each link (see #3 in Figure 9-5). (If you set an explicit width on the <a> tags in the nav bar, then you've already taken care of this IE bug. Skip steps 3 and 4.)

3. **Remove the gap in Internet Explorer.**

   To remove this space, you must add a style for the <li> tag:

   ```
   ul.nav li { display: inline; }
   ```

   This situation's one of many where you have to send Internet Explorer some nonsense CSS to make it behave. Fortunately, this workaround has no ill effects for other browsers.

4. **Expand the clickable area in Internet Explorer 6 and earlier.**

   Another IE bug (one that's been fixed in IE 7) appears whenever you set a link to display as a *block*. Even though other browsers make the entire block area clickable, IE 6 still limits clicking to just the text inside the link. To fix this, add a style that sets a height for the <a> tag. Because this new style would cause the links to shrink to an unreadable height in IE 7 and other browsers, you have to hide it from them. One way to do so is by using the * *html* hack you learned about in Chapter 7 (page 152):

   ```
   * html ul.nav a { height: 1px; }
   ```

Tip: Another way to create a style that applies only to IE 6 and earlier is to use conditional comments. You can read about them in depth in Chapter 14 (page 399).

Now that all this busywork is out the way, you can style the buttons to your heart's content. Add padding, background colors, margins, images, or whatever tickles your artistic fancy. If you want to spread the buttons out so they don't touch, then add a bottom (or top) margin to each link.

WORKAROUND WORKSHOP

When Borders Bump

If the buttons in your nav bar touch and you apply a border around each link, then the borders double up. In other words, the bottom border from one button touches the top border of the next button.

To get around this, add the border to only the *top* of each link. That way, you'll get just one border line where the bottom from each button touches the top from the next.

This workaround, however, leaves the entire nav bar borderless below the last link. To fix that problem, you can either create a class with the correct bottom border style and apply it to the last link, or better yet, add a bottom border to the <ul> tag that encloses the nav bar. (You'll see this trick in action in this chapter's tutorial, on page 243.)

Horizontal Navigation Bars

CSS lets you turn a set of stacked list items into a side-by-side presentation of links, like the one shown back in Figure 9-4. This section shows you two common ways to create a horizontal navigation bar from a list. The first—using the *display: inline* property—is easy, but it can't create equal-size buttons. If a uniform look is what you crave, then turn to the *floated <ul>* method described on page 225.

Whichever method you use, start by removing the bullets and left space from the <ul> tag, as illustrated in #1 of Figure 9-6.

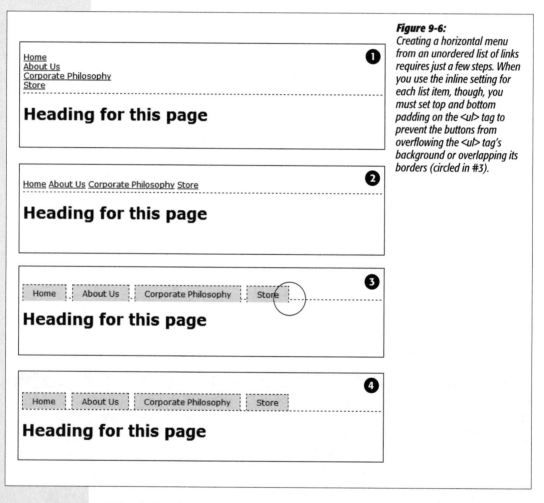

Figure 9-6:
Creating a horizontal menu from an unordered list of links requires just a few steps. When you use the inline setting for each list item, though, you must set top and bottom padding on the <ul> tag to prevent the buttons from overflowing the <ul> tag's background or overlapping its borders (circled in #3).

Using display: inline

The simplest method of creating a horizontal navigation bar involves changing the *display* property of the list items from *block* to *inline*. It's easy to do using CSS.

1. **Make the list items inline elements.**

   Inline elements don't create a line break before or after them as block-level elements do. Setting the *display* property of the <li> tags to *inline* makes them appear one beside the other (see #2 in Figure 9-6).

   ```
   ul.nav li { display: inline; }
   ```

   You need to make sure you don't have too many buttons, though. If they won't all fit side by side, some will drop down below the first row.

2. **Style the links.**

   You can remove the underline beneath the links and add a border around them instead. You can also add background color or a background image to provide visual depth. Add padding if you need more room around each link's text. If you want some space between each button, then apply a right margin. The following style gives links a button-like appearance, as shown in #3 and #4 in Figure 9-6:

   ```
   ul.nav a {
       border: 1px dashed #000;
       border-bottom: none;
       padding: 5px 15px 5px 15px;
       margin-right: 5px;
       background-color: #EAEAEA;
       text-decoration: none;
       color: #333;
   }
   ```

Note: When you use the inline method to create a horizontal nav bar, don't set the links' *display* property to *block*. If you do, then each link will appear one on top of the other and span the entire width of the page (or entire width of the list's containing block).

---

3. **Add top and bottom padding to the <ul> tag.**

   Because <a> tags are inline elements, adding top and bottom padding doesn't actually increase the height of a link. Instead, that padding just causes borders and backgrounds on links to overlap elements above and below the link, like the example shown way back in Figure 7-6. In Internet Explorer, the padding can also make top borders on your links disappear. In this case, the <a> tag's padding is also making the border on the bottom of the <ul> tag appear a little above and behind the links (circled in image #3 in Figure 9-6).

   The solution's to add padding to the <ul> tag, which creates space to accommodate the links' overflowing backgrounds and borders. For the<ul> tag's bottom padding, use the same value as the link's bottom padding. To determine the <ul> tag's top padding value, add 1 pixel to the link's top padding. (If you're using ems, just make sure the <ul> tag's top padding is greater than the top padding used for the link.) For example, the <ul> tag style to accompany the links in step 2 would look like this:

```
ul.nav {
    margin-left: 0;
    list-style: none;
    padding-left: 0;
    padding-top: 6px;
    padding-bottom: 5px;
    border-bottom: 1px dashed #000;
}
```

As you can see in #4 in Figure 9-6, the bottom padding lets the bottom border of a <ul> fit in place nicely. One problem with this approach is that there's always a gap between each button, so if you want buttons that touch, then you need to float the links or set a negative right margin on them. Read on for another solution.

Tip: To make this horizontal nav bar appear in the center of the page, add *text-align: center;* to the <ul> tag's style.

FREQUENTLY ASKED QUESTION

Pop-up Menus

How do I create those cool pop-up menus that display a submenu of links when someone rolls his mouse over a button?

Navigation bars that have multiple levels of menus that pop up or slide out are extremely popular. They're a perfect way to cram a lot of link options into a compact navigation bar. You can create them in a couple of ways.

First, there's the CSS-only approach. One popular drop-down menu technique is called Son of Suckerfish. (The earlier version was called Suckerfish.) You can learn about both here: *www.htmldog.com/articles/suckerfish/dropdowns/.*

As for creating a multi-level, horizontal drop-down menu, there's a nice easy tutorial at: *www.tanfa.co.uk/css/examples/menu/tutorial-h.asp.*

The same site provides a tutorial for creating vertical menus with pop-out submenus: *www.tanfa.co.uk/css/examples/menu/tutorial-v.asp.*

The one disadvantage to the CSS approach is that the submenus disappear instantly if your visitor's mouse strays. You can hope that all your visitors have excellent reflexes, or you can try a different approach: Use CSS to style the buttons and JavaScript to control the actions of the submenus. You can find various free JavaScript-driven dynamic menus at YADM (Yet Another Dynamic Menu): *http://www.onlinetools.org/tools/yadm/.*

For a continuously updated and very powerful commercial JavaScript-driven menu system, check out Ultimate Drop-down Menu (*www.udm4.com*). It's compliant with current CSS standards, and accessible to search engines, screen readers, and other alternate browsing devices. A commercial license costs around $70 for a single site. But educational and charitable organizations, as well as people running personal, non-commercial Web sites can get Ultimate Drop-down Menu for free.

Using floats for horizontal navigation

Although the *display: inline* technique for creating a horizontal nav bar is simple, it has one fundamental flaw: there's no way to create equally sized buttons. Setting a width on either the <li> or <a> tags has no effect, because they're inline elements. To get around this problem, you need to use a little trickier solution—floats.

Note: Nav bars made up of floated elements are hard to center horizontally in the middle of a page. When you need to do that, the *inline* method described on page 222 is better.

1. **Float the list items.**

   Adding a left float to the <li> tags removes them from the normal top-down flow of elements:

   ```
   ul.nav li { float: left; }
   ```

   The floated list items (along with their enclosed links) slide right next to each other, just like the images in the photo gallery tutorial on page 188. (You can just as easily float them right if you want those buttons to align to the right edge of the screen or containing sidebar.)

2. **Add *display: block* to the links.**

   Links are inline elements, so width values (as well as top and bottom padding and margins) don't apply to them. Making a browser display the links as block elements lets you set an exact width for the button and add a comfortable amount of white space above and below each link:

   ```
   ul.nav a { display: block; }
   ```

3. **Style the links.**

   Add background colors, borders, and so on. This part of the process is identical to step 2 on page 223.

4. **Add a width.**

   If you want the nav buttons to have identical widths, set a width for the <a> tag (page 146). When you set the *width* property, it's a good idea to use em units because they scale. That way, the link text won't get bigger than the buttons if a visitor increases the browser's font size. The exact width you use depends on how much text is in each button. Obviously for a link like Corporate Philosophy, you need a wider button.

Tip: To center the text in the middle of the button, add *text-align: center;* to the links' style.

5. **Float the <ul> tag.**

   If it has a border, background color, or image, you should also float the <ul> tag to the left. If you don't, the list items float outside the <ul> and cause it to collapse in height. (Preventing this overflow is known as *containing a float*, and it's discussed in depth on page 293.)

Note: You may want the floated <ul> to span the entire width of the page (or a containing block like a sidebar)–if you've added a background color to the <ul> tag that you'd like to span across the page to form a solid stripe. Just set the <ul> tag's width to 100 percent, as shown in the code following these numbered steps.

Finally, because the <ul> is floated, there's the potential that content following it may attempt to wrap around the right side of the navigation bar. To prevent this, you need to *clear* the float by applying the CSS clear property to whatever follows the <ul> tag.

6. **Clear stuff after the float.**

   One easy way is to create a class style named *.clear*, like this *.clear { clear: both; }* and then apply it to the first tag after the list.

Tip: You can learn more about clearing floats in Chapters 7 (page 155) and 11 (page 293).

Here are the styles required to create the navigation bar pictured in Figure 9-7. Notice that the buttons are the same width, and the button text is centered.

```
ul.nav {
    margin-left: 0px;
    padding-left: 0px;
    list-style: none;
    border-bottom: 1px dashed #000;
    float:left;
    width: 100%;
}
ul.nav li {
    float: left;
}
ul.nav a {
    width: 12em;
    display: block;
    border: 1px dashed #000;
    border-bottom: none;
    padding: 5px;
    margin-right: 5px;
    background-color: #EAEAEA;
    text-decoration:none;
    color: #333;
    text-align: center;
}
```

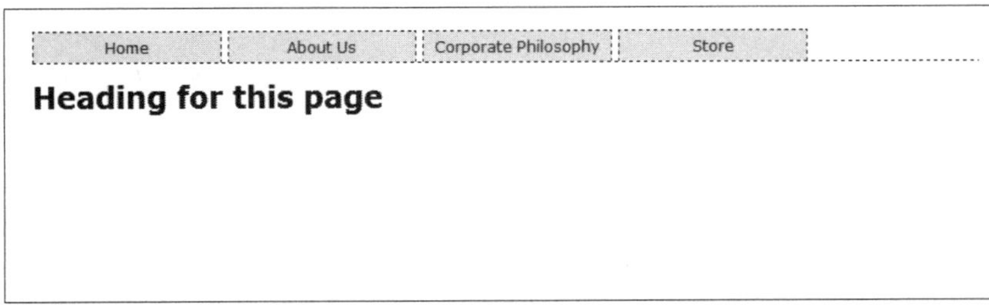

Home	About Us	Corporate Philosophy	Store

Heading for this page

Figure 9-7:
*Floating list items let you
create equal width
buttons for a navigation
bar like this one. You can
see the actual CSS that
created this bar on the
facing page.*

FREQUENTLY ASKED QUESTION

Where to Get Navigation Bar Help

*I've never made a nav bar before, but I really want my site
to have one. I just don't think I can put it all together on my
own. Is there something that walks me through the whole
process for the first time?*

Yes. In fact, there's a tutorial in this very chapter that shows
you step by step how to create a navigation bar. Just flip to
page 239.

Online, you can also find tutorials, plus tools that do some
of the work for you.

For more information on turning ordinary lists into extraordinary navigation elements, visit the step-by-step list tutorial at: *http://css.maxdesign.com.au/listutorial/*.

You can also find loads of cool list-based navigation designs
at *http://css.maxdesign.com.au/listamatic/*.

If you want to create tabs for your navigation (like the ones
at the top of every Amazon.com page), check out the
resources on this page: *http://css-discuss.incutio.com/
?page=ListTabs*.

Finally, if you just don't want to bother creating your own,
then try the List-O-Matic wizard at *www.accessify.com/
tools-and-wizards/developer-tools/list-o-matic/* or List-U-
Like CSS Generator at *www.listulike.com/generator/*. Both
sites ask for certain information, like fonts and colors, and
can create the CSS you need for list-based navigation.

Advanced Link Techniques

If you've mastered the basic *:hover* principle, and know how to add a background
image to a link, you're probably hungry for more elaborate ways to spruce up your
site's navigation. In the following sections, you'll meet a few of the most popular
techniques.

Big Clickable Buttons

The *:hover* pseudo-class is a great way to add an interactive feel to a Web page. But
what if you want to highlight an area that's bigger than just a two-word navigation
link? Suppose you have a list of news stories in a sidebar. Each item includes the
title on one line, followed by a paragraph summary of the story. And suppose you
want to highlight the area around both title and summary when a visitor mouses
over them (see Figure 9-8).

Fortunately, Internet Explorer 7, Firefox, Safari, and Opera all understand the *:hover*
pseudo-class when applied to all kinds of elements, not just links. So if you want to
highlight a paragraph when the mouse moves across it, you can do so like this:

```
p:hover { background-color: yellow;}
```

Figure 9-8:
*Give your visitors a big target. With a little clever CSS, you can make what looks like a headline
and a paragraph behave like one giant button.*

Look ma, no link! You can even apply hover effects to larger regions, like a div
containing headlines, photos, and text paragraphs. So, if each news item in a page's
sidebar is wrapped in a <div> tag and has a class of *newsItem* applied to it, this
style changes the background color of each:

```
.newsItem:hover { background-color: #333; }
```

Sadly, Internet Explorer 6 (and earlier) doesn't understand this style at all. That
browser can display a hover effect only when it's applied to a link. And since the
link tag is an inline element, you can't (at least according to the rules of HTML)
wrap it around a block-level element. So you can't wrap both the headline of a
story and the paragraph summary in the same link—exactly what you need to do
to make both the title and summary change appearance when hovered over.

You're not out of luck, though. You just need to apply a little creative thinking.
Don't put the title and summary into separate tags. Instead, keep them together in
the link and use CSS to make the title *look* like a headline. Here's an example of
marking up some HTML to achieve this effect. This snippet represents a single list
item inside an unordered list:

```
<li class="story">
<a href="virgo.html"><span class="title">Virgo: It's Your Month!</span>
The stars are aligned in your favor. Next month? Not so much.</a>
</li>
```

In this case, both the title and summary are together inside the link, so you can
highlight both with the same style:

```
li.story a:hover {
    background-image: url(highlight.gif);
}
```

In HTML, the story title ("Virgo, It's Your Month!") is wrapped in a <span> tag. You can make text look like a block-level headline with just a few simple rules:

```
.story span.title {
    display: block;
    text-weight: bold;
    font-size: 150%;
}
```

The key here's the *block* value, which makes the browser treat the text inside the span like its own headline with a line break before and after. Now, even though the title and summary look like they're separate block-level tags, they're still just part of the same inline <a> tag.

Tip: There's also a programming workaround for Internet Explorer 6's inability to apply hover styling to any tag but a link: *www.xs4all.nl/~peterned/csshover.html.*

CSS-Style Preloading Rollovers

In the bad old days, making a graphical link change to another graphic when moused over required JavaScript. With CSS, you can achieve similar effects with the *:hover* pseudo-class and a background image. However, there's one problem with the CSS method: Unless your visitor has already downloaded the rollover graphic, there's a noticeable delay while the browser sucks down the new graphic and displays it. The delay happens only the first time the visitor hovers over the link, but still, waiting for graphics to load is very 20th century.

The JavaScript solution can avoid this problem thanks to a technique called *preloading* which automatically downloads the rollover graphic well before it's needed. But CSS doesn't give you that option, so you need to enlist another clever maneuver called the *Pixy method*, which utilizes a single graphic to create different states for the same button.

Note: To read about the original Pixy method (the predecessor to what you're about to learn), visit *http://wellstyled.com/css-nopreload-rollovers.html.*

Here's how to implement the Pixy method:

1. **In your favorite image-editing program, create one image with different versions of the button.**

   You might create a regular state, a rollover state, and maybe even a "you are here" state. Place the images one on top of the other, with the regular link image on top, and the rollover image below.

2. **Measure the distances from the top of the entire graphic to the top of each image.**

   In Figure 9-9 (top) the rollover image's top edge is 39 pixels from the top of the graphic.

3. **Create a CSS style for the regular link. Include the image in the background and place it at the left top of the style (Figure 9-9, middle).**

   Your style may look something like this:

   ```
   a { background: #E7E7E7 url(images/pixy.png) no-repeat left top; }
   ```

4. **Create the *:hover* style.**

   Here's the trick: Use the background-position property to shift the graphic *upwards*, so the first image disappears and the rollover image becomes visible (Figure 9-9, bottom).

   ```
   a:hover { background-position:  0 -39px; }
   ```

Besides preventing the dreaded download delay, this technique helps you keep your navigation graphics organized in a single file.

Tip: CSS gives you other ways to preload the image. You can place the image into the background of an element that's covered by another element. Say your site's logo appears in the top-left corner of the Web page. You could place the rollover image in the top-left corner of the page's background: *body { background: url(rollover.gif) no-repeat left top; }*. When the page loads, the rollover graphic is sitting in the background of the page but your visitors won't see it because it's covered by the logo. Another method is to place the rollover image inside a <div> that you position off the page using CSS positioning (see page 325). In either case, the browser downloads the image and the CSS rollover won't have any delays.

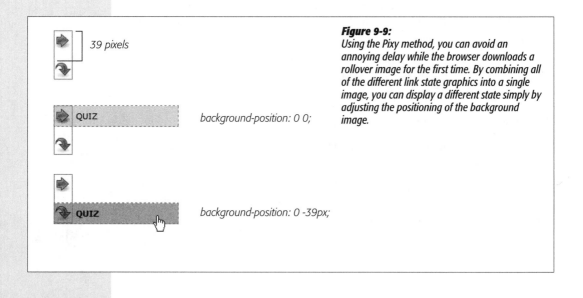

Figure 9-9:
Using the Pixy method, you can avoid an annoying delay while the browser downloads a rollover image for the first time. By combining all of the different link state graphics into a single image, you can display a different state simply by adjusting the positioning of the background image.

Note: Believe it or not, the Web site of one well-known designer uses *one* single graphic for 15–count 'em, *15*–different graphic navigation buttons. You can read about her technique at *http://veerle.duoh. com/index.php/blog/comments/the_xhtml_css_template_phase_of_my_new_blog_part_2/*. You can also see this technique in action in this chapter's tutorial, in step 3 on page 238.

Sliding Doors

Ever since Amazon popularized them years back, tabbed navigation buttons have become one of the most common ways to highlight the organization of a site. With good reason, too: Selecting a tab to open a new "folder" of information is a metaphor everyone recognizes. You have many ways to create tab buttons. It's still common to see tabs where the button and its text are one and the same graphic. However, updating a bunch of button images in Photoshop or Fireworks every time you change your site's navigation can get old quick. Furthermore, having different graphics for each button slows down the loading time of your site.

A slicker technique is to put a tab graphic in the background of each link, and use regular HTML for the text. That way, updating your site's navigation is a simple matter of updating some text in a Web page. Even someone with zero Photoshop experience can manage it. The only time a single graphic for a tab doesn't work well is when the text on each link varies in length. If one tab reads "Store," and the other reads "Contact Us Today!" the Store tab suffers from empty space and the Contact tab looks a little cramped (see #1 in Figure 9-10).

What you need in that case is a way to have the tab graphic shrink-wrap itself around the link text. Luckily, designer Douglas Bowman has come up with a creative technique that does just that. Dubbed the *Sliding Doors* method, it involves creating one very wide and tall tab graphic in your image editing program (#2 in Figure 9-10), and then slicing that image into two graphic files (#3 in Figure 9-10). The very thin graphic is the left edge of the tab. It should be only wide enough to reveal the sloping left edge of the tab. The second graphic is very wide—wider than you imagine any tab on the page would ever get—and forms the tab's main body and right edge.

Note: Douglas Bowman's Sliding Doors technique is a classic in CSS design. You can find his original article at the A List Apart Web site: *www.alistapart.com/articles/slidingdoors*. There's also a follow-up article covering more advanced techniques at *www.alistapart.com/articles/slidingdoors2*.

Now here's the tricky part. Since a tag can have only *one* background image, you need to apply the graphics as backgrounds to *two* different tags. Start by creating an unordered list and turning it into a horizontal navigation bar as described on page 222. At this point, each <a> tag is nested inside one <li> tag, so you've got two tags to play with.

First, add the wide background image to the <li> tag and place it at the top-right corner of the tag. Do that by adding the following property to the style formatting for that button's <li> tag:

```
background: url(images/right_tab.gif) no-repeat right top;
```

The Sliding Doors technique capitalizes on the fact that a background image never extends outside of the box created by its tag. In other words, even though this image is really, really wide and tall, you won't see any part of the graphic that extends outside the region of the <li> tag—either below it or outside its left edge.

Tip: If you like this technique, but aren't good at using Photoshop to create graphics, you can pick up free tab designs at *www.exploding-boy.com/2005/12/15/free-css-navigation-designs* and *www.exploding-boy.com/2005/12/21/more-free-css-navigation-menu-designs.*

Next, place the thin, left-hand graphic in the top-*left* background of the <a> tag by adding this property to the style for the link:

```
background: url(images/left_tab.gif) no-repeat left top;
```

Because the <a> tag is nested *inside* of the <li> tag, its background appears *above* the <li> tag's background. That left side tab graphic sits on top of the really wide tab graphic, creating the illusion of a single graphic. At this point, type whatever text you want for each link, in the process expanding the <li> tag and exposing more of the extra-wide graphic (see #4 Figure 9-10).

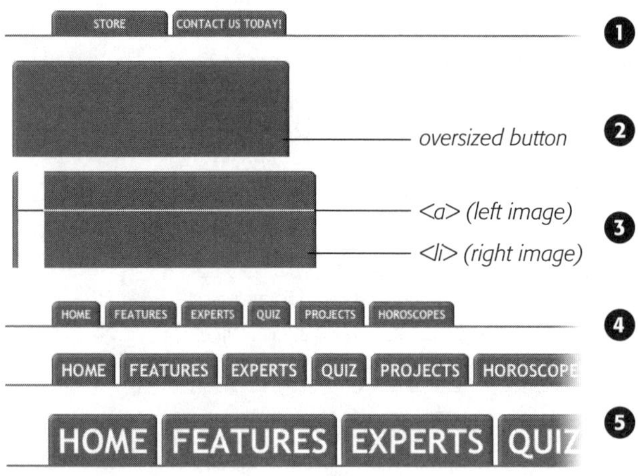

Figure 9-10:
With the Sliding Doors method, you can add graphical tabs to any link. By using oversized graphics (#3) that are taller and wider than the largest tab, you can make sure that your tabs look right even when visitors pump up the size of their text (#5).

Tip: You can find a Web page with an example of the Sliding Doors technique in the tutorial files for this chapter. The file's located in the *chapter_09 → sliding_doors* folder.

Tutorial: Styling Links

In this tutorial, you'll style links in a variety of ways, like adding rollovers and background graphics. You'll also create both vertical and horizontal navigation bars.

To get started, download the tutorial files from this book's companion Web site at *www.sawmac.com/css/*. Click the tutorial link and download the files. All the files are enclosed in a ZIP archive, so you need to unzip them first. (You'll find detailed instructions on the Web site.) The files for this tutorial are contained inside the *chapter_09* folder.

Basic Link Formatting

1. **Launch a Web browser and open the file** *chapter_09 → links → bathtub.html.*

    As usual, you'll be working on a page from CosmoFarmer.com. This page contains a variety of links (circled in Figure 9-11) that point to other pages on the site, links to pages on other Web sites, and an email address. Start by changing the color of the links in the main content area of this page.

2. **Open** *bathtub.html* **in a text editor and place your cursor between the opening and closing <style> tags.**

    The page already has an external style sheet attached to it with some basic formatting, plus the <style> tags for an internal style sheet.

3. **Add a new style to the internal style sheet:**

    ```
    <style type="text/css">
    #main a {
        color: #8C1919;
    }
    </style>
    ```

    This descendent selector changes the color of all <a> tags that are inside tags that have an ID of *#main*. The main body text on the page is wrapped in a <div> tag with an ID of *#main*. Adding and naming a <div> like this makes it easy to create styles that target just the HTML containing the page's main text. This style changes the color of the text for links, but only those inside this main body <div>. If you preview the page now, you'll see that the color of the link at the bottom of the page—which is contained in a separate <div> with a different ID—isn't affected.

    Now, time to remove that boring old underline beneath the link.

4. **Add** *text-decoration: none;* **to the** *#main a* **style you just created.**

    This removes the underline, but also makes the link less visible on the page. Remember you should always do something to make links stand out and seem clickable to your site's visitors.

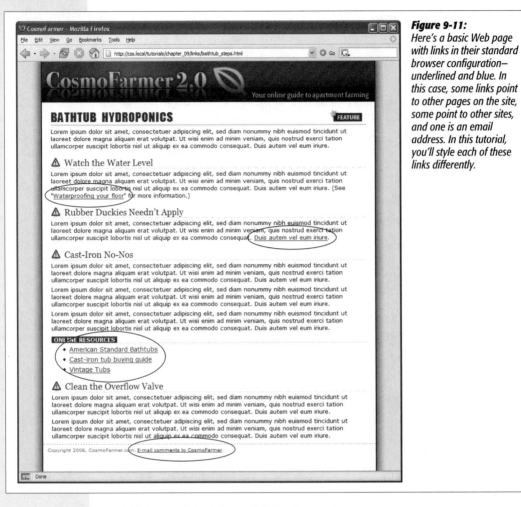

Figure 9-11:
*Here's a basic Web page
with links in their standard
browser configuration—
underlined and blue. In
this case, some links point
to other pages on the site,
some point to other sites,
and one is an email
address. In this tutorial,
you'll style each of these
links differently.*

5. Add *font-weight: bold;* to the *#main a* style.

   Now links appear in bold (other text may appear bold, too). Next you'll replace
   the underline, but you'll do it a bit more creatively, using a border instead of
   the *text-decoration* property.

6. Add a *border* declaration to the style, so it looks like this:

   ```
   #main a {
       color: #8C1919;
       text-decoration: none;
       font-weight: bold;
       border-bottom: 2px dotted #A5E410;
   }
   ```

The links really stand out, and using a border instead of the normal underline applied to links lets you change the line's color, size, and style (Figure 9-12, left). Time to take it a step further by adding a rollover effect, so the link's background changes color when the mouse moves over it.

7. Add a *:hover* pseudo-class style to the style sheet:

```
#main a:hover {
    background-color: #FCC423;
}
```

This pseudo-class applies only when the mouse is over the link. The interactive quality of rollovers lets visitors know the link does something (Figure 9-12, right).

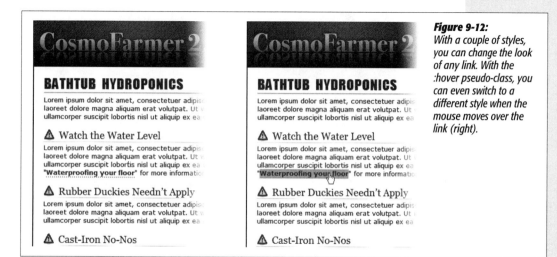

Figure 9-12:
With a couple of styles, you can change the look of any link. With the :hover pseudo-class, you can even switch to a different style when the mouse moves over the link (right).

Adding a Background Image to a Link

The email link at the bottom of the page remains unaffected by the styles you've created so far (Figure 9-13, top). That's fine—you have other plans for that *mailto* link. Since it points to an email address, clicking it doesn't take a visitor to another page, but instead launches an email program. To provide a visual cue emphasizing this point, you'll add a cute little email icon.

1. Add another descendent selector to the internal style sheet of the *bathtub.html* file:

```
#legal a {
    color: #666666;
    background: url(images/email.gif) no-repeat left center;
}
```

The email link's inside a <div> tag with an ID of *legal*, so this style affects only this link, and the *color* declaration makes it gray. The *background* property adds an image on the left edge of the link. Finally, the *no-repeat* value forces the graphic to appear just a single time. Trouble is, the graphic lies directly underneath the link, so it's hard to read the text (Figure 9-13, middle).

2. **Add 20 pixels of left padding to the *#legal a* style you just created:**

   ```
   padding-left: 20px;
   ```

   Remember that padding adjusts the space between content and its border. So adding some left padding moves the text over 20 pixels but leaves the background in place. One last touch: move the entire link a little away from the copyright notice.

3. **Add 10 pixels of left margin to the style, so it finally ends up like this:**

   ```
   #legal a {
       color: #666666;
       background: url(images/email.gif) no-repeat left center;
       padding-left: 20px;
       margin-left: 10px;
   }
   ```

   This small visual adjustment makes it clear that the icon's related to the link and not part of the copyright notice (Figure 9-13, bottom).

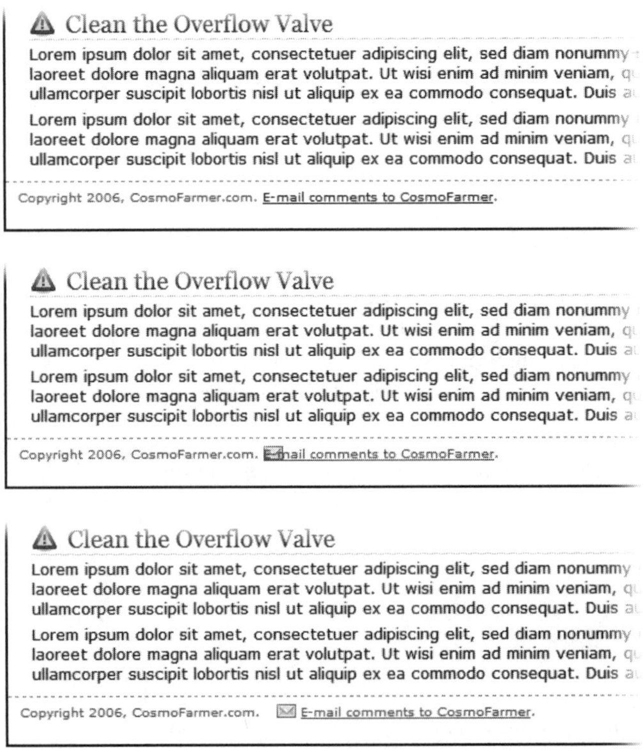

⚠ Clean the Overflow Valve

Lorem ipsum dolor sit amet, consectetuer adipiscing elit, sed diam nonummy laoreet dolore magna aliquam erat volutpat. Ut wisi enim ad minim veniam, q ullamcorper suscipit lobortis nisl ut aliquip ex ea commodo consequat. Duis a

Lorem ipsum dolor sit amet, consectetuer adipiscing elit, sed diam nonummy laoreet dolore magna aliquam erat volutpat. Ut wisi enim ad minim veniam, q ullamcorper suscipit lobortis nisl ut aliquip ex ea commodo consequat. Duis a

Copyright 2006, CosmoFarmer.com. E-mail comments to CosmoFarmer.

Figure 9-13:
Just a few subtle touches can help make a link's purpose obvious. In this case, a plain link (top) becomes clearly identifiable as an email link (bottom).

⚠ Clean the Overflow Valve

Lorem ipsum dolor sit amet, consectetuer adipiscing elit, sed diam nonummy laoreet dolore magna aliquam erat volutpat. Ut wisi enim ad minim veniam, q ullamcorper suscipit lobortis nisl ut aliquip ex ea commodo consequat. Duis a

Lorem ipsum dolor sit amet, consectetuer adipiscing elit, sed diam nonummy laoreet dolore magna aliquam erat volutpat. Ut wisi enim ad minim veniam, q ullamcorper suscipit lobortis nisl ut aliquip ex ea commodo consequat. Duis a

Copyright 2006, CosmoFarmer.com. ✉mail comments to CosmoFarmer.

⚠ Clean the Overflow Valve

Lorem ipsum dolor sit amet, consectetuer adipiscing elit, sed diam nonummy laoreet dolore magna aliquam erat volutpat. Ut wisi enim ad minim veniam, q ullamcorper suscipit lobortis nisl ut aliquip ex ea commodo consequat. Duis a

Lorem ipsum dolor sit amet, consectetuer adipiscing elit, sed diam nonummy laoreet dolore magna aliquam erat volutpat. Ut wisi enim ad minim veniam, q ullamcorper suscipit lobortis nisl ut aliquip ex ea commodo consequat. Duis a

Copyright 2006, CosmoFarmer.com. ✉ E-mail comments to CosmoFarmer.

Highlighting External Links

At times you may want to indicate that a link points to another Web site. In this way, you can give your visitors a visual clue that there's additional information elsewhere on the Internet, or warn them that they'll exit your site if they click the link. In the next few steps, you'll create a special style for external links.

1. **Add this style to the *bathtub.html* internal style sheet:**

```
#main a.external {
    background-image: url(images/globe.png);
    background-repeat: no-repeat;
    background-position: right top;
    padding-right: 18px;
    border-bottom: none;
}
```

As with the email link style you just created, this style adds a background image. It places the image at the right side of the link. Setting the *border-bottom* property to *none* eliminates the green, dashed border that appears under links pointing to other pages on the CosmoFarmer site.

None of the external links on the page have changed yet. Now that you've got your new class style—*.external*—you should apply it to any external links you want to format.

2. **In the page's HTML code, locate the three external links. (Hint: They're in an unordered list about two-thirds of the way down the page.) Add** *class="external"* **to each of the <a> tags:**

```
<li><a href="http://www.americanstandard-us.com/Products/products.
aspx?area=bath&cat=8" class="external">American Standard Bathtubs</a></li>
<li><a href="http://www.clawfootsupply.com/editor/cast-iron-buying-guide.php"
class="external">Cast-iron tub buying guide</a></li>
<li><a href="http://www.vintagetub.com/" class="external">Vintage Tubs</a>
</li>
```

If you preview the page in a Web browser, you'll see those three links have a small globe icon at their right (Figure 9-14, top). The links higher up on the page are globe-free. They point to other CosmoFarmer pages, so you didn't apply the external class to them.

Tip: You've been learning about the rules for CSS 2.1 (the most widely supported version of CSS). But you can use a CSS 3 selector to automatically target any link beginning with *http://*. Just change the name of the selector in step 1 above from *#main a.external* to *#main a[href^='http://']*. When you use this selector, you don't have to apply classes to individual links as in step 2. The downside: Only Internet Explorer 7, Safari, Firefox, and Opera 9 recognize the selector. IE 6 folks won't see the style at all.

Next, give these links a rollover effect using the Pixy method described on page 229. As a matter of fact, the background graphic you added in step 1—*globe.png*—actually contains two images. Currently, only the top image is visible, and you want the graphic's position to shift when a visitor mouses over the link.

3. **Immediately after the style you created in step 1, add the following style:**

   ```
   #main a.external:hover {
       background-position: right -24px;
       color: #152D6A;
   }
   ```

   This style both changes the color of the text and adjusts the position of the background image. It moves the graphic up -24 pixels, essentially moving the globe image out of view and exposing a new rollover image.

   There's one problem, however. The background color from the *#main a:hover* style (created in step 7 on page 235) also appears. As you can see Figure 9-14, middle, the graphic obscures part of the background. It'll look better when you remove that background color.

4. **Edit the style you just created by adding a background-color property:**

   ```
   #main a.external:hover {
       background-position: right -24px;
       color: #152D6A;
       background-image: url(images/globe_highlight.png);
       background-color: #FFF;
   }
   ```

   This declaration sets the background color to white, matching the white background of the page (Figure 9-14, bottom).

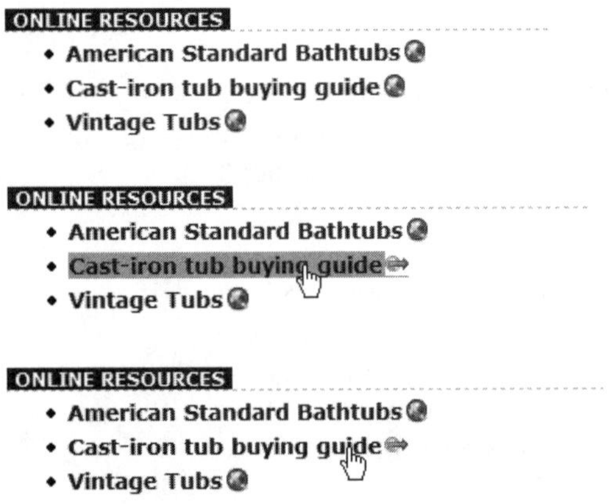

Figure 9-14:
Using a class style, you can format external links differently than other links on the page. A globe icon is one way to indicate that a link leads out into the greater Web (top). You may have to tweak a style to overcome properties inherited from other styles, like the background color inherited from a more generic style (middle). Here, the fix is removing a background color from the link's :hover style (bottom).

Marking Visited Pages

To round out the look of the links on this page, you'll add one more style. This one applies only in one certain case—when a link's been visited. Using the *:visited* pseudo-class, it's easy to add a graphic marker indicating pages someone has already been to.

1. **Add one last style to the style sheet:**

   ```
   #main a:visited {
       color: #999;
   }
   ```

   Now, when the Web browser has already visited one of the pages linked to from this page, it makes that link gray. By making the color duller and lighter than other links, you make the link visually recede from the page (Figure 9-15, top). But just in case that's not enough information to let people know they've been to the linked page before, you'll make it even more obvious with a checkmark.

2. **Edit the style you just created by adding a background property and some padding:**

   ```
   #main a:visited {
       color: #999;
       background: url(images/check.gif) no-repeat right center;
       padding-right: 18px;
   }
   ```

   Preview the page, click one of the links, and then hit your browser's back button to see how the link changes appearance once visited (Figure 9-15, bottom).

A finished version of this tutorial is in the *chapter_09_finished → links* folder.

Creating a Vertical Navigation Bar

In this exercise you'll turn a plain old list of links into a spectacular navigation bar complete with rollover effects and a "You are here" button effect.

1. **In a text editor, open *chapter_09 → nav_bar → nav_bar.html*.**

   As you can see, there's not much to this file yet. There's an internal style sheet with one rule setting up some basic properties for the <body> tag, and an unordered list consisting of six links. It looks like example one in Figure 9-16. Your first step is to add some HTML so you can target your CSS to format the links in this list.

2. **Locate the opening <ul> tag and add *id="mainNav"* to it, so it looks like this:**

   ```
   <ul id="mainNav">
   ```

   The ID attribute identifies this list as the main navigation area. Use this ID to build descendent selectors to format only these links (and not just any old link on the page). (See page 49 for the story on descendent selectors.)

Figure 9-15:
Let folks know they've clicked a link by employing the :visited pseudo-class. You can subtly identify visited links by making their color recede into the background (top), or give them a sense of completion by adding a checkmark graphic (bottom).

visited

unvisited

visited

unvisited

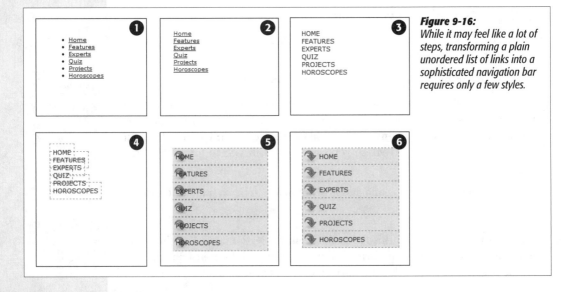

Figure 9-16:
While it may feel like a lot of steps, transforming a plain unordered list of links into a sophisticated navigation bar requires only a few styles.

3. **Below the** *body* **style in the internal style sheet, add a new style:**

```
ul#mainNav {
    margin: 0;
    padding: 0;
    list-style: none;
}
```

This style applies only to a <ul> tag with an ID of *mainNav*. It removes the indent and bullets that browsers apply to unordered lists, as shown in #2 in Figure 9-16. Next, you'll start formatting the links.

4. **Add a descendent selector to format the links in the list:**

```
#mainNav a {
    color: #000;
    font-size: 1.1em;
    text-transform: uppercase;
    text-decoration: none;
}
```

This style defines the basic text formatting for the links. It sets the color and font size, makes all letters uppercase, and removes the line usually found underneath links (# 3 in Figure 9-16). Now start making the links look like buttons.

5. **To the** *#mainNav a* **style, add the following** *border* **and** *padding* **properties:**

```
border: 1px dashed #999;
padding: 7px 5px;
```

If you preview the file now, you'll see a few problems (#4 in Figure 9-16): The borders overlap and the boxes aren't the same width. That's because the <a> tag is an inline element, so the width of the box is just as wide as the text in the link. In addition, top and bottom padding don't add any height to inline boxes, so the borders overlap. (See page 140 for a discussion of inline boxes.) You can fix these problems by changing how a browser displays these links.

6. **To the** *#mainNav a* **style, add** *display: block;.*

You've changed the basic display of the <a> tag so that it acts like a paragraph or other block-level element, with the links neatly stacked one on top of the other. The only problem now is that they also extend the full length of the browser window—a little too wide for a button. You can fix this by constraining the width of the <ul> tag's style.

Note: If you preview the page in Internet Explorer 6 or earlier, you'll notice a gap between each nav button. Remain calm. You'll fix this bug in step 1 on page 246.

---

7. In the internal style sheet, locate the *ul#mainNav* style and add *width: 175px;* to it.

With the list's width now set to 175 pixels, the links still expand, but they're limited to the width of their container (the <ul> tag). In many cases, you'll have a list of links inside some layout element (like a sidebar) that already has a set width, so you'll be able to skip this step. (You'll learn how to add sidebars in Part 3.)

Now for the fun part.

8. Add background properties to the *#mainNav a* style, like so:

```
#mainNav a {
    color: #000;
    font-size: 1.1em;
    text-transform: uppercase;
    text-decoration: none;
    border: 1px dashed #999;
    padding: 7px 5px;
    display: block;
    background-color: #E7E7E7;
    background-image: url(images/link.png);
    background-repeat: no-repeat;
    background-position: left center;
}
```

These lines add a gray background color to the links and a non-repeating image at the left edge of each button (#5 in Figure 9-16). You still have a couple of things to fix: The link text overlaps the icon, and the border between each button is 2 pixels thick. (Technically, the borders are still just 1 pixel thick, but the bottom and top borders of adjoining links are creating a 2-pixel line.)

Note: Using the *background* shorthand property you can write the code in step 8 like this: *background: #E7E7E7 url(images/link.png) no-repeat left center;*. See Chapter 8 (page 182) for the details.

---

9. Remove the top border and adjust the padding for the *#mainNav a* style, so it looks like this:

```
#mainNav a {
    text-decoration: none;
    color: #000000;
    font-size: 1.1em;
    text-transform: uppercase;
    border: 1px dashed #999999;
    border-bottom: none;
    padding: 7px 5px 7px 30px;
    display: block;
```

```
    background-color: #E7E7E7;
    background-image: url(images/link.png);
    background-repeat: no-repeat;
    background-position: left center;
}
```

The text of each link sits clear of the icon and the borders look great…except for one thing. The last link's bottom border is now gone. (Sometimes CSS feels like two steps forward, one step back!) But you have a few ways to fix this snafu. One way is to create a class style with the proper *border-bottom* setting, and then apply it to just that first link. But it would be easier to apply a bottom border to the <ul> tag containing the list of links. (Since there's no padding on that tag, there's no space separating the top of the <ul> from the top of that first link.)

10. **Add a top border to the *ul#mainNav* style so that it looks like this:**

```
ul#mainNav {
    margin: 0;
    padding: 0;
    list-style: none;
    width: 175px;
    border-bottom: 1px dashed #999;
}
```

There you have it: A basic navigation bar using borders, padding, background color and images (# 6 in Figure 9-16).

Adding Rollovers and Creating "You Are Here" Links

Now it's time to add some interactive and advanced features to this nav bar. First, you'll add a rollover effect to the buttons in your main navigation bar. That way, the buttons change to show your visitor which button she's about to click.

It's also considerate to let your visitor know which page of your site she's on. Using the same HTML nav bar you already have, you can make this bit of interactivity happen automatically. You simply make the button's format change to match the page's section. Sounds simple, but it does require a little planning and setup, as you'll see in the following steps.

The rollover effect is easy, so get that out of the way first:

1. **In the *nav_bar.html* file, add the following style to the end of the style sheet:**

```
#mainNav a:hover {
    font-weight: bold;
    background: #B2F511 url(images/go.png) no-repeat 5px 50%;
}
```

This style sets the button's hover state. It makes the text inside the button bold, and (using the *background* shorthand property) changes the background color and image (Figure 9-17). Now, moving the mouse over any of the buttons instantly changes its look. (Open the page in your Web browser and try it yourself.)

Figure 9-17:
With some basic CSS, it's easy to create interactive rollover effects for navigation buttons. You can even automatically highlight the section of the site in which the current page is located.

Note: You can also use the Pixy method, as in step 3 on page 238, to create the same rollover effect using just one graphics file. That approach has the added benefit of avoiding the slight delay that appears when a visitor first rolls over one of the links.

Next, make your navigation bar more informative by highlighting the button that matches the section in which the page is located. To do so, you need to identify two things in the nav bar's HTML: 1) the section a page belongs to, and 2) the section each link points to. For this example, assume that the page you're working on belongs to the Features section.

Note: Alternatively, you can create a class style that changes the appearance of a link, and apply it to the link representing the page's section. For a horoscope page, you'd apply the class to the Horoscope link in the nav bar: *<a href="/horoscopes/" class="u_r_here">Horoscopes</a>*.

2. **Locate the <body> tag, and then add *id="feature"*, like so:**

   ```
   <body id="feature">
   ```

   Now that you know what section this page belongs to, you can use a descendent selector to create special CSS rules that apply only to tags on pages within the Features section. Next, you need to identify the section each link applies to, which you accomplish by adding some IDs to those links.

3. **In the nav bar's HTML code, locate the Features link, and then add *id="featureLink"* so the tag looks like this:**

   ```
   <a href="/features/" id="featureLink">Features</a>
   ```

   This ID uniquely identifies this link, providing the information you need to create a style that applies only to that link.

   You need to ID the other links in the navigation bar as well.

4. **Repeat step 4 for each of the other links using the following IDs:** *homeLink,
   expertLink, quizLink, projectLink,* and *horoscopeLink.*

   You're done with the HTML part of this exercise. Now it's time to create some
   CSS. Because you've ID'd the page and the link, it's easy to create a descendent
   selector to highlight the Features link.

5. **Add another style to the page's style sheet:**

   ```
   body#feature a#featureLink {
       background: #FFFFFF url(images/bg_here.png) no-repeat 95% 50%;
       padding-right: 15px;
       padding-left: 30px;
       font-weight: bold;
   }
   ```

   You've seen all these properties before. The interesting part's the selector—
   body#feature a#featurelink. This is a very specific selector that applies only to a
   link with an ID of *featureLink* that's *also* inside a <body> tag with an ID of *feature.* If you change the ID of the page to *home,* for example, the link to the Features section's no longer highlighted.

   Preview the page in a browser to see the effect: The Features link now has a
   white background and a paperclip icon. To make this work for the other links,
   you need to expand this selector a little...OK, make that a *lot.*

6. **Edit the selector for the style you just added, like so:**

   ```
   body#home a#homeLink,
   body#feature a#featureLink,
   body#expert a#experLink,
   body#quiz a#quizLink,
   body#project a#projectLink,
   body#horoscope a#horoscopeLink {
       background: #FFFFFF url(images/bg_here.png) no-repeat 95% 50%;
       padding-right: 15px;
       padding-left: 30px;
       font-weight: bold;
   }
   ```

   Yes, that's a lot of CSS. But your set-up work here has a big payoff. This style
   now applies to every link in the nav bar, but only under certain conditions,
   which is exactly how you want it to behave. When you change the *id* attribute of
   the <body> tag to *quiz,* the link to the Quiz gets highlighted instead of the link
   to the Features section. Time to take your work for a test drive.

7. **Change the *id* attribute of the <body> tag to *quiz* like this:**

   ```
   <body id="quiz">
   ```

Preview the page, and wham! The Quiz link's now highlighted with a white background and a paperclip icon (Figure 9-17). The secret at this point is to just change the ID in the <body> tag to indicate which section of the site a page belongs to. For a horoscope page, change the id to *id="horoscope"* in the <body> tag.

Note: Ready to take this design further? Try adding a rollover effect to complement the style you created in step 6. (Hint: Use the *:hover* pseudo-class as part of the selector like this: *body#quiz a#quizLink:hover*.) Also try adding a different graphic for the Home link. (You have a *home.png* file in the *images* folder to use.)

Fixing the IE Bugs

What would a CSS tutorial be if there weren't any Internet Explorer bugs to fix? Unfortunately, the navigation bar doesn't work quite right in that browser. First, an annoying gap appears between each button (even in IE 7, as of this writing). In addition, IE 6 and earlier treat only the text—not the entire area of the button—as clickable (Figure 9-18). In other browsers, moving the mouse over any part of the background (including the empty space to the right of the link text) highlights the link.

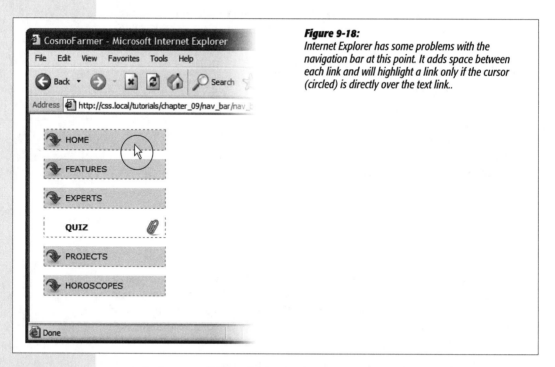

Figure 9-18:
Internet Explorer has some problems with the navigation bar at this point. It adds space between each link and will highlight a link only if the cursor (circled) is directly over the text link..

1. **At the bottom of the style sheet, add the following:**

```
#mainNav li {
    display: inline;
}
```

This bit of CSS changes the natural behavior of list items from block-level elements to inline elements. This workaround doesn't make much sense theoretically, but it at least removes the space between each link in the navigation bar without negatively affecting other browsers. The next style makes IE 6 and earlier treat the entire area of the button as clickable.

2. **After the style you just added, insert this IE-only style:**

```
* html #mainNav a {
    height: 1px;
}
```

This style uses the *html hack* to apply CSS properties to just IE 6 and earlier. IE 7 completely ignores this rule, as do all other browsers. The style declaration itself is nonsense: It attempts to set the height of the link to 1 pixel, something that IE ignores, but which forces that browser to see the background of the button as part of the link. (See the box on page 307 for the geeky details.)

3. **Preview the page in Internet Explorer on Windows.**

The navigation bar should now work as well in that browser as it does in more savvy browsers like Firefox, Opera, and Safari.

To see the completed version of this navigation bar, see the file *chapter_09_finished → nav_bar → nav_bar_vertical_finished.html*.

Note: When creating specific styles targeted to just Internet Explorer, it's a good idea to isolate them from your other styles. Not that they're contagious, but they usually include nonsense CSS that for weird reasons smoothes out IE kinks. You don't want to read your style sheet later and get confused about why you included some bizarre CSS. In fact, the preferred method is to put IE-only styles in external style sheets and attach them using Microsoft's conditional comments feature. Get the full story on page 399.

From Vertical to Horizontal

Suppose you want a horizontal navigation bar that sits at the top of the page. No problem—you did most of the hard work in the last part of this tutorial. Just modify that page a little to spread the buttons along a single line. (You'll use the *nav_bar.html* file you just completed, so if you want to keep the vertical nav bar, then save a copy of the file before proceeding.)

1. **Make sure you've completed all the steps above to create the vertical navigation bar, and have the file *nav_bar.html* open in your text editor.**

Now you'll see how easy it is to change the orientation of a navigation bar. Start by cleaning up some of the work you already did.

2. **In the *nav_bar.html* file's style sheet, remove the *#mainNav li* style you created in step 1 on page 246.**

That style was necessary only to remove the gap IE inserts between links when buttons are stacked one on top of the other, and that's no longer an issue when the buttons appear side by side.

Tip: Cleaning up a style sheet by removing unnecessary styles is a good habit to get into. If you don't, you can end up with unused styles in your style sheets, causing unnecessary file size and potential confusion down the line. And here's another reason to put IE-specific styles either together at the bottom of a style sheet or in their own external style sheets: When you no longer have to support a particular version of IE, you can clean up your CSS by simply removing those styles.

You also need to remove the width you set for the <ul> tag in step 7 on page 242. That width prevented the nav buttons from spanning the entire length of the page. But since the <ul> needs to spread out much wider to contain the side-by-side buttons, this width has to go.

3. **Find the *ul#mainNav* style, and then remove the *width: 175px;* declaration.**

    And now it's time for the big secret of vertical nav bars—placing the buttons side by side.

4. **Add a new style to your style sheet (directly below the *ul#mainNav* style is a good spot):**

    ```
    #mainNav li {
        float: left;
        width: 12em;
    }
    ```

    This style applies to the <li> tag (the list items that hold each link). The first declaration floats the tag to the left. In this way, each <li> tag attempts to wrap around to the right side of the previous <li> tag. (You saw the same effect in the photo gallery tutorial on page 188.) Also, setting the width of the <li> tag defines the width of each button. Here, a value of 12ems provides enough space to contain the longest link name—Horoscopes. When you're working with longer links, you need to increase this value.

Tip: Using an em value instead of a pixel value for the width of the buttons makes the width adjust to the visitor's browser. If the buttons' widths were set to pixels, and a visitor increased the browser's font size, then the text in the button might get wider than the button itself. When you use ems, the button simply gets wider as the font gets larger.

If you preview the page now, you'll see the basics are complete. All that's left are some cosmetic enhancements (see the circled areas of #1 in Figure 9-19). First, the bottom border you created in step 10 on page 243 runs the entire length of the <ul> tag—wider than the navigation buttons themselves. Even stranger, that bottom border's no longer on the bottom—it's on top of the navigation buttons! In addition, since the buttons sit side by side, their left and right borders combine to make a 2-pixel border between each button. You'll fix that problem now.

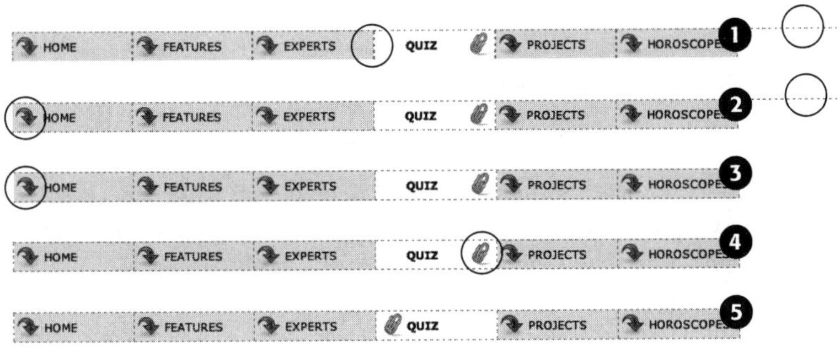

Figure 9-19:
*Changing a vertical stack
of navigation buttons into
the much shorter, side-by-
side format of a horizontal
navigation bar only takes a
couple of steps. Most of
your effort involves
tweaking styles for
cosmetic considerations
such as borders and
background image
placement.*

5. In the *#mainNav a* style change *border-bottom: none;* to *border*-left: *none;*.

   This change removes the left border so that the borders don't double up between buttons, and at the same time adds a border to the bottom of each button. But that <ul> tag's bottom border is still on top of the buttons, and now the nav bar is missing a border on the far left button (see circled areas of #2 in Figure 9-19). No problem—just change the border on the <ul> tag.

6. Locate the *ul#mainNav* style and change *border-bottom: 1px dashed #999999;* to *border*-left: *1px dashed #999999;*.

   If you preview the page now, you'll see that the border above the buttons is gone, but there's still no left border (#3 in Figure 9-19). You're witnessing one of the complications of using floats. That is, floating the list items removes them from the normal flow of the document, so Web browsers no longer see them as part of the <ul> tag, and the <ul> tag shrinks down to nearly no height—that's the reason the ul's bottom border appeared on top as well. (If this whole scenario sounds confusing, it is. That's why there's an entire section of Chapter 11 dedicated to dealing with the issue—see page 293 for the details.)

   Fortunately, while the problem is complex, the solution is simple. Just float the <ul> tag as well.

7. Add *float: left;* to the *ul#mainNav* style. The completed style should look like this:

```
ul#mainNav {
    margin: 0;
    padding: 0;
    list-style: none;
    border-left: 1px dashed #999999;
    float: left;
}
```

   Finally, that paperclip aligned to the right edge of the "You are here" button looks funny (#4 in Figure 9-19). You'll switch its position to the left edge of the button.

Note: Since the <ul> tag is floated, other page elements try to wrap around it. It's a good idea to set the *clear* property on the next element immediately after the navigation bar as described on page 155. That property forces whatever's following the navigation bar to sit below it rather than try to wrap to the nav bar's right side.

8. Locate the "You are here" style you created in step 6 on page 245. (It's the one with the crazy, long-winded selector.) Change its background position from *95% 50%* to *5px 50%*. The style should now look like this:

```
body#home a#homeLink,
body#feature a#featureLink,
body#expert a#experLink,
body#quiz a#quizLink,
body#project a#projectLink,
body#horoscope a#horoscopeLink {
    background: #FFFFFF url(images/bg_here.png) no-repeat 5px 50%;
    padding-right: 15px;
    padding-left: 30px;
    font-weight: bold;
}
```

Preview the page, and you'll find a fully functional horizontal navigation bar (#5 in Figure 9-19). And guess what? It works perfectly even in Internet Explorer.

To see the finished version, open the file *chapter_09_finished* → *nav_bar* → *nav_bar_horizontal_finished.html*.

Note: You may want to center the text inside each button. If so, you need to do two things: Add *text-align: center;* to the *#mainNav a* style, and adjust that style's *left-padding* until the text looks absolutely centered.

Formatting Tables and Forms

The formatting powers of CSS go way beyond text, images, and links. You can make tables of information like schedules, sports scores, and music playlists easier to read by adding borders, backgrounds, and other visual enhancements. Similarly, you can use CSS to organize the elements of a form to help your visitors through the process of ordering items, signing up for your newsletter, or using your latest Web application.

This chapter shows you how to display tables and forms with HTML and how to lay out and style them using CSS. In two tutorials at the end of the chapter, you'll create a table and a form, using the tricks you've learned along the way.

Using Tables the Right Way

HTML tables have seen a lot of use in the short history of the Web. Originally created to display data in a spreadsheet-like format, tables became a popular layout tool. Faced with HTML's limitations, designers got creative and used table rows and columns to position page elements like banner headlines and sidebars. As you'll see in Part III of this book, CSS does a much better job of laying out Web pages. You can concentrate on using (and formatting) tables for their original purpose—displaying data (Figure 10-1).

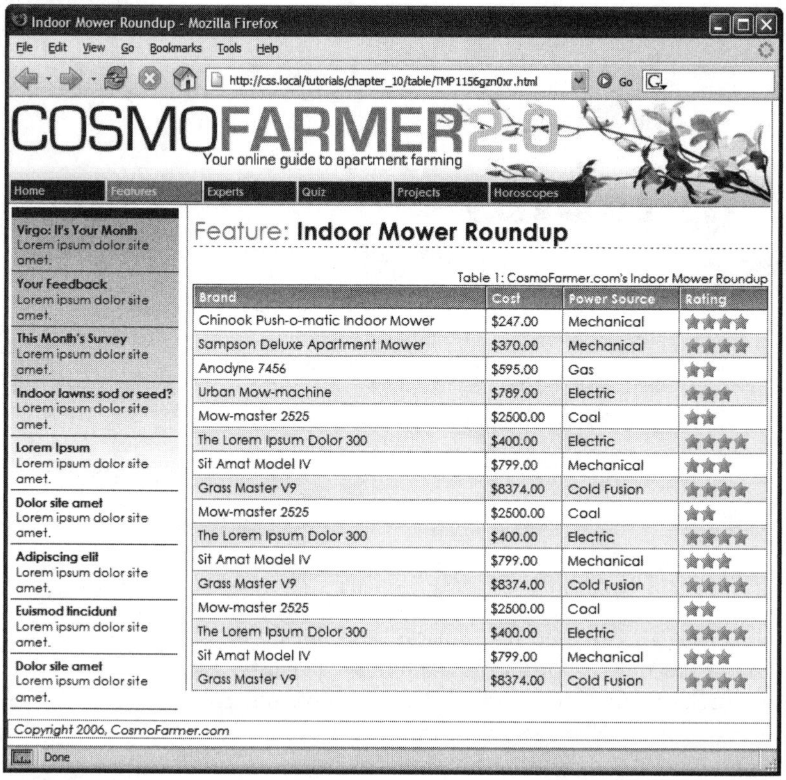

Figure 10-1:
You can do all of your page layout and design with CSS, and use tables for what they were intended—displaying rows and columns of information. CSS created the attractive fonts, borders, and background colors in this table about indoor lawn mowers, but the underlying structure is all thanks to HTML.

HTML (and XHTML) has a surprising number of tags dedicated to table building. This chunk of HTML creates the very simple table pictured in Figure 10-2.

```
<table>
<caption align="bottom">
Table 1: CosmoFarmer.com's Indoor Mower Roundup
</caption>
<colgroup>
<col id="brand" />
<col id="price" />
<col id="power" />
</colgroup>
<thead>
<tr>
    <th scope="col">Brand</th>
    <th scope="col">Price</th>
    <th scope="col">Power Source</th>
</tr>
</thead>
<tbody>
```

```
    <tr>
        <td>Chinook Push-o-matic Indoor Mower</td>
        <td>$247.00</td>
        <td>Mechanical</td>
    </tr>
    <tr>
        <td>Sampson Deluxe Apartment Mower</td>
        <td>$370.00</td>
        <td>Mechanical</td>
    </tr>
    </tbody>
    </table>
```

Even with only three rows and three columns, the table uses nine unique HTML tags: <table>, <caption>, <colgroup>, <col>, <thead>, <tbody> <tr>, <th>, and <td>. In general, more HTML isn't a good thing, but a table's various tags give you lots of useful hooks to hang CSS styles on. The headers of each column—the <th> tags—can look different from other table cells if you create a <th> tag style. This saves you the hassle of having to create lots of classes—*like .tableHeader*—and applying them by hand to individual table cells. In the next section, you'll see examples of how you can use these different tags to your advantage. 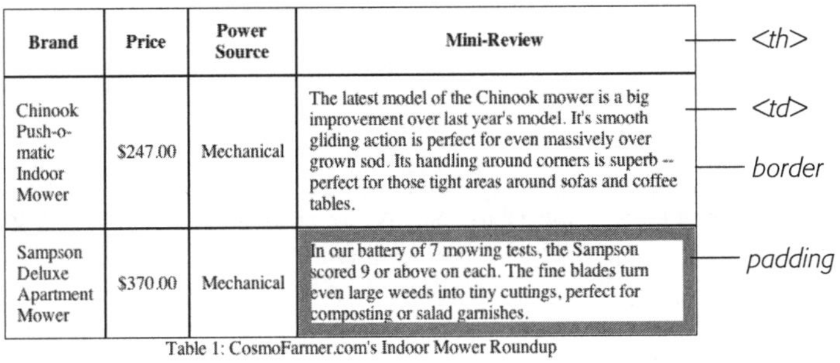

Brand	Price	Power Source	Mini-Review
Chinook Push-o-matic Indoor Mower	$247.00	Mechanical	The latest model of the Chinook mower is a big improvement over last year's model. It's smooth gliding action is perfect for even massively over grown sod. Its handling around corners is superb -- perfect for those tight areas around sofas and coffee tables.
Sampson Deluxe Apartment Mower	$370.00	Mechanical	In our battery of 7 mowing tests, the Sampson scored 9 or above on each. The fine blades turn even large weeds into tiny cuttings, perfect for composting or salad garnishes.

Table 1: CosmoFarmer.com's Indoor Mower Roundup

Figure 10-2:
Data tables, like this one, usually have headers created with the <th> tag. Header cells announce what type of information appears in a row or column. Price tells you that you'll find the cost of each lawn mower listed in the cells below. The actual data presented in a table is enclosed in <td> tags.

Note: For an in-depth article on the HTML used to create tables, visit *www.456bereastreet.com/archive/200410/bring_on_the_tables/*.

Styling Tables

You can use many of the CSS properties you've read about to dress up the appearance of a table and its contents. The *color* property, for example, sets a table's text color, just like anywhere else. You'll find a few properties, however, that are particularly useful with tables, as well as a couple aimed specifically at formatting tables.

Because tables are composed of several HTML tags, it helps to know which tag to apply a particular CSS property to. Applying padding to a <table> tag has no effect. The next few sections cover CSS properties for formatting tables and which HTML tags they get along with.

Adding Padding

As you read on page 135, padding is the space between an element's border and its content. You can use padding to provide a little space between the edges of a paragraph's text and its border. When it comes to tables, the borders are the *edges* of a cell, so padding adds space around any content you've placed inside of a table cell (see Figure 10-2). It works a lot like the <table> tag's *cellpadding* attribute, with the added benefit that you can individually control space between a cell's content and each of its four edges.

You apply padding to either a table header or a table cell tag, but *not* to the <table> tag itself. So, to add 10 pixels of space to the inside of all table cells, you'd use this style:

```
td, th { padding: 10px; }
```

You can also control the spacing separately for each edge. To add 10 pixels of space to the top of each table data cell, 3 pixels to the bottom of that cell, and 5 pixels on both the left and right sides, create this style:

```
td {
    padding-top: 10px;
    padding-right: 5px;
    padding-bottom: 3px;
    padding-left: 5px;
}
```

Tip: If you place an image into a table cell using the <img> tag, and notice that there's unwanted space below the image, then set its display property to *block* (see page 140). For more information, see *http:// developer.mozilla.org/en/docs/Images,_Tables,_and_Mysterious_Gaps.*

Adjusting Vertical and Horizontal Alignment

To control where content is positioned *within* a table cell, use the *text-align* and *vertical-align* properties. Text-align controls horizontal positioning, and can be set to *left*, *right*, *center*, and *justify* (see Figure 10-3). It's an inherited property. (See Chapter 4 for more on inheritance.) When you want to right align the contents of all table cells, create a style like this:

```
table { text-align: right; }
```

This property comes in handy with <th> tags, since browsers usually center align them. A simple style like *th { text-align: left; }* makes table headers align with table cells.

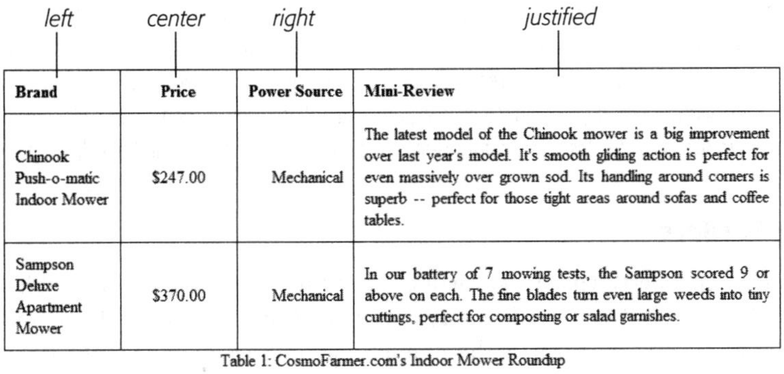

Figure 10-3:
When applied to table cells, the CSS text-align property works like the <td> tag's align attribute. Use the CSS approach, however, since it lets you store the style information in an external style sheet. That way, if you decide you need to change alignment in your table cells from right to left, then you need to update only the external style sheet, not 10,000 individual <td> tags.

Table cells have a height as well. Web browsers normally align content vertically in the middle of a table cell (see "middle" example in Figure 10-4). You can control this behavior using the vertical-align property. Use one of these four values: *top, baseline, middle,* or *bottom. Top* pushes content to the top of the cell, *middle* centers content, and *bottom* pushes the bottom of the content to the bottom of the cell. *Baseline* works just like *top,* except the browser aligns the baseline of the first line of text in each cell in a row (Figure 10-4). (Unless you're a real perfectionist, you won't even notice the subtlety of the baseline option. More importantly, neither will your visitors.) Unlike text-align, the vertical-align property isn't inherited, so you can use it only on styles that apply directly to <th> and <td> tags.

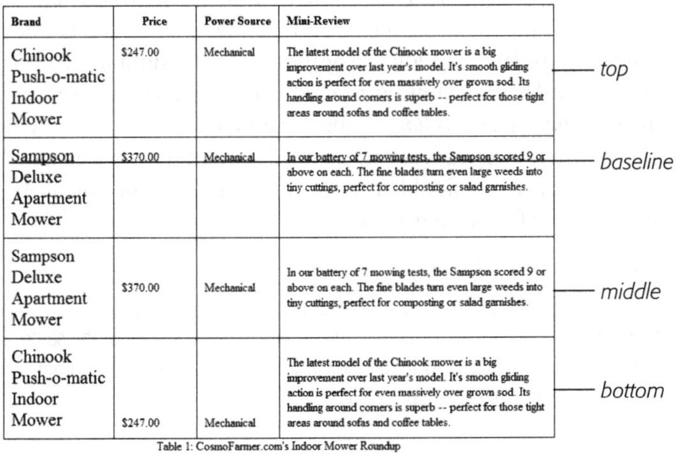

Figure 10-4:
The vertical-align property is the CSS equivalent of the <td> tag's align attribute. When padding is applied to a cell, the content never actually aligns to the bottom or top border lines: There's always a gap equal to the padding setting. You can control the size of the padding (see page 254).

Tip: So far, the table formatting you've learned applies to *all* your tables. When you want to style individual tables (or table cells), change the selector you use. To apply a special design to a certain table, give it a class name—*<table class="stocks">*—and create descendent selectors like *.stocks td*, or *.stocks th* to uniquely format individual cells. If you want to style a particular cell differently than other cells in a table, then apply a class to the tag—*<td class="subtotal">*—and create a class style to format that cell.

Creating Borders

The CSS *border* property (page 141) works pretty much the same with tables as with other elements, but you need to keep a couple of things in mind. First, applying a border to a style that formats the <table> tag outlines just the table, not any of the individual cells. Second, applying borders to cells (*td { border: 1px solid black; }*) leaves you with a visual gap between cells, as shown in Figure 10-5, top. To gain control of how borders appear, you need to understand the <table> tag's *cellspacing* attribute and the CSS *border-collapse* property.

- **Controlling the space between table cells.** Unless instructed otherwise, browsers separate table cells by a couple of pixels. This gap's really noticeable when you apply a border to table cells. CSS 2.1 gives you the *border-spacing* property to control this space, but since Internet Explorer (including IE 7) doesn't support border-spacing, you're better off using the <table> tag's cellspacing attribute. Here's the HTML to insert 10 pixels of space between each cell: *<table cellspacing="10px">*. (Setting the value to 0 eliminates the space entirely, but if you want to do that, then use the CSS border-collapse property, discussed next.)

- **Eliminating double borders.** Even if you eliminate the cell spacing of a table, borders applied to table cells double up. That is, the bottom border of one cell adds to the top border of the underhanging cell, creating a line that's twice as thick as the border setting (Figure 10-5, middle). The best way to eliminate this (and eliminate cell-spacing at the same time) is to use the border-collapse property. It accepts two values—*separate* and *collapse*. The separate option is normally how tables are displayed, with the cell spaces and doubled borders. Collapsing a table's borders eliminates the gaps and doubled borders (Figure 10-5, bottom). Apply the collapse value to a style formatting a table, like so:

```
table { border-collapse: collapse; }
```

Note: HTML tags that are used to build tables include attributes that accomplish a lot of the same tasks as CSS. The *border* attribute can add a border to the table and each cell. In general, you should avoid these attributes: CSS can do a much better job with less code.

Styling Rows and Columns

Adding stripes, like the ones in Figure 10-6, is a common table design technique. By alternating the appearance of every other row of data, you make it easier for people to spot the data in each row. Unfortunately, CSS (at least at this point) doesn't offer a way to say, "Hey browser, make *every other row* look this way!" The

Figure 10-5:
Browsers normally insert space between each table cell. (You probably won't notice this extra space unless you've added a border, as shown here, at top.) If you use the <table> tag's cellspacing attribute to remove the extra space, you're left with double border lines where adjoining borders touch (middle). The border-collapse property solves both dilemmas (bottom).

Brand	Price	Power Source	Mini-Review
Chinook Push-o-matic Indoor Mower	$247.00	Mechanical	The latest model of the Chinook mower is a big improvement over last year's model. It's smooth gliding action is perfect for even massively over grown sod. Its handling around corners is superb -- perfect for those tight areas around sofas and coffee tables.
Sampson Deluxe Apartment Mower	$370.00	Mechanical	In our battery of 7 mowing tests, the Sampson scored 9 or above on each. The fine blades turn even large weeds into tiny cuttings, perfect for composting or salad garnishes.

Table 1: CosmoFarmer.com's Indoor Mower Roundup

Brand	Price	Power Source	Mini-Review
Chinook Push-o-matic Indoor Mower	$247.00	Mechanical	The latest model of the Chinook mower is a big improvement over last year's model. It's smooth gliding action is perfect for even massively over grown sod. Its handling around corners is superb -- perfect for those tight areas around sofas and coffee tables.
Sampson Deluxe Apartment Mower	$370.00	Mechanical	In our battery of 7 mowing tests, the Sampson scored 9 or above on each. The fine blades turn even large weeds into tiny cuttings, perfect for composting or salad garnishes.

Table 1: CosmoFarmer.com's Indoor Mower Roundup

Brand	Price	Power Source	Mini-Review
Chinook Push-o-matic Indoor Mower	$247.00	Mechanical	The latest model of the Chinook mower is a big improvement over last year's model. It's smooth gliding action is perfect for even massively over grown sod. Its handling around corners is superb -- perfect for those tight areas around sofas and coffee tables.
Sampson Deluxe Apartment Mower	$370.00	Mechanical	In our battery of 7 mowing tests, the Sampson scored 9 or above on each. The fine blades turn even large weeds into tiny cuttings, perfect for composting or salad garnishes.

Table 1: CosmoFarmer.com's Indoor Mower Roundup

basic solution's to apply a class (like *<tr class="odd">*) to every other row, and then create a style to format that row:

```
tr.odd { background-color: red; }
```

You're not limited to colors either. You can use background images (see page 172) to create more sophisticated looks like the slight gradation in the table header row of Figure 10-6. (You'll see a similar example of this in the tutorial on page 267.) You can use a descendent selector to target cells in that row as well. This technique's great for when you style all of the cells in one column with their own class and look: *<td class="price">*, for example. To create a unique look for that cell when it appears in an odd row, create a style with this selector: *tr.odd td.price*.

Tip: For a quicker, JavaScript-driven approach to striping tables, check out *www.alistapart.com/articles/zebratables/*.

Formatting columns is a bit trickier. HTML provides the <colgroup> and <col> tags to indicate groups of columns and individual columns, respectively. You include one <col> tag for each column in the table and can identify them with either a class or ID. (See the HTML code on page 252.) Only two sets of properties

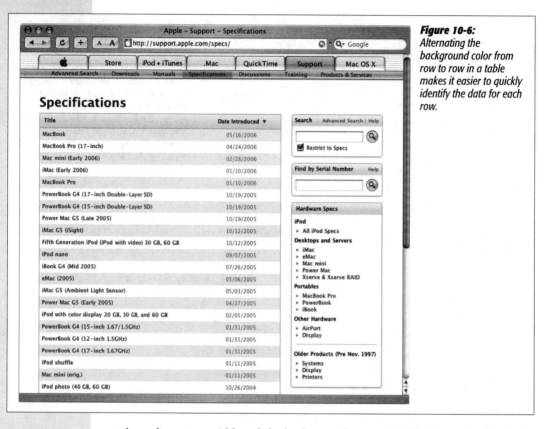

Figure 10-6:
Alternating the background color from row to row in a table makes it easier to quickly identify the data for each row.

work on these tags: *width* and the background properties (*background-color, background-image,* and so on). But they can come in mighty handy. When you want to set the width of all of the rows in a column, you can skip any HTML attributes and just style the columns using the <col> tag:

```
col#price { width: 200px; }
```

Of course, don't forget to add a class or ID to the <col> tag, like *#price* in this example.

Likewise, the <colgroup> tag groups several columns together. When you set a width for that tag, a Web browser automatically applies the specified width to *each* column in the group. A table displaying airline schedules might have several columns displaying the different dates a plane travels from Boston to Chicago. You can use <colgroup> to organize those columns and apply an ID to the tag to identify it: *<colgroup id="dates">*. Then, to set each date column to a set width of 10ems, you can create this style:

```
colgroup#dates{ width: 10em; }
```

Even though the *width* property here applies to the <colgroup> tag, a browser actually applies the value—*10em*—to *each* column in the group.

To highlight a column, you can use the background properties:

```
col#price { background-color: #F33; }
```

Keep in mind, however, that backgrounds for columns appear under table cells, so if you set a background color or image for <td> or <th> tags, then a column's background won't be visible.

Styling Forms

Web forms are the primary way visitors interact with a Web site. By supplying information on a form, you can join a mailing list, search a database of products, update your personal profile on MySpace, or order that Star Wars collector's plate you've had your eye on.

There's no reason your forms need to look like all the others on the Internet. With a little CSS, you can style form fields to share the same formatting as other site elements like fonts, background colors, and margins. There aren't any CSS properties specific to forms, but you can apply just about any property in this book to a form element.

The results, however, can be mixed (see Figure 10-7). Browser support for styling form elements varies greatly. Safari 2 and earlier limits styling to only a few form elements like text fields and the <fieldset> and <legend> tags. It won't let you change the look of buttons, checkboxes, radio buttons, or pull-down menus. Even Internet Explorer and Firefox may display the same form elements differently. The next section tells you which properties work best with which form tags, and also lists which browsers interpret them properly.

UP TO SPEED

Staying True to Form

Even without the varying browser support for CSS-styled forms (page 261), there are good reasons to tread lightly when altering the look of universally recognized interface elements like Submit buttons and pull-down menus. Most Web surfers are already very familiar with how forms look and work. The generic look of a Submit button's the same from site to site. When people see it, they instantly know what that button does and how to use it. If you alter the look of a form *too* much, you may make it harder for visitors to fill out your form correctly.

Adding a dotted border to a form field can turn an easily recognizable text field into an easily skipped box. (See the examples at bottom right and bottom center of Figure 10-7.) If that text box is intended to capture email addresses for your newsletter, you may lose a few visitors who skip right over it. At the very least, make sure people can recognize the forms on your sites as forms.

HTML Form Elements

A variety of HTML tags help you build forms. You can format some of them (like text fields) more successfully than others (submit buttons.) Here are a few common form tags and the types of properties they get along with:

- **Fieldset.** The <fieldset> tag groups related form questions. Most browsers do a good job of displaying background colors, background images, and borders for this tag. However, Internet Explorer lets the background flow up and over the top line of the fieldset. (Look at the top of the middle image in Figure 10-7, left column.) Padding places space from the edges of the fieldset to the content inside it. (Although Internet Explorer unfortunately ignores top padding, you can simulate it by adding a top *margin* to the first element inside the fieldset.)

Tip: Matt Heerema has found a way to prevent Internet Explorer from adding a background above a fieldset's top borderline. Read about it at *www.mattheerema.com/archive/getting-fieldset-backgrounds-and-legends-to-behave-in-ie.*

- **Legend.** The <legend> tag follows the HTML for the <fieldset> tag and provides a label for the group of fields. The legend appears vertically centered on the top borderline of a fieldset. If the form elements for collecting a shipping address appear inside the fieldset, you might add a legend like this: *<legend> Shipping Address</legend>*. You can use CSS to change the <legend> tag's font properties, add background colors and images, and add your own borders.

- **Text fields.** The <input type="text"> (<input type="text" /> in XHTML), <input type="password"> (<input type="password" />) and the <textarea> tags create text boxes on a form. These tags give you the most consistent cross-browser CSS control. You can change the font size, font family, color, and other text properties for text boxes, as well as add borders and background colors. IE, Firefox, and Opera also let you add background images to text boxes; Safari 2.0 doesn't. You can set the width of these fields using the CSS *width* property. However, only the <textarea> tag obeys the *height* property.

- **Buttons.** Form buttons—like <input type="submit"> (<input type="submit" />)— let your visitors submit a form, reset its contents, or set off some other action to occur. While Safari 2.0 and earlier doesn't recognize formatting of these elements, other browsers let you go wild with text formatting, borders, and backgrounds. You can also align the button's text to left, middle, or right using the text-align property (page 114).

- **Drop-down menus.** Drop-down menus created by the <select> tag also give you a fair amount of styling control. Safari 2.0 limits you to font family, color, and size, while most other browsers also let you set background color, image, and borders.

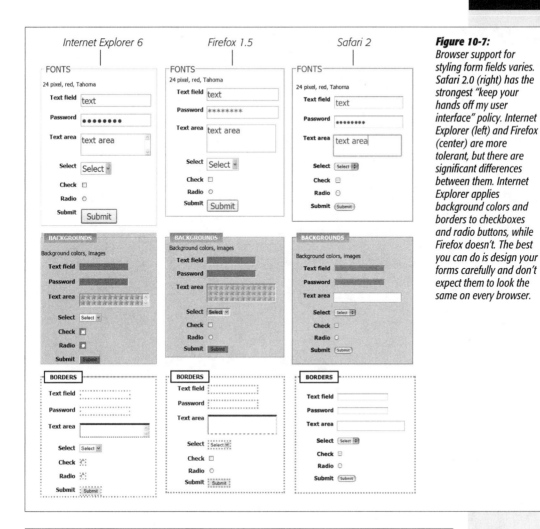

Figure 10-7:
Browser support for styling form fields varies. Safari 2.0 (right) has the strongest "keep your hands off my user interface" policy. Internet Explorer (left) and Firefox (center) are more tolerant, but there are significant differences between them. Internet Explorer applies background colors and borders to checkboxes and radio buttons, while Firefox doesn't. The best you can do is design your forms carefully and don't expect them to look the same on every browser.

Note: For more on the wide variety of browser results you get when applying CSS to form elements, visit *www.456bereastreet.com/archive/200409/styling_form_controls/* and *www.456bereastreet.com/archive/200410/styling_even_more_form_controls/*.

- **Checkboxes and radio buttons.** Most browsers don't allow formatting of these elements. Opera, however, lets you set a background color that appears *inside* the box or button. Internet Explorer adds a background color *around* the box or button. Because browsers vary widely in how they treat these elements, it's best to leave them alone.

Attribute: The Selector of the Future

When it comes to styling forms, tag styles just don't cut the mustard. After all, text boxes, radio buttons, checkboxes, password fields, and buttons all share the same HTML tag—<input>. While a width of 200 pixels makes sense for a text box, you probably don't want your checkboxes to be that big, so you can't use the <input> tag to format width. For now, the most reliable way of formatting just text fields would be to add a class name to each text field—like <input type="text" class="textfield" name="email" />—and then use the class style to style it.

Before long, you'll have a more advanced CSS selector—the *attribute selector*. An attribute selector targets an HTML tag based on one of the tag's attributes. The *type* attribute is responsible for determining what kind of form element the <input> tag produces. The type value for a form text field is *text*. To create a style that makes the background color of all single-line text fields blue, you'd create this selector and style:

```
input[type="text"] { background-color:
blue; }
```

Changing *text* in the above example to *submit* creates a style for submit buttons only, and so on.

Since Internet Explorer 7, Firefox, Safari, and Opera already understand attribute selectors, it won't be long before you can start using them full force. They're not just for form elements either. You can use an attribute selector to style *any* tag with a particular attribute. Here's the selector for styling links that point to *http://www.cosmofarmer.com/*: a[href="http://www.cosmofarmer.com"].

CSS 3 promises even more elaborate attribute selectors, including the ability to select attributes that *start* with a particular value (like *http://*) or which *end* with a particular value (like *.jpg* or *.pdf*).

Laying Out Forms Using CSS

All it takes to create a form is adding a bunch of labels and other form elements to a Web page. Visually, though, you may end up with a chaotic mess (see Figure 10-8, left). Forms usually look best when the questions and form fields are organized into columns (Figure 10-8, right).

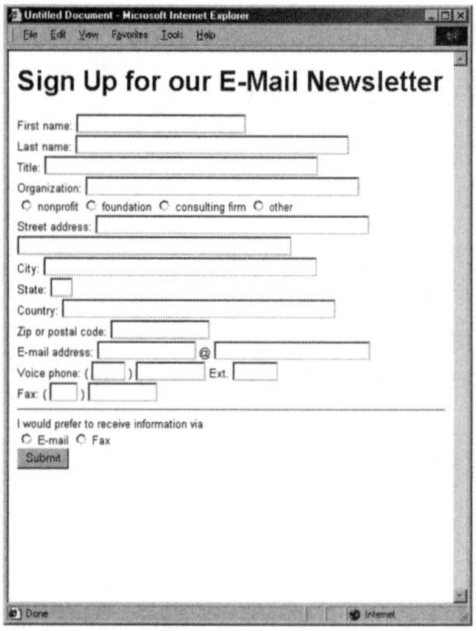

Figure 10-8:
The different shapes and sizes of text boxes, radio buttons, and other form objects don't naturally align well with text, often causing an ungainly zigzag pattern. This form isn't just ugly, it's hard to read (left). The solution's to organize your forms into columns (right), using either an HTML table or CSS styles.

You can achieve this effect in a couple of ways. The easiest approach is with an HTML table. Although form labels and fields aren't strictly table data, they lend themselves beautifully to a row/column format. Just put your labels ("First Name," "Phone Number," and so on) in one column, and form fields in a second column.

Using CSS, you can also create a two-column form like Figure 10-8 (with the added benefit of less HTML code.) Here's the basic approach:

1. **Wrap each label in a tag.**

   The obvious choice for a tag is <label>, since it's designed to identify form labels. But you can't *always* use <label> tags for all labels. Radio buttons usually have a question like "What's your favorite color?" followed by separate <label> tags for each button. So what tag do you use for the question? In this case, you must resort to wrapping the question in a <span> tag: *<span>What's your favorite color?</span>*. Then add a class to each of these tags: *<span class="label">*.

Note: Visit *www.htmldog.com/guides/htmladvanced/forms/* for a quick overview on the <label> tag.

---

2. **Float and set a width for the labels.**

   The secret to this technique lies in creating a style that floats the labels to the left and sets a width for them. The *width* value should provide enough space to accommodate the entire label on one line if possible. You can create a class style that looks something like this:

   ```
   .label {
       float: left;
       width: 20em;
   }
   ```

   The *width* and *float* turn the labels into little evenly-sized blocks and let the content that follows—the form field—wrap on the right side of the label.

3. **Adjust the style.**

   Just a couple more enhancements complete the job. You want to align the label text to the right, so each label appears next to each form field. Also, adding a *clear: left* property clears the floats (page 152), so that the labels fall one below the other instead of wrapping continuously. Finally, by adding a little bit of right margin, you can create a nice gutter of white space between the labels and form fields.

   ```
   .label {
       float: left;
       width: 20em;
       text-align: right;
       clear: left;
       margin-right: 15px;
   }
   ```

At this point, you've got yourself a simple, neat form. You can make other enhancements if you wish, like making the labels bold and a different color. The tutorial that starts on page 268 provides a step-by-step example of this technique.

Note: For a sophisticated demonstration of an all-CSS form layout, visit *http://jeffhowden.com/code/css/forms/*.

Tutorial: Styling a Table

HTML is great for building tables, but you need CSS to give them style. As you can see on page 252, it takes quite a bit of HTML to construct a simple table. Lucky for you, this book comes with a prebuilt HTML table for you to practice your CSS on. In this tutorial, you'll format the table's rows, columns, and cells, and give it an attractive font and background color.

To get started, download the tutorial files located on this book's companion Web site at *www.sawmac.com/css/*. Click the tutorial link and download the files. All the files are enclosed in a ZIP archive, so you need to unzip them first. (Go to the Web site for detailed instructions.) The files for this tutorial are in the *chapter_10 → table* folder.

1. **Launch a Web browser and open the file *chapter_10 → table → table.html.***

   This CosmoFarmer.com page contains a simple HTML table that rates this season's indoor lawn mowers. The table has a caption, a row of table headers, and eight rows of data contained in table cells (Figure 10-9).

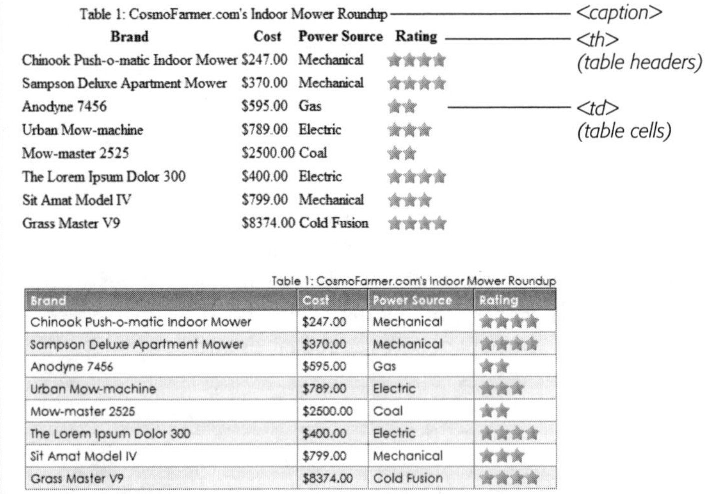

Table 1: CosmoFarmer.com's Indoor Mower Roundup

Brand	Cost	Power Source	Rating
Chinook Push-o-matic Indoor Mower	$247.00	Mechanical	★★★★
Sampson Deluxe Apartment Mower	$370.00	Mechanical	★★★★
Anodyne 7456	$595.00	Gas	★★
Urban Mow-machine	$789.00	Electric	★★★
Mow-master 2525	$2500.00	Coal	★★
The Lorem Ipsum Dolor 300	$400.00	Electric	★★★★
Sit Amat Model IV	$799.00	Mechanical	★★★
Grass Master V9	$8374.00	Cold Fusion	★★★★

Table 1: CosmoFarmer.com's Indoor Mower Roundup

Brand	Cost	Power Source	Rating
Chinook Push-o-matic Indoor Mower	$247.00	Mechanical	★★★★
Sampson Deluxe Apartment Mower	$370.00	Mechanical	★★★★
Anodyne 7456	$595.00	Gas	★★
Urban Mow-machine	$789.00	Electric	★★★
Mow-master 2525	$2500.00	Coal	★★
The Lorem Ipsum Dolor 300	$400.00	Electric	★★★★
Sit Amat Model IV	$799.00	Mechanical	★★★
Grass Master V9	$8374.00	Cold Fusion	★★★★

***Figure 10-9:** Formatting a table with borders, background colors, and other CSS properties not only makes a drab HTML table (top) look great, but also makes the table's data easier to read (bottom).*

2. **Open *table.html* in a text editor.**

   You'll start by creating a style that sets the table's width and text font.

Note: There are already a couple of external style sheets attached to this page, but you'll add your new styles to an internal style sheet.

---

3. **Click between the opening and closing <style> tags, and then add the following style:**

```
table {
    width: 100%;
    font-family: "Century Gothic", "Gill Sans", Arial, sans-serif;
}
```

   Unless you set the width of a table, it grows and shrinks to fit the size of the content inside it. In this case, you've set a 100 percent width, so the table stretches to fit the entire width of its containing <div>. (In this case, it's the area of the page containing the headline "Feature: Indoor Mower Roundup" and the table itself.) Setting the font family in the <table> uses inheritance to give all of the tags inside the table the same font—<caption>, table headers (<th>), table cells (<td>), and so on.

   Next you'll style the table's caption.

4. **Add another style below the table style you just created:**

```
caption {
    text-align: right;
    font-size: .75em;
}
```

   A <caption> tag indicates what a table is about. In this case, it shouldn't be the focus of attention, so you've shrunk the text and moved it to the right edge, out of the way.

   When you read information across a table row, it's easy to lose track of which row you're looking at. Good visual guides are essential. Adding borders around the cells, which you'll do next, visually delineates the information.

5. **Add the following group style to the internal style sheet:**

```
td,th {
    font-size: .8em;
    border: 1px solid #73afb7;
}
```

   This group selector formats the table header (<th>) and table cell (<td>) tags with smaller type and draws a border around each header and each cell. Browsers normally insert space between each cell, so at this point there are

---

small gaps between the borders (Figure 10-10, circled). Between the gaps and the borders, the whole table looks too boxy. You'll fix that next.

6. **Add the border-collapse property to the table style you created in step 3 so that it looks like this:**

```
table {
    width: 100%;
    font-family: "Century Gothic", "Gill Sans", Arial, sans-serif;
    border-collapse: collapse;
}
```

The border-collapse property removes the spacing between cells. It also merges borders that touch, which prevents thick, unattractive borders. Without border-collapse, the bottom border of a table header and the top border of the table cell would double up to make a 2-pixel border.

If you preview the table now, you'll see the data's better organized visually, but the information in each cell looks a little cramped. Add some padding to fix that.

7. **Add padding to the group selector you created in step 5:**

```
td,th {
    border: 1px solid #73afb7;
    padding: 3px 5px 2px 5px;
    font-size: .8em;
}
```

While the top, table-header row stands out because of its boldface text, there are a few things you can do to make it stand out even more and approve its appearance.

8. **Create a new style below the *td, th* style for formatting just table head cells:**

```
th {
    text-align: left;
    border-color: #14556b;
}
```

This style's a perfect example of effective cascading. The group selector *td, th* defines common formatting properties between the two types of cells. By introducing this *th*-only style, you can further tweak the look of *just* the table headers. Notice that the basic border properties, such as line style and thickness, come from the group selector, but the *th* style overrides the border color. That's why you must put this style *after* the *td,th* style in your code. Otherwise, this new border color has no effect.

The table headers still don't have enough oomph, and the table seems to recede into the background of the page. A background graphic can provide the necessary boost.

Table 1: CosmoFarmer.com's Indoor Mower Roundup

Brand	Cost	Power Source	Rating
Chinook Push-o-matic Indoor Mower	$247.00	Mechanical	★★★
Sampson Deluxe Apartment Mower	$370.00	Mechanical	★★★
Anodyne 7456	$595.00	Gas	★★
Urban Mow-machine	$789.00	Electric	★★★
Mow-master 2525	$2500.00	Coal	★★
The Lorem Ipsum Dolor 300	$400.00	Electric	★★★
Sit Amat Model IV	$799.00	Mechanical	★★★
Grass Master V9	$8374.00	Cold Fusion	★★★

Figure 10-10:
A browser's normal display of a table inserts space between each cell (top). It also lets borders double up where cells touch. Setting the border-collapse property to collapse solves both problems (bottom).

Table 1: CosmoFarmer.com's Indoor Mower Roundup

Brand	Cost	Power Source	Rating
Chinook Push-o-matic Indoor Mower	$247.00	Mechanical	★★★
Sampson Deluxe Apartment Mower	$370.00	Mechanical	★★★
Anodyne 7456	$595.00	Gas	★★
Urban Mow-machine	$789.00	Electric	★★
Mow-master 2525	$2500.00	Coal	★★
The Lorem Ipsum Dolor 300	$400.00	Electric	★★★
Sit Amat Model IV	$799.00	Mechanical	★★★
Grass Master V9	$8374.00	Cold Fusion	★★★

9. Edit the *th* style by adding a background image, and changing the text color:

```
th {
    background: url(images/th_bg.png) no-repeat left top;
    color: white;
    text-align: left;
    border-color: #14556b;
}
```

In this case, the graphic introduces a subtle top-down gradient while a white borderline at the top and left edges of the image contrasts nicely with the darker top and left borders around the cells, giving the cells a 3-D look.

Tip: By the way, you could just as easily set the background color of these cells to achieve a similar effect.

When tables have lots of data stuffed into many rows and columns, it's sometimes hard to quickly identify which data belongs to each row. One solution designers use is to alternate the color of every other row in a table. You create this effect with a class style that you apply to every other table row.

10. Add one last style to the Web page's internal style sheet:

```
tr.alt td {
    background: url(images/td_bg.png) no-repeat left top;
}
```

This selector places a background image into every table cell (<td> tag), but only when that <td> tag is nested inside a table row (<tr> tag) with a class of *alt* applied to it. So, next you have to apply the class to every other row for this style to have any effect.

11. **In the page's HTML, look for the <tr> tag that precedes the <td> containing "Sampson Deluxe Apartment Mower." Add** *class="alt"* **to that <tr> tag, like so:**

    ```
    <tr class="alt">
    <td>Sampson Deluxe Apartment Mower</td>
    ```

    You'll need to do this with every second row after this one as well. (Manually tagging each alternating row can be tedious, especially if you frequently add or reorder table rows. For an automated approach to striping table rows using a little JavaScript programming, see the Tip on page 257.)

12. **Repeat step 11 for the <tr> tags that precede table cells with the following text:** *Urban Mow-machine, The Lorem Ipsum Dolor 300,* **and** *Grass Master V9.*

Preview the page in a Web browser to see the results. Your page should look like the bottom image in Figure 10-9. You'll also find the completed exercise in the *chapter_10_finished → table* folder.

Tutorial: Styling a Form

This tutorial gives you some practice using CSS to organize a form and make it more attractive. If you open *chapter_10 → form → form.html* in a Web browser, then you'll see it contains a simple form for subscribing to CosmoFarmer.com (Figure 10-11). The form asks several questions and uses a variety of form elements for input, including text boxes, radio buttons, and pull-down menus.

As subscription forms go, it looks fine, but a little bland. In the steps on the following pages, you'll CosmoFarmer-ize the fonts, line up the questions and boxes better, and add a few other improvements.

1. **Open the file** *form.html* **in a text editor.**

   There's already an external style sheet attached to this page, but you'll add your new styles to an internal style sheet. Start by bringing down the size of the type in the form.

2. **Click between the opening and closing <style> tags, and then add the following style:**

   ```
   #subForm {
       font-size: .8em;
   }
   ```

   The subscription form has an ID of *subForm* applied to it, so this style sets the text size for all text between the <form> tags.

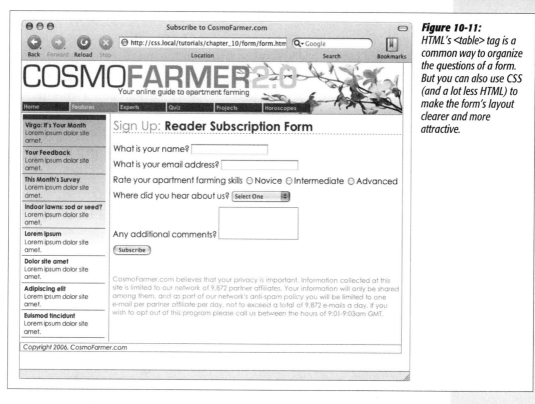

Figure 10-11:
HTML's <table> tag is a common way to organize the questions of a form. But you can also use CSS (and a lot less HTML) to make the form's layout clearer and more attractive.

Time to work on the layout. To better align the form elements, you'll create the appearance of two columns, one for the questions (labels) and another for the answers (form fields).

3. **Add another style to the internal style sheet:**

```
#subForm .label {
    float: left;
    width: 230px;
}
```

This descendent selector identifies any element with a class of *.label* within this form. The style sets a width of 230 pixels and floats the element to the left. Remember the *float* property lets you move elements to one side or the other of a containing block. It has the added benefit of letting you set a width and force elements that follow the style to wrap around it. As a result, when you apply this style to each of the questions in the form, you create an even-width column. But in order to see the effect, you must first apply the class to the appropriate page elements.

4. **In the page's HTML, locate this code** *<label for="name">* **and add** *class="label",* **so the tag looks like this:**

```
<label for="name" class="label">
```

You must do the same for each question in the form, so…

5. **Repeat step 5 for the following pieces of HTML code:** *<label for="email">*, *<label for="refer">*, *<label for="comments">*.

There's one additional question on the form—"Rate your apartment farming skills." It isn't inside a label tag, since its purpose is to introduce a series of radio buttons, each of which has its own label. You need to add a <span> tag to this text so you can apply the *label* style to it.

6. **Find the text** *Rate your apartment farming skills,* **and then wrap it in a** *<span>* **tag with a class of** *label,* **like so:**

   ```
   <span class="label">Rate your apartment farming skills</span>
   ```

   Now the questions appear to be in a single column (Figure 10-12, top). But they'd look better if they stood out more and lined up with the corresponding form fields.

7. **Edit the** *#subForm .label* **style you created in step 4, so it looks like this:**

   ```
   #subForm .label {
       float: left;
       width: 230px;
       margin-right: 10px;
       text-align: right;
       font-weight: bold;
   }
   ```

   Preview the page in a Web browser. The form should look like the bottom image in Figure 10-12.

   There's one last step for these labels. Because they're floated to the left, if the text runs more than one line, the question that follows will also try to wrap around to the right. Fix that by applying the *clear* property.

Note: You can see a similar problem illustrated in Figure 7-12. See "Stopping the Float" on page 155 for more detail on clearing floats.

---

8. **Add a** *clear* **property to the** *#subForm .label* **style:**

   ```
   #subForm .label {
       float: left;
       width: 230px;
       margin-right: 10px;
       text-align: right;
       font-weight: bold;
       clear: left;
   }
   ```

The form's shaping up, but that Subscribe button looks out of place over at the left edge. You'll align it with the other form elements next.

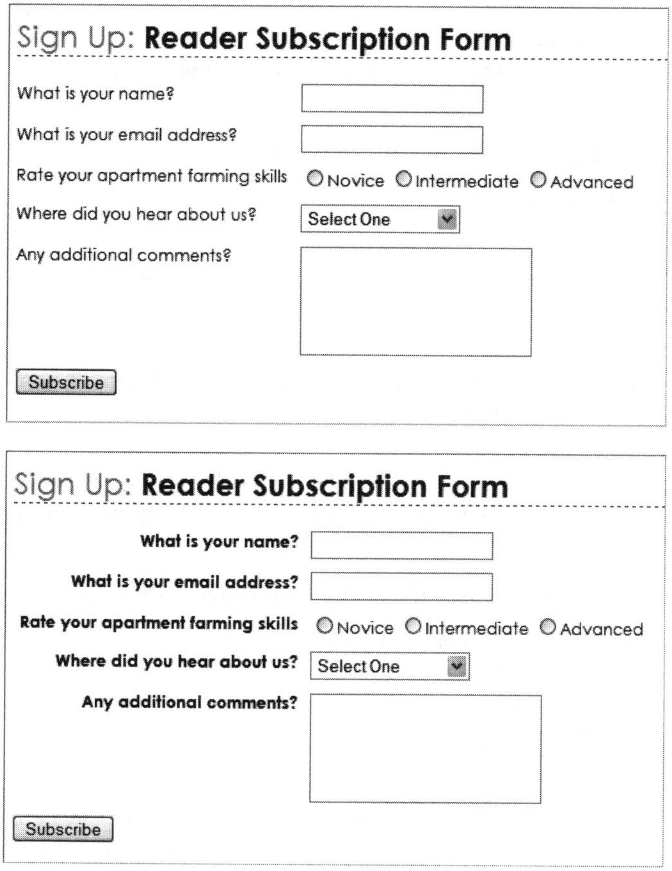

Figure 10-12:
Sometimes small and subtle changes can make a form more readable. Making the questions on the form bold, and aligning them with their corresponding form elements (bottom figure) immediately improves the look of the form.

9. **Add another style to the internal style sheet.**

```
input#subscribe {
    margin-left: 240px;
}
```

The <input> tag that creates this Subscribe button has an ID of *subscribe* already applied to it, so this style indents the button 240 pixels to match the width and right margin of the *#subForm .label* style.

Most browsers let you style buttons in other ways, too, so…

10. Edit the Subscribe button style by adding a background color and font to the style you just created:

```
input#subscribe {
    margin-left: 240px;
    background-color: #CBD893;
    font-family: "Century Gothic", "Gill Sans", Arial, sans-serif;
}
```

You can even change the font used in a pull-down menu.

11. Add a style for the form's select menu:

```
select#refer {
    font-family: "Century Gothic", "Gill Sans", Arial, sans-serif;
}
```

Note: You can style submit buttons and pull-down menus in Internet Explorer, Firefox, and Opera. Safari 2.0, as of this writing, doesn't let you change these basic form elements.

There! You've got the text labels and Subscribe button looking great, but why stop there? Time to jazz up the form fields. Begin by changing their font and background colors.

12. Create a new group selector for styling the three text boxes in the form:

```
input#name, input#email, textarea#comments {
    background-color: #FBEF99;
    font-family: "Lucida Console", Monaco, monospace;
    font-size: .9em;
}
```

This style gives the text boxes a light yellow background color and sets a new size and font for text visitors to type into them. The boxes look a little narrow, and they also appear a little low compared to their labels at right. Fixing these two problems with CSS is a snap:

13. Edit the style you just created by setting a width, and altering the top margin:

```
input#name, input#email, textarea#comments {
    background-color: #FBEF99;
    font-family: "Lucida Console", Monaco, monospace;
    font-size: .9em;
    width: 300px;
    margin-top: -2px;
}
```

You can make your form easier for your visitors to fill out by highlighting the active form element with the special *:focus* pseudo-class (page 210). You'll add that in the next step.

14. At the end of the internal style sheet, add one last style for the pull-down menu and the three text fields:

```
input#name:focus,
input#email:focus,
textarea#comments:focus,
select#refer:focus
{
    background-color: #FDD041;
}
```

The *:focus* pseudo-class works only in Firefox, Safari, and Opera at this writing, but since it doesn't do IE people any harm, adding a *:focus* style is a fun enhancement.

Preview the page in a Web browser. It should now look like Figure 10-13. You can find a completed version of this tutorial in the *chapter_10_finished → form* folder.

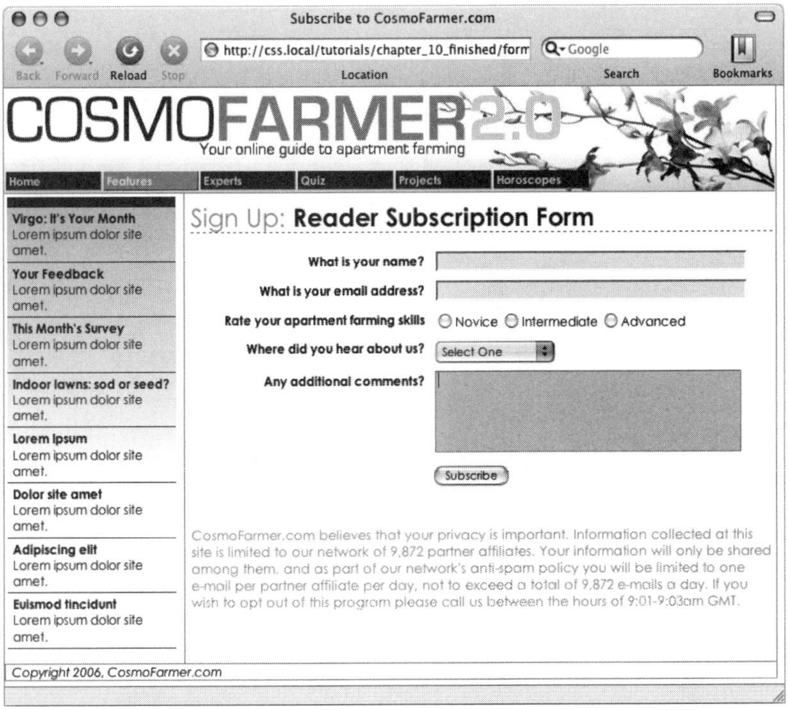

Figure 10-13:
Using the :focus pseudo-class, you can make your forms more interactive by highlighting form fields the visitor uses. Here, you can see you're about to type into the Comments field because of its darker background color.

Part Three:
CSS Page Layout

3

Building Float-Based Layouts

CSS leads a double life. As great as it is for formatting text, navigation bars, images, and other bits of a Web page, its truly awesome power comes when you're ready to lay out entire Web pages.

CSS layout comes in two flavors—*absolute positioning* and *floats*. Absolute positioning lets you position an element anywhere on the page with pixel-level accuracy—or so the theory goes. This kind of total control is exciting, as you'll see in the next chapter, but actually very difficult to achieve. That's why the vast majority of Web pages use float-based layouts, which are the subject of this chapter.

How CSS Layout Works

As discussed in Chapter 1, the limitations of HTML forced designers to develop clever ways to make their Web sites look good. The most common tool was the <table> tag, which was originally supposed to be used to create a spreadsheet-like display of information composed of rows and columns of data. Instead, designers used HTML tables to build a kind of scaffolding for organizing a page's contents (see Figure 11-1). But because the <table> tag wasn't meant for layout, designers often had to manipulate the tag in unusual ways—like placing a table inside the cell of *another* table—just to get the effect they wanted. This method was a lot of work, added a bunch of extra HTML code, and made it very difficult to modify the design later. But before CSS, that's all Web designers had.

If you're a longtime <table> tag jockey, you need to develop a new mindset when you begin to use CSS for layout. First, forget about rows and columns (a notion that's important when working with tables). There are no column spans or row

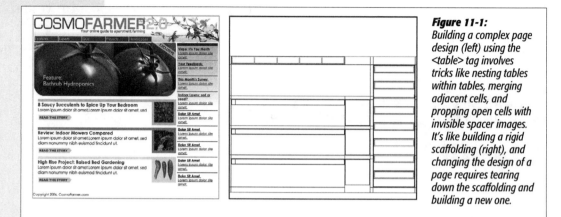

Figure 11-1:
Building a complex page design (left) using the <table> tag involves tricks like nesting tables within tables, merging adjacent cells, and propping open cells with invisible spacer images. It's like building a rigid scaffolding (right), and changing the design of a page requires tearing down the scaffolding and building a new one.

spans, and the grid-like structure of a table is nowhere to be found in CSS. You can, however, think of a <div> tag as a table cell. As with table cells, a <div> tag is the logical place to put content that you want to position in one area of the page. In addition, as you'll see, CSS designs often nest a div inside another div, much like you'd nest tables within tables to get certain effects—but, fortunately, the CSS method uses a *lot* less HTML code.

The Mighty <div> Tag

Whether you're using tables or CSS, Web page layout involves putting chunks of content into different regions of the page. With CSS, the element most commonly used for organizing content is the <div> tag. As you read on page 18, the <div> tag is an HTML element that has no inherent formatting properties (besides the fact that browsers treat the tag as a block with a line break before and after it); instead, it's used to mark a logical grouping of elements or a *division* on the page.

You'll typically wrap a <div> tag around a chunk of HTML that belongs together. The elements comprising the logo and navigation bar in Figure 11-1 occupy the top of the page, so it makes sense to wrap a <div> tag around them. At the very least, you would include <div> tags for all the major regions of your page, such as the banner, main content area, sidebar, footer, and so on. But it's also possible to wrap a <div> tag around one or more additional divs. One common technique is to wrap the HTML inside the <body> tag in a <div>. Then you can set some basic page properties by applying CSS to that *wrapper* <div>. You can set an overall width for the page's content, set left and right margins, or center all of the page's content in the middle of the screen. (You'll get a chance to work with a wrapper <div> in the tutorial on page 313.)

Once you've got your <div> tags in place, add either a class or ID to each one, which becomes your handle for styling each <div> separately. For parts of the page that appear only once and form the basic building blocks of the page, designers usually use an ID. The <div> tag for a page's banner area might look like this: *<div id="banner">*. You can use an ID only once per page, so when you have an element that appears multiple times, use a class instead. If you have several divs that position photos and their captions, then you can create a style like this: *<div class="photo">*.

With styles like these, you can position the various page elements. Using the CSS *float* property, you can position different blocks of content to the left or right of a page (or left or right edge of a containing block like another <div>).

WORD TO THE WISE

When More Isn't Better

Although divs are critical to CSS layout, don't go crazy pelting your page with divs. A common trap is to believe you must wrap *everything* on a Web page in a <div> tag. Say your main navigation bar is an unordered list of links (like the one described on page 218). Because it's an important element, you may be tempted to wrap a <div> around it: *<div id="mainNav"><ul>...</ul></div>*.

But there's no reason to add a <div> when the <ul> tag's just as handy. As long as the <ul> contains the main navigation bar links, you can simply add your ID style to that tag: *<ul id="mainNav">*. An additional <div> is just unnecessary code.

Types of Web Page Layouts

Being a Web designer means dealing with the unknown. What kind of browsers do your visitors use? Do they have the latest Flash Player plug-in installed? Perhaps the biggest issue designers face is creating attractive designs for different display sizes. Monitors vary in size and resolution: from petite 15-inch 640 × 480 pixel displays to 30-inch monstrosities displaying, oh, about 5,000,000 × 4,300,000 pixels.

Float-based layouts offer three basic approaches to this problem. Nearly every page design you see falls into one of two types—*fixed width,* or *liquid.* A fixed width gives you the most control over how your design looks, but can inconvenience some of your visitors. Folks with really small monitors have to scroll to the right to see everything, and those with large monitors have wasted space that could be showing more of your excellent content. Liquid designs make controlling the design of the page more challenging, but make the most effective use of the browser window. An elastic design combines some advantages of both.

- **Fixed Width.** Many designers prefer the consistency of a set width, like the page in Figure 11-2, top. Regardless of the browser window's width, the page content's width remains the same. In some cases, the design clings to the left edge of the browser window, or, more commonly, it's centered in the middle. With the fixed-width approach, you don't have to worry about what happens to your design on a very wide (or small) monitor.

Many fixed-width designs are about 760 pixels wide—a good size for 800 × 600 screens (since you need to leave a little room for scrollbars and other parts of the browsers "chrome"). However, more and more sites (especially ones aimed at a more tech-savvy crowd) are about 950 pixels wide, on the assumption that visitors have at least 1024 × 768 monitors.

Note: For examples of fixed-width designs aimed at larger monitors, visit *www.alistapart.com*, *www.espn.com*, or *www.nytimes.com*.

- **Liquid.** Sometimes it's easier to roll with the tide instead of fighting it. A liquid design adjusts to fit the browser's width—whatever it may be. Your page gets wider or narrower as your visitor resizes the window (Figure 11-2, middle). While this type of design makes the best use of the available browser window real estate, it's more work to make sure your design looks good at different window sizes. On very large monitors, these types of designs can look ridiculously wide.

Note: The *max-width* and *min-width* properties offer a compromise between fixed and liquid designs. See page 289.

- **Elastic.** An elastic design is really just a fixed-width design with a twist—type size flexibility. With this kind of design, you define the page's width using em values. An em changes size when the browser's font size changes, so the design's width is ultimately based on the browser's base font size (see page 105). If a visitor increases the size of the browser's display font (by pressing Ctrl-+ in Firefox, for example), then the page's width grows as well.

Figure 11-2, bottom, shows an elastic page with the browser's normal font size (left) and several font sizes larger (right). Increasing the font size makes all page elements wider as well. Elastic designs keep everything on your page in the same relative proportions, and make sure that when someone with poor vision has to pump up the text size, the columns holding the text grow as well.

In the tutorials at the end of this chapter, you'll create a fixed-width design and a liquid design.

Float Layout Basics

Float-based layouts take advantage of the *float* property to position elements side by side and create columns on a Web page. As described in Chapter 7 (page 152), you can use this property to create a wrap-around effect for, say, a photograph, but when you apply it to a <div> tag, *float* becomes a powerful page-layout tool. The *float* property moves a page element to one side of the page (or other containing block). Any HTML that appears below the floated element moves up on the page and wraps around the float.

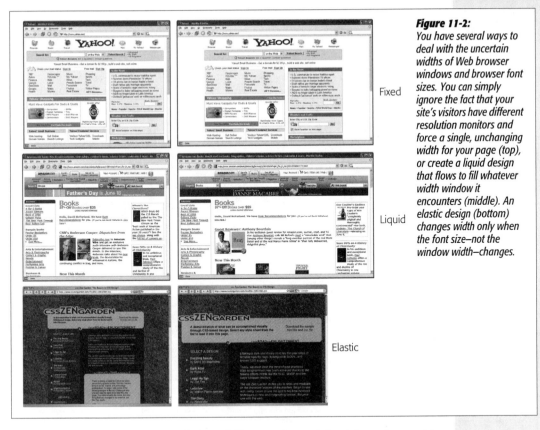

Figure 11-2:
You have several ways to deal with the uncertain widths of Web browser windows and browser font sizes. You can simply ignore the fact that your site's visitors have different resolution monitors and force a single, unchanging width for your page (top), or create a liquid design that flows to fill whatever width window it encounters (middle). An elastic design (bottom) changes width only when the font size—not the window width—changes.

Fixed

Liquid

Elastic

The *float* property accepts one of three different values—*left*, *right*, and *none*. To move an image to the right side of the page, you could create this class style and apply it to the <img> tag:

```
.floatRight { float: right; }
```

The same property applied to a <div> tag full of content can also create a sidebar:

```
#sidebar {
    float: left;
    width: 170px;
}
```

Figure 11-3 shows these two styles in action.

Note: The *none* value turns off any floating and positions the element like a normal, unfloated element. It's useful only for overriding a float that's already applied to an element. You may have an element with a particular class such as "sidebar" applied to it and that element floats to the right. But on one page you may want an element with that class to *not* float, but to be placed within the flow of the page, like this Note box. By creating a more specific CSS selector (see page 89) with *float: none,* you can prevent that element from floating.

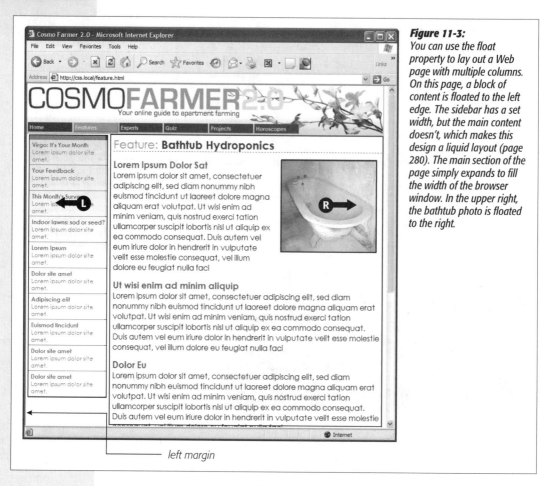

A simple two-column design like Figure 11-3 requires just a few steps:

1. **Wrap each column in a <div> tag with an ID or class attribute.**

   In Figure 11-3, the news items listed in the left sidebar are wrapped in one <div>—<div id="news">—and the main content in another div—<div id="main">.

2. **Float the sidebar <div> either right or left.**

   When you work with floats, the source order (the order in which you add HTML to a file) is important. The HTML for the floated element must appear *before* the HTML for the element that wraps around it.

   Figure 11-4 shows three two-column layouts. The diagrams on the left side show the page's HTML source order: A <div> for the banner, followed by a <div> for the sidebar and, lastly, a <div> for the main content. On the right side, you see the actual page layout. The sidebar comes *before* the main content in the HTML so it can float either left (top, bottom) or right (middle).

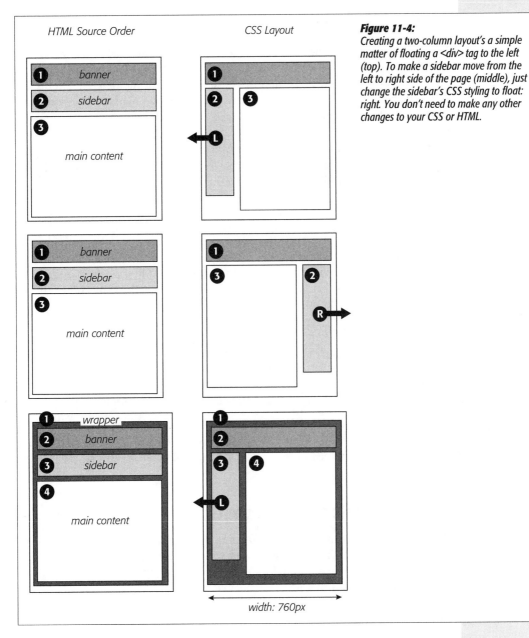

HTML Source Order   CSS Layout

Figure 11-4:
Creating a two-column layout's a simple matter of floating a <div> tag to the left (top). To make a sidebar move from the left to right side of the page (middle), just change the sidebar's CSS styling to float: right. You don't need to make any other changes to your CSS or HTML.

width: 760px

3. **Set a width for the floated sidebar.**

Unless you're floating an image with a predefined width, you should always give your floats a width. In this way, you create a set size for the floated element, letting the browser make room for other content to wrap into position.

The width could be a fixed size like 170px or 10em. You can also use percentages for a flexible design that's based on the width of the browser window. (See page 279 for more about the pros and cons of the different measurement units.) If the sidebar is 20 percent wide and the browser window is 700 pixels wide, then the sidebar will be 140 pixels wide. But if your visitor resizes the window to 1000 pixels, then the sidebar grows to 200 pixels. Fixed-width sidebars are easier to design for, since you don't have to consider all the different widths the sidebar might stretch to. However, percentages let you maintain the same proportions between the two columns, which can be more visually pleasing.

Note: When the overall page design is a fixed width (as described on page 279), percentage width values for the sidebar are based on the fixed-width containing element. The width isn't based on the window size and won't change when the browser window changes size.

4. **Add a left margin to the main content.**

   If the sidebar's shorter than the other content on the page, the text from the main column wraps underneath the sidebar, ruining the look of two side-by-side columns (see Figure 11-18 for an example). Adding a left margin that's equal to or greater than the width of the sidebar indents the main content of the page, creating the illusion of a second column:

   ```
   #main { margin-left: 180px ; }
   ```

   By the way, it's usually a good idea to make the left margin a little bigger than the width of the sidebar: This creates some empty space—a white gutter—between the two elements. So, when you use percentages to set the width of the sidebar, use a slightly larger percentage value for the left margin.

   Avoid setting a width for the main content div. It's not necessary, since browsers simply expand it to fit the available space. Even if you want a fixed-width design, you don't need to set a width for the main content div, as you'll see in the next section.

Applying Floats to Your Layouts

Now that you've learned a basic two-column liquid layout, you can adapt it in countless ways. Converting it into a fixed-width layout is a snap. Simply wrap all the tags within the page's body inside *another* <div> (like *<div id="wrapper">*). Then, create a style for that new container element that has a set width such as 760 pixels (see Figure 11-4, bottom). That width setting constrains everything inside the container box.

Expanding it into a three-column design isn't difficult, either (Figure 11-5). First, add another <div> between the two columns and float it to the right. Then add a right margin to the middle column, so that if the text in the middle column runs longer than the new right sidebar, it won't wrap underneath the sidebar.

The rest of this section explores more CSS layout techniques that use float-based layouts.

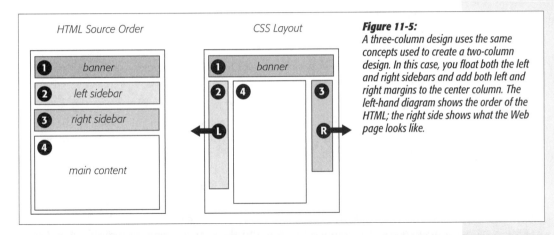

HTML Source Order

① banner

② left sidebar

③ right sidebar

④

main content

CSS Layout

① banner

② ④   ③

◄— L   R —►

Figure 11-5:
*A three-column design uses the same
concepts used to create a two-column
design. In this case, you float both the left
and right sidebars and add both left and
right margins to the center column. The
left-hand diagram shows the order of the
HTML; the right side shows what the Web
page looks like.*

Don't Reinvent the Wheel

If terms like *liquid layout* and *containing element* sound a little intimidating, don't give up. First of all, the tutorials beginning on page 307 walk you step by step through the process of laying out Web pages with CSS. But there's no law saying you have to create your own CSS layouts from scratch. On the Web you'll find plenty of pre-built and tested designs you can make your own. The Layout Gala site offers 40 different CSS designs that work in most common browsers, including Internet Explorer 5 (*http://blog.html.it/layoutgala/*). The designs are just basic skeletons consisting of <div> tags and the CSS that positions them. All you need to do is fill them with your own design touches like font styling and imagery.

For a sophisticated design including multiple templates, drop-down menus, and preformatted text and link styles, check out the Mollio templates at *www.mollio.org*. The site includes a style guide explaining how to use the templates, as well as the original Photoshop files so you can tweak the graphics' appearance to your liking.

Finally, for a total smorgasbord of CSS designs, check out Open Source Web Design (*www.oswd.org*). This site includes literally thousands of Web page designs that you can freely download and reuse.

Floating All Columns

It's perfectly possible to float *every* column, not just the left and right sidebars. You could float the first sidebar to the left, the middle column to the left, and the right sidebar to the right, as shown in Figure 11-6, top. This approach lets you put more than three columns in your design. You can float four or more columns, as long as there's room for all the floats to fit side by side.

When you float all columns in a design, you need to pay close attention to the widths of each column. If the total width of all the columns is less than the space available—for example, if the browser window is smaller, or the columns are placed inside another <div> with a set width—then the last column drops down, below the others. (You can read a solution to this dropping float problem on page 299.)

In addition, floating more than just the sidebars lets you change the order of your divs in the HTML. Take, for example, the left diagram in Figure 11-5, which shows the order of the <div> tags for that page. Because of the way floated elements work, they must appear before any content that wraps around them, so in this example, the main content area must go *after* the sidebars.

The order of the <div> tags in the HTML may not seem like a big deal until you try to browse the Web page *without* CSS, which is the case for many alternative browsers, including screen readers which read a page's content aloud to visually impaired visitors. Without CSS, all the sidebar material (which often includes navigational elements, ads, or other information that's not relevant to the main topic of the page) appears before the content the visitor came to read in the first place. The inconvenience of having to scroll past the same sidebar content on each page will turn off some visitors. Furthermore, your page is less accessible to vision-impaired visitors, who have to listen to their screen readers read off a long list of links and ads before coming to any real information.

And if that doesn't sway you, you've got the search engines to worry about. Most search engines limit the amount of HTML they read when searching a site. On a particularly long Web page, they simply stop at a certain point—possibly missing important content that *should* be indexed by the search engine. Also, most search engines give greater value to the HTML near the beginning of the file. So if you're worried about getting good placement in search engine results, it's in your best interest to make sure the important contents as close as possible to the top of the page's HTML code. Finally, floating every column also avoids a 3-pixel bug that affects Internet Explorer 6 and earlier (see page 304).

In the top-left diagram in Figure 11-6, the main content's HTML is between the left and right sidebars, which is better than having it after both sidebars. You can even put the main content before *both* sidebars' HTML by wrapping the main content and left sidebar in one <div>, floating that <div> left, and then floating the main content right and the left sidebar right *within* that <div> (Figure 11-6, bottom). Voilà—the main column's HTML falls before the other <div> tags.

Floats Within Floats

The bottom diagram in Figure 11-6 illustrates another useful technique—floating elements *within* floats. Imagine that the main content (3) and the left sidebar (4) divs didn't exist, and only the column wrapper (2) and the right sidebar (5) were left. You'd have just a basic two-column design with one column floated left and another floated right. In fact, it's still a 2-column design even with the two divs (3 and 4) placed back inside the column wrapper div. The difference is that the left column is itself divided into two columns.

Although this arrangement's a bit confusing, it's also helpful in a number of instances. First, it lets you add columns within a column. The three-column layout at the top of Figure 11-7 shows a small Tips box in the middle column that also has two columns inside it. By nesting floats inside floats, you can create some very complex designs.

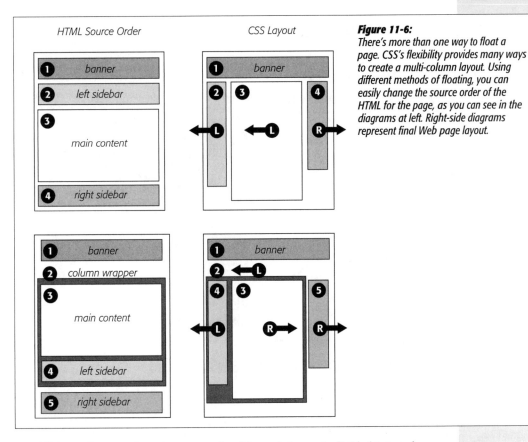

Figure 11-6:
*There's more than one way to float a
page. CSS's flexibility provides many ways
to create a multi-column layout. Using
different methods of floating, you can
easily change the source order of the
HTML for the page, as you can see in the
diagrams at left. Right-side diagrams
represent final Web page layout.*

In addition, when you have just a couple of floated elements divided into columns
with additional floated elements, it's easier to calculate the widths of page elements. That's a good thing when you need to control float drops (page 299) and
other problems that occur when columns get too wide.

Using Negative Margins to Position Elements

While the last section provided a few techniques that let you reorder the HTML for
each column in a design, there's an even more advanced technique that gives you
complete control over the placement of your columns. By using *negative* margins,
you can put your <div> tags in any order you wish in your HTML, and then position them in a different order onscreen—thereby keeping your pages accessible to
screen readers, text browsers, and search engines as described on the opposite
page. In addition, since you don't need to worry about the source order, you can
always change the design of a page—maybe float the main column to the far right,
and the two sidebars to the left—without having to change the HTML of the page.
Be warned, though, this method involves math and some mind-bending uses of
CSS. You can live a healthy, happy life using just the float methods presented earlier in this chapter. But if you're up for some adventure, read on. (The tutorial also
presents a hands-on demonstration of this method, starting on page 314.)

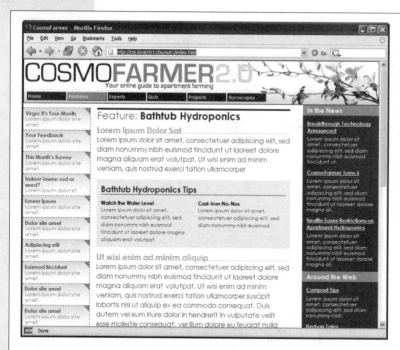

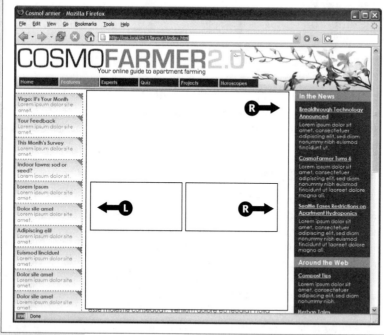

Figure 11-7:
*Top: create columns within
columns by floating elements
inside another floated
element. In the middle
column, the Tips box provides
a simple two-column note that
adds visual interest to the
page.*

*Bottom: it doesn't matter
which direction the container
is floated (in this instance, to
the right)—you simply float the
two additional columns left
and right.*

Finding the Middle Ground

The two types of layouts—fixed-width and liquid—have their pluses and minuses. A fixed-width design gives you a lot of control and lets you make sure that your layout looks exactly the same even on different sized monitors. However, on a particularly small monitor, a fixed-width page may force your visitor to scroll horizontally to view the whole page. On a really wide monitor, your lovely fixed-width design may look like a small sliver in a sea of empty space.

Liquid layouts solve these problems, but have their own limitations as well. On a small screen, a liquid layout may contract so much that the design falls apart. And on a really wide screen, your design may stretch so far that your visitors get eye cramps trying to read 30-inch-wide lines of text.

Several CSS properties aim to solve this problem: *min-width, min-height, max-width,* and *max-height.* The *min-* properties instruct a browser to make an element *at least* as wide or tall as the specified value. You can apply *min-width* to the <body> tag to control the total width of the page's content, like so: *body { min-width: 760px; }.* If a visitor expands his browser window to 1000 pixels, the page content stretches to fit the space. However, if he makes the window 500 pixels, then the content remains 760 pixels wide and the browser adds horizontal scrollbars. The *min-height* property does the same thing, but for an element's height.

On the other hand, the *max-* properties limit an element to a maximum size. The styled element can get smaller than that value, but never larger. With them, you can make sure your pages don't get too wide to be unreadable. Say you create a style for the <body> tag with this property: *max-width: 1200px.* Now, if a visitor expands her browser window to 1800 pixels wide (on her unbelievably expensive 30-inch monitor), the page content doesn't sprawl all over the screen, but remains 1200 pixels wide. *Max-height* does the same thing, but for the height of a style.

By combining the two properties, you can create a style that expands and contracts only within set dimensions, so your design never gets too small or too big:

```
body {
    min-width: 760px;
    max-width: 1200px;
}
```

The only problem with these otherwise useful properties: Internet Explorer 6 and earlier ignores them completely. If you're feeling adventurous, try one of the workarounds at *www.cssplay.co.uk/boxes/width3.html* or *www.antix.co.uk/code/css/imposing_minimum_width/.* Both workarounds are experimental, but they work fairly well. There's also a JavaScript technique that dynamically changes the dimensions of Web page elements based on the size of the browser window: *www.doxdesk.com/software/js/minmax.html.*

Note: The technique described on these pages works only for fixed-width layouts, where you know the exact width of each column. For another method that achieves the same results with a liquid layout (where you don't know the exact width of the middle column), visit *www.alistapart.com/articles/holygrail/.*

Here's how to lay out a page using negative margins:

1. **Add a wrapper <div> around all of the page content.**

   This step provides a container for setting a fixed width for all of the content on the page, and gives you an easy way to make the banner, columns, and footer the same width.

2. **Set a width for the wrapper <div>.**

Create a style for the wrapper div that gives it a set width. For example, 760 pixels is a typical size that accommodates visitors with 800 × 600 pixel monitors.

3. **Wrap each column in a <div> tag with an ID or class attribute.**

This part of the process is the same as creating any float-based layout. It defines the basic layout blocks (Figure 11-8, top left).

4. **Float the divs for each column.**

You must float each of the columns in your design. When you float them all to the left, they sit side-by-side. Another option's to float the left sidebar and main content left and the right sidebar right. (Since all columns are enclosed in the wrapper <div> from step 1, the right sidebar stays close to the central column.)

Note: If you're not using a wrapper div as described in step 1, then you *must* float the right sidebar *left*. Otherwise, it clings to the right edge of the browser window, potentially creating a large empty space between the right sidebar and the main content.

---

5. **Set widths for each column.**

You should always specify a width for a floated element. Depending on your design, you can also add padding, margins, and borders. Keep in mind, though, that the total width of the three columns in the browser window is the sum of the CSS *width* property values *and* the left and right margins, padding, and borders for each column. (And remember that, as described on page 150, Internet Explorer 5 on Windows has its own ideas about what *width* means.) Yep, here's where the math comes in. If you're not careful, the total width of the columns may exceed the width provided by the wrapper <div>, causing the dreaded float drop (see page 299).

Note: The *width* property doesn't define the total width that an element takes up onscreen. Margins, padding, and borders count, too. If this stuff doesn't sound familiar, then read page 133 to brush up on the CSS box model theory.

---

6. **Add a left margin to the main column.**

Here's where the negative margin technique differs from the layout methods described earlier in this chapter. The left margin should *equal the space required for the left sidebar*. If the left sidebar is 160 pixels wide, then set the left margin of the main column to 160 pixels: *margin-left: 160px*. The top-right diagram in Figure 11-8 shows the page so far. The crosshatched area to the left of the main column (3) represents that column's left margin.

Or, say the left sidebar is 160 pixels wide and you want 10 pixels of space between it and the main content. In that case, add 10 pixels to the main column's left margin: *margin-left: 170px*.

IMP.

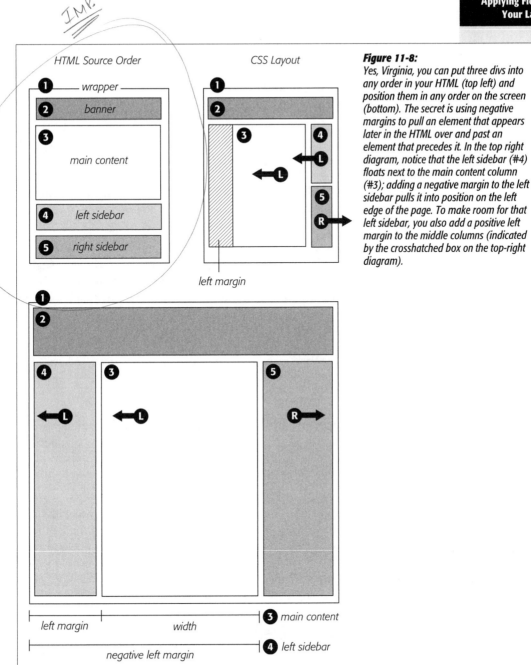

Figure 11-8:
Yes, Virginia, you can put three divs into any order in your HTML (top left) and position them in any order on the screen (bottom). The secret is using negative margins to pull an element that appears later in the HTML over and past an element that precedes it. In the top right diagram, notice that the left sidebar (#4) floats next to the main content column (#3); adding a negative margin to the left sidebar pulls it into position on the left edge of the page. To make room for that left sidebar, you also add a positive left margin to the middle columns (indicated by the crosshatched box on the top-right diagram).

Finally, when the left sidebar has padding and borders, you need to factor those in as well. Suppose the left sidebar is 160 pixels wide, has a 2-pixel right border and 10 pixels of left and right padding, and you want 10 pixels of space between it and the main column. Add all of these together to get the left margin value for the main column. So, 160 (width value) + 2 (right border) + 10

(left padding) + 10 (right padding) + 10 (gutter between sidebar and main column) = 192 pixels (*margin-left: 192px*).

7. **Apply a negative margin to the left sidebar <div>.**

At this point, the left sidebar's floated to the left, but since it comes after the
main column in the HTML's source order, it appears on the right edge of the
main column (Figure 11-8, top right). To get it into position, use a negative
margin, which—believe it or not—pulls the sidebar clear across the main column to the left edge of the page. The only trick is figuring out what that negative margin value should be to move the sidebar the exact distance required to
position it at the left side of the page. In other words, the left margin must equal
the distance from the right edge of the main column to the left edge of the
wrapper <div>.

To determine that value, add the main column's width, left and right margins,
left and right padding, and left and right borders. Say the main column is 400
pixels wide, has a 1 pixel border around it, has 10 pixels of left padding and 15
pixels of right padding, and has a 160 pixels left margin to accommodate the left
sidebar. Just add the values together to get the left sidebar's left-margin value:
400 + 1 + 1 + 10 + 15 + 160 = 587. Then add a left margin to the style formatting the left sidebar, but make its value negative: *left-margin: -587px;*. The
minus sign is the critical piece that makes the whole thing work.

8. **Fix the Internet Explorer bugs.**

When you use negative margins, Internet Explorer 6 and earlier exhibits a weird
bug—the *double-margin* bug. In this case, IE doubles the left margin applied to
the main column, totally disrupting the design. The fix is to add *display: inline*
to the style formatting the *main column*. (Read more about the double-margin
bug on page 302.)

Once you get past the math, the negative margin approach rewards you with flexibility. If you want to swap the sidebars so the left sidebar moves to the right and
right sidebar moves to the left, then simply swap the styles for those two divs. In
other words, set the first sidebar to float right, and the second sidebar to float left
using a negative left margin. You'll see negative margins in action in the tutorial on
page 314.

Overcoming Float Problems

As you get more adventurous with CSS, you'll probably encounter—like many
Web designers before you—some of the weird intricacies of working with floats.
This section describes a few common problems and their solutions. (And if you
ever stumble upon a problem not listed here, you can always take it to one of the
online forums or discussion lists in Appendix C.)

Note: When it comes to designing pages that work in Internet Explorer, there are even more potential pitfalls. So many, in fact, that this chapter has a separate section dedicated to dealing with that one browser. See page 302.

Clearing and Containing Floats

Floats are powerful design tools because they let content flow around them. Floating a photo lets text below it move up and wrap around the image (Figure 11-3). When you're creating float-based column designs, though, sometimes you *don't* want content to move up and next to a floated element. For example, you frequently want to keep copyright notices, contact information, or other housekeeping details at the bottom of your Web page, below all other content.

In the two- and three-column designs you've seen so far, if the main column is shorter than either of the floated sidebar columns, a footer can move up and around the left floated column (Figure 11-9, left). To make the footer stay down below the sidebars, you can use the *clear* property (page 155). This property prevents an element from wrapping around floats. You can make an element drop below a left-floated object (*clear: left;*), or a right floated object (*clear: right;*). For footers and other items that need to appear at the bottom of the page, you should clear *both* left and right floats, like this:

```
#footer { clear: both; }
```

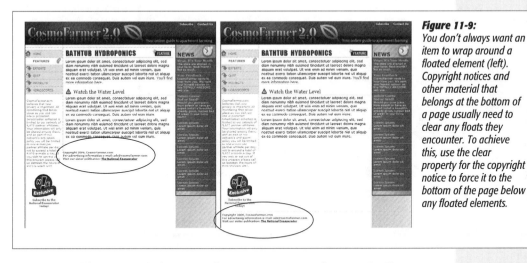

Figure 11-9:
You don't always want an item to wrap around a floated element (left). Copyright notices and other material that belongs at the bottom of a page usually need to clear any floats they encounter. To achieve this, use the clear property for the copyright notice to force it to the bottom of the page below any floated elements.

Another problem occurs when you float one or more elements inside a non-floated containing tag like a <div> tag. When the floated element is taller than the other content inside the div, it sticks out of the bottom of the enclosing element. This snafu is especially noticeable if that tag has a background or border. The top of the web page in Figure 11-10 shows a <div> tag that has an <h1> tag ("Bathtub

Hydroponics Tips") and two columns created by floating two divs. The background and border, which appear only around the <h1> tag, are actually applied to the entire enclosing <div>, including the area where the two columns are. However, since the columns are floated, they pop out of the bottom instead of expanding the borders of the box.

Note: For a good explanation of why floated elements can break outside of their containing blocks, read *www.complexspiral.com/publications/containing-floats/*.

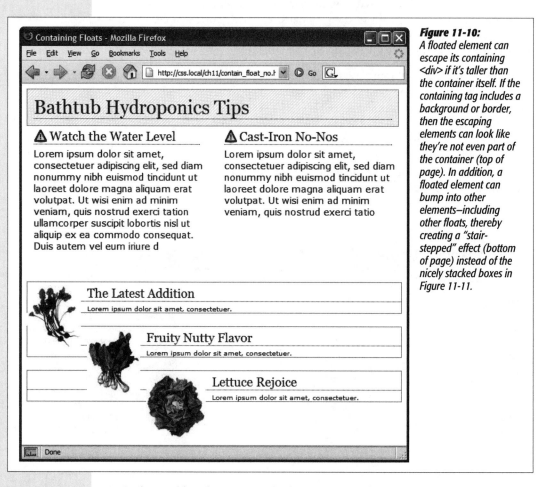

Figure 11-10:
A floated element can escape its containing <div> if it's taller than the container itself. If the containing tag includes a background or border, then the escaping elements can look like they're not even part of the container (top of page). In addition, a floated element can bump into other elements—including other floats, thereby creating a "stair-stepped" effect (bottom of page) instead of the nicely stacked boxes in Figure 11-11.

A similar problem happens in the bottom example in Figure 11-10. In this case, each image is floated left inside a containing <div> that has a border. Because the images are taller than their boxes, they pop out of the bottom. Unfortunately, this example's even worse than the previous one, because each image causes the image below it to wrap to the right, creating an ugly staggered effect.

You have three ways to tackle the problem of these renegade floating elements:

- **Add a clearing element at the bottom of the containing div.** This solution's the most straightforward, although it adds extra HTML code. Simply add a tag—like a line break or horizontal rule—as the last item in the <div> containing the floated element (that is, right before the closing </div> tag). Then use the *clear* property to force that extra tag below the float. This trick makes the enclosing div expand, revealing its background and border. You can add a line break—
 (HTML) or
 (XHTML)—before the closing </div> tag and add a class to it: *<br class="clear" />*. Then create a style for it, like this:

  ```
  br.clear { clear: both; }
  ```

- **Float the containing element.** An easier way is to just float the <div> containing the floated elements as well. A floated container <div> expands to fully contain any floated elements inside it. In Figure 11-11, top, the <div> containing the heading and two floated columns is floated to the left of the page. In the process, its entire box—background and borders—expands to fit everything inside it, including the floated elements. Strange, but true.

- **Use the "easy clearing method."** With this technique, created by Tony Aslett of CssCreator.com, you add just a few styles and a class name to the <div> tag containing the floated element. Of course, the name "easy clearing method" is a bit of a misnomer, since the CSS behind it is anything but easy. You must add three different styles to your style sheet: One applies to Firefox, Safari, Opera and other modern browsers; another style applies to IE 7 (which doesn't yet understand the first style); and the last style makes IE 6 and IE 5 behave. The whole shebang looks like this:

  ```
  .clear:after {
      content: ".";
      display: block;
      height: 0;
      font-size: 0;
      clear: both;
      visibility: hidden;
  }
  .clear {
      min-height: 1px;
  }
  * html .clear {
      height: 1px;
  }
  ```

The last two styles make IE 5, 6, and 7 "have layout" as described in the box on page 307.

Once you've added these styles to a style sheet, you simply add the class name to the div *containing* the escaping floats: *<div class="clear">*. See the bottom of Figure 11-11.

Tip: You can simplify this code by replacing the last two styles with this CSS: *.clear { zoom: 1; }*. This single style knocks all versions of IE into shape, but since it uses the non-standard *zoom* property, it makes your page flunk the CSS validator check. To get around *that*, you can put this rule (along with any other IE-only styles) into an external style sheet and attach it to your Web pages using any of the tricks described in Chapter 14 (page 399).

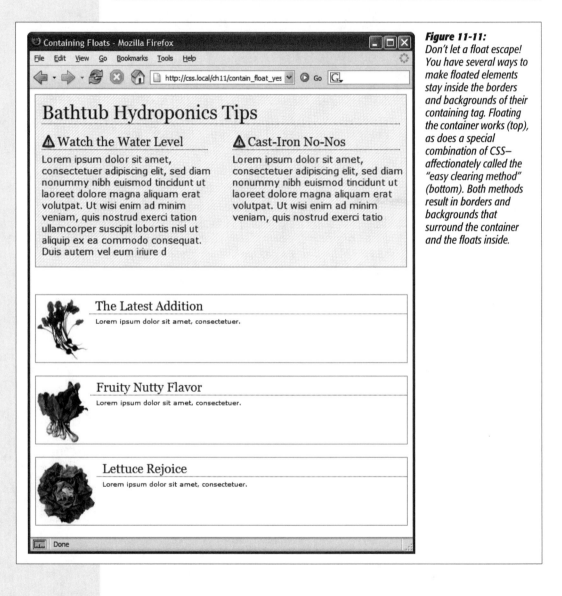

Figure 11-11:
Don't let a float escape! You have several ways to make floated elements stay inside the borders and backgrounds of their containing tag. Floating the container works (top), as does a special combination of CSS— affectionately called the "easy clearing method" (bottom). Both methods result in borders and backgrounds that surround the container and the floats inside.

Creating Full-Height Columns

HTML tables aren't great for Web page layout for several reasons. They add lots of code, are difficult to update, and don't work well on alternative browsers like those used by cellphones. But tables have one thing going for them in the layout department—the ability to create columns of equal height. Equal-height columns let you add a background color or graphic to one column and have it fill the entire height of the page. The backgrounds of the two sidebars in the top image of Figure 11-12 fill the screen height, creating solid, bold stripes on either side of the page.

CSS floats, on the other hand, fall a bit short in this regard. Table cells in a row are always the same height, which isn't true of divs. The height of a float is usually dictated by the content inside it. When there's not a lot of content, the float's not very tall. Since a background image or background color fills only the float, you can end up with solid-colored columns that stop short of the page bottom, as in the circled areas in Figure 11-12, bottom.

As with most problems related to CSS, there's a workaround. The secret's to add background images to a tag that *wraps around* the stubby sidebar and the other columns on the page. Say your HTML has two <div> tags that contain the content for a left sidebar and the page's main content:

```
<div id="sidebar">Sidebar content here</div>
<div id="main">Main content for page, this column has a lot of text and is
much taller than the sidebar.</div>
```

The sidebar <div> is floated to the left edge of the page and has a width of 170 pixels. Because there's less content in the sidebar, it's shorter than the main text. Suppose you wrap that HTML in a wrapper <div> tag, like so:

```
<div id="wrapper">
<div id="sidebar">Sidebar content here</div>
<div id="main">Main content for page, this column has a lot of text and is
much taller than the sidebar.</div>
</div>
```

That outer div grows to be as tall as the tallest element inside it, so even if the *#main* div is very tall, that wrapper div will be just as tall. Here's the magic: Create a style for the wrapper <div> with a background image the width of the sidebar, in the background color you want for the sidebar. That way, if the background image tiles vertically, it forms a solid bar the height of the wrapper <div> (Figure 11-13, top).

```
#wrapper { background: url (images/col_bg.gif) repeat-y left top; }
```

Web browsers display that background image directly *under the sidebar*, creating the illusion that the sidebar has a background color. In essence, you create a "faux column" in the words of Dan Cederholm, the fellow who first publicized this technique.

Figure 11-12:
*Full-height columns with bold
background colors are a common
design technique. The left and right
sidebars (top) show how solid
backgrounds can help visually define
the different areas of a page. When a
sidebar's background stops abruptly
(circled at bottom), you get extra
white space that's both distracting
and unappealing.*

Tip: You're not limited to solid colors either. Since you're using an image anyway, you can make a decorative pattern that tiles seamlessly down the left side of the page.

Reproducing this result for two columns is just a little more involved. First, add two wrapper divs:

```
<div id="wrapper1">
<div id="wrapper2">
<div id="sidebar1">Sidebar content here</div>
<div id="sidebar2">Second sidebar</div>
<div id="main">Main content for page, this column has a lot of text and is
much taller than the two sidebars.</div>
</div>
</div>
```

Tip: If the wrapper and each column are all fixed widths, you can create this "faux" column look for both the left and right columns with just a single image and wrapper div. Just make the graphic as wide as the wrapper, with the left side of the graphic being the color and width of the left sidebar, the right side of the graphic the color and width of the right sidebar, and the center part of the graphic matching the background color of the center column.

If the first sidebar appears on the left side of the page and the second sidebar appears on the right side, you create two styles. Apply one style to the first wrapper <div> tag to add a background to the left sidebar; apply one to the second wrapper <div> to add a background to the right sidebar (Figure 11-13, bottom).

```
#wrapper1 { background: url(images/col1_bg.gif) repeat-y left top; }
#wrapper2 { background: url(images/col2_bg.gif) repeat-y right top; }
```

When adding a background image to the right-hand column, make sure you position the background image in the top-right of the second wrapper, so that it falls underneath the second sidebar on the right side of the page.

Note: If you use percentages to define the width of columns, then it's more difficult to create the illusion of full-height columns using graphics. But it's not impossible. To learn how, go to *www.communitymx. com/content/article.cfm?page=1&cid=AFC58.*

Preventing Float Drops

Suddenly, one of your columns simply drops down below the others (Figure 11-14, top). It looks like there's plenty of room for all the columns to coexist perfectly side by side, but they just don't. You've got the dreaded float drop.

A floated column drops down because there's not enough room to fit it. Be careful if you set widths for *each* column. If the available space in the browser window (or the containing block in a fixed-width design) is less than the *total* widths of the columns, then you're asking for a float drop. Also, keep the CSS box model in mind: As discussed on page 147, the width of an element displayed in the browser window isn't the same as its *width* property. The displayed width of any element is a combination of its width, left and right border sizes, left and right padding, and

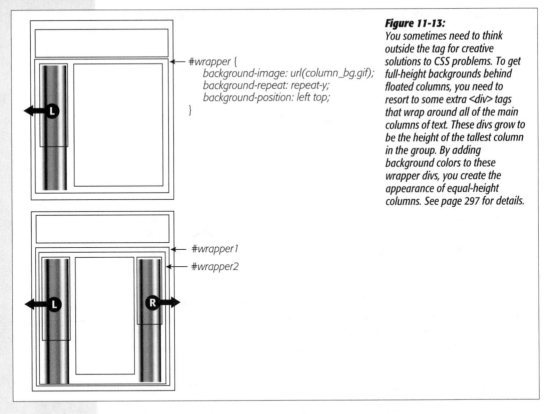

#wrapper {
    background-image: url(column_bg.gif);
    background-repeat: repeat-y;
    background-position: left top;
}

#wrapper1
#wrapper2

Figure 11-13:
You sometimes need to think outside the tag for creative solutions to CSS problems. To get full-height backgrounds behind floated columns, you need to resort to some extra <div> tags that wrap around all of the main columns of text. These divs grow to be the height of the tallest column in the group. By adding background colors to these wrapper divs, you create the appearance of equal-height columns. See page 297 for details.

left and right margins. For the columns to fit, the browser window (or containing block) must accommodate the combined total of all those widths.

Take, for example, the simple three-column layout in Figure 11-14. As you can see in the top example, the three columns don't fit. Here's a breakdown of the math behind the problem:

- **Wrapper div.** A fixed-width wrapper <div> tag encloses the entire design. Its *width* property is set to *760 pixels*, so all three columns can't total more than that.

- **Sidebar 1 (left side).** Its width is 150 pixels, but it also has 10 pixels of padding, making its total onscreen width *170 pixels*. (150 + 10 pixels of left padding + 10 pixels of right padding.)

- **Main content.** The main content <div> is *390 pixels* wide, with a 1-pixel border and 15 pixels of left and right margin for a total width of *422 pixels*. (You may need a calculator for this one: 390 + 1 [left border] +1 [right border] + 15 [left margin] + 15 [right margin].)

- **Sidebar 2 (right side).** This element has a *width* property set to 150 pixels, with 10 pixels of left and 10 pixels of right padding: *170 pixels*, just like Sidebar 1.

The actual widths of each element add up to a grand total of *762 pixels*. That's two pixels more than the width of the wrapper <div>. The middle image of Figure 11-14 shows an outline around the main content <div> indicating its total width plus margins. Just those measly two extra pixels of width (circled) are enough to cause a column to drop down. The solution: Remove two pixels of space from any of the elements. Changing the main content div's left and right margins from 15 to 14 pixels buys you the extra room needed for all three columns to fit side by side (bottom).

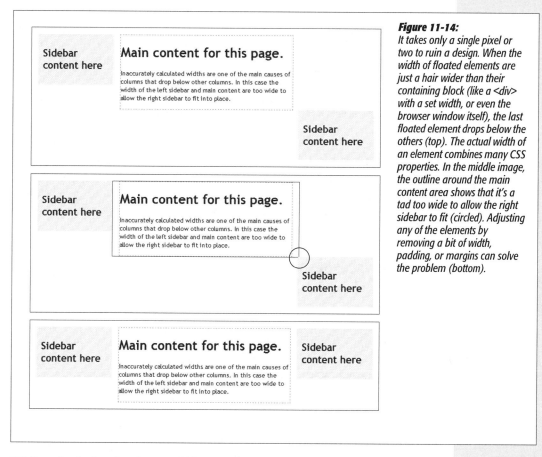

Figure 11-14:
It takes only a single pixel or two to ruin a design. When the width of floated elements are just a hair wider than their containing block (like a <div> with a set width, or even the browser window itself), the last floated element drops below the others (top). The actual width of an element combines many CSS properties. In the middle image, the outline around the main content area shows that it's a tad too wide to allow the right sidebar to fit (circled). Adjusting any of the elements by removing a bit of width, padding, or margins can solve the problem (bottom).

While miscalculated column widths are the most common cause of dropping floats, they're not the only cause. Here are a few other culprits:

• **Rounding errors in percentage widths.** Be careful when setting widths in percentages. Browsers sometimes make mistakes when calculating the actual number of pixels needed to display something on the screen. That is, they can round numbers up, making elements slightly too large for the available space. So err on the side of caution and make your percentage widths total slightly less than 100 percent.

- **Internet Explorer's double-margin bug.** Under some conditions, Internet Explorer 6 and earlier doubles the margin applied to a floated element, making the element wider than in other browsers. When you have a float drop occurring only in IE 6 or earlier, this bug may be the culprit. See page 302 for a solution.

- **Internet Explorer's 3-pixel gap.** Sometimes IE 6 and earlier adds an extra 3 pixels to the side of a float. Again, if you see a float drop only in IE, then this bug could be the reason. See page 304 for an explanation and solution.

- **Italic text.** IE strikes again. If a floated element contains italicized text, then IE 6 sometimes makes the float wider. When there's a float drop and italics inside the float, check to see if the problem's happening in all browsers or only IE. For a solution, you can remove any italics from the sidebar, or add *overflow: hidden* to the style formatting the sidebar.

Tip: For the definitive treatise on dropping floats (and how to solve them), visit *http://nemesis1.f2o.org/ aarchive?id=11.*

Bottom line: Float drops are always caused by not enough room to hold all of the columns. Rather than striving to use every last pixel of onscreen space, give all your elements a little more wiggle room. Get in the habit of making the overall column widths a bit smaller than necessary, and you'll spend less time troubleshooting float drops.

Handling Internet Explorer Bugs

The Windows version of Internet Explorer has a long history of CSS bugs, especially (and unfortunately) when it comes to float-based layouts. These bugs can affect the placement of floats and the overall width allotted to floated elements. If you're lucky, you may just get a slightly annoying difference in how your Web page looks in Internet Explorer versus other browsers. At worst, these bugs can cause significant display problems like the float drops discussed in the previous section. This section tells you the most common problems and how to get around them.

Tip: When a floated element has padding or a border, it appears thinner in IE 5 than in other browsers. There's more detail on this IE 5 bug—and its solution—on page 150.

Double-Margin Bug

Internet Explorer 6 and earlier sometimes *doubles* the size of a margin you've applied to a floated element. The problem occurs only when the margin's in the same direction as the float—a left margin on a left-floated element or a right margin on a right-floated element. In Figure 11-15, there's a left-floated sidebar holding the site's navigation. To add a bit of space between it and the left edge of the browser window, the sidebar has a left margin of 10 pixels.

CSS: The Missing Manual

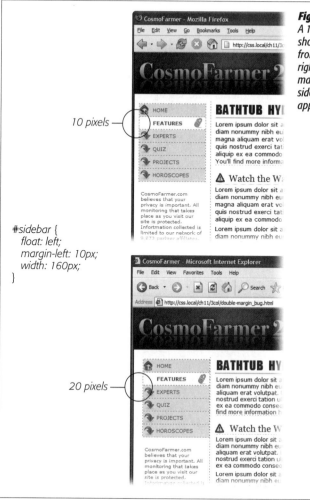

Figure 11-15:
A 10-pixel left margin applied to a left-floated element should, in theory anyway, indent the float 10 pixels from the left edge of the page. Firefox (above) gets it right. But IE 6 (bottom) incorrectly doubles that margin. By adding 20 pixels to the left edge of the sidebar, IE 6 significantly changes the page's appearance.

Most browsers, including Internet Explorer 7, Safari, and Firefox (Figure 11-15, top) add the requested 10 pixels of space. However, Internet Explorer 6 (bottom) doubles that margin to 20 pixels. Even with relatively small margins like 10 pixels, the visual difference is significant. Furthermore, if the layout's very tight, with precisely measured floated elements sitting side by side, then the doubled margin can easily trigger a float drop (page 299).

Note: This margin doubling happens only when the element's margin touches the edge of its containing block, so when an element is floated left against another left-floated element, its left margin *won't* double.

The solution's simple: Add *display:inline;* to the CSS style for the floated element:

```
#sidebar {
    float: left;
```

```
    margin-left: 10px;
    width: 160px;
    display: inline;
}
```

In this case, the display property doesn't do anything except fix IE's bug. Floated elements are always block-level elements, and changing a style's display to inline won't alter that. (See page 140 for more on the display property.) However, even though this added style declaration doesn't adversely affect any other browsers, you may want to put it in an IE-only style using the *html* hack:

```
#sidebar {
    float: left;
    margin-left: 10px;
    width: 160px;
}
* html #sidebar {
    display: inline;
}
```

Tip: Internet Explorer's conditional comments feature provides an even better way to isolate IE-only styles than the * html hack. An external style sheet attached to a page using a conditional comment is read only by Internet Explorer; it's ignored by all other browsers. See page 399 for the details.

3-Pixel Gaps

Internet Explorer 6 and earlier inserts an additional three pixels of space between a floated column and a non-floated column. The exact placement of that gap depends on a couple of conditions:

- **The non-floated column doesn't have a set width or height.** If the column next to the float doesn't have any dimensions defined, then you'll see a 3-pixel indent between the edge of the column and the text inside that column. This space appears only along the float, so when the float ends, the text moves back to the left edge of the column (Figure 11-16).

In this case, the best solution's to live with it. The extra indent isn't terribly distracting and doesn't do anything else weird to the page. But if the perfectionist in you can't let go of this bug, you can fix it by doing what's known as "adding layout" to the non-floated element, as described in the box on page 307. Add an IE6-only style for that column:

```
* html #mainColumn { height; 1px; }
```

The downside to fixing this bug is that it triggers the bug discussed next. (See what you get for being a perfectionist?)

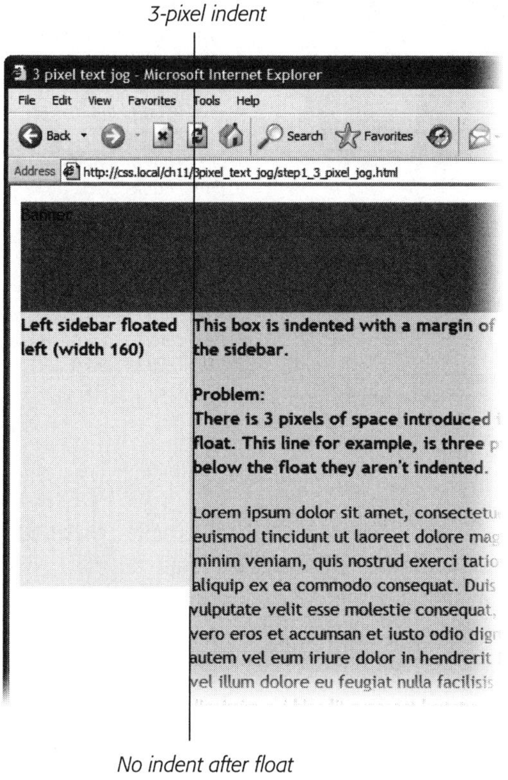

3-pixel indent

No indent after float

Figure 11-16:
On this page, the left-hand sidebar is floated left, while the central column isn't floated at all. A left margin on the central column indents it far enough to the left so that it won't wrap around the bottom of the sidebar. (This technique is described on page 284.) Unfortunately, Internet Explorer 6 and earlier also adds a small indent to the text in the non-floated column.

• **The non-floated column has a set width or height.** When the column next to the float has a set layout dimension (like *height* in the previous example), another 3-pixel error appears—a small gap between the two columns (Figure 11-17, left). This bug is more serious than the one in Figure 11-16, since this 3-pixel gap can force the second column to drop below the floated element (Figure 11-17, right).

The solution to this problem is two-fold. First, you must eliminate the left margin of the non-floated column (but for IE 6 and earlier only):

```
* html #mainColumn { margin-left: 0; }
```

Then, you must set the right margin for the floated column to *-3* pixels. This pulls the non-floated column back into position:

```
* html #sidebar { margin-right: -3px; }
```

In any normal browser, these styles make no sense. Some determined CSS experts (with time on their hands, apparently) came up with them to make IE behave. For more info on this phenomenon, check out *www. positioniseverything.net/explorer/threepxtest.html.*

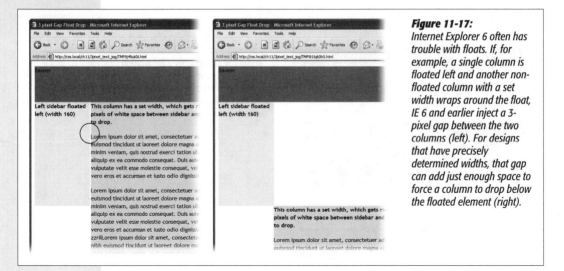

Figure 11-17:
Internet Explorer 6 often has trouble with floats. If, for example, a single column is floated left and another non-floated column with a set width wraps around the float, IE 6 and earlier inject a 3-pixel gap between the two columns (left). For designs that have precisely determined widths, that gap can add just enough space to force a column to drop below the floated element (right).

Another option is to float *all* of the columns. In the examples pictured in Figure 11-16 and Figure 11-17, removing any left margins from the non-floated column and floating it either left or right eliminates *both* 3-pixel problems:

```
#mainColumn {
    float: left;
}
```

This solution seems quick, but it adds a little more complexity, since you have to manage yet another float in the design.

Other IE Problems

A few more bugs plague float-based layouts in Internet Explorer 6. Many of them are so rare you may *never* come across them in your Web design projects. But just in case, here are a couple of weird things that can happen when viewing a page in IE 6 or earlier.

- **If the bottom part of a floated element just disappears,** it may be the *guillotine bug.* For information on the cause and solution (which fortunately has nothing to do with sharp, dangerous objects), visit *www.positioniseverything.net/explorer/guillotine.html.*

- **Content inside a floated element doesn't appear,** but sometimes reappears if you resize the browser window or scroll. This oddity is aptly called the *peek-a-boo bug.* Learn about it at *www.positioniseverything.net/explorer/peekaboo.html.*

POWER USERS' CLINIC

Got Layout?

As you've probably gathered by now, Internet Explorer for Windows has a long history of browser bugs. Some basic CSS that looks fine in Firefox or Safari crumbles in Internet Explorer 6. As it turns out, you can fix many IE bugs by switching on a special IE-only property known as *layout*. This isn't a CSS concept, nor does it have anything to do with the rules of HTML. It's just a concept built into Internet Explorer by the engineers who created IE (who, rumor has it, were under mind control by extraterrestrial beings at the time, which explains a *lot*). As far as IE is concerned, each page element either has layout or it doesn't.

In IE, floats, list items, and absolutely positioned elements display differently depending on whether or not they have layout. In the last chapter (page 246), you saw how IE 6 doesn't make the entire area of a link clickable when the link is set to display as a block. You can fix that problem by creating an IE-only style that sets the links to 1 pixel tall:

```
* html a .nav a { height: 1px; }
```

The point of that style isn't to make the links 1 pixel tall: IE 6 ignores the height specification anyway and expands the links to the height of the links' content. But the *height* property triggers layout in IE 6. For reasons known only to Microsoft (and the extraterrestrials), switching on layout makes IE treat the entire area of block-level links as clickable.

Height isn't the only property that switches on layout in IE. Several other CSS properties also give an element layout: *position: absolute; float: left; float: right; display: inline-table;* any *width* value, any *height* value, and an IE-only property called *zoom*. You can add that last property to a style like this: *zoom: 1;*. *Zoom* doesn't affect how the element looks in any other browser, and if you use *zoom: 1*, all it does in IE is give the element layout. The downside of using this property is that it isn't valid CSS, so it won't pass W3C validation (page 32).

Internet Explorer 7 (as of this writing) still has a few bugs you have to fix by adding layout. Any of the properties listed above add layout to an element in IE 7, as will the following: *min-width, max-width, min-height,* and *max-height* (see page 289).

Throughout this book, you use layout to overcome many different IE bugs. For an in-depth (so deep, you may need a life preserver) discussion of the topic, go to *www.satzansatz.de/cssd/onhavinglayout.html.* Microsoft offers a friendly introduction at *http://msdn.microsoft.com/library/default.asp?url=/library/en-us/IETechCol/cols/dnexpie/expie20050831.asp.*

Tutorial: Multiple Column Layouts

In this tutorial, you'll create a multi-column, float-based layout. In the process, you'll create two- and three-column liquid designs, as well as a fixed-width design.

To get started, download the tutorial files located on this book's companion Web site at *www.sawmac.com/css/*. Click the tutorial link and download the files. All the files are in a ZIP archive, so you need to unzip them first. (Find detailed instructions on the Web site.) The files for this tutorial are in the *chapter_11 → layout1* folder.

Structuring the HTML

The first step in creating a CSS-based layout is identifying the different layout elements on the page. You do this by wrapping chunks of HTML inside of <div> tags, each of which represents a different part of the page.

---

1. **Open the *start.html* file in a text editor, and click in the empty line following the HTML comment:** `<!--sidebar goes here-->`

   As you can see, some of the HTML work is already done: currently there's a banner and footer. Before you create any styles, you need to add the structure and content for the page. You'll next add the <div> tag for the left sidebar.

2. **Add an opening <div> for the sidebar:** *<div id="sidebar">*. **Then press Enter (Return) to create a new, empty line.**

   If you were creating a Web page from scratch, at this point you'd add the HTML for the page's sidebar, perhaps a list of articles on the site, links to related Web sites, and so on. In this case, the HTML's already taken care of. The code for an unordered list of links is waiting for you in another file. You just need to copy and paste it into this page.

3. **Open the file *sidebar.txt*, copy all of the contents, and then return to the *start. html* file. Paste the HTML after the <div> tag you created in step 2.**

   The HTML for the sidebar is nearly complete. You just need to close the <div> tag.

4. **Immediately after the code you just pasted, type** *</div>*.

   You've just added the first layout element on the page. In a little bit you'll style this HTML so that it looks like a column. But first, you need to add some more content.

5. **Place your cursor in the empty line after this HTML comment:** *<!--main content goes here-->*, **and then type** *<div id="main">*.

   This div holds the page's main content. You'll get that HTML from another file, too.

6. **Open the file *story.txt*, copy all of the contents, return to the *start.html* file, and then paste the code after the <div> tag you just created. Add the closing </ div> tag exactly as in step 4.**

   That's all the HTML you need to create your design. Now it's time to turn your attention to building the CSS.

Creating the Layout Styles

If you preview the page now, you'll see that the banner, navigation buttons and text are already styled. That's because this page has an external style sheet attached to it with some basic formatting. Next, you'll create styles to format the page's columns.

1. **In your text editor, click in the empty space directly before the closing </head> tag near the top of the file. Type** *<style type="text/css">*, **and then hit Enter (Return).**

This code is the opening tag for an internal style sheet. As with the other tutorials in this book, you'll create your styles in an internal style sheet, which makes creating and testing your styles easier. Once you're done, you should move the styles into an external style sheet, as described on page 31.

2. **Add a style for the sidebar element, like so:**

```
#sidebar {
    float: left;
    width: 160px;
    margin-top: 10px;
}
```

This class style floats the sidebar div to the left of the page, gives it a width of 160 pixels, and adds a bit of space to separate the sidebar from the banner above. The *width* property is important in this style: Unless you're floating an image that has a set width, you should always set a width for a floated element. Otherwise, the browser sets the width based on the content inside the float, leading to inconsistent results.

3. **Press Enter (Return), and then type** *</style>* **to finish the internal style sheet. Preview the page in a Web browser.**

The sidebar now forms a left-hand column…sort of. When the text in the main column reaches the bottom of the sidebar, it wraps around the bottom of the sidebar, as shown in Figure 11-18. While that's normally how floats work, it's not what you want in this case. To make the main body text appear like a column of its own, you have to add enough left margin to indent the main text beyond the right edge of the sidebar.

4. **Create a style for the second column:**

```
#main {
    margin-left: 180px;
}
```

Since the sidebar is 160 pixels wide, a margin of 180 pixels indents the main content an additional 20 pixels, creating a gutter between the two columns. This additional white space not only makes the text easier to read, but also makes the page look better.

Preview the page now and you'll see you've got yourself a two-column layout.

Adding Another Column

As you can see, a two-column design isn't hard. Adding a third column so you can treat your visitors to even more information isn't any harder. In fact, the steps are quite similar to the previous part of this tutorial.

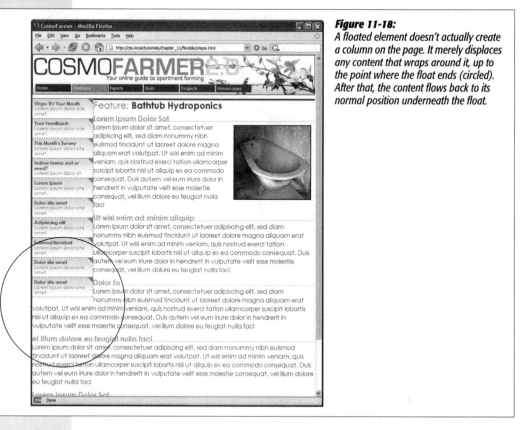

Figure 11-18:
A floated element doesn't actually create a column on the page. It merely displaces any content that wraps around it, up to the point where the float ends (circled). After that, the content flows back to its normal position underneath the float.

1. Open the file *secondary.txt*. Copy all the HTML from that file, and then return to the *start.html* file.

   The HTML for this next column goes between the page's two divs.

2. Click just after the closing </div> for the sidebar element (right before the HTML comment *<!--main content goes here-->*). Then press Enter (Return) to create an empty line.

   It's often hard to find the right closing </div> when you use a lot of divs to structure a page. That's why HTML comments—like this one—can really help you identify and keep track of the HTML in your page.

3. Type *<div id="secondary">*, press Enter (Return), and then paste the HTML you copied in step 1. Hit Enter (Return) again, and then type *</div>*.

   When you close the <div> tag, you've completed the HTML for the page's third column. Start styling it next.

4. Below the *#main* style you created in step 4 on page 309, add a new style to the internal style sheet:

```
#secondary {
    float: right;
```

```
    width: 180px;
}
```

You're floating this column to the right side of the page to flank the main content with sidebars on either side. The problem with the first column (Figure 11-18) appears here as well—the main content wraps underneath this new sidebar. To fix it, add a right margin to the *#main* style.

5. **Edit the *#main* style so that it looks like this:**

```
#main {
    margin-left: 180px;
    margin-right: 200px;
}
```

Now the page is a full, 3-column layout. Test the page in a browser. When you resize the window, you'll see that the page adjusts to fit the window.

Tip: In this design, the left and right sidebars are a fixed width, so even when you make the browser window much larger, they stay the same size. You can make those columns change width as well, simply by setting their widths to percentage values and changing the *#main* style's left and right margins to percentages as well.

That new column you just added doesn't look very good, so polish it up in the next section.

Adding a "Faux Column"

The right hand sidebar doesn't stand out enough visually. You'll fix that with a dark background color and some text formatting.

1. **Edit the *#secondary* style you created earlier by adding a dark background color. The complete style should look like this:**

```
#secondary {
    float: right;
    width: 180px;
    background-color: #294E56;
}
```

Now the right sidebar's background color really stands out, but the text, which is also dark, doesn't.

2. **Add another style to the bottom of the internal style sheet to make all the text in this sidebar white:**

```
#secondary * {
    color: #FFF;
}
```

This style takes advantage of the "universal selector" (page 54). It essentially says "set the text color for every tag inside *#secondary* to white." It's a short-hand way of creating what would normally be a very long group selector: *#secondary h1, #secondary h2, #secondary p, #secondary a*, and so on.

Next, you'll create a few styles to help adjust the font size, margins, and other display properties of the text.

3. **Add the following styles to the internal style sheet:**

```
#secondary h3 {
    font-size: 1.5em;
    background: #73AFB7;
    padding: 3px 5px 3px 10px;
}
#secondary h4 {
    font-size: 1.2em;
    margin: 10px 10px 5px 10px;
}
#secondary p {
    font-size: 1.2em;
    margin: 3px 10px 10px 10px;
    line-height: 110%;
}
```

Each of these styles adjusts the font size for the different text tags used in the sidebar. In addition, you've added a background color to the headings that introduce each section in the sidebar. If you preview the page in a Web browser now, it should look like Figure 11-19.

***

Note: The *#secondary* style—the one that defines the layout of this sidebar—has no padding added. But the text doesn't bump right up to the edges of the sidebar because the other styles add space between the edges of the sidebar and the text inside. Specifically, the padding in the *h3* style and the margins in the *h4* and *p* styles add the needed space, which has two benefits. First, you avoid IE 5's box model problem, so the width of the sidebar is the same in that browser as others (see page 150). Also, without padding on the sidebar, you can make the background color of the main headers in the sidebar ("In the News" and "Around the Web") span the entire width of the sidebar.

***

The sidebar presents one more hurdle—its background color stops short of the bottom of the page. Things would look much better if that dark color extended all the way down the window's right side.

4. **In the *#secondary* style, remove the background declaration *background-color: #294E56;*.**

You want that color behind the right sidebar, but the *background-color* property isn't the way to go. Instead, you need to put a graphic in the background of the page itself and tile it vertically, so no matter how tall the page gets, the background image stays visible.

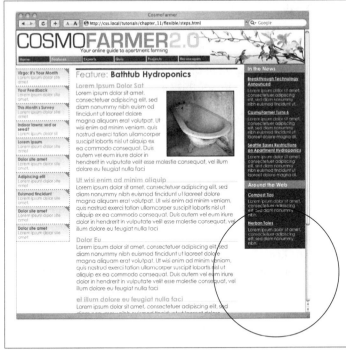

Figure 11-19:
One of the biggest challenges with CSS layouts is making columns of equal height. In this example, the right-hand sidebar has a dark background that would look much better if it extended down the page. However, since there's more content in the middle section of the page, the right sidebar's background stops short (circled). Using a background image (instead of the background-color property) is the answer.

5. **Add a *body* tag style to the top of the internal style sheet:**

```
body {
    background: url(images/bg/bg_column.gif) repeat-y right top;
}
```

The *bg_column.gif* file is a simple, solid color graphic that's the same width as the right sidebar. The *repeat-y* property makes the graphic tile up and down only, and the *right* value places the graphic on the right edge of the page.

Fixing the Width

Currently, the page is a liquid design (page 280), meaning that it expands to fill the entire width of the browser window. But say you'd rather have the page stay the same width all the time—because you hate how it looks on cinema display monitors, or you don't like what happens to the design when the browser window is shrunk too small. Changing a liquid design to a fixed-width design is easy. Start by adding a little more HTML.

1. **Directly after the opening <body> tag (*<body id="feature">*) add a new <div> tag:**

```
<div id="wrapper">
```

You're wrapping the entire page inside a div, which you'll use to control the page's width. You need to make sure that tag's closed.

2. Add the closing </div> just before the closing </body> tag:

```
</div>
</body>
```

Now that there's a div surrounding all of the content on this page, you can control the page's width by setting a width for this tag.

3. **Just below the body tag style you created earlier, add a style that defines a set width for the new div:**

```
#wrapper {
    width: 760px;
}
```

Preview the page in a browser, and you'll see that the banner, footer, and other content on the page stays locked at 760 pixels. However, the image that adds the background to the right sidebar jumps around depending on the width of the browser window. That's because that graphic is aligned in relation to the right edge of the window. To fix this, just place the graphic as a background on the *#wrapper* instead.

4. **Delete the** *body* **style you created in step 5 on page 313. Add the background declaration to the** *#wrapper* **style, so it looks like this:**

```
#wrapper {
    width: 760px;
    background: url(images/bg/bg_column.gif) repeat-y right top;
}
```

Preview the page in a browser. It should now look like Figure 11-20.

There's a completed version of this tutorial in the *chapter_11_finished/layout1/* folder.

Tutorial: Negative Margin Layout

In this tutorial, you'll explore how to create a multi-column, float-based layout using the negative margin technique discussed on page 287. Download the files as described for the previous tutorial. The files for this tutorial are contained inside the folder named *chapter_11* → *layout2*.

Centering a Layout

Unlike the last exercise, all the HTML is already in place for this page. All you have to do is add CSS to create the layout. There are six major sections to the page, each enclosed in a <div> tag with an ID applied.

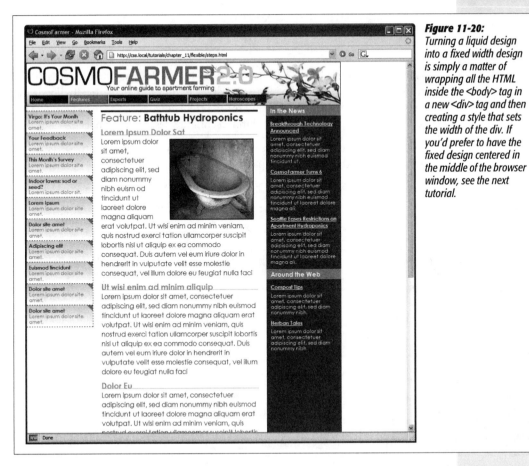

Figure 11-20:
*Turning a liquid design
into a fixed width design
is simply a matter of
wrapping all the HTML
inside the <body> tag in
a new <div> tag and then
creating a style that sets
the width of the div. If
you'd prefer to have the
fixed design centered in
the middle of the browser
window, see the next
tutorial.*

1. **In a text editor, open the** *chapter_11 → layout2 → start.html* **file.**

   Figure 11-21 shows the basic structure of the HTML (left) and the final result
   you're aiming for (right). Currently, the divs just stack one on top of the other,
   because you haven't added any CSS layout—yet.

   Begin by creating a fixed width layout and centering it in the middle of the
   browser window.

2. **In the <head> region of the HTML, place your cursor between the opening
   and closing <style> tags.**

   There's already an external style sheet attached to the page, with most of the
   visual formatting in it. You'll add the layout styles to this internal style sheet,
   which you can always move to an external style sheet later as described on page
   33.

3. **Add a new style for the** *wrapper* **div:**

   ```
   #wrapper {
       border-right: 2px solid #000000;
   ```

```
    border-left: 2px solid #000000;
    background: #FFFFFF url(images/column_bg.png) repeat-y right top;
}
```

These declarations add a border to either side of the page and place a background image in the right side of the div. The image tiles vertically down the page, and provides the background for the right sidebar in the final design. This setup's an example of the faux column technique described on page 297.

Because the wrapper div encloses the other tags on the page, setting its width defines the width for the entire page.

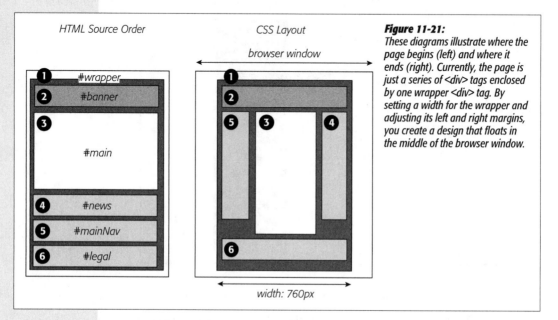

HTML Source Order CSS Layout browser window width: 760px

Figure 11-21:
These diagrams illustrate where the page begins (left) and where it ends (right). Currently, the page is just a series of <div> tags enclosed by one wrapper <div> tag. By setting a width for the wrapper and adjusting its left and right margins, you create a design that floats in the middle of the browser window.

4. Edit the *#wrapper* style you just created. Add a width and left and right margins so the style looks like this:

```
#wrapper {
    width: 760px;
    margin-right: auto;
    margin-left: auto;
    border-right: 2px solid #000000;
    border-left: 2px solid #000000;
    background: #FFFFFF url(images/column_bg.png) repeat-y right top;
}
```

The *width* property sets the overall width of the page content to 760 pixels. To center the wrapper div, set the left and right margins to *auto*. The *auto* value tells the browser that it should calculate the margins automatically. Also, since the value is applied to both left and right margins, the browser should split the difference between the two margins. In other words, the browser adds the same amount of space on either side of the wrapper div, whatever the window's width.

Preview the page now in a Web browser. Resize the browser window, and you'll see that the page stays centered in the middle of the window. But you can still improve on the page's looks.

5. **At the beginning of the internal style sheet, add a new style for the <body> tag:**

```
body {
    margin: 0;
    padding: 0;
    background: #E6E6E6 url(images/page_bg.png) repeat-y center top;
}
```

The first two declarations eliminate any space around the page content, allowing the wrapper div to freely touch the edges of the browser window. The *background* property is where the real fun is. First, it changes the page's background to a sophisticated gray (#E6E6E6). Second, it adds a graphic and tiles it vertically from page top all the way to the bottom. The *center* value places the graphic in the middle of the window. That way, no matter how wide the window, the graphic stays centered (see page 176). The graphic itself is slightly wider than the 760 pixels of the wrapper div, and has a shadow effect on both the right and left sides. This gives the appearance that the wrapper is floating above the page, as shown in Figure 11-22.

Figure 11-22:
Placing an image centered in the background of a page's <body> tag creates the illusion of a drop shadow underneath the page's contents.

There's one more task. When you view the page in Internet Explorer 5 for Windows, you see the page content isn't centered, since that browser doesn't understand the *auto* value you set in step 4. It just ignores those values and leaves the wrapper div aligned against the left edge of the window.

6. Add *text-align: center* to the body style you just created:

```
body {
    margin: 0;
    padding: 0;
    background: #E6E6E6 url(images/page_bg.png) repeat-y center top;
    text-align: center;
}
```

This tricks IE into centering the wrapper div in the middle of the window. Unfortunately, since *text-align* is an inherited property, every paragraph of text is also aligned in the center of the page.

7. Add *text-align: left* to the *#wrapper* style, so that the style looks like this:

```
#wrapper {
    width: 760px;
    margin-right: auto;
    margin-left: auto;
    border-right: 2px solid #000000;
    border-left: 2px solid #000000;
    background: #FFFFFF url(images/column_bg.png) repeat-y right top;
    text-align: left;
}
```

Aligning the text within the *wrapper* div to the left, gets it back into the proper position.

Floating the Columns

Now it's time to create the three columns of this design. In the left diagram of Figure 11-21, notice the HTML for the *main* div containing the page's main content appears *before* the HTML for either the left sidebar with an ID of *mainNav* or right sidebar with an ID of *news*. A couple of factors make this design different from the basic float layout you created in the previous tutorial. First, since the HTML for the *main* div comes first, you have to float it to make the sidebars wrap around either side of it. Second, the *main* div appears in the middle, between the two sidebars. Normally, that kind of arrangement isn't possible. But you'll cleverly use negative margins (page 287) to make it work.

1. Add a style to the internal style sheet for the *main* div:

```
#main {
    float: left;
    width: 419px;
```

```
    padding-left: 10px;
    border-left: 1px dashed #999999;
}
```

So far, this style's pretty basic. It positions the div at the left edge of the wrapper div, sets its width, adds a left border, and adds a little space between the text and the border. You'll position the *news* div next.

2. **Add another style to position the right sidebar:**

```
#news {
    float: right;
    width: 160px;
}
```

Lastly, you need to position the nav sidebar.

3. **Add one more style to the internal style sheet:**

```
#nav {
    float: left;
    width: 160px;
}
```

The page should look like Figure 11-23. Sure enough, there are three side-by-side columns, but they're not in the right order. The large column on the left belongs in the middle.

Figure 11-23:
Normally, the placement of floated elements is completely dependent on the order of their HTML in the source code of the HTML file. The large, main content (left) is first in the source code, so it doesn't appear between the two sidebars. But you can change that with negative margins.

Here's where the negative margins come in. The basic process goes like this: First, you want to add enough left margin to the main column to push it into its final location in the middle of the page. Then, you need to add enough *negative* margin to the navigation sidebar to *pull it over* to the left of the main content area.

4. **In the #*main* style, add *margin-left: 160px*:**

```
#main {
    float: left;
    width: 419px;
    margin-left: 160px;
    padding-left: 10px;
    border-left: 1px dashed #999999;
}
```

Back in step 3, the *nav* div (which is supposed to be the far left column) is 160 pixels, just like you used for the left margin. By indenting the *main* div 160 pixels, you've made room for the *nav* sidebar.

5. **Add a negative left margin to the #*nav* style so that it looks like this:**

```
#nav {
    float: left;
    width: 160px;
    margin-left: -590px;
}
```

Here's the story behind the -590 pixel value: Currently the *nav* div and *main* div are both floated left. But because the *nav* div's HTML comes after that of the *main* div, it can float only as far left as the right edge of the *main* div. In order for the *nav* div to get to the left edge of the wrapper, it has to move all the way from the right edge of the *main* div to the left edge of the wrapper. In other words, it has to travel left the same distance (in pixels) from the left edge of the wrapper to the right edge of the *main* div.

The right edge of the *main* div is the grand total of its width, left and right margins, left and right padding, and left and right border. That is, 160 (left margin) + 10 (left padding) + 1 (left border) + 419 (width) = 590 pixels. So, giving the *nav* div a left margin of –590 pixels moves it over and past the *main* div, and into position.

Preview the page in a Web browser and you'll see something like Figure 11-24. It works if you use Firefox or Safari. It's a different story with Internet Explorer 5 or 6. In those browsers, you'll see a large empty space to the left of the middle column, and no navigation bar anywhere in sight. That's the nasty double margin bug in action (page 302). Because the *main* div is floated left *and* it has a left margin, IE 5 and 6 double the margin, ruining the layout. Luckily, there's an easy fix.

Figure 11-24:
Using negative margins, you can place columns in any order on the page. Doing so requires floating all of the columns, which can cause problems for content that comes after the columns, like the copyright notice (circled). That element tries to wrap around the floats, and in the process it gets crammed into a corner rather than positioned at the bottom of the page. To fix it, add clear: both to the copyright notice's style.

6. Add *display: inline* to the *#main* style:

```
#main {
    display: inline;
    float: left;
    width: 419px;
    margin-left: 160px;
    padding-left: 10px;
    border-left: 1px dashed #999999;
}
```

Now if you preview the page in IE 6, everything works fine (Figure 11-24). But there's still one last glitch in IE 5, which gets the width of the *main* div wrong. Due to IE 5's box model problem, it miscalculates the width of any element that has padding and borders, messing up the display of the columns.

7. **Add an IE-only style to the internal style sheet:**

```
* html #main {
    width: 430px;
    w\idth: 419px;
}
```

This little bit of trickery fools IE 5 into making the *main* div the correct width onscreen, and then tells IE 6 to set that div back to its proper width. (See page 151 for a full explanation of what this style's doing.)

Final Adjustments

The next couple of steps demonstrate how flexible CSS layout really is. First, you'll take care of the copyright notice that should appear at the bottom of the page. Currently, it's caught up in all of that floating stuff. It needs to clear the floats to get into position.

1. **At the end of the internal style sheet, add one last style:**

```
#legal {
    clear: both;
    margin-right: 160px;
    padding: 5px 160px 20px;
    border-top: 1px dashed #999999;
    font-weight: bold;
    color: #666666;
}
```

   This style applies a variety of formatting rules to the copyright notice. The most important is the *clear* declaration, which drops the copyright below all of the floats. The right margin pushes the copyright notice away from the right sidebar, so the top border (also defined in this style) doesn't overlap the background graphic.

   The page is basically done, and as a reward, you get to do one last thing to demonstrate how cool CSS really is. Think you can swap the two sidebars so that the news appears on the left and the navigation on the right? It's easier than it sounds—just a couple of changes to two styles.

2. **Edit the *#nav* style by removing the negative margin and changing its float value from left to right. The finished style should look like this:**

```
#nav {
    float: right;
    width: 160px;
}
```

   The navigation bar moves to the right side. Now move the news to the left.

3. **In the *#news* style, add *margin-left: -590px* and set the float to *left* like this:**

```
#news {
    float: left;
    width: 160px;
    margin-left: -590px;
}
```

Save the page and preview it in a Web browser (Figure 11-25). The columns have swapped with no messy HTML changes. All you did was swap the two styles. If you want to take this a bit further, you can move the background graphic applied to the wrapper from the right to the left, and switch the border that appears on the left edge of the main content div to its right edge so that it butts up against the navigation div.

Figure 11-25:
CSS's flexibility is one of its biggest benefits. By changing just a few CSS styles, you can move elements to completely different areas of a page. In this case, swapping two styles made the left and right sidebars switch position—without any changes to the HTML.

Positioning Elements on a Web Page

When the World Wide Web Consortium introduced *CSS-Positioning,* some designers understandably thought they could make Web pages look just like print documents created in programs like PageMaker, InDesign, or Quark XPress. With just a couple of CSS properties, CSS-Positioning lets you position an element in a precise location on a page—say 100 pixels from the top of the page and 200 pixels from the left edge. The pixel-accurate placement possible with CSS-P (as it was called way back when) seemed to promise that, at last, you could design a page simply by putting a photo here, a headline there, and so on.

Unfortunately, the level of control designers expected from CSS-P never materialized. There have always been differences in how various browsers display CSS positioned elements. But, even more fundamentally, the Web doesn't work like a printed brochure, magazine, or book. Web pages are much more fluid than printed pages. Once a magazine rolls off the press, readers can't change the page size or font size. About the only way they can change the look of the magazine is to spill coffee on it.

Web visitors, on the other hand, can tinker with your handcrafted presentation. They can increase their browsers' font size, potentially making text spill out of precisely placed and sized layout elements. But the news isn't all bad: As long as you don't try to dictate the exact width, height, and position of *every* design element, you'll find CSS's positioning properties powerful and helpful. You can use these properties to make a text caption appear on top of a photo, create multi-column page layouts, place a logo anywhere on the page, and much more.

How Positioning Properties Work

The CSS *position* property lets you control how and where a Web browser displays particular elements. Using *position* you can, for example, place a sidebar anywhere you wish on a page, or make sure a navigation bar at the top of the page stays in place even when visitors scroll down the page. CSS offers four types of positioning:

- **Absolute.** Absolute positioning lets you determine an element's location by specifying a *left, right, top,* or *bottom* position in pixels, ems, or percentages. (See Chapter 6 for more on picking between the different units of measurement.) You can place a box 20 pixels from the top and 200 pixels from the left edge of the page, as shown in Figure 12-1, middle. (More in a moment on how you actually code these instructions.)

  In addition, absolutely positioned elements are completely detached from the flow of the page as determined by the HTML code. In other words, other things on the page don't even know that the absolutely positioned element exists. They can even disappear completely underneath absolutely positioned items, if you're not careful.

Note: Don't try to apply both the *float* property and any type of positioning other than static (explained below) or relative to the same style. *Float* and *absolute* or *fixed* positioning can't work together on the same element.

- **Relative.** A relatively positioned element is placed relative to its current position in the HTML flow. So, for example, setting a top value of 20 pixels and left value of 200 pixels on a relatively positioned headline moves that headline 20 pixels down and 200 pixels from the left *from wherever it would normally appear.*

  Unlike with absolute positioning, other page elements accommodate the old HTML placement of a relatively positioned element. Accordingly, moving an element with relative positioning leaves a "hole" where the element would have been. Look at the dark strip in the bottom image of Figure 12-1. That strip is where the relatively positioned box *would have* appeared, before it was given orders to move. The main benefit of relative positioning isn't to move an element, but to set a new point of reference for absolutely positioned elements that are nested inside it. (More on that brain-bending concept on page 332.)

- **Fixed.** A fixed element is locked into place on the screen. It does the same thing as the *fixed* value for the *background-attachment* property (page 181). When a visitor scrolls the page, fixed elements remain onscreen as paragraphs and headlines, while photos disappear off the top of the browser window.

  Fixed elements are a great way to create a fixed sidebar or replicate the effect of HTML frames, where only a certain portion (frame) of the page scrolls.

- **Static** positioning simply means the content follows the normal top-down flow of HTML (see Figure 12-1, top). Why would you want to assign an element static positioning? The short answer: You probably never will.

CSS: The Missing Manual

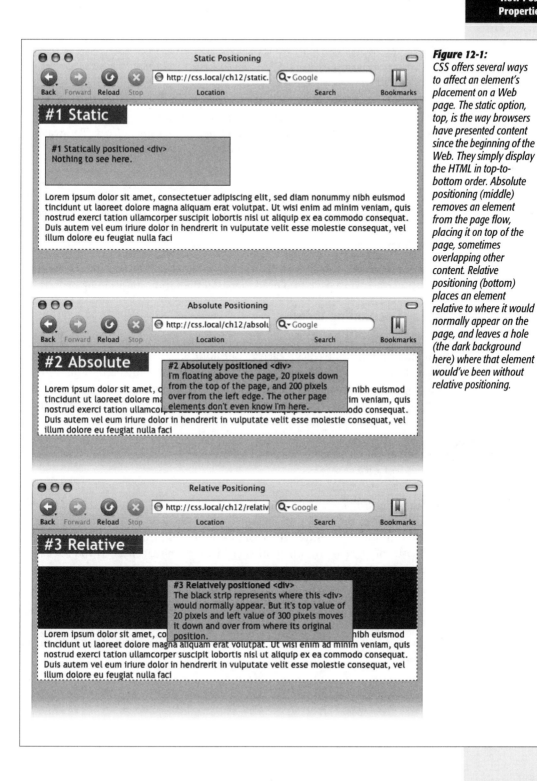

Figure 12-1:
CSS offers several ways to affect an element's placement on a Web page. The static option, top, is the way browsers have presented content since the beginning of the Web. They simply display the HTML in top-to-bottom order. Absolute positioning (middle) removes an element from the page flow, placing it on top of the page, sometimes overlapping other content. Relative positioning (bottom) places an element relative to where it would normally appear on the page, and leaves a hole (the dark background here) where that element would've been without relative positioning.

Note: Internet Explorer 6 (and earlier versions) doesn't understand the *fixed* setting and ignores it. Since IE 6 is still the most popular browser out there, this book doesn't deal much with *fixed* positioning. But you can find a quick overview on page 345.

To change the positioning of any element, simply use the *position* property followed by one of the four keywords: *static, absolute, relative, fixed.* To create an absolutely positioned element, add this property to a style:

```
position: absolute;
```

Static is the normal positioning method, so unless you're overriding a previously created style that already has a position of *absolute, relative* or *fixed,* you won't need to specify that. In addition, static elements don't obey any of the positioning values discussed next.

Setting a positioning value is usually just part of the battle. To actually place an element somewhere on a page, you need to master the various positioning properties.

Setting Positioning Values

The display area of a Web browser window—also called the *viewport*—has top, bottom, left, and right edges. Each of the four edges has a corresponding CSS property: *top, bottom, left,* and *right.* But you don't need to specify values for all four edges. Two are usually enough to place an item on the page. You can, if you want, place an element 10ems from the left edge of the page and 20ems from the top.

Note: Internet Explorer sometimes misplaces elements that are positioned with the *bottom* or *right* properties. See the box on page 335.

To specify the *distance* from an edge of a page to the corresponding edge of the element, use any of the valid CSS measurements—pixels, ems, percentages, and so on. You can also use negative values for positioning like *left: -10px;* to move an element partly off the page (or off another element) for visual effect, as you'll see later in this chapter (page 340).

After the *position* property, you list two properties (*top, bottom, left,* or *right*). If you want the element to take up less than the available width (to make a thin sidebar, for example), then you can set the *width* property. To place a page's banner in an exact position from the top and left edges of the browser window, create a style like this:

```
#banner {
    position: absolute;
    left: 100px;
    top: 50px;
    width: 760px;
}
```

This style places the banner as pictured in Figure 12-2, top.

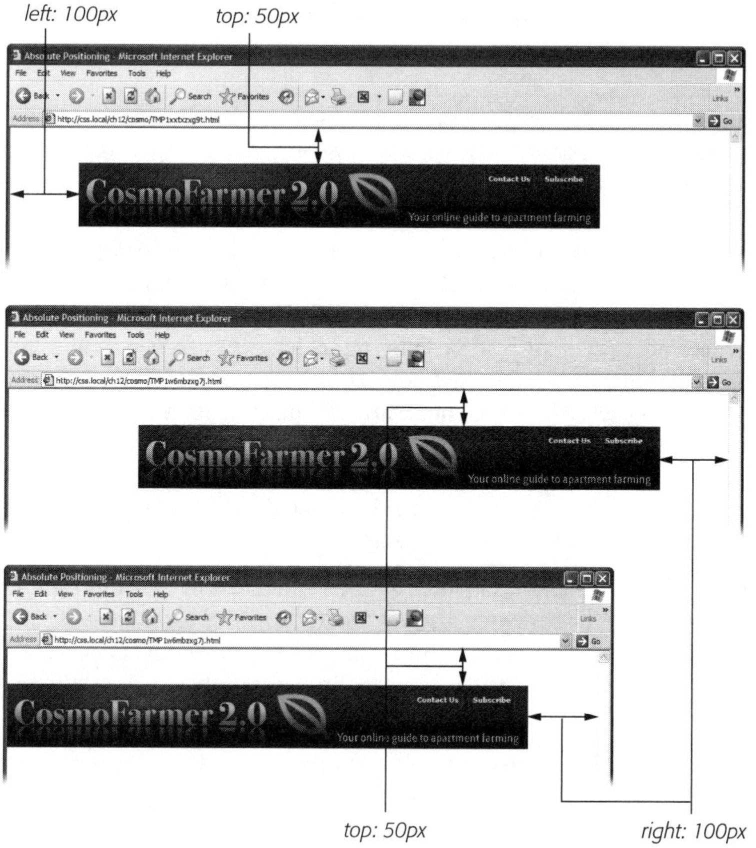

left: 100px　　　　*top: 50px*

Figure 12-2:
One useful aspect of absolute positioning is the ability to place an item relative to the right edge of the browser window (middle). Even when the width of the browser changes, the distance from the right edge of the window to the right edge of the positioned element stays the same (bottom).

top: 50px　　　　　　*right: 100px*

Here's another example: placing an element so it always remains a fixed distance from the right side of the browser. When you use the *right* property, the browser measures the distance from the right edge of the browser window to the right edge of the element (Figure 12-2, middle). To position the banner 100 pixels from the right edge of the window, you'd create the same style as above, but simply replace *left* with *right*:

```
#banner {
    position: absolute;
    right: 100px;
    top: 50px;
    width: 760px;
}
```

Since the position's calculated based on the right edge of the browser window, adjusting the size of the window automatically repositions the banner, as you can see in Figure 12-2, bottom. Although the banner moves, the distance from the right edge of the element to the right edge of the browser window remains the same.

Note: When you use percentages to specify top and bottom distances, the distance is calculated as a percentage of the *width* of the browser window (or, as you'll see in the next section, a positioned parent), not its height. See the box on page 146 for more detail.

Technically, you can specify *both* left and right position properties and let a browser determine the width of the element. Say you want a central block of text positioned 100 pixels from the top of the window and 100 pixels from both the left and right edges of the window. To position the block, you can use an absolutely positioned style that sets the *top, left,* and *right* properties to 100 pixels. In a browser window, the left edge of the box starts 100 pixels from the left edge of the window and the right edge extends to 100 pixels from the right edge (Figure 12-3, top). The exact width of the box, then, depends on how wide the browser window is. A wider window makes a wider box; a thinner window, a thinner box. The left and right positions, however, remain the same.

Unfortunately, though, Internet Explorer 6 (and earlier) doesn't get this right (see Figure 12-3, bottom). That browser displays the left position correctly, but simply ignores any right value. So until IE 6 isn't around anymore, you're better off sticking with either *left* or *right* and using the *width* property to specify the width of an absolutely positioned element.

The *width* and *height* properties, which you learned about in Chapter 7, work exactly the same way for positioned elements. To place a 50 x 50 pixel gray box in the top-right corner of the browser window, create this style:

```
.box {
    position: absolute;
    right: 0;
    top: 0;
    width: 50px;
    height: 50px;
    background-color: #333;
}
```

The same caveat mentioned on page 148 applies here as well: Be careful with setting heights on elements. Unless you're styling a graphic with a set height, you can't be sure how tall any given element will be on a page. You might define a sidebar to be 200 pixels tall, but if you end up adding enough words and pictures to make the sidebar taller than 200 pixels, then you end up with content spilling out of the sidebar. Even if you're sure the content fits, a visitor can always pump up the size of her browser's font, creating text that's large enough to spill out of the box.

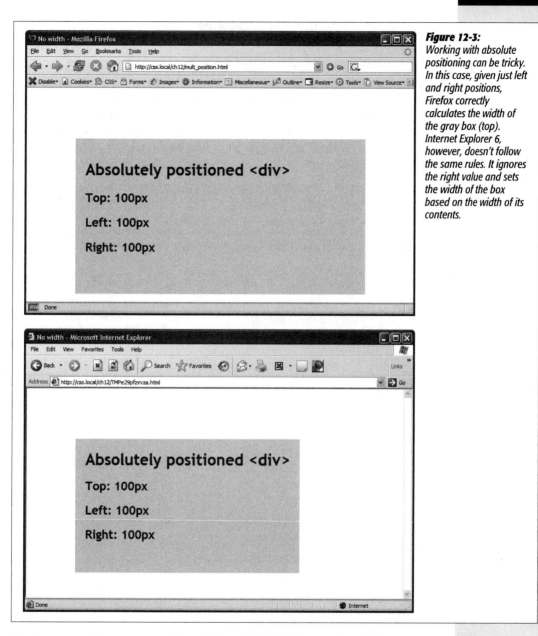

Figure 12-3:
*Working with absolute
positioning can be tricky.
In this case, given just left
and right positions,
Firefox correctly
calculates the width of
the gray box (top).
Internet Explorer 6,
however, doesn't follow
the same rules. It ignores
the right value and sets
the width of the box
based on the width of its
contents.*

Furthermore, when you specify a width and height in a style and the contents inside the styled element are wider or taller, strange things can happen. (See the box on page 148 for a discussion of how to use the CSS *overflow* property to control this situation.)

When Absolute Positioning Is Relative

So far, this chapter has talked about positioning an element in an exact location in the browser window. However, absolute positioning doesn't always work that way. In fact, an absolutely positioned element is actually placed *relative* to the boundaries of its closest positioned ancestor. Simply put, if you've already created an element with absolute positioning (say a <div> tag that appears 100 pixels down from the top of the browser window), then any absolutely positioned elements with HTML *inside* that <div> tag are positioned relative to the div's top, bottom, left, and right edges.

Note: If all this talk of parents and ancestors doesn't ring a bell, then turn to page 50 for a refresher.

In the top image of Figure 12-4, the light grey box is absolutely positioned 5ems from the top and left edges of the browser window.

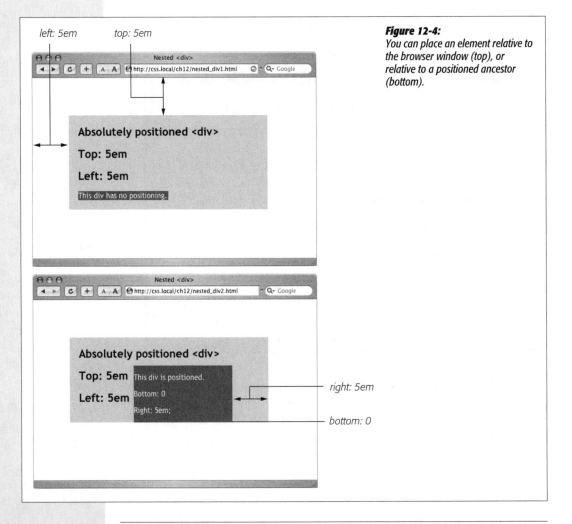

Figure 12-4:
You can place an element relative to the browser window (top), or relative to a positioned ancestor (bottom).

There's also a <div> tag nested inside that box. Applying absolute positioning to that <div> positions it *relative to its absolutely positioned parent*. Setting a *bottom* position of *0* doesn't put the box at the bottom of the screen; it places the box at the bottom of its parent. Likewise, a *right* position for that nested <div> refers to the right of the edge of its parent (Figure 12-4, bottom).

Whenever you use absolute positioning to place an element on the page, the exact position depends upon the positioning of any other tags the styled element is nested in. Here are the rules in a nutshell:

• **A tag is positioned relative to the browser window** if it has an absolute position *and* it's not inside any other tag that has absolute, relative, or fixed positioning applied to it.

• **A tag is positioned relative to the edges of another element** if it's inside another tag with absolute, relative, or fixed positioning.

When (and Where) to Use Relative Positioning

You get one big benefit from placing an element relative to another tag: If that tag moves, the positioned element moves along with it. Say you place an image inside an <h1> tag and you want the image to appear on the right edge of that <h1> tag. If you simply position the image in an exact spot in the browser window on the left edge of the <h1> tag, you're taking your chances. If the <h1> moves, the absolutely positioned image stays glued to its assigned spot. Instead, what you want to do is position the image relative to the <h1> tag, so that when the headline moves, the image moves with it (bottom two images in Figure 12-5).

Note: Use the *background-image* property (see page 172) to place an image into the background of an <h1> tag. But if the graphic's taller than the <h1> tag, or you want the graphic to appear *outside* the boundaries of the headline (see the example third from the top in Figure 12-5), then use the *relative* positioning technique described here.

You could use the *position* property's relative value to place the image, but that has drawbacks, too. When you set an element's position to relative and then place it— maybe using the left and top properties—the element moves the set amount from where it would normally appear in the flow of the HTML. In other words, it moves relative to its current position. In the process, it leaves a big hole where it would've been if you hadn't positioned it at all (Figure 12-1, bottom). Usually that's not what you want.

A better way to use relative positioning is to create a new positioning context for nested tags. For instance, the <h1> tag in the example at the beginning of this section is an ancestor of the <img> tag inside it. By setting the position of the <h1> tag to *relative*, any absolute positioning you apply to the <img> tag is relative to

Figure 12-5:
Top: A graphical button (circled) is placed inside an <h1> tag.

Second from top: Adding absolute positioning to the button—right: -35px; top: -35px;—moves it outside of the <h1> tag area and places it in the top-right corner of the browser window (circled). (In fact, it's placed a little outside of the browser window thanks to the negative positioning values.)

Third from top: Adding position: relative to the <h1> creates a new positioning context for the <img> tag. The same top and right values move the <img> tag to the <h1> tag's top-right corner.

Bottom: When you move the heading down the page, the graphic goes along for the ride.

the four edges of the <h1> tag, not the browser window. Here's what the CSS looks like:

```
h1 { position: relative; }
h1 img {
    position: absolute;
    top: 0;
    right: 0;
}
```

Setting the image's *top* and *right* properties to *0* places the image in the upper-right corner of the headline—not the browser window.

In CSS, the term *relative* doesn't exactly mean the same thing as in the real world. After all, if you want to place the <img> tag relative to the <h1> tag, your first instinct may be to set the image's position to relative. In fact, the item that you want to position—the image—gets an *absolute* position, while the element you want to position the element *relative to*—the headline—gets a setting of relative. Think of the relative value as meaning "relative to me." When you apply relative positioning to a tag, it means "all positioned elements inside of me should be positioned relative to my location."

Note: Because you'll often use relative positioning merely to set up a new positioning context for nested tags, you don't even need to use the left, top, bottom, or right settings with it. The <h1> tag has *position: relative*, but no left, top, right, or bottom values.

BROWSER BUG

IE Forgets Its Place

Sometimes, you'll use the *bottom* and *right* positioning properties to place something at a page's lower-right corner or to put something in a low corner of another element. Say you want to place a Contact Us link in the lower-left corner of a banner. If the style for the banner has either absolute or relative positioning and you position the link absolutely, then most browsers position the link relative to the banner's edges, as they should.

But not Internet Explorer 6 and earlier. Seemingly straightforward properties like *bottom* and *right* can confound this ornery browser. IE sometimes continues to use the bottom and right edges of the Web page as a reference, so you'll end up with a positioned element way lower or further to the right than you expected.

Like most other IE bugs, this one's been fixed in Internet Explorer 7.

The fix is to give the containing element (the element you want to position something *relative* to, like the banner in this example) a special IE-only property known as *layout*.

If you use the *bottom* or *right* properties on an absolutely positioned element, and IE places that element in a different location than other browsers, turn to page 307 in Chapter 11 and apply one of the solutions described there. You'll see examples of this problem (and its solution) throughout this chapter.

Stacking Elements

As you can see in Figure 12-6, absolutely positioned elements sit "above" your Web page, and can even reside on top of (or underneath) other positioned elements. This stacking of elements takes place on what's called the *z-index*. If you're familiar with the concept of layers in Photoshop, Fireworks, or Adobe InDesign, then you know how the z-index works: It represents the order in which positioned elements are stacked on top of the page.

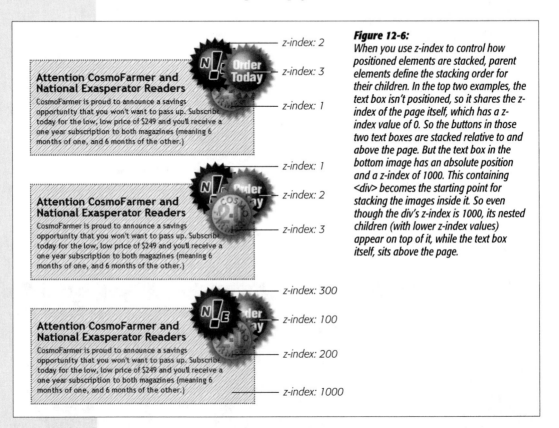

z-index: 2

z-index: 3

z-index: 1

z-index: 1

z-index: 2

z-index: 3

z-index: 300

z-index: 100

z-index: 200

z-index: 1000

Figure 12-6:
When you use z-index to control how positioned elements are stacked, parent elements define the stacking order for their children. In the top two examples, the text box isn't positioned, so it shares the z-index of the page itself, which has a z-index value of 0. So the buttons in those two text boxes are stacked relative to and above the page. But the text box in the bottom image has an absolute position and a z-index of 1000. This containing <div> becomes the starting point for stacking the images inside it. So even though the div's z-index is 1000, its nested children (with lower z-index values) appear on top of it, while the text box itself, sits above the page.

To put it another way, think of a Web page as a piece of paper and an absolutely positioned element like a sticky note. Whenever you add an absolutely positioned element to a page, it's like slapping a sticky note on it. Of course, when you add a sticky note, you run the risk of covering up anything written on the page below.

Normally, the stacking order of positioned elements follows their order in the page's HTML code. On a page with two absolutely positioned <div> tags, the <div> tag that comes second in the HTML appears *above* the other <div>. But you can control the order in which positioned elements stack up using the CSS z-index property. The property gets a numeric value, like this:

```
z-index: 3;
```

The larger the value, the closer to the top of the stack an element appears. Say you have three absolutely positioned images, and parts of each image overlap. The one with the larger z-index appears on top of the others (see Figure 12-6, top). When you change the z-index of one or more images, you change their stacking order (Figure 12-6, middle).

Tip: It's perfectly OK to have gaps in z-index values. In other words, *10, 20, 30* does the exact same things as *1, 2, 3*. In fact, spreading out the numerical values gives you room to insert more items into the stack later. And, when you want to make sure nothing ever appears on top of a positioned element, give it a really large z-index, like this: *z-index: 10000;*.

Hiding Parts of a Page

Another CSS property often used with absolutely positioned elements is *visibility*, which lets you hide part of a page (or show a hidden part). Say you want a label to pop into view over an image when a visitor mouses over it. You make the caption invisible when the page first loads (*visibility: hidden*), and switch to visible (*visibility: visible*) when the mouse moves over it. Figure 12-7 shows an example.

The visibility property's *hidden* value is similar to the *display* property's *none* value (see page 141), but there's a fundamental difference. When you set an element's display property to *none*, it literally disappears from the page without a trace. However, setting the visibility property to hidden prevents the browser from displaying the element's contents, but leaves an empty hole where the element would have been. When applied to absolutely positioned elements which are already removed from the flow of the page, *visibility: hidden* and *display: none* behave identically.

The most common way to switch an element from hidden to displayed and back again is with JavaScript. But you don't have to learn JavaScript programming to use the visibility property (or, for that matter, the display property). You can use the *:hover* pseudo-class (see page 54) to make an invisible element visible.

Tip: For a basic CSS method of adding pop-up tool tips—additional information that appears when someone mouses over a link—check out: *http://psacake.com/web/jl.asp*. You also have many JavaScript options to choose from: solarDreamStudios offers a simple tutorial at *http://solardreamstudios.com/learn/css/qtip*. For a version that's a bit fancier, but still easy to add to a Web page, go to *http://web-graphics.com/mtarchive/001717.php*.

Powerful Positioning Strategies

As explained at the beginning of this chapter, you can run into trouble when you try to use CSS positioning to place *every* element on a page. Because it's impossible to predict all possible combinations of browsers and settings your visitors will use, CSS-controlled positioning works best as a tactical weapon. Use it sparingly to provide exact placement for specific elements.

Figure 12-7:
The visibility property is useful for hiding part of a page that you later want to reveal. The top image shows movie listings. Moving the mouse over one of the images makes a previously invisible pop-up message appear. Programmers usually use JavaScript to create this kind of effect, but you can use the CSS :hover pseudo-class to make an invisible element visible when a visitor mouses over a link.

In this section, you'll learn how to use absolute positioning to add small but visually important details to your page design, how to absolutely position certain layout elements, and how to cement important page elements in place while the rest of the content scrolls.

Positioning Within an Element

One of the most effective ways to use positioning is to place small items relative to other elements on a page. Absolute positioning can simulate the kind of right-alignment you get with floats. In example 1 of Figure 12-8, the date on the top headline is a bit overbearing, but with CSS you can reformat it and move it to the right edge of the bottom headline.

In order to style the date separately from the rest of the headline, you need to enclose the date in an HTML tag. The <span> tag (page 47) is a popular choice for applying a class to a chunk of inline text to style it independently from the rest of a paragraph.

```
<h1><span class="date">Nov. 10, 2006</span> CosmoFarmer Bought By Google</h1>
```

Now it's a matter of creating the styles. First, you need to give the containing element—in this example, the <h1> tag—a relative position value. Then, apply an absolute position to the item you wish to place—the date. Here's the CSS for the bottom image in example 1 of Figure 12-8:

```
h1 {
    position: relative;
    width: 100%;
    border-bottom: 1px dashed #999999;
}
h1 span.date {
    position: absolute;
    bottom: 0;
    right: 0;
    font-size: .5em;
    background-color: #E9E9E9;
    color: black;
    padding: 2px 7px 0 7px;
}
```

Some of the properties listed above, like *border-bottom*, are just for looks. The crucial properties are bolded: *position, bottom,* and *right.* Once you give the headline a relative position, you can position the <span> containing the date in the lower-right corner of the headline by setting both the *bottom* and *right* properties to *0.*

Note: Internet Explorer 6 and earlier can get the placement of an element wrong when you use the *bottom* or *right* properties. In this example, the *width: 100%;* declaration in the *h1* tag style fixes the problem, as discussed in the box on page 335.

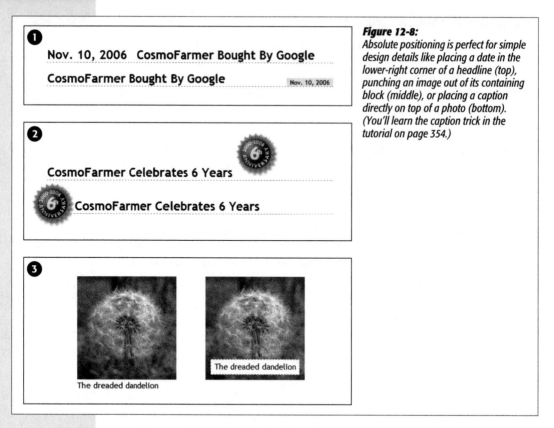

Figure 12-8:
Absolute positioning is perfect for simple design details like placing a date in the lower-right corner of a headline (top), punching an image out of its containing block (middle), or placing a caption directly on top of a photo (bottom). (You'll learn the caption trick in the tutorial on page 354.)

Breaking an Element Out of the Box

You can also use positioning to make an item appear to poke out of another element. In example 2 in Figure 12-8, the top image shows a headline with a graphic. That is, the <img> tag is placed inside the <h1> tag as part of the headline. Using absolute positioning and negative *top* and *left* property values moves the image to the headline's left and pushes it out beyond the top and left edges. Here's the CSS that produces that example:

```
h1 {
    position: relative;
    margin-top: 35px;
    padding-left: 55px;
    border-bottom: 1px dashed #999999;
}
h1 img {
    position: absolute;
    top: -30px;
    left: -30px;
}
```

The basic concept's the same as the previous example, but with a few additions. First, the image's *top* and *left* values are negative, so the graphic actually appears 30 pixels above the top of the headline and 30 pixels to the left of the headline's left edge. Be careful when you use negative values. They can position an element partially (or entirely) off a page, or make the element cover other content on the page. To prevent a negatively positioned element from sticking out of the browser window, add enough margin or padding to either the body element or the enclosing, relatively positioned tag—the <h1> tag in this example. The extra margin provides enough space for the protruding image. In this case, to prevent the image from overlapping any content above the headline, add a significant top margin. The left padding of 55 pixels also moves the text of the headline out from under the absolutely positioned image.

As in the previous example, Internet Explorer's ready to make trouble. What's worse, adding *width: 100%* doesn't even fix things this time. Since there's padding on the <h1> tag, setting its width to 100 percent actually makes the <h1> wider than 100 percent of the page (see page 147 for the reason why). There's a solution, but it uses a non-standard CSS property—*zoom*. Simply add *zoom: 1* to the <h1> tag style:

```
h1 {
    position: relative;
    margin-top: 35px;
    padding-left: 55px;
    border-bottom: 1px dashed #999999;
    zoom: 1;
}
```

Tip: The *zoom* property doesn't cause harm in other browsers, although it prevents your CSS from validating correctly (page 32). You can use Internet Explorer's conditional comments to hide the non-standard property, as discussed on page 399. An even better solution's to create a separate external style sheet just for IE (page 399).

Using CSS Positioning for Page Layout

As mentioned on page 325, trying to position every last element on a page in exact spots in a browser window is usually an exercise in frustration. Using absolute positioning judiciously, you can build many standard Web page layouts (like the ones you saw in the last chapter). This section shows you how to build a three-column, fluid layout using absolute positioning. The page will have a banner, left and right sidebars, a main content area, and a footer for copyright notices.

Note: This section teaches you a generic approach to absolute positioning that you can apply to almost any page layout. For a real hands-on exercise in creating a layout with absolute positioning, turn to the tutorial on page 357.

Whenever you use absolute positioning, keep this rule of thumb firmly in mind: *Don't try to position everything.* To achieve a good layout, you usually have to use absolute positioning on only a couple of page elements.

Here's a simple technique you can use to figure out which elements need positioning. Say you want to build a three-column design, like Figure 12-9, right. First, study how the different sections of the page follow the normal HTML flow, without any CSS positioning (Figure 12-9, left). Then, for each layout element on your page, ask yourself, "Would this be in the right place if I didn't position it at all?"

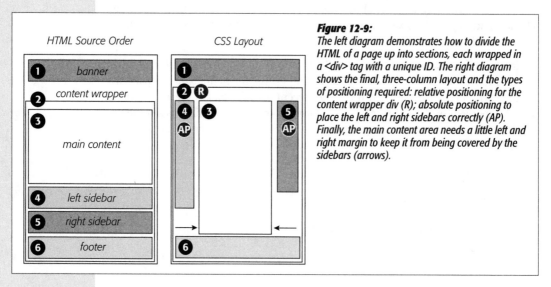

Figure 12-9:
The left diagram demonstrates how to divide the HTML of a page up into sections, each wrapped in a <div> tag with a unique ID. The right diagram shows the final, three-column layout and the types of positioning required: relative positioning for the content wrapper div (R); absolute positioning to place the left and right sidebars correctly (AP). Finally, the main content area needs a little left and right margin to keep it from being covered by the sidebars (arrows).

Here's a walk through the page elements in the left image of Figure 12-9:

- **The banner.** The banner (1) is at the top of the page. That's right where you want it, so it doesn't require absolute positioning. You can use a combination of margins and padding to scoot the content around a little (maybe add some white space above or to the left of the banner).

- **The content wrapper.** This <div> is a special element that holds all other elements on the page (2). Since it holds the page's contents, just ask yourself whether you want the contents to appear below the banner. You do, so you don't need to apply absolute positioning here, either.

Note: This content wrapper's role in life is to help you position page elements—like the sidebars—within it. See step 4 on page 357.

- **The main content.** The main part of the page is also directly under the banner (3). You'll have to indent it on the left and right sides to make room for the sidebars, but you don't need absolute positioning to do that.

- **The left sidebar.** In Figure 12-9, left, it appears way down the page underneath the main content (4). Is that where it should be? Definitely not, so this section needs absolute positioning.

- **The right sidebar.** Instead of on the right as its name implies, this one (5) appears way down the page below the left sidebar. Here again, you need absolute positioning to put this element in its rightful place—under the banner and on the right side of the page.

- **The footer.** In the left image, the footer appears at the bottom of the page (6)— just where you want it, so no need for any special positioning.

Note: It's usually a bad idea to use absolute positioning to place a footer at the bottom of the browser window. If the page's content runs longer than the height of the browser window, then the footer scrolls along with—and rides on top of—other page elements when your visitor scrolls. A better solution is *fixed* positioning, as described on page 345.

Now that you know how to decide where to use CSS positioning in your design, here's an overview of the process for building a three-column layout:

1. **Add <div> tags for each section of the page.**

   These tags let you divide the page's content into different layout containers for the banner, sidebar, and so on. As with float layouts discussed in the previous chapter, you'll add IDs to these container divs so you can create specific CSS styles to format each part of the page (like *<div id="banner">*).

   The left image in Figure 12-9 shows the order in which the different <div> tags for a three-column layout appear in the HTML. One nice thing about absolute positioning is that you don't have to worry (as you do with float layouts) about the order of the <div> tags in the HTML. The HTML for any absolutely positioned element can appear anywhere in the flow of the file—directly after the opening <body> tag, just before the closing </body> tag, or somewhere in between. It's the *positioning* properties that determine where an absolutely positioned element appears onscreen, not its place in the HTML.

2. **Wrap *all* the HTML for the main content, sidebars, and footer in another <div> tag.**

   This <div> (Figure 12-9, #2) gathers all of those content sections in one wrapper. Add an ID to the tag so you can style it (*<div id="contentWrapper">*, for example). This <div> provides a context for positioning the sidebars, as you'll see next.

3. **Give the wrapper <div> a relative position.**

   Use the *position* property and the *relative* value to create a style like this:

   ```
   #contentWrapper { position: relative; }
   ```

Remember, if you don't supply a *top, left, bottom,* or *right* value for a relatively positioned element, then it appears where it normally would—in this case, directly below the banner. The relative position *does* change the positioning of elements *inside* the <div>. Now when you use absolute positioning to place the sidebars—that's the next step—you can set *top* values relative to the wrapper, not the browser window. That way, if you add more content to the banner and make it taller, the wrapper <div> and everything inside it moves neatly down the page. Without the <div>, your sidebars would be placed relative to the top of the browser window and you'd have to adjust their *top* values to accommodate the change.

4. **Apply absolute positioning to the sidebars.**

Since all other content on the page fits fine where it is, you need to position only the sidebars. Since you're positioning the sidebars relative to the wrapper <div> that you set up in step 3, you can simply use *top* and *left* positions of *0* for the left sidebar and *top* and *right* positions of *0* for the right sidebar.

```
#leftSidebar {
    position: absolute;
    left: 0;
    top: 0;
    width: 175px;
}
#rightSidebar {
    position: absolute;
    right: 0;
    top: 0;
    width: 180px;
}
```

Tip: You can also adjust the *top, right,* and *left* values to your liking. If the left sidebar would look a little better indented a bit from the left and top of the wrapper, then change the *left* and *top* values to, say, *10px,* or *.9em,* or whatever value looks good to you.

5. **Specify a width for each sidebar using pixels, ems, or percentages.**

The widths constrain the sidebar boxes. When you don't set a width, the sidebars expand to fill as much space as possible, leaving no room for the page's main content.

6. **Adjust margins on the main content.**

Since the left and right sidebars have absolute positioning, they're removed from the flow of the page. The main content doesn't even know they exist, so it simply goes about its business and flows right under them. But since the main content's in the right place on the page—below the banner—you don't need to reposition it. All you have to do is scoot it in a bit from the left and right edges to clear the sidebars.

To do so, apply left and right margins to the main content <div>. Set the value of each margin to equal or greater than the sidebar's width:

```
#mainContent {
    margin-left: 185px;
    margin-right: 190px;
}
```

In this code, the margins are slightly larger than the widths of each sidebar. It's usually a good idea to increase the margins a little so that there's some visual space between the different elements of the page.

Handsome though it is, this layout has an Achilles heel. Whenever you use absolutely positioned columns (like these sidebars), the columns can potentially grow to cover up part of a footer or other lower HTML elements (see Figure 12-10, top right and bottom). Unlike with float-based layouts, where you can clear an element and force it to appear below a floated column, CSS gives you no way to clear the bottom of a positioned column. The best you can do is find a workaround, as in the next step.

7. **If necessary, add margins to the footer to prevent the sidebars from covering it up.**

Your other option: just make sure that any absolutely positioned columns are *never* taller than the main content. When the main content's long enough, it pushes the footer down below the columns and you avoid the problem.

Tip: If you like to live on the edge of Web innovation, you can try a JavaScript solution to this problem: *www.shauninman.com/plete/2006/05/clearance-position-inline-absolute.php*.

You can modify this basic page layout technique in any number of ways. Remove the right sidebar and eliminate the *right-margin* on the main content <div>, and you've got a two-column layout. Or eliminate the left sidebar instead to create a two-column layout, but with the thinner column on the right. You can also use this basic design in a fixed-width layout. Just set a width for the banner, and a width for the content wrapper <div>, like this:

```
#banner, #contentWrapper { width: 760px; }
```

Creating CSS-Style Frames Using Fixed Positioning

Since most Web pages are longer than one screen, you often want to keep some page element constantly visible—like a navigation panel, search box, or your site logo. HTML frames were once the only way to keep important fixtures handy as other content scrolled out of sight. But HTML frames have major drawbacks. Since each frame contains a separate Web page file, you have to create several HTML files to make one complete Web page (called a *frameset*). Not only are framesets time-consuming for the designer, they also make your site hard for search engines

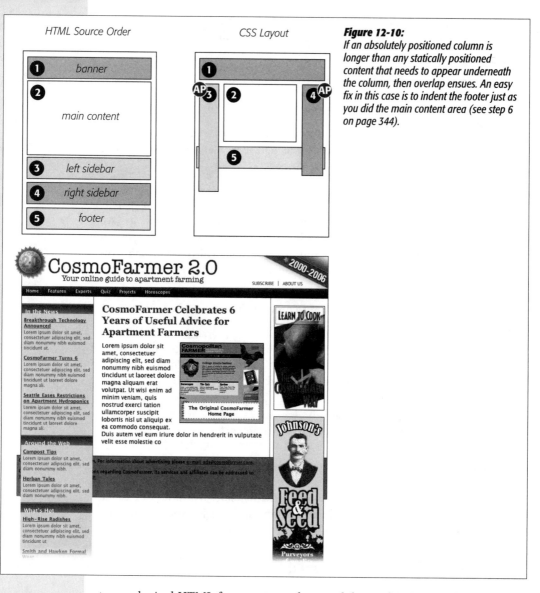

HTML Source Order

CSS Layout

Figure 12-10:
If an absolutely positioned column is longer than any statically positioned content that needs to appear underneath the column, then overlap ensues. An easy fix in this case is to indent the footer just as you did the main content area (see step 6 on page 344).

to search. And HTML framesets can also wreak havoc for visitors who use screen readers due to vision problems, or who want to print pages from your site.

Nevertheless, the idea behind frames is still useful, so CSS offers a positioning value that lets you achieve the visual appearance of frames with less work. You can see a page created using the *fixed* value in Figure 12-11.

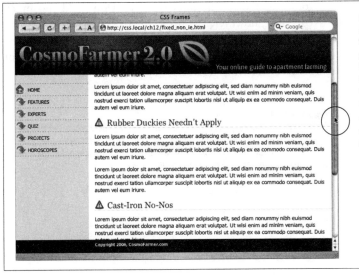

Figure 12-11:
*Revisit the Web of yesteryear, but with
a lot less code. Using the position
property's fixed value, you can emulate
the look of HTML frames by fixing
some elements in place, but still letting
visitors scroll through the content of a
very long Web page. The scrollbar
(circled) moves only the large text
area; the top and bottom banners and
the sidebar stay fixed.*

Note: As mentioned on page 328, fixed positioning doesn't work with Internet Explorer 6 or earlier. However, with just a little extra CSS (described in step 5 on page 349), you can make the page look fine in IE 6
(although the "fixed" elements end up scrolling along with everything else). And since Internet Explorer 7
does support fixed positioning, it's only a matter of time before you can use this technique and get similar
results for all of your site's visitors.

Fixed positioning works much like absolute positioning in that you use the *left,
top, right,* or *bottom* properties to place the element. Also like absolutely positioned elements, fixed positioning removes an element from the flow of the
HTML. It floats above other parts of the page, which simply ignore it.

Here's how you can build the kind of page pictured in Figure 12-11, which has a
fixed banner, sidebar and footer, and a scrollable main content area:

1. **Add <div> tags with ID attributes for each section of the page.**

   You can have four main <div> tags with IDs like *banner, sidebar, main,* and
   footer (Figure 12-12). The order in which you place these tags in the HTML
   doesn't matter. Like absolute positioning, fixed positioning lets you place elements on a page regardless of their HTML order.

Note: One exception: In order for the page to look normal for Internet Explorer 6 folks, the HTML for the
footer should appear *below* the HTML for the main content area, as you'll see in step 5.

2. **Add your material to each <div>.**

   In general, use the fixed divs for stuff that a visitor should always have access to
   in the areas you wish to be locked in place. In this example, the banner, sidebar,
   and footer contain the site logo, global site navigation, and copyright notices.

The main content goes into the remaining <div> tag. Don't add too much information to a fixed <div>, however. If a fixed sidebar is taller than the visitor's browser window, he won't be able to see the entire sidebar. And since fixed elements don't scroll, there'll be no way (short of buying a bigger monitor) for that visitor to see the sidebar content that doesn't fit in his browser window.

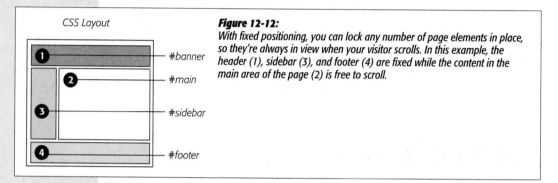

CSS Layout

Figure 12-12:
With fixed positioning, you can lock any number of page elements in place, so they're always in view when your visitor scrolls. In this example, the header (1), sidebar (3), and footer (4) are fixed while the content in the main area of the page (2) is free to scroll.

3. **Create styles for all fixed elements.**

   The left, right, top, and bottom values are relative to the browser window, so just determine where on the screen you'd like them to go and plug in the values. Specify a width for the elements as well.

Note: Unlike absolute positioning, fixed positioning is *always* relative to the browser window, even when an element with fixed positioning is placed inside another tag with relative or absolute positioning.

The styles to position the elements numbered 1, 3, and 4 in Figure 12-12 look like this:

```
#banner {
    position: fixed;
    left: 0;
    top: 0;
    width: 100%
}
#sidebar {
    position: fixed;
    left: 0;
    top: 110px;
    width: 175px;
}
#footer {
    position: fixed;
    bottom: 0;
    left: 0;
    width: 100%;
}
```

4. **Create the style for the scrollable content area.**

Since fixed positioning elements are removed from the flow of the HTML, other tags on the page have no idea the fixed position elements are there. So, the <div> tag with the page's main content, for example, appears underneath the fixed items. The main task for this style is to use margins to move the contents clear of those areas. (The concept is the same as for absolutely positioned layouts, as discussed on page 344.)

```
#main {
    margin-left: 190px;
    margin-top: 110px;
}
```

5. **Fix the layout for Internet Explorer 6 and earlier.**

IE 6 doesn't understand fixed positioning. It treats fixed elements like *static* elements, in that it doesn't try to place them in exact spots on the page. Depending on how you've ordered your HTML, in IE 6 your page may just look weird with big margins between the banner and sidebar, or worse—the navigation bar and banner may end up *below* the main content.

The trick is to tell IE 6 to treat the fixed elements like absolutely positioned elements, which takes those elements out of the flow of the page and places them in their rightful places in the browser window.

```
* html #banner { position: absolute; }
* html #sidebar { position: absolute; }
```

Note: These styles use the * *html hack* to hide their properties from browsers other than IE 6 and earlier (page 152). You can also use IE's conditional comments (page 399).

You'll notice that the *#footer* style isn't listed. You don't want to position the footer absolutely—otherwise it'll travel up the browser window when scrolled, sitting directly on top of the other scrolling content.

In this case, it's best to have the footer appear at the bottom of the page and scroll up into view, just as any un-positioned footer would. (That's why, as mentioned in step 1, you should put the HTML for the footer below the HTML for the main content so it appears at the bottom of the page in IE 6.)

This technique doesn't make IE 6 handle fixed positioning correctly, but it at least places the banner and sidebar in their proper places when the page loads. When someone using IE 6 scrolls the page, the banner and sidebar scroll off the top of the window like other content. In other words, in IE 6 your page works like any ordinary Web page, and in IE 7, Firefox, Safari, and Opera it works even better.

Note: To see examples of frame-like Web pages that *do* work in Internet Explorer 6, visit *www.456bereastreet.com/lab/cssframes/* and *http://jessey.net/simon/articles/007.html*.

Tutorial: Positioning Page Elements

This tutorial lets you explore a few different ways to use absolute positioning, like creating a three-column layout, positioning items within a banner, and adding captions on top of photos. Unlike the previous chapter, where you wrapped chunks of HTML in <div> tags and added ID or class names to them, in these exercises most of the HTML work has already been done for you. You can focus on honing your new CSS skills.

To get started, download the tutorial files located on this book's companion Web site at *www.sawmac.com/css/*.

Enhancing a Page Banner

First, you'll make some small but visually important changes to a page banner. You'll create styles that refer to HTML tags with IDs or classes applied to them. (Again, that part's been taken care of for you.)

1. **Launch a Web browser and open the file** *chapter_12 → index.html.*

   On this CosmoFarmer.com Web page (Figure 12-13), start by repositioning several parts of the banner.

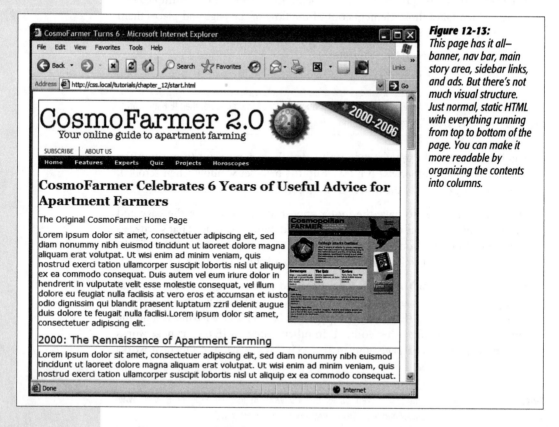

Figure 12-13:
This page has it all— banner, nav bar, main story area, sidebar links, and ads. But there's not much visual structure. Just normal, static HTML with everything running from top to bottom of the page. You can make it more readable by organizing the contents into columns.

2. **Open the *index.html* file in a text editor. Place your cursor between the opening and closing <style> tags.**

   Along with the <style> tags for an internal style sheet, the page already has an attached external style sheet with some basic formatting. Start by moving the small CosmoFarmer 2.0 badge to the left side of the banner. To help break up the boxy look that's typical of CSS designs, break this graphic out of the banner's borders, so it looks like a slapped-on sticker.

3. **In the internal style sheet, add this new style:**

   ```
   <style type="text/css">
   #banner #badge {
       position: absolute;
       left: -18px;
       top: -18px;
   }
   </style>
   ```

   The graphic is inside of a <div> with an ID of *banner,* and the graphic itself has an ID of *badge.* This style positions the top left corner of the graphic 18 pixels to the left and 18 pixels above the top of the page.

   Preview the page now and you'll see a couple of problems. First, the graphic hangs off the edge of the page but you really want it to hang off the edge of the banner area. You'll tackle that problem now.

4. **Add this style *above* the one you just created:**

   ```
   #banner {
       position: relative;
   }
   ```

   It's good practice to place the CSS code for styles that control a general section of a page (like this *#banner* style) *above* the code for styles that format just parts of that section (like the style you created in step 3). Also, grouping styles for related sections makes it easier to find styles when you need to analyze or edit a page's CSS. In this case, the *#banner* style goes first in the internal style sheet because it applies to a large chunk of HTML. But you should keep the *#banner #badge* style near it as you add more styles to the page. (You can read more about techniques for organizing your CSS on page 384.)

   The *#banner* style creates a new positioning context for any nested tags. In other words, the *relative* setting makes any other positioned elements inside this tag place themselves relative to the edges of the banner. This change in positioning shifts the placement of the style you created in step 3. Now it's 18 pixels above and to the left of the banner box. The badge still hangs off the page just a little bit, so you'll add some margins around the page to accommodate the graphic.

5. **Add a style for the *body* tag. Place it in the internal style sheet *above* the other two styles you created:**

```
body {
    margin: 20px;
}
```

This margin adds enough space around the edges of the page so the entire graphic is visible (Figure 12-14). But now you have another problem—the CosmoFarmer logo is partially hidden underneath the badge. Overlapping elements is one of the hazards of absolute positioning. In this case, you can fix the problem by adding a little margin to the logo.

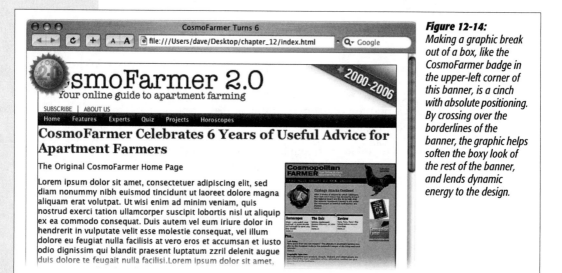

Figure 12-14:
Making a graphic break out of a box, like the CosmoFarmer badge in the upper-left corner of this banner, is a cinch with absolute positioning. By crossing over the borderlines of the banner, the graphic helps soften the boxy look of the rest of the banner, and lends dynamic energy to the design.

6. **Add a new style for the logo to the internal style sheet. Place it below the other styles you've created so far:**

```
#banner #logo {
    margin-left: 60px;
}
```

Like the badge graphic, the logo already has an ID applied to it—*logo*. This style moves the logo far enough to the left so that it's out of the way of the absolutely positioned graphic. However, a weird thing happens if you view this in Internet Explorer (including IE 7, as of this writing): When you mouse over the navigation bar, the logo jumps *back* to where it was before. Huh? Fortunately, the problem's easily fixed.

7. Edit the *#banner #logo* style you just created by changing its positioning to *relative*:

```
#banner #logo {
    margin-left: 60px;
    position: relative;
}
```

Adding relative positioning doesn't actually move the logo anywhere—that would happen only if you added a *left*, *top*, *right*, or *bottom* value. For reasons known only to Microsoft, though, it knocks IE upside the head and makes it behave.

The banner's looking good so far, but the two links—*Subscribe* and *About Us*—look awkward sandwiched between the logo and the nav bar. There's plenty of space in the right side of the banner, so you'll move them there. (The links are actually an unordered list that gets its formatting from the page's external style sheet. See page 218 for details on how to turn an unordered list into a horizontal navigation bar.)

8. **Add this new style to the bottom of the internal style sheet:**

```
#banner ul {
    position: absolute;
    right: 60px;
    bottom: 5px;
}
```

This style is a descendent selector that targets unordered lists inside the banner. (There's just one list in this case.) Since the <ul> is absolutely positioned, it's removed from the flow of the page, letting the nav bar scoot up just under the banner.

Also, remember this tag is inside the banner, which you earlier set to a *relative* position. Accordingly, the Subscribe and About Us links are positioned relative to the tag. They're placed an exact amount from the right and bottom edges of the banner...unless you're viewing this in—you guessed it—Internet Explorer 6 or earlier. As discussed on page 335, IE 6 has problems positioning elements using the bottom coordinates of relatively positioned elements (like this banner). It ends up using the bottom coordinates of the entire page. Luckily, the fix is easy.

Tip: If you're following along in IE, you can actually see the links in IE if you scroll down to the very bottom of the Web page.

9. **Add an IE-only style below the *#banner* style you created in step 4:**

```
* html #banner {
    height: 1px;
}
```

This style uses the * *html* hack (page 152) to create a style that only Internet Explorer 6 and earlier pay attention to. It's really just nonsense code, but in IE 6, it fixes the problem.

10. **Preview the page in a Web browser.**

The finished banner should look like Figure 12-15. This exercise is a good example of using absolute positioning to achieve small, subtle changes that add a lot to a page's visual appeal.

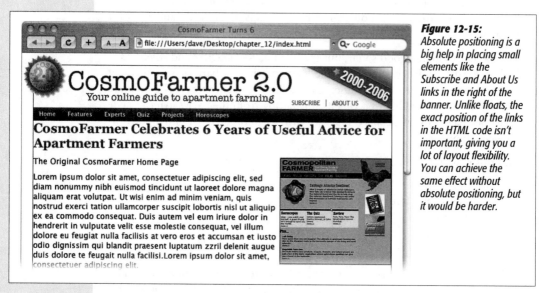

Figure 12-15:
Absolute positioning is a big help in placing small elements like the Subscribe and About Us links in the right of the banner. Unlike floats, the exact position of the links in the HTML code isn't important, giving you a lot of layout flexibility. You can achieve the same effect without absolute positioning, but it would be harder.

Adding a Caption to a Photo

In Chapter 8, you learned one way to add a caption to a photo (page 186). In the examples from that chapter, the captions sat underneath the photos, which is what you want most of the time. But someday, you may want to add a caption directly *on* a photo, like the subtitles TV news shows love to display across the lower third of the screen.

1. **Open *index.html* in your text editor.**

Notice the graphic of the original CosmoFarmer home page. Currently it's aligned to the right using the *align* attribute of the <img> tag, but that's *so* 2001. You'll align it using CSS instead, but first you need to edit some HTML.

2. **Locate the <img> tag that inserts the graphic *old_home.jpg*, and then delete the HTML code *align="right"*.**

Here's what the entire tag looks like. You want to remove the part that's bolded:

```
<img src="images/old_home.jpg" alt="The Original Cosmo Home Page" width="200"
height="186" align="right" />
```

Now that you've gotten rid of the old HTML, you need to create a container—a <div> tag—to hold the CSS for both the image and its caption.

3. **Immediately before the <img> tag, add *<div class="figure">*. After the closing </p> of the caption (which appears right after the <img> tag), add the closing </div>. When you're done, the HTML should look like this:**

   ```
   <div class="figure">
   <img src="images/old_home.jpg" alt="The Original Cosmo Home Page" width="200"
   height="186"/>
   <p>The Original CosmoFarmer Home Page</p>
   </div>
   ```

   All the code for the photo and caption are in one box that you can align and format as a unit.

4. **Create a style to format the newly added <div>:**

   ```
   #main .figure {
       float: right;
       width: 200px;
       margin-bottom: 2px;
       margin-left: 10px;
   }
   ```

   The properties in this style should be old news by now (especially if you read Chapter 8). This style aligns the box to the right edge of the page, and the bottom and left margins add a little space between the photo box and the text that wraps around it.

   The plan is to move the caption paragraph out of the normal flow of the page and place it on top of the photo. To do so, you'll position the caption relative to the edges of the photo. However, since the <img> tag is *self-closing* (meaning it doesn't have both an opening and closing tag), you must position the caption relative to another element. Here's another use of the *figure* <div> you just added—to provide the positioning context for the caption.

5. **Add *position: relative* to the style you just created:**

   ```
   #main .figure {
       float: right;
       width: 200px;
       margin-bottom: 2px;
       margin-left: 10px;
       position: relative;
   }
   ```

   Now you can position the caption relative to the <div>, which for all intents and purposes is the same as positioning it relative to the photo.

---

6. **Add a new style after the #*main .figure* style you created in the last step:**

```
#main .figure p {
    position: absolute;
    width: 168px;
    left: 10px;
    bottom: 10px;
    background-color: #FFF;
}
```

This new style positions the paragraph 10 pixels from the bottom and 10 pixels from the left edge of the <div> tag. The *width* property constrains the paragraph so it doesn't span across the entire photo, and *background-color* makes the text legible. All that's left are a few formatting details to improve the look of the caption.

7. **Edit the style you just created, so that it looks like this:**

```
#main .figure p {
    position: absolute;
    width: 168px;
    left: 10px;
    bottom: 10px;
    background-color: #FFF;
    border: 1px dashed #666666;
    font-size: 1.1em;
    font-weight: bold;
    text-align: center;
    padding: 5px;
    margin: 0;
}
```

You need to attend to one small detail. It's something you may never notice, but some browsers position the caption just a few pixels lower than other browsers. (To see for yourself, check the page out in IE and then in Firefox.) Browsers position inline elements (like images) differently relative to the baseline of other elements around them (page 255). (Also, you can see a similar problem with images in table cells on page 254.) At any rate, the fix is simple: Using CSS, force the image to display as a block-level element.

8. **Add one more style to the internal style sheet:**

```
#main .figure img {
    display: block;
}
```

Preview the page. The caption should appear centered across the lower portion of the photo, as in Figure 12-16.

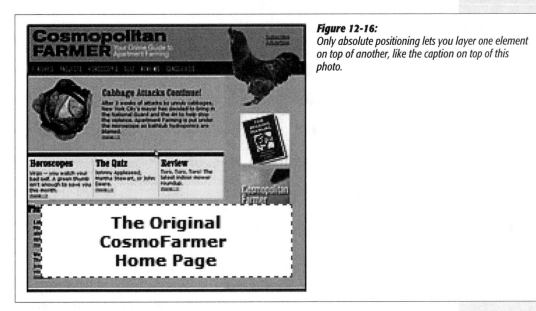

Figure 12-16:
Only absolute positioning lets you layer one element on top of another, like the caption on top of this photo.

Laying Out the Page

Now it's time to turn your attention to the structure of this page. As it is now, you need to scroll down the page to read the latest news in the sidebar, and scroll even farther to see the ads. (Advertisers hate that.) In this section, you'll use absolute positioning to create a three-column flexible layout that brings all content up to the top of the page (and keeps your sponsors from canceling their accounts).

Before you get started, get an overview of the page structure—see Figure 12-17. Each section of the page is wrapped in its own <div> tag, with an appropriate ID applied. The page's main contents, sidebar, ads, and copyright notice are enclosed in a <div> with the ID *contentWrapper* (#4 in Figure 12-17). All of the tags in the page's body are wrapped in a <div> with an ID of *wrapper* (#1). That may seem like a lot of <div> tags, but they each serve an important purpose.

Your mission is to arrange the three <divs> (*sidebar*, *main*, and *adverts*) into three columns. You need to use absolute positioning on only two elements—the sidebar and the advertising section (see #6 and #7 in Figure 12-17). You'll take them out of the normal flow of the page (where they appear near the bottom) and stick them at the left and right edges of the page just below the banner. Absolute positioning also causes those elements to float above the page, and on top of the main content area (see #5). To make room for the sidebars, you have to add a little margin to the left and right of the main area.

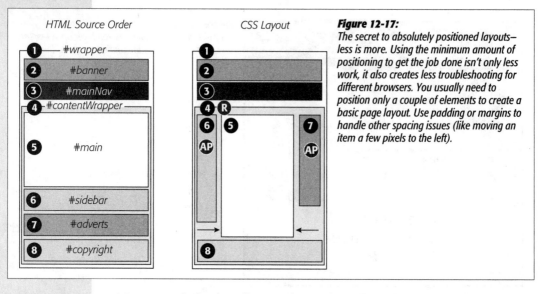

HTML Source Order   CSS Layout

Figure 12-17:
The secret to absolutely positioned layouts—less is more. Using the minimum amount of positioning to get the job done isn't only less work, it also creates less troubleshooting for different browsers. You usually need to position only a couple of elements to create a basic page layout. Use padding or margins to handle other spacing issues (like moving an item a few pixels to the left).

1. **Create a style for the <div> tag that encloses the main contents of the page (#3 in Figure 12-17). Add it as the last style in the internal style sheet:**

   ```
   #contentWrapper {
       clear: both;
       position: relative;
   }
   ```

   The *clear* property helps the *#contentWrapper* clear the navigation bar, which was created using a left float. (As explained on page 155, you should always clear elements that need to appear under a float.)

   The position property comes in handy for placing the sidebars. Setting its value to *relative* lets you position both sidebars relative to the four edges of the content wrapper, not the four edges of the browser window. (See step 3 on page 343 for more on why this is useful.)

2. **Create a style for the left sidebar, placing the CSS code under the style you created in step 1:**

   ```
   #sidebar {
       position: absolute;
   }
   ```

   This style takes the sidebar out of the normal flow of the page, but it doesn't yet position it anywhere. It's still near the bottom of the page, but if you view it in a browser, you'll see it's floating on top of the advertisements. To position it, use the *top* and *left* properties.

3. **Add top and left properties to the style you just created by:**

```
#sidebar {
    position: absolute;
    top: 15px;
    left: 0;
}
```

Since this sidebar is positioned relative to the content wrapper <div>, a *left* position of *0* places it flush with the left edge. The top value is determined by aesthetic judgment (otherwise known as trial and error). A top value of *0* would make the sidebar touch the bottom of the nav bar; the 15 pixels of space bring the sidebar's top more in line with the story headline.

One thing's missing: Most of the time when you position something, you also want to give it a width. That's true in this case, since at this point the sidebar spreads almost across the entire page, covering nearly all of the content.

4. **Add a width to the *#sidebar* style.**

The final style looks like this:

```
#sidebar {
    position: absolute;
    top: 15px;
    left: 0;
    width: 170px;
}
```

Next, repeat the process to position the advertising area of the page.

5. **Add an *#adverts* style to the bottom of the style sheet:**

```
#adverts {
    position: absolute;
    top: 15px;
    right: 5px;
    width: 125px;
}
```

This style works just like the one for the sidebar, except that you place the ads relative to the *right* edge of the page. That works much better than trying to put the ads at some point relative to the *left* edge of the page. When you specify a *right* value, the ads always stay the same distance from the right edge of the content wrapper. If you change the width of the browser window, the ads stay in position.

At this point, the page should look like Figure 12-18, with both the sidebar and ads covering the main story of the page. Adjust that main area's margins to prevent this overlap.

---

6. **Below the** *#adverts* **style you just created, add a style for the main story area of the page:**

```
#main {
    margin-left: 170px;
    margin-right: 135px;
}
```

This *#main* style indents the main story area so that it clears the left and right sidebars. Now just a few design enhancements remain.

7. **Add some padding and borders to the** *#main* **style:**

```
#main {
    margin-left: 170px;
    margin-right: 135px;
    padding: 0 15px 15px 20px;
    border: 1px solid #666666;
    border-top: none;
    border-bottom: none;
}
```

The padding adds some space inside of the div, so the text doesn't touch the sidebars or the bottom of the div. You can actually achieve the same thing by increasing the left and right margins from the previous step, but this way you also get to add a nice border to the left and right edges of the div, helping to visually divide the three columns.

Notice the little productivity shortcut in this style. First, the *border* style declaration sets up a border on *all four edges* of the div; the last two declarations turn *off* the border at the top and bottom. You can achieve the exact same effect with two style declarations (*border-left* and *border-right*), but then you'd have to repeat the values (*1px solid #666666*). If you want to change the color, thickness, or style of both borders, then you have to edit *two* properties. This way, only one declaration takes care of both the left and right borders.

The layout's nearly complete. There's just one last thing: When you preview the page in IE 6, you see the left sidebar is off by a lot—185 pixels too far to the right to be exact! Yep, another IE bug. Fortunately, there's an easy fix. To make the left sidebar line up and fly right (#4 in Figure 12-17), give its containing <div> tag that mysterious IE-only property known as *layout* (see page 307).

8. **Add a width to the** *#contentWrapper* **style:**

```
#contentWrapper {
    position: relative;
    clear: both;
    width: 100%;
}
```

CSS: The Missing Manual

Figure 12-18:
Absolute positioning can pose some problems. Since absolutely positioned elements (like the two sidebars here) float on top of the page, separate from the main flow of the HTML, they can cover up and hide other elements.

The page now falls correctly into three columns (Figure 12-19), with fewer steps than the modifications you made to the banner. Preview the page in a Web browser and expand the browser window. You'll see the page's flexible design lets it fit any width window.

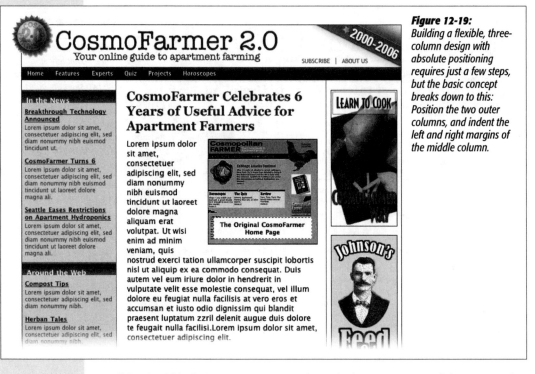

Figure 12-19:
Building a flexible, three-column design with absolute positioning requires just a few steps, but the basic concept breaks down to this: Position the two outer columns, and indent the left and right margins of the middle column.

If fixed-width designs are your cup of tea, the basic structure of this page makes it easy to set a fixed width. Just set a width for the <div> that wraps all of the other tags on the page (#1 in Figure 12-17) like this:

```
#wrapper {
    width: 760px;
}
```

A completed version of this tutorial is in the *chapter_12_finished* folder.

Part Four:
Advanced CSS

4

CSS for the Printed Page

Not everyone likes to sit in front of a computer and read. More and more, Web surfers are printing out pages for offline reading. Plenty of folks enjoy Web sites while sitting at the dinner table, on a train, or lying on the grass in a park on a sunny day. So what becomes of your carefully crafted designs when the ink hits the paper? White text on a black background can waste gallons of toner, and some browsers may not even print the background. Do visitors really need to see your site's navigation bar on the printed page? Probably not. And complex CSS can make a page simply unprintable (see Figure 13-1).

Web designers used to solve this dilemma by creating separate "printer-friendly" versions of their sites—essentially creating a duplicate site formatted just for printing. Not only is that a lot more work than building one version of the site, it also means changing multiple files each time a page needs editing. Fortunately, CSS offers a better way—the ability to make a page look one way when displayed on a screen and a different way when printed. The secret? Media style sheets.

How Media Style Sheets Work

The creators of CSS were pretty thorough when they envisioned all the different ways people might view Web sites. They knew while most people view the Web using a computer and monitor, sometimes people want to print out a page. In addition, new Web surfing devices like mobile phones, handhelds, and televisions have their own unique requirements when it comes to Web design.

To accommodate these different methods of surfing, CSS lets you create styles and style sheets that specifically target a particular *media type*. CSS recognizes ten different media types: *all, Braille, embossed, handheld, print, projection, screen,*

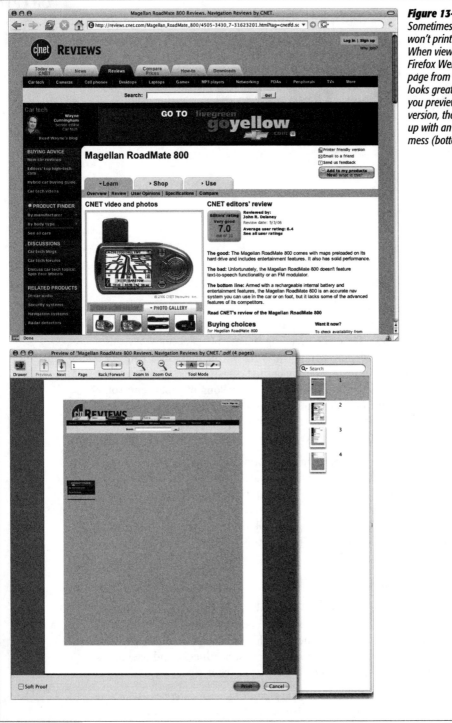

Figure 13-1:
*Sometimes a Web page
won't print correctly.
When viewed in the
Firefox Web browser, a
page from CNET.com
looks great (top). When
you preview the printed
version, though, you end
up with an unreadable
mess (bottom).*

speech, *tty*, and *tv*. The browser applies the style sheet only when that media type is active. In other words, the browser applies one style sheet for the screen and a different one when printing. Many of these media types are for very specialized applications like a Braille reader for the blind, a speech reader (for those who want or need to hear a page in spoken form), or a teletype machine. Most of these types don't yet work in the real world, as there are no devices programmed to understand them. You should be aware, however, of three: *all*, *screen*, and *print*.

- **All** applies to every type of device. When a style or style sheet applies to *all* media types, every device accessing the page uses those same styles. Printers and monitors alike attempt to format the page the same way. (Styles actually work this way already when you embed them in the page or link them from an external style sheet.)

- **Screen** styles display only on a monitor. When you specify the *screen* media type, the browser ignores those styles when it prints the page. This media type lets you isolate styles that look good on screen but awful on paper, like white text on a black background.

- **Print** styles apply only when the page is printed. Print styles let you create styles that use printer-friendly font sizes, colors, graphics, and so on.

Note: The Opera Web browser understands the *projection* media type when it's in Full Screen mode. For a tutorial on this cool feature, visit *www.opera.com/support/tutorials/operashow/*.

One approach is to build styles with your monitor in mind first, and attach them using one of the methods described below (methods like internal or external, linked or imported). At the outset, these styles work for both the monitor and the printer. Then, you create a printer-only style sheet that applies only when printing. It overrides any of the main styles that negatively affect the look of the page when printed. You'll learn this technique starting on page 369. Alternatively, you can create two different media style sheets—one for screen and the other for print—and attach them to your Web pages, as described next.

How to Add Media Style Sheets

Media style sheets are simply CSS style sheets: They can be either internal or external. However, when you want a Web browser to apply the styles only for a particular device such as a screen or printer, you need to add the style sheet to your Web page in a slightly different way than usual.

Specifying the Media Type for an External Style Sheet

To attach an external style sheet while specifying a particular media type, use the <link> tag with a *media* attribute. To link a style sheet that should be used only for printing, add this HTML to your Web page:

```
<link rel="stylesheet" type="text/css" media="print" href="print.css"/>
```

Note: Technically, the rules of CSS also let you define a media type when using the @import method of attaching an external style sheet (see page 33), like so: *@import url(print.css) print;*. But since Internet Explorer refuses to understand this code, you should avoid using it.

If you don't specify any media, a Web browser assumes you're targeting all media, so it uses the style sheet for screen display, printing, and so on. In addition, you can specify *multiple* media types by separating them with commas. A linked external style sheet targeting multiple media might look like:

```
<link rel="stylesheet" type="text/css" media="screen, projection, handheld"
href="screen.css"/>
```

You probably won't need to specify more than one until browsers start recognizing multiple media types.

Tip: When you build and test printer style sheets, leave off the *media="print"* attribute, and turn off any screen-only style sheets. For example, change *media="screen"* to *media="speech"*. This technique lets you view the page in a Web browser but have it display as if it were formatted for a printer. Once the printer style sheet looks good, make sure to set its media type to *print* and turn on any screen-only style sheets.

Specifying the Media Type Within a Style Sheet

You can also include media-specific styles directly inside a style sheet using the *@media* directive. Maybe you want to add a couple of print-specific styles to an internal style sheet. Or perhaps you'd like to keep all your styles in a single external style sheet and just add a few printer-only styles. You can do so using the *@media* directive, like so:

```
@media print {
    /* put your styles for the printer in here */
}
```

Be careful to include that closing brace character (on the last line) otherwise the directive won't work. Here's an example of using *@media* to include two printer-only styles:

```
@media print {
    h1 {
        font-size: 24pt;
    }
    p {
        font-size: 12pt;
    }
}
```

Technically, it doesn't really matter whether you put all styles in a single file and use the *@media* method, or put media-specific styles in their own external style sheets (like *screen.css,* and *printer.css*). Putting all your printer-only styles in their own external style sheet named something like *printer.css* makes it a lot easier to find and edit styles for print only.

Creating Print Style Sheets

You should see how pages on your site print before embarking on a print-specific redesign. Often, all the information on a Web page prints without problems, so you may not have to add a printer style sheet to your site. But in some cases, especially when using heavy doses of CSS, pages look awful printed, like the example in Figure 13-1. But even if a page looks the same in print as it does on the screen, you have many ways to improve the quality of the printed version by adding custom printer-only styles (see Figure 13-2).

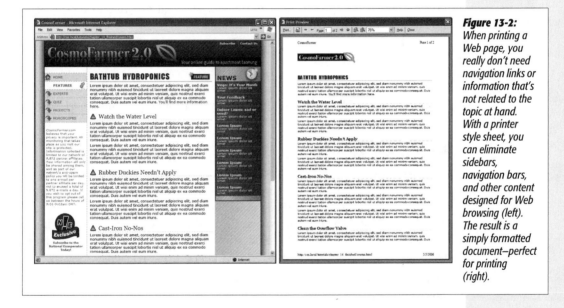

Figure 13-2:
When printing a Web page, you really don't need navigation links or information that's not related to the topic at hand. With a printer style sheet, you can eliminate sidebars, navigation bars, and other content designed for Web browsing (left). The result is a simply formatted document—perfect for printing (right).

Tip: A quick way to see how a page will print without wasting a lot of paper and toner, is to use your browser's *Print Preview* command. On Windows this is usually available from a Web browser's File → Print Preview menu. On Macs, you usually first choose File → Print, and then in the window that appears click Preview. Using Print Preview you can check to see whether a page is too wide to fit on one page and see where page breaks occur.

Using !important to Override Onscreen Styling

As mentioned earlier, it's often useful to create a style sheet without specifying a media type (or by using *media="all"*). When you're ready to define some print-specific rules, you can just create a separate style sheet to override any styles that don't look good in print.

Say you've got an <h1> tag that's styled to appear blue onscreen and you've also chosen rules controlling letter spacing, font weight, and text alignment. If the only thing you want to change for your printed pages is to use black rather than blue, then you don't need to create a new style with a whole new set of properties. Just create a main style sheet that applies in both cases, and a print style sheet that overrides the blue color for the <h1> tag.

One problem with this approach is that you need to make sure the printer styles actually *do* override the main style sheet. To do this successfully, you have to carefully manage the *cascade*. As discussed in Chapter 5, styles can interact in complex ways: Several styles may apply to the same element and those styles' CSS properties can merge and override each other. There's a surefire way to make sure one property trumps all others—the *!important* declaration.

When you add *!important* after the value in a CSS declaration, that particular property overrides any conflicts with other styles. Add this rule to a print style sheet to ensure that all <h1> tags print black:

```
h1 {
    color: #000 !important ;
}
```

This *h1* style overrides even more specific styles, including *#main h1*, *h1.title*, or *#wrapper #main h1* from the main style sheet.

Reworking Text Styles

You may not necessarily want to have text look the same onscreen as it does in print. A good place to start when creating a printer style sheet is by modifying the *font-size* and *color* properties. Using pixel sizes for text doesn't mean much to a printer. Should it print 12-pixel type as 12 dots? If you've got a 600 DPI printer, that text will be illegibly small. And while bright green text may look good onscreen, it may come out a difficult-to-read pale gray when printed.

Pixels and ems (page 104) make sense for onscreen text, but the measurement of choice for printing is *points*. Points are how Word and other word processing programs measure font sizes, and they're what printers expect. In practice, most Web browsers translate pixel and ems to something more printer friendly anyway. The base onscreen font size for most browsers—16-pixels—prints out as 12 points. But there's no consistent way to predict how every browser will resize text, so for maximum printing control, set the font size specifically to points in your print style sheets.

To make all paragraphs print in 12-point type (a common size for printing), use the following rule:

```
p {
    font-size: 12pt;
}
```

Note: As with ems, you don't add an 's' when setting the font to a point size: 12pt *not* 12pts.

Likewise, screen colors don't often translate well when printed on a black and white laser printer. Crisp black text on white paper is much easier to read, for instance, than light gray letters. What's more, as you'll see in the next section, white text on a black background—though very legible onscreen—often doesn't print well. To make text most readable on paper, it's a good idea to make all text print black. To make all paragraph text black, add this style to your print style sheet:

```
p {
    color: #000;
}
```

As mentioned on page 369, if your print style sheet competes with styles from another attached style sheet, then use *!important* to make sure your printer styles win:

```
p {
    font-size: 12pt !important;
    color: #000 !important;
}
```

To make sure *all* text on a page prints black, use the universal selector (page 54) and *!important* to create a single style that formats every tag with black text:

```
* { color: #000 !important }
```

Of course, this advice applies only if your site's printed out in black and white. If you think most visitors to your site use color printers, then you may want to leave all the text color in, or change the colors to be even more vibrant when printed.

Styling Backgrounds for Print

Adding background images and colors to navigation buttons, sidebars, and other page elements adds contrast and visual appeal to your Web pages. But you can't be sure if the background will come through when those pages are printed. Because colored backgrounds eat up printer ink and toner, most Web browsers don't normally print them and most Web surfers don't turn on backgrounds for printing even if their browser has this feature.

In addition, even if the background *does* print, it may compete with any text that overlaps it. This is especially true if the text contrasts strongly with a colorful background on a monitor, but blends into the background when printed on a black-and-white printer.

Note: White text on a black background used to pose the biggest problem—your visitor would end up with a blank white page. Fortunately, most current Web browsers have the smarts to change white text to black (or gray) when printing without backgrounds.

Removing background elements

The easiest way to take care of backgrounds is to simply remove them in your print style sheet. Say you reverse out a headline so that the text is white and the background's a dark color. If the style that creates that effect is named *.headHighlight*, then duplicate the style name in your print-only style sheet, like this:

```
.headHighlight {
    color: #000;
    background: white;
}
```

This style sets the background to white—the color of the paper. In addition, to get crisp printed text, this style sets the font color to black.

GEM IN THE ROUGH

Two Birds with One Stone

You can use the *background-color* property to set a background color to white like this: *background-color: white*. You get the same effect using the *background* shorthand method: *background: white*. Remember that the background property (page 182) can also specify a background image, how the image repeats, and its position.

But when you leave out any values using the shorthand method, the Web browser resets to its normal value.

In other words, by omitting a background image value, the Web browser sets that value to its normal setting—*none*. So a declaration like *background: white;* not only sets the background color to white but also removes any background images. By using the *background* shorthand property, you kill two birds—setting a white background and removing images—with very little code.

Leaving background elements in

If you don't want to get rid of the background, you can leave it in and hope that visitors set their browsers to print them. If you leave background elements in your print style sheet and text appears on top of them, then make sure the text is legible with the backgrounds on *and* off.

Another thing to consider when using background images: Do you *need* the image to print out? Say you place a company's logo as a background image of a <div> tag used for the banner of a page. Because the logo's in the background, it may not print. Your company or client may not be happy when every page printed from their site lacks a logo. In this case, you've got a few options. You can insert the logo as a regular <img> tag instead of a background image. This technique works, but what if the logo looks great on a full-color monitor but no good at all when printed on a black-and-white printer? Another technique is to leave the logo in as a background image, and add *another,* more printer-friendly logo using the <img> tag. You then hide that <img> tag onscreen but show the printer-friendly logo when printed. You'll learn this second technique in the tutorial on page 380.

Tip: If you want to be absolutely sure that a background image prints, there's another tricky CSS workaround for overcoming a browser's reluctance to print background images. You can find it here: *http://web-graphics.com/mtarchive/001703.php*.

Revealing Links in Print

Imagine a coworker hands you a printout of a fascinating article she found on the Web. You're reading along and come to this passage: "And that's when I found the secret to eternal life here." The underline tells you there's a clickable link that reveals the secret. But on a piece of paper, of course, you have no way to follow where the link leads.

To prevent this conundrum on your own pages, you can make linked URLs print along with the rest of the text: "secret to eternal life here (http://www.pyramind_scam.com/)." Using an advanced selector—*:after*—and an advanced CSS property called *content*, you can print text that doesn't appear onscreen at the end of a styled element. Unfortunately, the *:after* selector and *content* property trick doesn't work in Internet Explorer 6 or earlier (nor in IE 7, as of this writing). But it does work in Firefox and Safari, so you can at least spell out URLs for the benefit of visitors using those browsers.

To do so, add a style to the print style sheet that prints the URL after each link.

You can even add other text items like parentheses to make it look better:

```
a:after {
  content: " (" attr(href) ") ";
}
```

However, this CSS doesn't distinguish between external or internal links, so it also prints unhelpful document-relative links to other pages on the same site: "Visit the home page (../../index.html)." Using a bit of CSS 3 magic, you can force the style to print only absolute URLs (the ones that begin with *http://*), like so:

```
a[href^="http://"]:after {
  content: " (" attr(href) ") ";
}
```

Since this style uses yet-to-be-finalized CSS 3 rules, it works only in really new browsers like Firefox and Safari, and even the CSS Validator (page 32) doesn't know about it. So if you use root-relative links on your site, you can use another technique to print the correct, full URLs. See this article for more information: *www.alistapart.com/articles/goingtoprint/*.

Hiding Unwanted Page Areas

Web pages are often loaded with informational and navigational aids like navigation bars, sidebars full of helpful links, search boxes, and so on. These elements are great for surfing the Web, but don't do much good on a piece of paper. Your Web pages may also contain ads, movies, and other doodads that people don't like to waste expensive ink and toner on. You can do your visitors a favor by stripping these onscreen frills out of the content they really want to print.

As you learned in the first part of this book, one way to lay out a page is to wrap <div> tags around different layout elements—banner, main navigation, content, copyright notice, and so on. By styling each <div> using floats or absolute positioning, you can place various page elements right where you want them. You can use that same structure to create a print-only style sheet that hides unwanted elements using the *display* property (page 141).

By setting the *display* value to *none*, you can make a Web browser remove a styled element from a page. So to prevent a sidebar from printing, simply redefine that style in a print style sheet and set its display property to *none*:

```
#sidebar {
    display: none;
}
```

For most pages, you want the print style sheet to display only the most basic informational elements—like the logo, the main content, and a copyright notice—and hide everything else. You can easily hide multiple elements with a group selector, like so:

```
#banner, #mainNav, #sidebar, #ads, #newsLinks {
    display: none;
}
```

Remember, these styles go into your *print style sheet*, not the main style sheet. Otherwise, you'd never see the navigation, banner, or other important areas of your page onscreen. However, at times you'll want to hide something from your main style sheet and reveal it *only* when printed.

Say you place your site's logo as a background image inside the banner area of a page. You may want to do this to have text or links appear on top of an empty area of the logo graphic. You (or your boss or client) certainly want the logo to appear on any printed pages, but since not all browsers print background images, you can't be sure the logo will appear when printed. One solution's to insert an <img> tag containing a modified, printer-friendly version of the logo graphic; add an ID to the image; create an ID style in the main style sheet with the *display* property set to *none*; and then set the *display* property for the same ID style in the print style sheet to *block*. Voilà! The logo appears only when printed. You'll see an example of this trick in the tutorial on page 380.

Tip: If you're using float-based layouts (see Chapter 12), then you may also want to fix a Firefox bug that plagues long passages of floated text—like the part of your page containing the main story or article. When printing, Firefox gets confused about the placement of really long floated blocks. In this case, you should *unfloat* that block in the print-only style sheet, like this: *float: none;*.

Adding Page Breaks for Printing

Version 2.1 of the Cascading Style Sheet standard includes many CSS properties aimed at better formatting a printed Web page: from setting the orientation of the page to defining margins and paper size. (You can see the full list at *www.w3.org/TR/CSS21/page.html*.) Unfortunately, today's Web browsers recognize very few of these print styles.

Two widely recognized properties are *page-break-before* and *page-break-after*. Page-break-before tells a Web browser to insert a page break before a given style. Say you want certain headings to always appear at the top of a page, like titles for different sections of a long document (see Figure 13-3). You can add *page-break-before: always* to the style used to format those headings. Likewise, to make an element appear as the last item on a printed page add *page-break-after: always* to that element's style.

The page-break-before property is also useful for large graphics, since some browsers let images print across two pages, making it a little tough to see the whole image at once. If you have one page with three paragraphs of text followed by the image, then the browser prints part of the image on one page and the other part on a second page. You don't want your visitors to need cellophane tape to piece your image back together, so use the page-break-before property to make the image print on a new page, where it all fits.

Here's a quick way to take advantage of these properties. Create two class styles named something like *.break_after* and *.break_before*, like so:

```
.break_before { page-break-before: always; }
.break_after { page-break-after: always; }
```

You can then selectively apply these styles to the elements that should print at the top—or bottom—of a page. If you want a particular heading to print at the top of a page, then use a style like this: *<h1 class="break_before">*. Even if the element already has a class applied to it, you can add an additional class like this: *<h1 class="sectionTitle break_before">*. (You'll learn about this useful technique in the next chapter on page 385.)

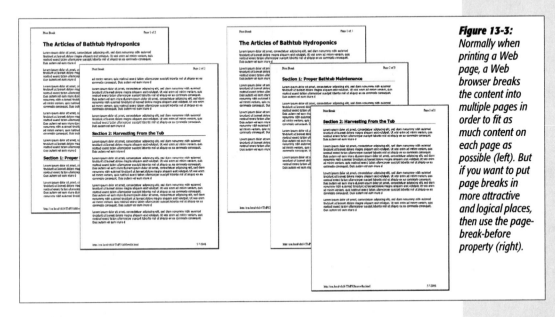

Figure 13-3:
Normally when printing a Web page, a Web browser breaks the content into multiple pages in order to fit as much content on each page as possible (left). But if you want to put page breaks in more attractive and logical places, then use the page-break-before property (right).

Tutorial: Building a Print Style Sheet

In this tutorial, you'll create a print style sheet. To make the printed version of a Web page look better, you'll add styles that remove unwanted page elements and backgrounds, change text formatting, add a printable logo, and print the URLs attached to any links on the page.

To get started, download the tutorial files from this book's companion Web site at *www.sawmac.com/css/*. Click the tutorial link, and then download the files. All of the files are in a ZIP archive, so you need to unzip them first (You'll find detailed instructions on the Web site.) The files for this tutorial are in the *chapter_13* folder.

Remove Unneeded Page Elements

To get started, you first need to understand how the page is laid out so you can decide which elements you want printed.

1. **Launch a Web browser and open** *chapter_13 → cosmo.html.*

   This CosmoFarmer Web page is a float-based layout consisting of several <div> tags (see Figure 13-4). In all likelihood, anyone printing this page is most interested in the main content—the Bathtub Hydroponics story. Printing the Subscribe and Contact links, the navigation bar, and the news links is just a waste of toner, so your print style sheet should hide these parts of the page.

2. **In a text editor, create a new file named** *print.css* **and save it in the** *chapter_13* **folder.**

   In your new print style sheet, the first order of business is to hide the navigation bar and other parts of the page that you don't want to print.

3. **Using the** *display* **property, create a new group selector that hides site tools, navigation bar, and news sidebar, like so:**

   ```
   #sitetools, #nav, #news {
       display: none;
   }
   ```

   With the *display* property set to *none*, Web browsers hide those elements so they won't print. But first you need to attach this external style sheet to your Web page so browsers can find it.

4. **In your text editor, open** *chapter_13 → cosmo.html.*

   This page already has an attached style sheet—*global.css*. This external style sheet provides all of the formatting for the page when it's displayed in a browser. Also, since the style sheet is attached using the <link> tag with no media attribute specified, it applies when the page is printed as well. Your print style sheet, then, needs to override any styles from the *global.css* file that won't look good in print. The first step in that process is attaching the print style sheet *after* the *global.css* file in the html of this page.

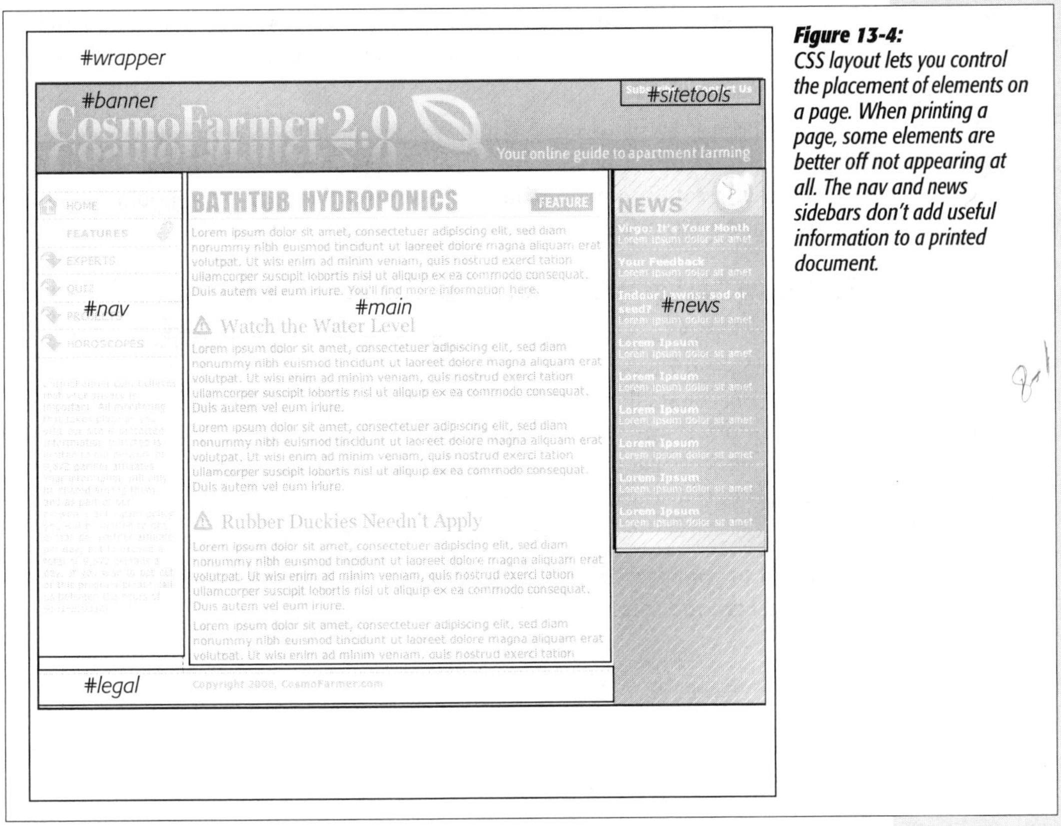

Figure 13-4:
CSS layout lets you control
the placement of elements on
a page. When printing a
page, some elements are
better off not appearing at
all. The nav and news
sidebars don't add useful
information to a printed
document.

5. **Locate the <link> tag in the head of the page used to attach the *global.css* file.
Insert a blank line after that tag, and then add the following:**

```
<link href="print.css" rel="stylesheet" type="text/css" media="print" />
```

If properties from two styles with the same name conflict, the properties from
the style sheet *last linked on the page* wins, so this <link> must go *after* the other
<link>. That way, if the *global.css* file has a class named *.copyright* that creates
white, 10 pixel type on a black background, you can create another style named
.copyright in the *print* style sheet with black, 12-point type on a white background. Even though the two styles share the same name, the properties from
the print style sheet win because it's the last one linked. (See page 87 for more
detail on this cascading rule.)

6. **Save the *print.css* and *cosmo.html* files, and then preview *cosmo.html* in a Web
browser.**

The page should look no different than it did in step 1 above. That's because
you haven't printed it yet. You can see the effect of the print style sheet by using
your Web browser's Print Preview command.

7. If you're using Windows, choose File → Print Preview. Mac fans should choose File → Print, and then, in the Print window that appears, click the Preview button.

In the Print Preview window, you'll see that the left and right sidebars as well as the two links in the banner area have disappeared. But the design still doesn't look that great. The main content doesn't fill the page as it should. You'll fix that—and a few other things—next.

Removing Backgrounds and Adjusting the Layout

Sometimes background images and colors print out, but often they don't. It all depends on the browser and the visitor's settings. Some browsers don't print background elements at all; others can print them but give folks the option of turning them on or off. Printing backgrounds is useful when it's important for the printed page to look just like the screen version. But when you have backgrounds that would only be a distraction and a waste of ink, do your visitors a favor and disable them.

1. Return to your text editor and the *print.css* file. Add two new styles to remove the background color and banner:

```
body {
    background: #FFF;
}
#banner {
    background: #FFF;
}
```

When viewed onscreen, this page has a gray background and a graphic that creates the drop shadow effect to the left and right edges of the content. The banner has a graphic that includes the site's logo. These two styles set the background color of the page and banner to white *and* remove the graphic. (See page 183 for the story on why the background image disappears as well.)

Now it's time to adjust the layout a bit, so that the text fills an entire printed page. Start by changing the *#wrapper* ID style that sets the entire width of the content area of the page to 760 pixels.

2. Add another style to the *print.css* style sheet:

```
#wrapper {
    background: #FFF;
    border-style: none;
    width: auto;
}
```

The first declaration in this style works just like the previous step: It sets the background to white and removes any background images. The second property removes the black border that appears on both the left and right edges of the wrapper.

The last declaration—*width:auto*—affects the overall layout of the page. It overrides the 760-pixel width setting from the *global.css* file and leaves the exact width up to the Web browser. *Auto* simply lets the <div> fill the entire available width, so no matter the paper size—letter, A4, or whatever—the content fills the width of the printed page.

The next problem's the part of the page containing the article. It's a <div> tag called *#main*, as you can see in Figure 13-4.

3. **Add a new style to the *print.css* file:**

```
#main {
    border: none;
    padding: 0;
    width: auto;
}
```

The first two properties eliminate the borders and the extra white space visible in the onscreen version of the page. The third declaration lets the text fill the width of the page, just like the *width: auto* setting you added for the *#wrapper* in step 2.

Now it's time to get a little picky. The copyright notice at the bottom of the page is indented left using a large *padding-left* value. This element would look better if it lined up at the left with the other text on the page.

4. **Add a style for the copyright region of the page:**

```
#legal {
    padding-left: 0px;
}
```

Feel free to save this file, preview the *cosmo.html* file in a Web browser, and use the Print Preview function to see how the printed version's coming along.

Reformatting the Text

While colored text and pixel-sized fonts may work on the screen, laser printers understand point sizes better. Also, solid black text looks better on white paper. In this section, you'll adjust the text accordingly to look better in print.

1. **In the *print.css* file, add the following CSS rule:**

```
* {
    color: #000000 !important;
}
```

This style is the CSS equivalent of a sledgehammer. It essentially tells every tag to use black text no matter what. The * (universal selector) is a quick way of specifying a style for every single element on a page (see page 54), while the *!important* declaration cancels out any conflicts caused by the cascade. So even though * isn't a very specific style, the color property here trumps the same property in much more specific styles like *#main h1* or *#nav #mainNav a*.

Next you'll set new font sizes for the text.

2. **Add the following three styles:**

```
h1 {
    font-size: 18pt !important;
}
h2 {
    font-size: 14pt !important;
    font-weight: bold !important;
}
p {
    font-size: 10pt !important;
}
```

These styles make each of these tags use a more printer-friendly font size. The addition of *!important* makes these sizes *always* apply to those tags regardless of any style conflicts with the *global.css* style sheet.

Note: In this case, h1, h2, and p are the only tags that print from the *cosmo.html* page. Your pages may require you to redefine text sizes for other tags like lists, blockquote, and so on.

Displaying the Logo

Since the logo in the banner is a background-image, not all browsers will print it. Because the powers that be at CosmoFarmer international headquarters don't want to lose any opportunity to promote their brand, they've devised another way to get their logo on the printed page. In the HTML of the *cosmo.html* Web page is an <img> tag that includes a smaller black and white version of the logo. However, it doesn't appear onscreen because the *global.css* file hides it using the *display: none* trick just like step 3 on page 376. Now it's time to make it visible.

1. **In the *print.css* file, add a style to make the logo appear:**

```
#logo {
    display: block;
}
```

Block is the value required to counter the effects of the display property's *none* value. That's all it takes. Now when your visitor prints the page, the simplified logo appears.

Displaying URLs

For a final flourish, you'll add one more style that prints the URL next to the text of each link on the page. That way, the onscreen text "Click here to found out more" will print as "Click here to found out more (http://www.outmore.com/)" so anyone reading the printed version can visit the site referenced by the link. This technique uses some advanced CSS that Internet Explorer 6 (and 7 as of this writing) doesn't understand, but it doesn't do any harm in those browsers, either. And it *is* a great enhancement for visitors who print from your site with Firefox and Safari.

1. **Add one last style to the *print.css* style sheet:**

   ```
   a:after {
       content: " (" attr(href) ") ";
   }
   ```

   In the *content:* line, this style adds the URL (the *attr(href)* part) at the end of each link (the *a:after* part).

2. **Save the *print.css* file. In your Web browser, open *cosmo.html* and print it.**

   The printed page should look something like Figure 13-5—a simple, barebones, just-the-facts page.

   You'll find a completed version of the page in the *chapter_13_finished* folder.

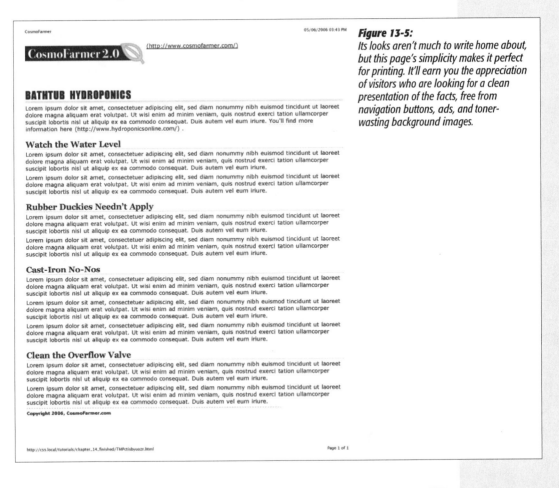

Figure 13-5:
Its looks aren't much to write home about, but this page's simplicity makes it perfect for printing. It'll earn you the appreciation of visitors who are looking for a clean presentation of the facts, free from navigation buttons, ads, and toner-wasting background images.

Improving Your CSS Habits

At this point, we've covered most aspects of Cascading Style Sheets. With the addition of CSS-based layout, which you learned about in Part III, you're now an unstoppable Web-designing machine. But even after you've mastered all the properties CSS offers, nailed those annoying browser bugs, and learned great tricks for producing beautiful Web pages, you can still stand to learn a few techniques that'll make your CSS easier to create, use, and maintain.

This chapter covers some recommendations for creating and using CSS. None of them count as "must know" CSS essentials, but they can make your CSS work go faster, leading to less frustration and greater productivity.

Adding Comments

When it's time to edit a style sheet weeks, months or even years after creating it, you may find yourself wondering "Why'd I create that style? What does it do?" As with any project, when building a Web site, you should keep notes of what you did and why. Fortunately, you don't need a pad of paper to do this. You can embed your notes right into your style sheets using CSS comments.

A CSS comment is simply a note contained within two sets of characters, /* and */. As with HTML comments, CSS comments aren't read or acted on by a Web browser, but they do let you add helpful reminders to your style sheets. Say you created a style intended to solve an Internet Explorer bug:

```
* html .imageFloat {
    display: inline;
}
```

At the time you wrote the style, you knew what you were doing, but will you still remember three months later? Add a comment and it'll be easy for you or someone else who needs to work on the site to figure out what the style does and why it was created:

```
/* Fix IE 5 and 6 double-margin bug */
* html .imageFloat {
    display: inline;
}
```

If you have a lot to say, comments can span multiple lines as well. Just begin with /*, type all the comments you'd like, then end with */. This is handy when adding background information at the beginning of a style sheet as pictured in Figure 14-1.

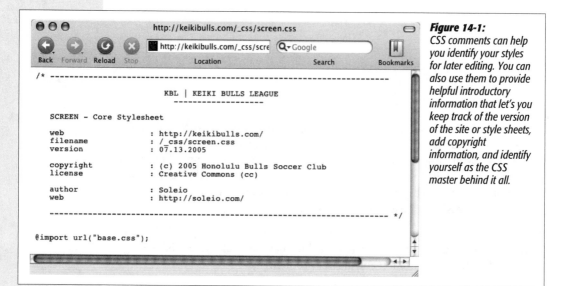

Figure 14-1:
CSS comments can help you identify your styles for later editing. You can also use them to provide helpful introductory information that let's you keep track of the version of the site or style sheets, add copyright information, and identify yourself as the CSS master behind it all.

Organizing Styles and Style Sheets

You've learned a lot in this book about creating styles and style sheets. But when you're designing a site that's meant to last, you can incorporate a few other steps to help you out in the future. The day will come when you need to change the look of the site, tweak a particular style, or hand off your hard work to someone else who'll be in charge. In addition to leaving notes for yourself and others, a little planning and organization within your CSS will make things go more smoothly down the road.

Name Styles Clearly

You've already learned the technical aspects of naming different types of selectors—class selectors begin with a . (period) to identify the styles as a class, and ID styles begin with the # symbol. In addition, the names you give IDs and classes must begin with a letter, and can't contain symbols like &, *, or !. But beyond those requirements, following some rules of thumb can help you keep track of your styles and work more efficiently:

Name styles by purpose not appearance. It's tempting to use a name like *.redhighlight* when creating a style to format eye-catching, fire-engine red text. But what if you (or your boss or your client) decide that orange, blue, or chartreuse look better? Let's face it: a style named *.redhighlight* that's actually chartreuse is confusing. It's better to use a name that describes the *purpose* of the style. For example if that "red" highlight is intended to indicate an error that a visitor made while filling out a form, then use the name *.error*. When the style needs to alert the visitor of some important information, a name like *.alert* would work. Either way, changing the color or other formatting options of the style won't cause confusion, since the style's still intended to point out an error or alert the visitor—regardless of its color.

Don't use names based on position. For the same reason you avoid naming styles by appearance, you should avoid naming them by position. Sometimes a name like *#leftSidebar* seems like an obvious choice—"I want all this stuff in a box placed at the left edge of the page!" But it's possible that you (or someone else) will want the left sidebar moved to the right, top, or even bottom of the page. All of a sudden, the name *#leftSidebar* makes no sense at all. A name more appropriate to the *purpose* of that sidebar—like *#news*, *#events*, *#secondaryContent*, *#mainNav*—serves to identify the sidebar no matter where it gets moved. The names you've see so far in this book—*#gallery*, *.figure*, *.banner*, *#wrapper* and so on—follow this convention.

Avoid cryptic names. Names like *.s*, *#s1*, and *#s2* may save you a few keystrokes and make your files a bit smaller, but they can cause trouble when you need to update your site. You could end up scratching your head, wondering what all those weird styles are for. Be succinct, but clear: *.sidebar*, *#copyright*, and *#banner* don't take all that much typing, and their purpose is immediately obvious.

Note: For more tips on naming styles, check out *www.stuffandnonsense.co.uk/archives/whats_in_a_name_pt2.html*. You can also learn a lot from checking out the naming conventions used on other sites. The Web Developer's Toolbar, discussed in the box on page 39, gives you a quick way to reveal the style names.

Use Multiple Classes to Save Time

Often, two or more items on a Web page share many similar formatting properties. You may want to use the same border styles to create a frame around a bunch of images on a page. But there may be some formatting differences between those items as well. Maybe you want some images to float to the left and have a right margin, while some photos float to the right and have a left margin (Figure 14-2).

The most obvious solution's to create two class styles, each having the same border properties but different float and margin properties. You then apply one class

---

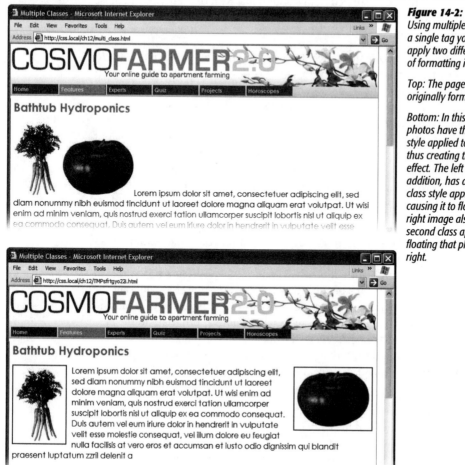

Figure 14-2:
Using multiple classes on a single tag you can apply two different sets of formatting instructions.

Top: The page as originally formatted.

Bottom: In this case, both photos have the same style applied to them, thus creating the border effect. The left image, in addition, has another class style applied, causing it to float left; the right image also has a second class applied to it floating that photo to the right.

to the images that should float left and another to the images that should float right. But what if you need to update the border style for all of these images? You'll need to edit *two* styles, and if you forget one, the images on one side of the page will all have the wrong frames!

There's a trick that works in all browsers and surprisingly few designers take advantage of—*multiple classes* applied to the same tag. This just means that when you use the class attribute for a tag, you add two (or more) class names like this: *<div class="note alert">*. In this example, the <div> tag receives formatting instructions from both the *.note* style and the *.alert* style.

Say you want to use the same border style for a group of images, but some of the images you want floating left and others you want floating right. You'd approach the problem like this:

1. **Create a class style that includes the formatting properties shared by all the images.**

   This style could be called *.imgborder* and have a 2-pixel, solid black border around all four edges.

2. **Create two additional class styles, one for the left floated images, and another for the right floated images.**

   For example, *.floatLeft* and *.floatRight*. One style would include properties unique to one set of images (floated left with a small right margin), while the other style includes properties specific to the second group of images.

3. **Apply both classes to each tag, like so:**

   ```
   <img src="photo1.jpg" width="100" height="100" class="imgborder floatLeft" />
   ```

   or

   ```
   <img src="photo1.jpg" width="100" height="100" class="imgborder floatRight" />
   ```

   At this point, two classes apply to each tag, and the Web browser combines the style information for each class to format the tag. Now if you want to change the border style, then simply edit one style—*.imgborder*—to update the borders around both the left and right floated images.

Tip: You can list more than two classes with this method; just make sure to add a space between each class name.

This technique's useful when you need to tweak only a couple of properties of one element, while leaving other similarly formatted items unchanged. You may want a generic sidebar design that floats a sidebar to the right, adds creative background images, and includes carefully styled typography. You can use this style throughout your site, but the width of that sidebar varies in several instances. Perhaps it's 300 pixels wide on some pages and 200 pixels wide on others. In this case, create a single class style (like *.sidebar*) with the basic sidebar formatting and separate classes for defining just the width of the sidebar—for example, *.w300* and *.w200*. Then apply two classes to each sidebar: *<div class="sidebar w300">*.

Organize Styles by Grouping

Adding one style after another is a common way to build a style sheet. But after a while, what was once a simple collection of five styles has ballooned into a massive 150-style CSS file. At that point, quickly finding the one style you need to change is like looking for a needle in a haystack. (Of course, haystacks don't have a Find command, but you get the point.) If you organize your styles from the get-go, you'll make your life a lot easier in the long run. There are no hard and fast rules for *how* to group styles together, but here are two common methods:

- **Group styles that apply to related parts of a page.** Group all the rules that apply to text, graphics, and links in the banner of a page in one place, the rules that style the main navigation in another, and the styles for the main content in yet another.

- **Group styles with a related purpose.** Put all the styles for layout in one group, the styles for typography in another, the styles for links in yet another group, and so on.

Using comments to separate style groups

Whatever approach you take, make sure to use CSS comments (page 383) to introduce each grouping of styles. Say you collected all the styles that control the layout of your pages into one place in a style sheet. Introduce that collection with a comment like this:

```
/*   *** Layout *** */
```

or

```
/* --------------------------
              Layout
-------------------------- */
```

As long as you begin with /* and end with */, you can use whatever frilly combination of asterisks, dashes, or symbols you'd like to help make those comments easy to spot. You'll find as many variations on this as there are Web designers. If you're looking for inspiration, then check out how these sites comment their style sheets: *www.wired.com*, *www.mezzoblue.com*, and *http://keikibulls.com.* (Use the Web Developer's Toolbar described in the box on page 391 to help you peek at other designers' style sheets.)

Tip: For a method of naming comments that makes it easy to find a particular section of a style sheet you're editing, check out *www.stopdesign.com/log/2005/05/03/css-tip-flags.html.*

Using Multiple Style Sheets

As you read in Chapter 13, you can create different style sheets for different types of displays—maybe one for a screen and another for a printer. But you may also want to have multiple onscreen style sheets, purely for organizational purposes. This takes the basic concept from the previous section—grouping related styles— one step further. When a style sheet becomes so big that it's difficult to find and edit styles, it may be time to create separate style sheets that each serve an individual function. You can put styles used to format forms in one style sheet, styles used for layout in another, styles that determine the color of things in a third, another style sheet for keeping your Internet Explorer hacks, and so on. Keep the number of separate files reasonable since having, say, 30 external CSS files to weed through may not save time at all.

CSS: THE MISSING MANUAL

At first glance, it may seem like you'll end up with more code in each Web page, since you'll have that many more external style sheets to link to or import—one line of code for each file. Ah, but there's a better approach: Create a single external style sheet that uses the *@import* directive to include multiple style sheets. Figure 14-3 illustrates the concept.

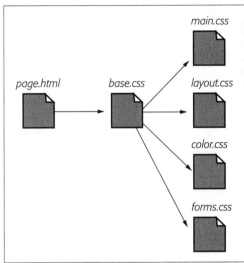

main.css

layout.css

color.css

forms.css

page.html

base.css

Figure 14-3:
Let a single external style sheet serve as gatekeeper for your site's CSS. Each HTML page in the site can link to a single CSS file (base.css in this example). The HTML never has to change, even if you want to add or remove additional external style sheets. Just update the base.css file by adding or removing @import directives.

Here's how to set up this type of arrangement:

1. **Create external style sheets to format the different types of elements of your site.**

   For example a *color.css* file with styles that control the color of the site, a *forms.css* file that controls form formatting, a *layout.css* file for layout control, and a *main.css* file which covers everything else (see the right side of Figure 14-3).

Note: These suggestions are just a few possibilities. Organize your styles and style sheets in whatever seems most logical and works best for you. For more suggestions, check out this article on modular CSS design: *www.contentwithstyle.co.uk/Articles/12/modular-css/*.

---

2. **Create an external style sheet and import each of the style sheets you created in step 1.**

   You can name this file *base.css*, *global.css*, *site.css* or something generic like that. This CSS file won't contain any rules. Instead use the *@import* directive to attach the other style sheets like this:

   ```
   @import url(main.css);
   @import url(layout.css);
   @import url(color.css);
   @import url(forms.css);
   ```

That's the only code that needs to be in the file, though you may add some comments with a version number, site name, and so on to help identify this file.

Tip: For a better way to attach an "IE-only" style sheet, see page 399.

---

3. **Finally, attach the style sheet from step 2 to the HTML pages of your site using either the <link> tag or the @import method. (See page 33 for more on using these methods.) For example:**

```
<link rel="stylesheet" href="base.css" type="text/css" />
```

Now, when a Web page loads, the Web browser loads *base.css,* which in turn tells the browser to load the four other style sheets.

It may feel like there's a whole lot of loading going on here, but once the browser's downloaded those files and stored them in its cache, it won't have to retrieve them over the Internet again. (See the box on page 35.)

There's another benefit to using a single external style sheet to load several other style sheets: If you decide later to further divide your styles into additional styles sheets, then you won't have to muck around with the HTML of your site. Instead, just add one more *@import* directive to that gatekeeper style sheet (see step 2). If you decide to take all the styles related to type out of the *main.css* file and put them in their own *type.css* file, then you won't need to touch the Web pages on your site. Simply open the style sheet with all of the *@import* directives in it and add one more: *@import url(type.css)*.

This arrangement also lets you have some fun with your site by swapping in different style sheets for temporary design changes. Say you decide to change the color of your site for the day, month, or season. If you've already put the main color-defining styles into a separate *color.css* file, then you can create another file (like *summer_fun.css*) with a different set of colors. Then, in the gatekeeper file, change the *@import* directive for the *color.css* file to load the new color style file (for example, *@import url(summer_fun.css)*.

Tip: Have you ever seen sites that have buttons that let you change the appearance of the site instantly? This is done with several different style sheets and a little JavaScript kung fu. You can find out how the basic concept works here: *www.alistapart.com/articles/bodyswitchers/*. For the latest and greatest version of the JavaScript required to make this magic, visit *www.stuffandnonsense.co.uk/resources/iotbs.html*.

Eliminating Browser Style Interference

When you view a non "CSS-ified" Web page in a Web browser, HTML tags already have some minimal formatting: headings are bold, the <h1> tag is bigger than other text, links are underlined and blue, and so on. In some cases, different Web browsers apply slightly different formatting to each of these elements. You may experience some frustrating "it *almost* looks the same in Internet Explorer and Firefox and Safari" moments.

The Web Developer's Toolbar

Web designers have to stay on top of a lot of things: HTML, CSS, links, graphics, forms, and so on. Troubleshooting problems with any of these items can sometimes be a real challenge. The Web Developer's Toolbar (*http:// chrispederick.com/work/webdeveloper/*), created by Chris Pederick, is a Firefox extension that's like the Swiss-army knife of Web design (see Figure 14-4). If you don't have Firefox, you should install it for this toolbar alone (*www. mozilla.com/firefox*).

Download the extension, install it, and spend a little time with the different options. You have many features available to you, but here are a few worth noting:

- Choose CSS → **View CSS**, and you'll see all of the styles for the current page, even styles imported from multiple style sheets. If you've ever been to a Web site and wondered "How'd they do that?" this tool gives you a free backstage tour.

- Choose CSS → **Edit CSS**, and you can edit the styles of the current Web page. This doesn't do any permanent damage to the real Web page, but it does let you tweak a page's styles and immediately see the results. Think of it as the ultimate WYSIWYG editor.

- The **Information** menu provides a wealth of detailed and often geeky under-the-hood details. The *Display Block Size* option displays the dimensions of block-level elements such as tables and divs. *Display Element Information* provides info on any element you hover over (including HTML attributes, CSS properties, and its position on the page). And *Display Id & Class Details* is a great way to see the names of styles applied to tags on the page. Use it to see how other sites name their <div> tags.

- The **Tools** menu gives you access to online tools for validating HTML and CSS, and even checking links. These tools work only for pages that are online, not ones you're currently working with on your computer.

Microsoft offers a similar tool for Internet Explorer. You can find it by visiting *www.microsoft.com* and entering *IE Developer Toolbar* in the search box.)

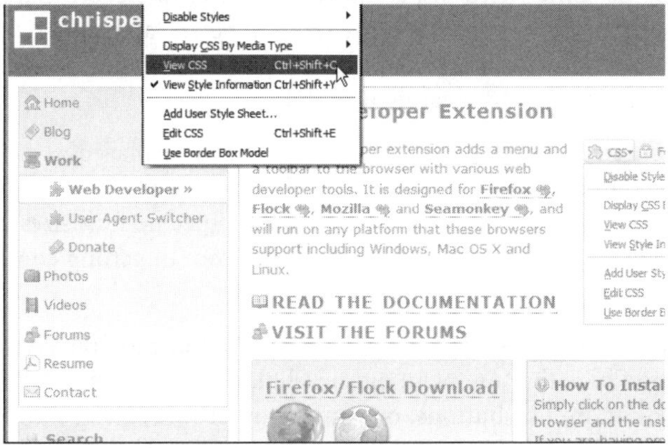

Figure 14-4:
The Web Developer's Extension is a must-have tool for any Web designer. This Firefox extension lets you view the styles of any site on the Web, identify the structure of a page's HTML, find out more information on how any element on a page is styled, validate a page and its CSS in one easy operation, and even edit the CSS of a page and see how the changes you make affect the appearance of the page.

Note: Firefox actually uses a CSS style sheet to format HTML tags. To see it on a Mac, locate the Firefox application file, right click it and then select "Show package contents." Then navigate to Contents → MacOS → res and open the *html.css* file in a text editing program. In Windows, you'll find that file at *C:\Program Files\Mozilla Firefox\res\html.css*. As you can see, it takes a lot of styles to make regular HTML look boring.

Because of these browser differences, it's a good idea to "zero out" the formatting for commonly used tags so your audience can see the beautiful styling you worked so hard to create (see Figure 14-5). All you have to do is set up some basic styles at the beginning of your style sheet that remove the offensive formatting.

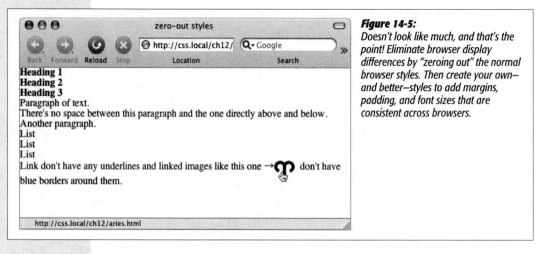

Figure 14-5:
Doesn't look like much, and that's the point! Eliminate browser display differences by "zeroing out" the normal browser styles. Then create your own—and better—styles to add margins, padding, and font sizes that are consistent across browsers.

Here are some things you may want to do to make browsers stop meddling with your designs:

- **Remove padding and margins.** Browsers add top and bottom margins to most block-level elements—the familiar space that appears between <p> tags, for example. This can cause some weird display issues like when the exact margin amount is inconsistently applied across browsers. A better approach is to remove padding and margins from the block-level tags you use and then purposely add the amount you want by creating new styles.

- **Apply consistent font sizes.** While text inside a <p> tag is displayed as 1em, Web browsers apply different sizes to other tags. You can force all tags to be 1em to begin with, and then create additional styles with specific font sizes for the different tags. That way, you stand a much better chance of getting consistent font sizes across browsers.

- **Remove underlines from links.** As you saw in Chapter 9, you can create visually exciting navigation bars that use plain old text links. In fact, if most of the links in your site look more like buttons, or you use other formatting to indicate an element's clickability (maybe by adding hover effects), then start off by removing the underlines. You can later selectively add underlines when you want them. (See "Using Descendent Selectors" on page 394.)

- **Remove borders from linked images.** Internet Explorer, Firefox, and other browsers add a colored border around any image inside of a link. If you're like most people, you find this border both unattractive and unnecessary. Remove it and start fresh.

To put these ideas into action, here are a few basic styles you can add at the beginning of your style sheet:

```
body, h1, h2, h3, h4, h5, h6, p, ol, ul, form, blockquote {
    padding: 0;
    margin: 0;
}
h1, h2, h3, h4, h5, h6, pre, code {
    font-size: 1em;
}
a {
    text-decoration: none;
}
a img {
    border: none;
}
```

The first two styles here are group selectors that apply the same formatting to every one of the tags listed. Add these styles to the beginning of your style sheet, and then, further down the style sheet, override them on a case-by-case basis. After zeroing out the margins and font-size for the <h1> tag, you may want to give the <h1> tag a specific top margin value and font size. Just add another style, like so:

```
h1 {
    margin-top: 5px;
    font-size: 2.5em;
}
```

Thanks to the cascade, as long as this *h1* style appears in the style sheet *after* the group selectors removing the margins and changing the font size, the new values take precedence.

Note: Web luminary Tantek Celic is often credited with introducing the very useful technique of undoing the standard Web browser formatting of HTML. You can see his basic set of undo styles at *http://tantek. com/log/2004/undohtml.css*.

Using Descendent Selectors

Descendent selectors are a powerful tool for efficient Web site building. As discussed in Chapter 3, they let you pinpoint the tags you want to style with greater accuracy than tag styles and with less work than class styles. Most of the time you want to format *all* the links in a navigation bar the same way, but that doesn't mean you want to format all of the links in the entire *page* the same way. What you need is a way to say (in CSS) "format *only* the links in the nav bar this way" without having to apply a class style to each of those links. In other words, you need the ability to format the same HTML in different ways depending on where it's located—and that's exactly what descendent selectors offer (see Figure 14-6).

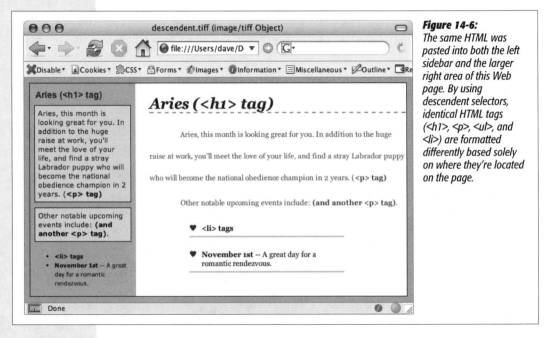

Figure 14-6:
The same HTML was pasted into both the left sidebar and the larger right area of this Web page. By using descendent selectors, identical HTML tags (<h1>, <p>, <ul>, and <li>) are formatted differently based solely on where they're located on the page.

Compartmentalize Your Pages

One of your biggest allies in using descendent selectors effectively is the <div> tag. Since this HTML tag lets you create logical *divisions* in a page, you can use it to identify different layout elements like a banner, a sidebar, a column of text, and so on. As discussed on page 47, you can organize the content of your page into different areas by wrapping HTML in a <div> tag.

Group the title of a story and a list of links used to navigate the story's pages like this:

```
<div>
<h2>The CosmoFarmer Revolution</h2>
<ul>
<li><a href="page1.html">Page 1</a></li>
```

```
<li><a href="page2.html">Page 2</a></li>
<li><a href="page3.html">Page 3</a></li>
</ul>
</div>
```

After adding the <div>, identify it for CSS purposes with either a *class* or *ID* attribute: *<div class="pullQuote">* or *<div id="banner">*. When you want to include the same type of layout element more than once on a page—multiple pull quotes in a single story perhaps—use a class. For regions that appear only once per page—like the banner—an ID is the common choice.

Suppose the list of links in the HTML above appears twice on a page—at the beginning of the text and at the end. You'd apply a class to it like this:

```
<div class="storyNav">
    <h2>The CosmoFarmer Revolution</h2>
<ul>
<li><a href="page1.html">Page 1</a></li>
<li><a href="page2.html">Page 2</a></li>
<li><a href="page3.html">Page 3</a></li>
</ul>
</div>
```

Tip: You don't always need to add a <div> tag to style a group of elements. If the HTML above had only an unordered list of links and didn't include the <h2> tag, then you could just as easily skip the <div> tag and simply add a class to the unordered list: *<ul class="storyNav">*.

Once you identify each <div> on a page, it becomes very easy to use a descendent selector to target tags inside a particular <div>. Say you want to create a unique look for each of the links in the above HTML. You'd create a descendent selector like this:

```
.storyNav a {
    color: red;
    background-color: #ccc;
}
```

Now links will appear as red text on a light gray background, but *only* when they appear *inside* another tag with the *storyNav* class applied to it. Best of all, if you want to add another link (like *page4.html*) to this list, then you don't have to lift a finger to format it like the other links. The browser handles all of that automatically when it applies the descendent selector.

Formatting other tags inside that <div> is a simple matter of creating a descendent selector that begins with the class name—*.storyNav*, for instance—followed by a space and the tag you want to style. To format the <h2> that appears inside the <div>, create the descendent selector *.storyNav h2*.

Identify the Body

Because descendent selectors provide such specific targeting of styles, you can easily create styles that not only apply to one particular area of a page, but also apply only to particular *types* of pages on your site. Say you want to style the <h1> tag differently on the home page than on other pages of the site. An easy way to distinguish <h1> tags on the home page is to add a class or ID to the <body> tag of the home page:

```
<body id="home">
```

or

```
<body class="home">
```

You can style the <h1> tag on the home page using a descendent selector: *#home h1* (if you're using an ID) or *.home h1* (if you're using a class). With this technique, you can create entirely different looks for any tag on any particular page of your site. One approach is to identify the section of the site each page is in. Say your site's divided into four sections—news, events, articles, and links. On each page within a section, add either a class or ID to the <body> tag. So each page in the news section might have the following HTML: *<body class="news">*, while pages in the events section would have *<body class="events">*.

Tip: You can also use a class to identify the type of layout you want for a particular page (like a one-, two-, or three-column design).

One great use for identifying a page's section in the site is to highlight that section's button in a navigation bar. The highlighted button acts as a kind of "you are here" marker, as shown in Figure 14-7. If a page is in the news section of your site, you can highlight the "news" button so visitors can tell immediately which section they're in.

Here's how to format a navigation button differently depending on which section of your site it's in:

1. **Add an identifier to the <body> tag indicating the section the page is in.**

   For example, *<body id="home">*. Do the same thing for each section, so pages in the news section of the site would have code like this: *<body id="news">*.

2. **Add a navigation bar to the page.**

   Step by step instructions are on page 218.

3. **Identify each link within the navigation bar.**

   For a link to the home page, you might have this code: *<a href="/index.html" id="homeLink">Home</a>*. The ID lets you identify that particular link as the one going to the home page. (You could do the same thing using a class instead of an ID.) Repeat for the other links: *<a href="/news/" id="newsLink">News</a>*, and so on.

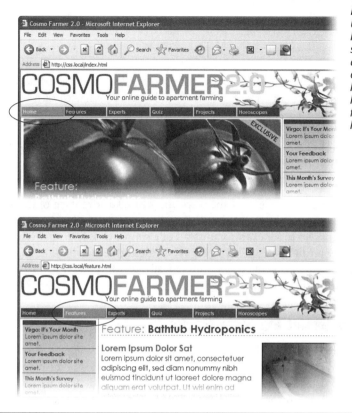

Figure 14-7:
Using descendent selectors, you can highlight a button in a navigation bar simply by changing the class or ID applied to the <body> tag. In this example, when the body tag has the ID home applied to it, the Home button lights up (circled, top). Change the ID to feature, and the Features button highlights (circled, bottom).

At this point, you have enough information in your HTML to uniquely format each section's link using CSS. In this example, you know that the Home page link is nested inside a <body> tag with the ID of home *only* on the home page.

4. **Create a descendent selector to format each section's link differently when the link is inside a page for that section.**

For the home page in this example, the descendent selector would look like this:

```
#home a#homeLink
```

This selector formats the *#homeLink* only when it's inside another tag with the ID *#home*. In most cases, you'll want the look of the "you are here" button to be the same for each section of the site, so you can use a group selector (page 53) to group all the descendent selectors for each section's button. That way, you can apply the same formatting to each button without creating separate rules for each button. A group selector to highlight the current section's navigation button with a light yellow background may look like this:

```
#home a#homeLink,
#news a#newLink,
```

```
#articles a#articlesLink,
#links a#linksLink {
    background-color: #FBEF99;
}
```

Tip: When creating a group selector that includes several descendent selectors, keep each selector on its own line as in this example. It's easier to identify each selector in the group this way when you need to go back and edit your style sheet.

Using the same technique, make additional styles to apply different looks for the links when you hover over them, click them, or when they've been visited. See page 209 for the details.

These few examples are just some of the ways you can take advantage of descendent selectors. They can make your style sheets a little more complex. You'll have styles like *#home .navbar a*, for example, instead of a simple class like *.navLink*. But once the styles are set up, you'll need to do very little further formatting. HTML pasted into different areas of the page automatically gets formatted in strikingly different ways. Almost like magic.

Managing Internet Explorer Hacks

Browsers don't always behave the way you, or the rules of CSS, expect. Browsers like Safari, Firefox, and Internet Explorer 7 handle CSS quite well and display CSS-based Web pages consistently and predictably. Getting your designs to work in Internet Explorer 5 and 6 for Windows is much more of a challenge. Although these browsers are old by today's standards, they still make up the majority of Web browsers in use.

Throughout this book, you've seen some of the most horrific IE 5 and 6 bugs—and their solutions. There's the double-margin bug (page 302) and IE 5's box model problem (page 150). Techniques for managing these problems include the ** html* hack (page 152). But knowing the techniques isn't enough. You've got to consider your entire Web audience and make sure your IE fixes don't get in the way and spoil the fun for other viewers.

Tip: You can find a list of pages describing various CSS bugs in many different browsers at *http://css-discuss.incutio.com/?page=BrowserBugs*.

Design for Contemporary Browsers First

Because Internet Explorer 6 is so common, many Web designers use it for testing their site design. When they find a problem with the way the page looks in this browser, they manipulate their CSS until the page looks fine. Unfortunately, because IE 6 doesn't always get CSS right, the "solutions" designers use for that browser cause more modern, CSS-savvy browsers like Firefox and Safari to display pages incorrectly.

The backward-looking approach of designing for Internet Explorer 6 would be fine if everyone visits your site on Windows with Internet Explorer 6 for the rest of eternity. But as more people upgrade to Internet Explorer 7 or switch to state-of-the-art browsers like Firefox or Safari, your fine-tuned IE 6 pages will begin to break. A better approach is to design with Internet Explorer 7, Firefox, and Safari in mind. Make sure your CSS works in those browsers and you can be reasonably confident that you're using CSS correctly. Then, after your site looks great in those browsers, it's time to fix the problems that crop up in Internet Explorer 5 and 6.

Tackling all those problems may sound like an overwhelming task, but take heart. You'll repeatedly encounter the same set of bugs, which in turn require the same set of fixes. So once you become an old hand at identifying and fixing the peek-a-boo bug or the double-margin bug, it won't be hard for you to add the necessary hacks to fix your pages for IE 5 and 6.

Tip: For more terrifying information on how Internet Explorer can mangle your carefully designed Web pages visit: *www.positioniseverything.net/explorer.html* and *www.positioniseverything.net/ie-primer.html*.

Isolate CSS for IE with Conditional Comments

The * *html* hack in Chapter 7 (page 152) is one way to send the "this'll fix your stupid bug" styles to just Internet Explorer 6 and earlier without adversely affecting other browsers. But as your style sheets get larger, all those little fixes start to create clutter. Even if you isolate those changes into one part of your style sheet (as described in step 8 on page 192), you may still end up inserting some invalid CSS code (like *zoom: 1*) that prevents your main CSS file from validating (page 32).

Another way to collect IE-only styles in a single place is to use Internet Explorer's *conditional comments* feature (Figure 14-8). This Microsoft invention provides a way of inserting HTML that only Internet Explorer understands. Other browsers simply see the code as an HTML comment and ignore it.

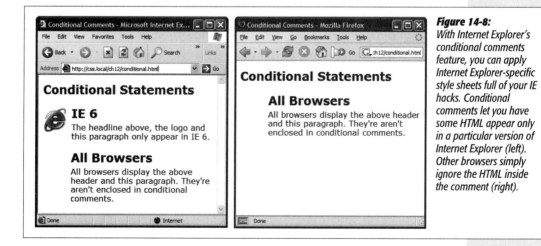

Figure 14-8:
With Internet Explorer's conditional comments feature, you can apply Internet Explorer-specific style sheets full of your IE hacks. Conditional comments let you have some HTML appear only in a particular version of Internet Explorer (left). Other browsers simply ignore the HTML inside the comment (right).

Conditional comments can even target different versions of IE. You can put all of your IE-5 only styles in a single external style sheet (like *IE5_styles.css*) and use a conditional comment to link it to IE 5 browsers only. This approach also makes it a snap to eliminate those styles when IE 5 finally goes the way of the dinosaurs. Just remove the external style sheet. Your non-IE visitors will benefit too. When you use conditional comments, other browsers don't download those external style sheets at all. As a result, your site opens and runs faster for these lucky folks.

Here's the basic structure of a conditional comment:

```
<!--[if IE]>
Some HTML code that only applies to IE goes here.
<![endif]-->
```

The *<!--[if IE]>* is the *condition* itself. It translates to: "if this browser is Internet Explorer then process the following HTML." So any Internet Explorer browser acts on the HTML that comes after this line of code and stops when it gets to the *<![endif]-->* statement. In this way, you can add any HTML—text, images, styles and even links to external style sheets—to Internet Explorer only.

Note: Non-IE-browsers simply view conditional statements as HTML comments and ignore them.

Conditional comments and IE 7

Internet Explorer 7 understands CSS much better than earlier versions, so you may have to hide some IE hacks from that browser as well. Fortunately, conditional comments also let you specify which *version* of Internet Explorer the style sheet applies to. Say you want to have a particular style sheet load only for Internet Explorer 6 or earlier. Add the following conditional comment to your Web page's head:

```
<!--[if lte IE 6]>
<link href="IE_styles.css" rel="stylesheet" type="text/css" />
<![endif]-->
```

Or, using the *@import* method:

```
<!--[if lte IE 6]>
<style type="text/css">
@import url(IE_styles.css)
</style>
<![endif]-->
```

The *lte* stands for "less than or equal to," so *if lte IE 6* means "if this browser is version 6 or earlier of Internet Explorer."

Conditional comments and the cascade

Use whatever method you prefer for linking an external style sheet (page 31), but add any conditional comments *after* any other linked style sheets. Most IE hacks tend to redefine styles already present in the style sheet—styles that work for other browsers. And, due to the nature of the cascade, rules defined later in a page can override earlier defined styles. In order to make sure your redefined "IE-only" styles successfully take hold in Internet Explorer, they should appear after any other style sheets attached to the page.

Here's the code you might use to link a) a style sheet for all browsers, b) a style sheet just for IE 6, and c) a style sheet for version 5 or earlier of IE:

```
<link href="global_styles.css" rel="stylesheet" type="text/css" />
<!--[if IE 6]>
<link href="IE6_styles.css" rel="stylesheet" type="text/css" />
<![endif]-->
<!--[if lte IE 5]>
<link href="IE5_styles.css" rel="stylesheet" type="text/css" />
<![endif]-->
```

Note: For more information on Internet Explorer's conditional comments, visit the source: *http://msdn. microsoft.com/workshop/author/dhtml/overview/ccomment_ovw.asp.*

Part Five: Appendixes

5

Appendix A: CSS Property Reference

Appendix B: CSS in Dreamweaver 8

Appendix C: CSS Resources

CSS Property Reference

Mastering Cascading Style Sheets involves knowing how to use a large number of CSS properties that control the appearance of text, images, tables, and forms. To help you in your quest, this appendix gives you a summary of the properties and values you'll use to create your own styles. This list covers nearly all of the CSS 2.1 standard properties—the ones that most Web browsers support.

Note: This appendix leaves out properties that no (or hardly any) browsers recognize. Otherwise, the following descriptions mention the browsers with which each property works. For full details straight from the horse's mouth, visit the World Wide Web Consortium's CSS 2.1 specification at *www.w3.org/TR/CSS21/*.

CSS Values

Every CSS property has a corresponding value. The *color* property, which formats font color, requires a color value to specify which color you want to use. The property *color: #FFF;* creates white text. Different properties require different types of values, but they come in four basic categories: colors, lengths and sizes, keywords, and URLs.

Colors

You can assign colors to many different properties, including those for font, background, and borders. CSS provides several different ways to specify color.

Keywords

A color keyword is simply the name of the color, like *white* or *black*. There are currently 17 recognized color keywords: *aqua, black, blue, fuchsia, gray, green, lime, maroon, navy, olive, orange, purple, red, silver, teal, white,* and *yellow*. Some browsers accept more keywords, and CSS 3 promises to offer many more in the future (*http://www.w3.org/TR/css3-color/*).

RGB values

Computer monitors create colors using a mixture of red, green, and blue light. These RGB values can create (nearly) the full spectrum of color. Almost every design, illustration, and graphics program lets you specify colors using RGB, so it's easy to transfer a color from one of those programs to a CSS property. CSS represents RGB values in several ways:

- **Hex values.** The method most commonly used on the Web for identifying color, hex color values consist of three two-character numbers in the hexadecimal (that is, base 16) system. *#FF0033* represents an RGB value composed of red (FF, which equals 255 in normal, base 10 numbers), green (00), and blue (33). The # tells CSS to expect hex numbers ahead, and it's required. If you leave off the #, a Web browser won't display the correct color.

Tip: If all three two-digit values have repeated digits, you can shorten the hex value by using just the first number of each pair. For example #361 means the same thing as #336611.

- **RGB percentages.** You can also specify a color using percentage values, like this: *rgb(100%, 0%, 33%)*. You can get these numbers from image editing and design programs that can define colors using percentages (which is most of them).

- **Decimal values.** Finally, you can use decimal RGB values to specify a color. The format is similar to the percentage option, but you use a number from 0 to 255 to indicate each color: *rgb(255, 0, 33)*.

It doesn't matter which method you use—they all work. For consistency's sake, you should pick one way of specifying RGB values and stick with it. The Windows and Mac operating systems both have color pickers which let you find the perfect color from a palette of millions, and then show you the RGB value. Alternatively, you can use this free online color picker: *www.ficml.org/jemimap/style/color/wheel.html*.

Tip: Many Mac programs such as TextEdit, let you open the color picker by pressing ⌘-Shift-C.

Lengths and Sizes

CSS provides many different ways to measure the size of type, the width of a box, or the thickness of a borderline. To indicate type size, you can use inches, picas, points, centimeters, millimeters, em-heights, ex-heights, pixels, and percentages.

CSS: THE MISSING MANUAL

However, even though there are a lot of options, most don't apply to the world of onscreen display, for reasons discussed on page 104. You really need to think about these three only—pixels, ems, and percentages.

Pixels

A pixel is a single dot on a computer screen. Pixels give you a consistent method of identifying lengths and font sizes from computer to computer: 72 pixels on one monitor is 72 pixels on another monitor. That doesn't mean the actual, real-world length is the same for everyone, though. Since people set their monitors to different resolutions—800 ×600, 1024 × 768, 1600 × 1200, or whatever—72 pixels may take up 1 inch on one monitor, but only half an inch for someone else. Nevertheless, pixels give you the most consistent control over presentation.

Note: There's just one drawback to using pixels: folks using Internet Explorer 6 or earlier can't resize any type that's sized using pixels. If your text is too small for someone's eyes, the visitor won't be able to enlarge it to make it more readable. (See page 105 for more on pixel measurements.)

Ems

Originally from the typographic world, an *em* is a unit that represents the height of the capital letter M for a particular font. In Web pages, one em is the height of the Web browser's base text size, which is usually 16 pixels. However, anyone can change that base size setting, so 1em may be 16 pixels for one person, but 24 pixels in someone else's browser. In other words, ems are a relative unit of measurement.

In addition to the browser's initial font size setting, ems can inherit size information from containing tags. A type size of .9em would make text about 14 pixels tall on most browsers with a 16 pixel base size. But if you have a <p> tag with a font size of .9ems, and then a <strong> tag with a font size of .9ems inside that <p> tag, that <strong> tag's em size isn't 14 pixels—it's 12 pixels (16 × .9 × .9). So keep inheritance in mind when you use em values.

Percentages

CSS uses percentages for many different purposes, like sizing text, determining the width or height of an element, and specifying the placement of an image in the background of a style, to name a few. Now, what you're taking a percentage *of* varies from property to property. For font sizes, the percentage is calculated based on the text's inherited value. Say the general font size for a paragraph is 16 pixels tall. If you created a style for one special paragraph and set its font size to 200 percent, that text is displayed at 32 pixels tall. When applied to width, however, percentages are calculated based on the width of the page, or on another parent element with a set width. You specify a percentage with a number followed by the percent sign: *100%*.

Keywords

Instead of color or size, many properties have their own specific values that affect how the properties display and are represented by keywords. The *text-align* property, which aligns text on screen, can take one of four keywords: *right*, *left*, *center*, and *justify*. Since keywords vary from property to property, read the property descriptions that follow to learn the keyword appropriate to each property.

One keyword, however, is shared by all properties—*inherit*. This keyword lets you force a style to inherit a value from a parent element. You can use the inherit keyword on any property. This keyword gives you the power to make styles inherit properties that aren't normally inherited from parent tags. For instance, say you use the *text-decoration* property to underline a paragraph. Other tags, such as <em> and <strong>, inside the <p> tag don't inherit this value, but you can force them to do so with the *inherit* keyword:

```
em, strong {
    text-decoration: inherit;
}
```

That way, the em and strong tags display the same text-decoration value as their parent <p> tag—underline, in this case. So the <em> and <strong> elements of the paragraph each get underlined as does the entire paragraph so you'd end up with double underlines under emphasized text (a good reason why that property *isn't* inherited normally). If you change the <p> tag's *text-decoration* value to *overline* instead of underline, the <em> and <strong> tags inherit that value and display overlines, too.

Note: Underline/overline isn't a very useful example, mainly because *inherit* isn't a very useful value. But this wouldn't be a Missing Manual if it didn't give you all the facts.

URLs

URL values let you point to another file on the Web. For example, the *background-image* property accepts a URL—the path to the file on the Web—as its value, which lets you assign a graphic file as a background for a page element. This technique is handy for adding a tiling image in the background of a page or for using your own graphic for bulleted lists (see page 172).

In CSS, you specify an URL like this: *url(images/tile.gif)*. A style that adds an image called *tile.gif* to the background of the page would look like this:

```
body { background-image: url(images/tile.gif); }
```

Unlike HTML, in CSS, quotes around the URL are optional, so *url("images/tile.gif")*, *url('images/tile.gif')*, and *url(images/tile.gif)* are equivalent.

Note: The URL itself is just like the HTML *href* attribute used for links, meaning you can use an absolute URL like *http://www.missingmanuals.com/images/tile.gif,* a root-relative path like */images/tile.gif,* or a document-relative URL like *../../images/tile.gif.* See page 175 for the full story on these kinds of paths.

Text Properties

The following properties affect how text is formatted on a Web page. Since most of the properties in this category are inherited, you don't necessarily have to apply them to tags specifically intended for text (like the <p> tag). You can apply these properties to the <body> tag, so that other tags inherit and use the same settings. This technique is a quick way to create an overall font, color, and so on for a page or section.

color (inherited)

Sets the color of text. Since it's inherited, if you set the color of the <body> tag to red, for example, all text inside of the body—and all other tags inside the <body> tag—is red, too.

- **Values:** any valid color value

- **Example:** `color: #FFFF33;`

Note: The preset link colors for the <a> tag override color inheritance. In the above example, any links inside the <body> tag would still be standard hyperlink blue. See page 210 for ways to change preset link colors.

font (inherited)

This is a shortcut method for cramming the following text properties into a single style declaration: *font-style*, *font-variant*, *font-weight*, *font-size*, *line-height*, and *font-family*. (Read on for the individual descriptions.)

You must separate each value by a space and include at least *font-size* and *font-family, and* those two properties must be the last two items in the declaration. The others are optional. If you don't set a property, the browser uses its own preset value, potentially overriding inherited properties.

- **Values:** Any value that's valid for the specific font property. When including a line-height, add a slash followed by the line-height after the font size like this: *1.25em/150%.*

- **Example:** `font: italic small-caps bold 1.25em/150% Arial, Helvetica, sans-serif;`

font-family (inherited)

Specifies the font the browser should use to display text. Fonts are usually specified as a series of three to four options to accommodate the fact that a particular font may not be installed on a visitor's computer. See page 101.

- **Values:** A comma-separated list of font names. When a font has a space in its name, surround that font name with quotes. The last font listed is usually a generic font type instructing browsers to choose a suitable font if the other listed fonts aren't available: serif, sans-serif, monotype, fantasy, or cursive.

- **Example:** font-family: "Lucida Grande", Arial, sans-serif;

font-size (inherited)

Sets the size of text. This property is inherited, which can lead to some weird behaviors when using relative length measurements like percentages and ems.

- **Values:** Any valid CSS measurement unit (page 406), plus the following keywords: *xx-small, x-small, small, medium, large, x-large, xx-large, larger,* and *smaller. Medium* represents the Web browser's normal, preset font size, and the other sizes are multiples of medium. The exact numbers depend on the browser, but they're generally a factor of 1.2. For example, *large* is 1.2 times as big as *medium.* Due to the uncertainty of how each browser handles these keywords, many designers use pixels, ems, or percentages instead.

- **Example:** font-size: 1.25em;

Note: When the *font-size* property is inherited from another tag, these keywords multiply the *inherited* font size by the same factor (1.2 in most browsers).

---

font-style (inherited)

Makes text italic. Applied to italic text, it turns it back to plain text. The options *italic* and *oblique* are functionally the same.

- **Values:** *italic, oblique, normal*
- **Example:** font-style: italic;

font-variant (inherited)

Makes text appear in small caps, like this: SPECIAL PRESENTATION. The value *normal* removes small caps from text already formatted that way.

- **Values:** *small-caps, normal*
- **Example:** font-variant: small-caps;

---

font-weight (inherited)

Makes text bold, or removes bolding from text already formatted that way.

- **Values:** CSS actually provides 14 different *font-weight* keywords, but only a couple actually work with today's browsers and computer systems—*bold* and *normal*.

- **Example:** `font-weight: bold;`

letter-spacing (inherited)

Adjusts the space between letters to spread out letters (adding spacing between each) or cram letters together (removing space).

- **Values:** Any valid CSS measurement unit, though ems and pixels are most common. For this property, percentages don't work in most browsers. Use a *positive* value to increase the space between letters and a *negative* value to remove space (scrunch letters together). The value *normal* resets *letter-spacing* to its regular browser value of 0.

- **Examples:** `letter-spacing: -1px; letter-spacing: 2em;`

line-height (inherited)

Adjusts space between lines of text in a paragraph (often called *line spacing* in word processing programs). The normal line height is 120 percent of the size of the text (page 112).

- **Values:** Most valid CSS lengths (page 406), though ems and pixels and percentages are most common.

- **Example:** `line-height: 200%;`

text-align (inherited)

Positions a block of text to the left, right, or center of the page or container element.

- **Values:** *left, center, right, justify* (the *justify* option often makes text difficult to read on monitors).

- **Example:** `text-align: center;`

text-decoration

Adds lines above, under, and/or through text. Underlining is common with links, so it's usually a good idea *not* to underline text that isn't a link. The color of the underline, overline, or strike-through line is the same as the font color of the tag being styled. The property also supports a *blink* value that makes text flash off and on obnoxiously.

- **Values:** *underline, overline, line-through, blink, none.* The *none* value turns off all decoration. Use this to hide the underline that normally appears under links. You can also add multiple decorations by listing the name of each type (except *none*) separated by a space.

- **Example:** `text-decoration: underline overline line-through;`

text-indent (inherited)

Sets the indent size of the first line of a block of text. The first line can be indented (as in many printed books) or outdented, so that the first line hangs off and over the left edge of the rest of the text.

- **Values:** Any valid CSS measurement unit. Ems and pixels are most common; percentages behave differently than with the *font-size* property. Here, percentages are based on the width of the box containing the text, which can be the width of the entire browser window. So *50%* would indent the first line half of the way across the window (see page 146 for a detailed explanation). To outdent (hang the first line off the left edge), use a negative value. This technique works well in conjunction with a positive *left-margin* property (page 418), which indents the left side of the other lines of text a set amount.

- **Example:** `text-indent: 3em;`

text-transform (inherited)

Changes the capitalization of text, so text appears in all uppercase letters, all lowercase, or only the first letter of each word capitalized.

- **Values:** *uppercase, lowercase, capitalize, none.* The *none* option returns the text to whatever case is in the actual HTML code. If *aBCDefg* are the actual letters typed in HTML, then *none* removes any other inherited case set by an ancestor tag and displays *aBCDefg* onscreen.

- **Example:** `text-transform: uppercase;`

vertical-align

Sets the baseline of an inline element relative to the baseline of the surrounding contents. With it, you can make a character appear slightly above or below surrounding text. Use this to create superscript characters like ™, ®, or ©. When applied to a table cell, the values *top, middle, bottom,* and *baseline* control the vertical placement of content inside the cell (page 255).

- **Values:** *baseline, sub, super, top, text-top, middle, bottom, text-bottom,* a percentage value, or an absolute value (like pixels or ems). Percentages are calculated based on the element's *line-height* value (page 411).

- **Examples:** `vertical-align: top; vertical-align: -5px; vertical-align: 75%;`

white-space

Controls how the browser displays space characters in the HTML code. Normally, if you include more than one space between words—"Hello   Dave"—a Web browser displays only one space—"Hello Dave." You can preserve any white space exactly as is in the HTML using the *pre* value, which does the same as the HTML <pre> tag. In addition, Web browsers will split a line of text at a space, if the line won't fit within the window's width. To prevent text from wrapping, use the *nowrap* value. But the *nowrap* value makes *all* of the paragraph's text stay on one line, so don't use it with long paragraphs (unless you like the idea of making your visitors scroll endlessly to the right).

- **Values:** *nowrap, pre, normal.* Two other values—*pre-line* and *pre-wrap*—don't work in many browsers.

- **Example:** white-space: pre;

word-spacing (inherited)

Works like the *letter-spacing* property (page 411), but instead of letters, it adjusts space between words.

- **Values:** Any valid CSS measurement unit, though ems and pixels are most common; percentages don't work in most browsers. Use a *positive* value to increase the space between words and a *negative* value to remove space (scrunch words together). The value *normal* resets word spacing to its regular browser value of 0.

- **Examples:** word-spacing: -1px; word-spacing: 2em;

List Properties

The following properties affect the formatting of bulleted lists (<ul>) and numbered lists (<ol>).

list-style (inherited)

This property is a shorthand method of specifying the three properties listed next. You can include a value for one or more of those properties, separating each by a space. You can even use this property as a shortcut for writing a single property and save a couple of keystrokes: *list-style: outside*, instead of *list-style-position: outside*. If you specify both a type and an image, a Web browser will display the bullet type (disc, square, and so on) *only* if it can't find the image. This way, if the path to your custom bullet image doesn't work, you don't end up with a bulletless bulleted list.

- **Values:** Any valid value for *list-style-type, list-style-image,* and/or *list-style-position.*

- **Example:** list-style: disc url(images/bullet.gif) inside;

list-style-image (inherited)

Specifies an image to use for a bullet in a bulleted list.

- **Values:** an URL value (page 408) or *none*.

- **Example:** list-style-image: url(images/bullet.gif);

Tip: The *background-image* property does the custom bullet job just as well and offers more control (see page 172).

---

list-style-position (inherited)

Positions the bullets or numbers in a list. These markers can appear outside of the text, hanging off to the left, or inside the text (exactly where the first letter of the first line normally begins). The *outside* position is how Web browsers normally display bullets and numbers.

- **Values:** *inside, outside*

- **Example:** list-style: inside;

list-style-type (inherited)

Sets the type of bullet for a list—round, square, roman numeral, and so on. You can theoretically turn an unordered (bulleted) list into an ordered (numbered) list by changing the *list-style-type* property, but it doesn't work in all browsers (including Internet Explorer for Windows). Use the *none* option to completely remove bullets or numbers from the list.

- **Values:** *disc, circle, square, decimal, decimal-leading-zero, upper-alpha, lower-alpha, upper-roman, lower-roman, lower-greek, none*

- **Example:** list-style-type: square;

Padding, Borders, and Margins

The following properties control the space around an element, and let you add border lines to a style.

border

Draws a line around the four edges of an element.

- **Values:** The width (thickness) of the border line in any valid CSS measurement unit (except percentages).

  You can also specify a style for the line: *solid, dotted, dashed, double, groove, ridge, inset, outset, none,* and *hidden.* (See Figure 7-7 on page 142 for an illustration of the different styles.) The *none* and *hidden* values do the same thing—remove any border.

Finally, you can specify a color using any valid CSS color type (a keyword like *green* or a hex number like *#33fc44*).

- **Example:** border: 2px solid #f33;

border-top, border-right, border-bottom, border-left

Adds a border to a single edge. For example, *border-top* adds a border to the top of the element.

- **Values:** same as for *border*.
- **Example:** border-left: 1em dashed red;

border-color

Defines the color used for all four borders.

- **Values:** Any valid CSS color type (a keyword like *green* or a hex number like *#33fc44*).
- **Example:** border-color: rgb(255,34,100);

border-top-color, border-right-color, border-bottom-color, border-left-color

Functions just like the *border-color* property but sets color for only one edge. Use these properties to override the color set by the *border* property. In this way, you can customize the color for an individual edge while using a more generic *border* style to define the basic size and style of all four edges.

- **Values:** see *border-color* above.
- **Example:** border-left-color: #333;

border-style

Defines the style used for all four borders.

- **Values:** One of these key words: *solid, dotted, dashed, double, groove, ridge, inset, outset, none,* and *hidden*. See Figure 7-7 on page 142 for an illustration of the different styles. The *none* and *hidden* values act identically—they remove any border.
- **Example:** border-style: inset;

border-top-style, border-right-style, border-bottom-style, border-left-style

Functions just like the *border-style* property, but applies only to one edge.

- **Values:** see *border-style* above.
- **Example:** border-top-style: none;

---

border-width

Defines the width or thickness of the line used to draw all four borders.

- **Values:** Any valid CSS measurement unit except percentages. The most common are ems and pixels.

- **Example:** border-width: 1px;

border-top-width, border-right-width, border-bottom-width, border-left-width

Functions just like the *border-width* property but applies only to one edge.

- **Values:** see *border-width* above.

- **Example:** border-bottom-width: 3em;

outline

This property is a shorthand way to combine *outline-color, outline-style,* and *outline-width* (listed next). An outline works just like a border, except the outline takes up no space (that is, it doesn't add to the width or height of an element), and it applies to all four edges. It's intended more as a way of highlighting something on a page than as a design detail. *Outline* works in Firefox, Safari, and Opera, but not in Internet Explorer.

- **Values:** The same as for *border* with one exception—see *outline-color* next.

- **Example:** outline: 3px solid #F33;

outline-color

Specifies the color for an outline (see *outline* above).

- **Values:** Any valid CSS color, plus the value *invert*, which merely reverses the color the outline is sitting on. If the outline is drawn on a white background, the invert value makes the outline black. Works just like *border-color* (page 415).

- **Example:** outline-color: invert;

outline-style

Specifies the type of line for the outline —dotted, solid, dashed, and so on.

- **Values:** Same as *border-style* (page 415).

- **Example:** outline-style: dashed;

outline-width

Specifies the thickness of the outline. Works just like *border-width* (page 416).

- **Values:** Any valid CSS measurement unit except percentages. The most common are ems and pixels.

- **Example:** `outline-width: 3px;`

padding

Sets the amount of space between the content and border and edge of the background. Use it to add empty space around text, images, or other content. (See Figure 7-1 on page 134 for an illustration.)

- **Values:** Any valid CSS measurement unit, like pixels or ems. Percentage values are based on the width of the containing element. A headline that's a child of the <body> tag uses the width of the browser window to calculate a percentage value, so a padding of 20 percent adds 20 percent of the window's width. If the visitor resizes his browser, the padding size changes proportionately. You can specify the padding for all four edges by using a single value, or set individual padding sizes per edge using this order: *top, right, bottom, left.*

- **Examples:** `padding: 20px; padding: 2em 3em 2.5em 0;`

padding-top

Works just like the *padding* property, but sets padding for top edge only.

- **Example:** `padding-top: 20px;`

padding-right

Works just like the *padding* property, but sets padding for right edge only.

- **Example:** `padding-right: 20px;`

padding-bottom

Works just like the *padding* property, but sets padding for bottom edge only.

- **Example:** `padding-bottom: 20px;`

padding-left

Works just like the *padding* property, but sets padding for left edge only.

- **Example:** `padding-left: 20px;`

margin

Sets the amount of space between an element's border and the margin of other elements (see Figure 7-1 on page 134). It lets you add white space between two elements—between one picture and another picture, or between a sidebar and the main content area of a page.

Note: Vertical margins between elements can *collapse*. That is, browsers use only the top or bottom margin and ignore the other, creating a smaller gap than expected (see page 137).

- **Values:** Any valid CSS measurement unit like pixels or ems. Percentage values are based on the width of the containing element. A headline that's a child of the body tag uses the width of the browser window to calculate a percentage value, so a margin of 10 percent adds 10 percent of the window's width to the edges of the headline. If the visitor resizes his browser, the margin size changes. As with padding, you specify the margin for all four edges using a single value, or set individual margins in this order: *top, right, bottom, left.*

- **Examples:** `margin: 20px; margin: 2em 3em 2.5em 0;`

margin-top

Works just like the *margin* property, but sets margin for top edge only.

- **Example:** `margin-top: 20px;`

margin-right

Works just like the *margin* property, but sets margin for right edge only.

- **Example:** `margin-right: 20px;`

margin-bottom

Works just like the *margin* property, but sets margin for bottom edge only.

- **Example:** `margin-bottom: 20px;`

margin-left

Works just like the *margin* property, but sets margin for left edge only.

- **Example:** `margin-left: 20px;`

Backgrounds

CSS provides several properties for controlling the background of an element, including coloring the background, placing an image behind an element, and controlling how that background image is positioned.

background

Provides a shorthand method of specifying properties that appear in the background of an element, like a color, an image, and the placement of that image. It combines the five background properties (described next) into one compact line, so you can get the same effect with much less typing. However, if you don't set one of the properties, browsers use that property's normal value instead. For example, if you don't specify how a background image should repeat, browsers will tile that image from left to right and top to bottom (see page 175).

- **Values:** The same values used for the background properties listed next. The order of the properties isn't important (except for positioning as described below) but usually follow the order of *background-color, background-image, background-repeat, background-attachment, background-position.*

- **Example:** `background:  #333  url(images/logo.gif)  no-repeat  fixed  left top;`

background-attachment

Specifies how a background image reacts when your visitor scrolls the page. The image either scrolls along with the rest of the content or remains in place. You can add a logo to the upper-left corner of a very long Web page, using the *background-attachment* property's *fixed* value, and make that image stay in the upper-left corner even when the page is scrolled. (In Internet Explorer 6 and earlier, this property works only for the <body> tag.)

- **Values:** *scroll* or *fixed*. Scroll is the normal behavior: An image will scroll off the screen along with text. Fixed locks the image in place.

- **Example:** `background-attachment:  fixed;`

background-color

Adds a color to the background of a style. The background sits underneath the border and underneath a background image, a fact to keep in mind if you use one of the non-solid border styles like *dashed* or *dotted*. In these cases, the background color shows through the gaps between the dashes or dots.

- **Values:** any valid color value (page 405).

- **Example:** `background-color:  #FFF;`

background-image

Places an image into the background of a style. Other page elements sit on top of the background image, so make sure that text is legible where it overlaps the image. You can always use padding to move content away from the image, too. The image tiles from left to right and top to bottom, unless you set the *background-repeat* property as well.

- **Values:** The URL of an image.

- **Examples:** background-image: url(images/photo.jpg); background-image: url(http://www.example.org/photo.jpg);

background-position

Controls the placement of an image in the background of a page element. Unless you specify otherwise, an image begins in the element's top-left corner. If the image tiles, *background-position* controls the image's start point (see *background-repeat* next). If you position an image in the center of an element, the browser puts the image there, and then tiles the image up and to the left *and* down and to the right. In many cases, the exact placement of an image doesn't cause a visible difference in the background tiling, but it lets you make subtle changes to the positioning of a pattern in the background.

- **Values:** You can use any valid CSS measurement unit like pixels or ems, as well as keywords or percentages. The values come in pairs, with the first being the horizontal position, and the second being vertical. Keywords include *left, center*, and *right* for horizontal positioning and *top, center*, and *bottom* for vertical. Pixel and em values are calculated from the top-left corner of the element, so to place a graphic 5 pixels from the left edge and 10 pixels from the top, you'd use a value of *5px 10px*.

  Percentage values map one point on the image to one point in the background of the element, calculated by the specified percentage from the left and top edges of the image and the specified percentage from the left and top edges of the element. *50% 50%* places the point that's 50 percent across and 50 percent down the image on top of the point that's 50 percent across and 50 percent down the element. In other words, it puts the image directly in the middle of the element (see page 179). You can mix and match these values: If you want, use a pixel value for horizontal placement and a percentage value for vertical placement.

- **Examples:** background-position: left top; background-position: 1em 3em; background-position: 10px 50%;

background-repeat

Controls whether, or how, a background image repeats. Normally, background images tile from the top left to the bottom right, filling the element's entire background.

- **Values:** *repeat, no-repeat, repeat-x, repeat-y*. The *repeat* option is the normal method—tiling left to right, top to bottom. *No-repeat* places the image a single time in the background with no tiling. *Repeat-y* tiles the image top to bottom only—perfect for adding a graphical sidebar. *Repeat-x* tiles the image from left to right only, so you can add a graphical bar to an element's top, middle, or bottom.

- **Example:** background-repeat: no-repeat;

Page Layout Properties

The following properties control the placement and size of elements on a Web page.

bottom

This property is used with *absolute*, *relative*, and *fixed* positioning (see page 425). When used with absolute or fixed positioning, *bottom* determines the position of the bottom edge of the style relative to the bottom edge of its closest positioned ancestor. If the styled element isn't inside of any positioned tags, then the placement is relative to the bottom edge of the browser window. You can use this property to place a footnote at the bottom of the browser window. When used with relative positioning, the placement is calculated from the element's bottom edge (prior to positioning). See page 332.

- **Values:** Any valid CSS measurement unit, like pixels, ems, or percentages. Percentages are calculated based on the width of the containing element.

- **Example:** bottom: 5em;

Note: Internet Explorer 6 and earlier can have a problem when positioning an element using the *bottom* property. See page 335 for details.

---

clear

Prevents an element from wrapping around a floated element. Instead, the cleared element drops below the bottom of the floated element.

- **Values:** *left, right, both, none*. The *left* option means the element can't wrap around left-floated elements. Similarly, *right* drops the element below any right-floated items. The *both* value prevents an element from wrapping around *either* left- or right- floated elements. *None* turns the property off, so you use it to override a previously set *clear* property. This trick comes in handy when a particular tag has a style that drops below a floated element but you want the tag to wrap in just one case. Create a more specific style (page 89) to override the float for that one tag.

- **Example:** clear: both;

clip

Creates a rectangular window that reveals part of an element. If you had a picture of your high-school graduating class, and the class bully was standing on the far right edge of the photo, you could create a display area that crops out the image of your tormentor. The full image is still intact, but the clipping area only displays the bully free portion of it. The *clip* property is most effective when used with JavaScript programming to animate the clip. You can start with a small clipping area and expand it until the full photo is revealed.

- **Values:** Coordinates of a rectangular box. Enclose the coordinates in parenthe-ses and precede them by the keyword *rect*, like so: *rect(5px,110px,40px,10px);*.

  Here's how the order of these coordinates works: The first number indicates the top offset—the top edge of the clipping window. In this example, the offset is *5px*, so everything in the first four rows of pixels is hidden. The last number is the left offset—the left edge of the clipping window. In this example, the offset is *10px*, so everything to the left (the first 9 pixels of the element) is hidden. The second number is the width of the clipping window plus the last number; if the left edge of the clip is 10 pixels and you want the visible area to be 100 pixels, the second number would be *110px*. The third number is the height of the clip-ping region plus the top offset (the first number). So, in this example, the clip-ping box is 30 pixels tall (30px + 10px = *40px*).

- **Example:** clip: rect(5px,110px,40px,10px);

Tip: Since the order of the coordinates is a little strange, most designers like to start with the first and last numbers, and then compute the two other numbers from them.

---

display

Determines the kind of box used to display a page element—block-level or inline (page 140). Use it to override how a browser usually displays a particular element. You can make a paragraph (block-level element) display without line breaks above and below it—exactly like, say, a link (inline element).

- **Values:** *block, inline, none.* The display property accepts 17 values, most of which have no effect in the browsers available today. *Block, inline,* and *none,* however, work in almost all browsers. *Block* forces a line break above and below an element, just like other block-level elements (like paragraphs and headers). *Inline* causes an element to display on the same line as surrounding elements (just as text within a <strong> tag appears right on the same line as other text). *None* makes the element completely disappear from the page. Then, you can make the element reappear with some JavaScript programming or the *:hover* pseudo-class (see page 54).

- **Example:** display: block;

float

Moves (floats) an element to the left or right edge of the browser window, or, if the floated element's inside another element, to the left or right edge of that contain-ing element. Elements that appear after the floated element move up to fill the space to the right (for left floats) or left (for right floats), and then wrap around the floated element. Use floats for simple effects, like moving an image to one side of the page, or for very complex layouts like those described in Chapter 11.

- **Values:** *left, right, none. None* turns off floating entirely, which comes in handy when a particular tag has a style with a left or right float applied to it, and you want to create a more specific style to override the float for that one tag.

- **Example:** *float: left;*

height

Sets the height of the *content area*—the area of an element's box that contains content like text, images, or other tags. The element's actual onscreen height is the total of height, top and bottom margins, top and bottom padding, and top and bottom borders.

- **Values:** Any valid CSS measurement unit such as pixels, ems, or percentages. Percentages are calculated based on the height of the containing element.

- **Example:** height: 50%;

Note: Sometimes, your content ends up taller than the set height–if you type a lot of text, for instance, or your visitor increases text size in her browser. Browsers handle this situation differently: IE 6 and earlier simply make the box bigger, while other browsers make the content extend outside of the box. The *overflow* property controls what happens in this case (see page 148).

---

left

When used with absolute or fixed positioning (page 326), this property determines the position of the left edge of the style relative to the left edge of its closest positioned ancestor. If the styled element isn't inside of any positioned tags, then the placement is relative to the left edge of the browser window. You can use this property to place an image 20 pixels from the left edge of the browser window. When used with relative positioning, the placement is calculated from the element's left edge (prior to positioning).

- **Values:** Any valid CSS measurement unit such as pixels, ems, or percentages.

- **Example:** left: 5em;

max-height

Sets the *maximum* height for an element. That is, the element's box may be shorter than this setting, but it can't be any taller. If the element's contents are taller than the *max-height* setting, they overflow the box. You can control what happens to the excess using the *overflow* property (page 148). Internet Explorer 6 (and earlier) doesn't understand the *max-height* property.

- **Values:** Any valid CSS measurement unit, like pixels, ems, or percentages. Browsers calculate percentages based on the height of the containing element.

- **Example:** max-height: 100px;

max-width

Sets the *maximum* width for an element. The element's box can be narrower than this setting, but no wider. If the element's contents are wider than the *max-width* setting, they overflow the box, which you can control with the *overflow* property (page 148). You mostly use *max-width* in liquid layouts (page 280) to make sure a page design doesn't become unreadably wide on very large monitors. This property doesn't work in Internet Explorer 6 (or in earlier versions).

- **Values:** Any valid CSS measurement unit, like pixels, ems, or percentages. Percentages are calculated based on the width of the containing element.

- **Example:** max-width: 950px;

min-height

Sets the *minimum* height for an element. The element's box may be taller than this setting, but it can't be shorter. If the element's contents aren't as tall as the *min-height* setting, the box's height shrinks to meet the *min-height* value. Internet Explorer 6 (and earlier) doesn't recognize this property.

- **Values:** Any valid CSS measurement unit, like pixels, ems, or percentages. Percentages are based on the containing element's height.

- **Example:** min-height: 20em;

min-width

Sets the *minimum* width for an element. The element's box may be wider than this setting, but it can't be narrower. If the element's contents aren't as wide as the *min-width* value, the box simply gets as thin as the *min-width* setting. You can also use *min-width* in liquid layouts, so that the design doesn't disintegrate at smaller window widths. When the browser window is thinner than *min-width*, it adds horizontal scroll bars. Internet Explorer 6 (and earlier) doesn't understand this property.

- **Values:** Any valid CSS measurement unit, like pixels, ems, or percentages. Percentages are based on the containing element's width.

- **Example:** min-width: 760px;

Note: You usually use the *max-width* and *min-width* properties in conjunction when creating liquid layouts. See Chapter 11 (page 289).

overflow

Dictates what should happen to text that overflows its content area, like a photo that's wider than the value set for the *width* property.

Note: IE 6 (and earlier) handles overflow situations differently than other browsers. See page 148.

- **Values:** *visible, hidden, scroll, auto. Visible* makes the overflowing content extend outside the box—potentially overlapping borders and other page elements on the page. IE 6 (and earlier) simply enlarges the box (borders and all) to accommodate the larger content. *Hidden* hides any content outside of the content area. *Scroll* adds scroll bars to the element so a visitor can scroll to read any content outside the content area—sort of like a mini-frame. *Auto* adds scrollbars *only* when they're necessary to reveal more content.

- **Example:** `overflow: hidden;`

position

Determines what type of positioning method a browser uses when placing an element on the page.

- **Values:** *static, relative, absolute, fixed. Static* is the normal browser mode—one block-level item stacked on top of the next with content flowing from the top to the bottom of the screen. *Relative* positions an element in relation to where the element currently appears on the page—in other words, it can offset the element from its current position. *Absolute* takes an element completely out of the page flow. Other items don't see the absolute element and may appear underneath it. It's used to position an element in an exact place on the page, or to place an element in an exact position relative to a parent element that's positioned with *absolute*, *relative* or *fixed* positioning. *Fixed* locks an element on the page, so that when the page is scrolled, the fixed element remains on the screen—much like HTML frames. Internet Explorer 6 (and earlier) ignores the *fixed* option.

- **Example:** `position: absolute;`

Note: You usually use *relative*, *absolute*, and *fixed* in conjunction with *left*, *right*, *top*, and *bottom*. See Chapter 12 for the full details on positioning.

---

right

When used with absolute or fixed positioning (page 326), this property determines the position of the right edge of the style relative to the right edge of its closest positioned ancestor. If the styled element isn't inside of any positioned tags, then the placement is relative to the right edge of the browser window. You can use this property to place a sidebar a set amount from the right edge of the browser window. When used with relative positioning, the placement is calculated from the element's right edge (prior to positioning).

- **Values:** Any valid CSS measurement unit, like pixels, ems, or percentages.

- **Example:** `left: 5em;`

Note: Internet Explorer 6 (and earlier) can have problems when positioning an element using the *right* property. See page 335 for details.

top

Does the opposite of the *bottom* property (page 421). In other words, when used with absolute or fixed positioning, this property determines the position of the top edge of the style relative to the top edge of its closest positioned ancestor. If the styled element isn't inside of any positioned tags, then the placement is relative to the top edge of the browser window. You can use this property to place a logo a set amount from the top edge of the browser window. When used with relative positioning, the placement is calculated from the element's top edge (prior to positioning).

• **Values:** Any valid CSS measurement unit, like pixels, ems, or percentages.

• **Example:** top: 5em;

visibility

Determines whether a Web browser displays the element. Use this property to hide part of the content of the page, such as a paragraph, headline, or <div> tag. Unlike the *display* property's *none* value—which hides an element and removes it from the flow of the page—the visibility property's *hidden* option doesn't remove the element from the page flow. Instead, it just leaves an empty hole where the element would have been. For this reason, you most often use the *visibility* property with absolutely positioned elements, which have already been removed from the flow of the page.

Hiding an element doesn't do you much good unless you can show it again. JavaScript programming is the most common way to toggle the *visibility* property to show and hide items on a page. You can also use the *:hover* pseudo-class (page 209) to change an element's visibility property when a visitor hovers over some part of the page.

• **Values:** *visible, hidden.* You can use the *collapse* value to hide a row or column in a table as well.

• **Example:** visibility: hidden;

width

Sets the width of the content area (the area of an element's box that contains text, images, or other tags). The amount of onscreen space actually dedicated to the element may be much wider, since it includes the width of the left and right margin, left and right padding, and left and right borders. IE 6 (and earlier) handles overflow situations differently than other browsers. (See page 148.)

- **Values:** Any valid CSS measurement unit, like pixels, ems, or percentages. Percentages are based on the containing element's width.

- **Example:** `width: 250px;`

z-index

Controls the layering of positioned elements. Only applies to elements with a position property set to *absolute, relative,* or *fixed* (page 326). It determines where on the Z-axis an element appears. If two absolutely positioned elements overlap, the one with the higher *z-index* appears to be on top.

- **Values:** An integer value, like *1, 2,* or *10.* You can also use negative values, but different browsers handle them differently. The larger the number, the more "on top" the element appears. An element with a *z-index* of *20* appears below an element with a *z-index* of *100* (if the two overlap). However, when the element is inside another positioned element, it's "positioning context" changes and it may not appear above another element—no matter what its *z-index* value. See Figure 12-6.

- **Example:** `z-index: 12;`

Tip: The values don't need be in exact integer order. If element A has a *z-index* of *1*, you don't have to set element B's *z-index* to *2* to put it on top. You can use *5, 10,* and so on to get the same effect, as long as it's a bigger number. So, to make sure an element *always* appears above other elements, simply give it a very large value, like *10000.*

Table Properties

There are a handful of CSS properties that relate solely to HTML tables. Chapter 10 has complete instructions on using CSS with tables.

border-collapse

Determines whether the borders around the cells of a table are separated or collapsed. When they're separated, browsers put a space of a couple of pixels between each cell. Even if you eliminate this space by setting the *cellspacing* attribute for the HTML <table> tag to 0, browsers still display double borders. That is, the bottom-border of one cell will appear above the top border of the cell below causing a doubling of border lines. Setting the *border-collapse* property to *collapse* eliminates both the space between cells and this doubling up of borderlines (page 256). This property works only when applied to a <table> tag.

- **Values:** *collapse, separate*

- **Example:** `border-collapse: collapse;`

border-spacing

Sets the amount of space between cells in a table. It replaces the <table> tag's *cell-spacing* HTML attribute. However, Internet Explorer doesn't understand the *border-spacing* property, so it's best to continue to use the cellspacing attribute in your <table> tags to guarantee space between cells in all browsers.

Note: If you want to eliminate the space browsers normally insert between cells, just set the *border-collapse* property to *collapse*.

* **Values:** Two CSS length values. The first sets the horizontal separation (the space on either side of each cell) and the second sets the vertical separation (the space separating the bottom of one cell from the top of the one below it).

* **Example:** border-spacing: 0 10px;

caption-side

When applied to a table caption, this property determines whether the caption appears at the top or bottom of the table. (Since, according to HTML rules, the <caption> tag must immediately follow the opening <table> tag, a caption would normally appear at the top of the table.)

* **Values:** *top, bottom*

* **Example:** caption-side: bottom;

Note: Unfortunately, this property has no effect in any versions of Internet Explorer (as of this writing), so it's safest to stick with the HTML equivalent: *<caption align="bottom"> or <caption align="top">*.

empty-cells

Determines how a browser should display a table cell that's completely empty, which in HTML would look like this: *<td></td>*. The *hide* value prevents any part of the cell from being displayed. Instead, only an empty placeholder appears, so borders, background colors, and background images don't show up in an emptied cell. Apply this property to a style formatting the <table> tag.

* **Values:** *show, hide*

* **Example:** empty-cells: show;

Note: The *empty-cells* property has no effect if the *border-spacing* property is set to *collapse*.

table-layout

Controls how a Web browser draws a table, and can slightly affect the speed at which the browser displays it. The *fixed* setting forces the browser to render all columns the same width as the columns in the first row, which (for complicated

CSS: The Missing Manual

technical reasons) draws tables faster. The *auto* value is the normal "browser just do your thing" value, so if you're happy with how quickly your tables appear on a page, don't bother with this property. If you use it, apply *table-layout* to a style formatting the <table> tag.

- **Values:** *auto, fixed*

- **Example:** `table-layout: fixed;`

Miscellaneous Properties

CSS 2.1 offers a few additional—and sometimes interesting—properties. They let you enhance your Web pages with special content and cursors, offer more control over how a page prints, and so on. (Unfortunately, browser understanding of these properties is spotty at best.)

content

Specifies text that appears either before or after an element. Use this property with the *:after* or *:before* pseudo-elements. You can add an opening quotation mark in front of quoted material and a closing quotation after the quote. This property isn't supported by Internet Explorer (not even IE 7 as of this writing), so its use is limited.

- **Values:** Text inside of quotes *"like this"*, the keywords *normal, open-quote, close-quote, no-open-quote, no-close-quote.* You can also use the value of an HTML attribute. (See "Revealing Links in Print" on page 373 for an example.)

- **Examples:** `p.advert:before  {  content:  "And  now  a  word  from  our sponsor…"; }`

  `a:after { content: " (" attr(href) ") "; }`

Note: Adding text in this way (like the opening and closing quote example) is called generated content. Read a simple explanation of the generated content phenomenon at *www.westciv.com/style_master/ academy/css_tutorial/advanced/generated_content.html*. For a deeper explanation, visit *www.w3.org/TR/ CSS21/generate.html*.

---

cursor

Lets you change the look of the mouse pointer when it moves over a particular element. You can make a question mark appear next to the cursor when someone mouses over a link that provides more information on a subject (like a word definition).

- **Values:** *auto, default, crosshair, pointer, move, e-resize, ne-resize, nw-resize, n-resize, se-resize, sw-resize, s-resize, w-resize, text, wait, help, progress.* You can also use an URL value to use your own graphic as a cursor (but see the Note below).

- **Example:** `cursor: help; cursor: url(images/cursor.cur);`

Note: Only Internet Explorer and Firefox recognize URL cursor values, and only in Windows. For more information, visit *www.echoecho.com/csscursors.htm* and *www.quirksmode.org/css/cursor.html*.

---

orphans

Specifies the minimum number of lines of text that can be left at the bottom of a printed page. Suppose you're printing your Web page on a laser printer, and a five-line paragraph is split between two pages, with just one line at the bottom of page one, and the four remaining lines at the top of page two. Because a single line all by itself looks odd (sort of like a lost *orphan*—get it?), you can tell the browser to break a paragraph *only* if at least, say, three lines are left on the bottom of the page. (At this writing, only the Opera browser understands this property.)

- **Values:** a number like *1, 2, 3,* or *5*.

- **Example:** `orphans: 3;`

page-break-after

Determines whether a page break (in printing) occurs after a particular element. With it, you can make sure that a particular paragraph is always the last item to appear on a printed page.

- **Values:** *auto, always, avoid, left, right. Auto* represents the normal value and lets the browser determine when and how to break content across printed pages. *Always* forces the element that follows to appear at the top of a separate printed page, and it's the only value that works consistently across browsers. *Avoid* prevents a page break after an element; it's a great way to keep a headline *with* the paragraph that follows it, but unfortunately, most browsers don't understand it. *Left* and *right* determine whether the element following appears on a left- or right-handed page, which may force the browser to print an extra empty page. But since no browsers understand these values, don't worry about wasting paper. Browsers treat *left* and *right* the same as *always*.

- **Example:** `page-break-after: always;`

page-break-before

Works like *page-break-after,* except the page break appears before the styled element, placing it at the top of the next printed page. You can use this property to make sure headlines for different sections of a long Web page each appear at the top of a page.

- **Values:** same as *page-break-after.*

- **Example:** page-break-before: always;

page-break-inside

Prevents an element from being split across two printed pages. If you want to keep a photo and its caption together on a single page, wrap the photo and caption text in a <div> tag, and then apply a style with *page-break-inside* to that <div>. (At this writing, only Opera understands this property.)

- **Values:** *avoid*

- **Example:** page-break-inside: avoid;

widows

The opposite of *orphans* (page 430), it specifies the minimum number of lines that must appear at the *top* of a printed page. Say the printer can manage to fit four out of five lines of a paragraph at the bottom of a page and has to move the last line to the top of the next page. Since that line might look weird all by itself, use *widows* to make the browser move at least two or three (or whatever number of) lines together to the top of a printed page. (Only Opera understands this property, so it's of limited use.)

Values: a number like *1, 2, 3* or *5.*

Example: widows: 3;

CSS in Dreamweaver 8

Adobe's Dreamweaver 8 is a Web site-building program that takes the drudgery out of creating HTML/XHTML and CSS. Instead of typing lines of code into a text editor, you can click convenient onscreen buttons and menus and watch your design unfold before your eyes. The program even has powerful site-management tools that help you keep track of your site's pages and links.

Although this book gives you everything you need to know to create your own CSS from scratch, there's nothing wrong with turning to a visual editor like Dreamweaver to save time. In fact, knowing how CSS works, as this book shows you, is a big help when tweaking or troubleshooting pages created in Dreamweaver.

Note: This appendix focuses solely on Dreamweaver 8's CSS features. To learn everything Dreamweaver can do for your Web site design and maintenance, check out *Dreamweaver 8: The Missing Manual*.

Creating Styles

You begin most CSS-related tasks in the CSS Styles panel, which is Dreamweaver's command center for creating styles. To open it, choose Window → CSS Styles (or press Shift-F11).

Using Figure B-1 as a guide, here's how to find your way around the CSS Styles panel:

- The All button at the top of the panel lists all internal and external styles for the currently open document. The other button—Current—lets you take a closer look at individual styles (page 449).

Tip: Clicking the minus (-) icon to the left of the style sheet collapses the list of styles, hiding them from view. (On a Mac, the button looks like a little triangle instead, but it does the same thing.)

- An internal style sheet is indicated by <style> in the panel. In this example, there's one tag style (for the <body> tag).

- External style sheets are listed by file name (*headlines.css*). The external style sheet's rules are listed below the file name (*p*, *h1*, *.celebrity*, and so on). The first two styles are tag styles (notice that the names match various HTML tags), while the last five are class styles (note the period at the beginning of each name).

- The Properties list in the bottom half of the panel lets you edit a style as described on page 442. The three buttons at the bottom-left of the panel (circled in Figure B-1) control how the property list is displayed.

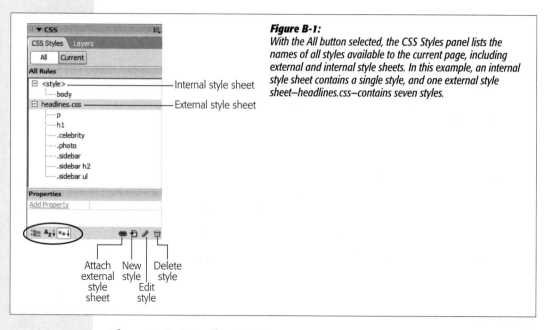

Figure B-1:
With the All button selected, the CSS Styles panel lists the names of all styles available to the current page, including external and internal style sheets. In this example, an internal style sheet contains a single style, and one external style sheet–headlines.css–contains seven styles.

Phase 1: Set Up the CSS Type

To create a new style, choose Text → CSS Styles → New. Or, on the CSS Styles panel, you can click the New Style button, or right-click anywhere in the panel and select New from the shortcut menu. The New CSS Rule dialog box appears (Figure B-2), where you begin creating your new style:

- **Selector Type.** Click the appropriate radio button for the kind of style you're creating: Class, to create your own style from scratch; or Tag, to create an HTML tag style that Dreamweaver will automatically apply to each occurrence of the tag.

To create IDs, pseudo-classes, and descendent selectors, click Advanced. (And if you need help remembering what all these kinds of selectors do, then flip back to Chapter 3.)

- **Name.** If you clicked the Class button, type a name for the new style. If you're in a desperate hurry, then you can leave out the period that goes at the beginning of every class style, since Dreamweaver adds it automatically when it puts the style in the style sheet.

Tip: Class style names must *begin* with a letter, too, and can contain only letters and numbers. Dreamweaver lets you know if you use any invalid characters for the name.

If you chose Tag instead, select the HTML tag you want to redefine from the Tag pop-up menu (which appears when you click the Tag radio button). Or, if you're an old hand at HTML, just type the tag name without the brackets. When you want to create a style for all unordered (bulleted) lists, type *ul*.

If you clicked the Advanced button, Dreamweaver lets you type any valid CSS selector type, including plain old tag and class styles.

- **Define in.** Click "This document only" if you want the styles to apply only to the current Web page, creating an *internal* style sheet. To create a new *external* style sheet, choose New Style Sheet File from the "Define in" pop-up menu. This option not only creates a new external CSS file (which you can save anywhere in your site folder), but adds the necessary code in the current document to link it to that file.

If you've previously linked this document to an external style sheet (see page 437), that style sheet's name appears in the pop-up menu, indicating that Dreamweaver will store the new style in that sheet. (See Chapter 2 for a review of internal and external style sheets.)

Tip: If you create a bunch of internal styles in a particular page, and later realize you'd like to turn them into an external style sheet that you can use in other pages, then you're in luck. Dreamweaver has a command for this very task. Open the page containing the internal styles you want to reuse and choose File → Export → Export CSS Styles. A dialog box opens, letting you save the file as an external style sheet. Don't forget to add the .css extension to the end of the file name.

If you indicated that you want to create an external style sheet, clicking OK makes a Save Style Sheet As dialog box appear. Navigate to your site's folder and type a name for the new external CSS file. (Don't forget the *.css* on the end.)

Tip: If you'll be using this style sheet for all of the pages in your site, then you may want to save it in the root folder of your site, or in a folder specifically dedicated to style sheets and give it a general name like *site_styles.css* or *global.css*. (You don't have to type the .css file name extension, by the way. In this case, Dreamweaver adds it.)

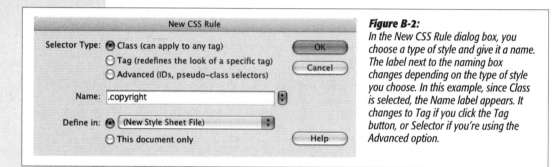

Figure B-2:
*In the New CSS Rule dialog box, you
choose a type of style and give it a name.
The label next to the naming box
changes depending on the type of style
you choose. In this example, since Class
is selected, the Name label appears. It
changes to Tag if you click the Tag
button, or Selector if you're using the
Advanced option.*

No matter what "Define in" option you selected, clicking OK eventually brings you
to the CSS Rule Definition window.

Phase 2: Defining the Style

The CSS Rule Definition window provides access to all of the formatting options
available to you and your Web page text and graphics (Figure B-3). Here you can
click to choose which properties to add to your style, instead of typing them. Look,
ma—no spelling errors!

Figure B-3:
*For ultimate formatting control,
Dreamweaver lets you set 67 different
Cascading Style Sheet properties from
the CSS Rule Definition window. But it
doesn't give you access to all the
available CSS properties and, in some
cases, Dreamweaver uses different
names for CSS properties than are
used in this book and in the CSS rules.
Turn to page 452 for more details.*

Once you've defined the style, click OK at the bottom of the Rule Definition window. Dreamweaver adds the style to the specified style sheet, and displays it in the
CSS Styles panel.

Adding Styles to Web Pages

Once you've created styles, applying them is easy. In fact, if you created HTML tag
styles, then you don't need to do anything to apply them because their selectors
automatically dictate which tags they affect. When you put your styles in an external style sheet, Dreamweaver automatically links it to the current document. To

use its styles in a *different* Web page, you must *attach* it to the page, as described next.

Linking to an External Style Sheet

When you add a new Web page to your site, usually you want to use the same CSS styles as you did in existing pages, for a consistent look. But you need to tell Dreamweaver which style sheet you're using by *attaching* it to the page. To do so, open the Web page to which you wish to add the style sheet. Then click the Attach Style Sheet button (see Figure B-1) on the CSS Styles panel. (If the CSS Styles panel isn't open, choose Window → CSS Styles or press Shift-F11.)

Tip: You can also use Dreamweaver's Property inspector (at the bottom of the window) to attach a style sheet. Just choose Attach Style Sheet from the Style menu.

When the Attach External Style Sheet window appears (Figure B-4), click Browse. In the Select Style Sheet File dialog box that appears, navigate to and double-click the CSS (.css) file you wish to attach to the document. If Dreamweaver offers to copy the style sheet file into your site's root folder, then click Yes.

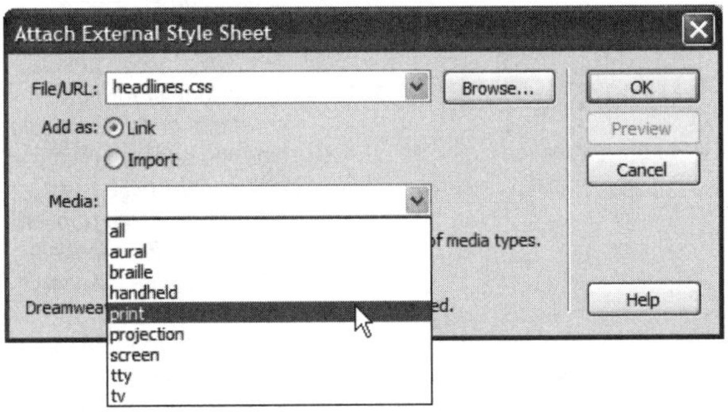

Figure B-4:
Most of the options in the Media menu aren't very useful, since there aren't any devices programmed to work with them. However, "printer" and "screen" are handy ways to control how your page displays when viewed on a monitor and when printed on paper.

The Attach External Style Sheet window provides two other options: how to attach the style sheet, and what type of media you want the styles to apply to.

- When attaching an external style sheet, you can choose to either **Link** or **Import** it. These two choices are nearly identical, as described on page 30.

- The **Media** menu defines which type of output device or display should use the style sheet. Selecting "print" means that the style sheet will *only* apply when the document is printed. Most of these options—such as TV for televisions, or TTY for teletype machines—aren't of any use to the average Web designer. You can read about these different media types and the two most important ones, "printer" and "screen," starting on page 365. Most of the time, you can safely ignore this menu.

The "all" option in the Media menu is the same as not selecting anything—the style sheet applies when printed, viewed on a monitor, felt on a Braille reader, and so on. (Dreamweaver 8 also includes a helpful toolbar for controlling the display of style sheets aimed at different media—see Figure B-5).

Tip: You can preview the effect of the style sheet on your page by clicking the Preview button on the Attach External Style Sheet window.

After choosing your options, click OK. Dreamweaver adds the necessary HTML code to the head of the Web page, and automatically formats any tags in the document according to the style sheet's HTML tag styles. You'll see the formatting changes take place in the document window immediately after attaching the external style sheet.

If the style sheet contains *class* styles, on the other hand, you won't see their formatting effects until you apply them to an element on the page, as described next.

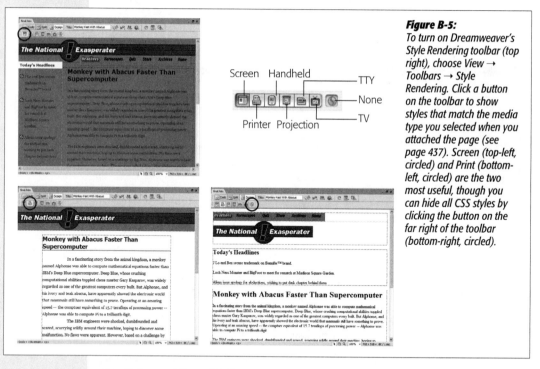

Figure B-5:
To turn on Dreamweaver's Style Rendering toolbar (top right), choose View → Toolbars → Style Rendering. Click a button on the toolbar to show styles that match the media type you selected when you attached the page (see page 437). Screen (top-left, circled) and Print (bottom-left, circled) are the two most useful, though you can hide all CSS styles by clicking the button on the far right of the toolbar (bottom-right, circled).

Applying a Class Style

You can apply class styles to any selection in the document window, whether it's a word, an image, or an entire paragraph. (You can apply any class style to any element, although doing so doesn't always make sense. If you format a graphic with a style that specifies bold, red Courier type, then it won't look any different.)

Suppose your company's name appears in a paragraph of text on a Web page that includes a class style named *.company* (either in an internal style sheet, or in a linked, external style sheet). To format that text using the class style, you select the name in the document window and apply the style, as described below.

Similarly, to format larger selections, such as an entire paragraph, you'd select the paragraph and apply the class style. In fact, you can apply a class style to any HTML tag, such as the <p> (paragraph), <td> (table cell), or <body> tags.

When you apply a class style (like *.company*) to a tag, Dreamweaver adds a special *class* property to the page's code, like this: *<p class="company">*. On the other hand, when you apply a class to a selection that isn't a tag—like a single word that you've double-clicked—Dreamweaver wraps the selection within a <span> tag like this: *<span class="company">The National Exasperator</span>*. This tag, in other words, applies a style to a *span* of text that can't be identified by a single tag.

To apply a class style to text, select some words. Then, from the Style menu in the Property inspector, select the style name (Figure B-6, top). To style an entire paragraph, place the cursor anywhere inside the paragraph (or heading) before using the Property inspector.

To apply a class style to an object like an image, select the object (the tag selector in the bottom of the document window is a great way to select a tag). Then use the Class pop-up menu on the Property inspector (Figure B-6, bottom) to select the style name.

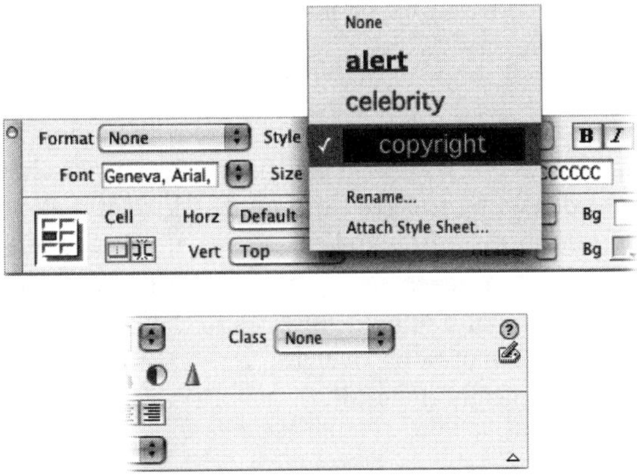

Figure B-6:
Using the Property inspector is the easiest way to apply a class style. Depending on what you've selected on the page (text, an image, or some other HTML tag), you'll encounter one of two different menus—the Style menu (top) or the Class menu (bottom). Either way, it's the same menu with the same options, and you use it to select the name of a style to apply it to whatever you've selected in the document window. You can also remove a style by selecting None from the menu.

You can also apply a class style by selecting whatever element you wish to style, choosing Text → CSS Styles, and then selecting the style from the submenu. (Alternative method for the anti-menu crowd: right-click [Control-click] the style's name in the CSS Styles panel, and then choose Apply from the shortcut menu.) Finally, you can also apply a class from the document window's tag selector, as shown in Figure B-7.

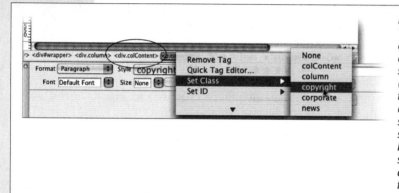

Figure B-7:
You can apply a class style directly to a tag using the document window's tag selector. Just right-click (Control-click) the tag you wish to format, and then select the class style from the Set Class submenu. In addition, the tag selector lets you know if a tag has a class style applied to it. If so, you'll see the style's name at the end of the tag. In this figure, a class style named .colContent has been applied to a <div> tag (circled).

Un-Applying a Class Style

To remove a style from an object on a Web page, simply select the element and then select None from the Property inspector's Style menu (see Figure B-6). You can also choose Text → CSS Styles → None to remove a style from any selection (even non-text elements like images or tables).

Tip: If you've applied a class style to a selection of text, then you don't actually have to select all the text to remove the style. Just click anywhere inside it and select None from the Property inspector's Style menu (or choose Text → CSS Styles → None). If you applied the style to a tag, then Dreamweaver removes the Class property from the tag. If you applied the style using the <span> tag, then Dreamweaver removes that tag.

You can't remove *tag* styles from HTML tags. Suppose you've redefined the <h1> tag using the steps outlined on page 434. If your page has three Heading 1 (<h1>) paragraphs, and you want the third heading to have a different style than the other two, then you can't simply "remove" the <h1> style from the third paragraph. Instead, what you'd need to do is create a new *class* style with all of the formatting options you want for that third heading and apply it directly to the <h1> tag (by the magic of CSS, the class formatting options override any existing tag style options—see page 86 for more on this sleight of hand).

Editing Styles

While building a Web site, you continually refine your designs. That chartreuse color you assigned to the background of your pages may have looked great at 2 a.m., but it loses something in the light of day. In fact, one of Dreamweaver's greatest selling points is how easy it makes updating the formatting on a Web site.

Dreamweaver 8 provides many ways to edit styles:

FREQUENTLY ASKED QUESTION

When Formatting Disappears

Sometimes when I copy text from one Web page and paste it into another Web page, all the formatting disappears. What's going on?

When you use Cascading Style Sheets, keep in mind that the actual style information is stored either in the <head> of the Web page (for internal style sheets) or in a separate CSS file (an external style sheet). If a page includes an internal style sheet, when you copy text, graphics, or other page elements, then Dreamweaver copies those elements and any class style definitions used by that content. When you paste the HTML into another page, the styles are written into the <head> of that page. This feature, new in Dreamweaver 8, can save you some time, but won't solve all of your woes. It doesn't, for example, copy any tag styles you've *created* or most advanced styles you might create (see page 58). So if you copy and paste some text, say an <h1> tag styled with an *h1* tag style, then the <h1> tag and its contents will paste into another page, but not the tag style.

In addition, if a page uses an external style sheet, then when you copy and paste text, the styles themselves don't go along for the ride.

When you copy a paragraph that has a class style applied to it and paste it into another document, the code in the paragraph is pasted (*<p class="company">*, for instance), but the actual *.company* style, with all its formatting properties, is not.

The best solution is to use a common external style sheet for all pages on your site. That way, when you copy and paste text, all the pages share the same styles and formatting. So in the example above, if you copy a paragraph that includes a class style—*class="company"*—into another page that shares the same style sheet, then the paragraphs will look the same on both pages.

• Select a style in the CSS Styles panel, and then click the Edit Style button to open the Rule Definition window (the same window you used when first creating the style). Make your changes, and then click OK to return to the document window. Dreamweaver reformats the page to reflect any changes you made to styles used in the current document.

• Double-clicking the name of a style in the CSS panel also opens the Rule Definition window. This is a change from the previous version of Dreamweaver (MX 2004), which switched to Code view so you could edit the raw CSS code. You can resurrect that behavior, by opening the Preferences window (Ctrl+U [⌘-U]), clicking the CSS Styles category, and selecting the last button "Edit using Code View."

• Right-click (Control-click) the name of a style in the CSS Styles panel and choose Edit from the shortcut menu, which also opens the Rule Definition Window. Make your changes to the style, and then click OK to return to the document window.

• Select a style to edit in the CSS Styles panel, and then use the Properties list (page 442) to edit the style's properties.

A Time to Design

A Dreamweaver feature called Design Time style sheets lets you quickly "try out" different CSS style sheets while developing your Web page. Using the simple dialog box shown here, you can hide the (external) style sheets you've attached to a Web page and substitute in new ones.

Design Time style sheets come in handy when working on HTML that, later on, you intend to make part of a complete Web page. Dreamweaver Library items are a good example; this feature lets you create a chunk of HTML that you can use on any number of pages on your site (see *Dreamweaver 8: The Missing Manual* for instructions on how to use this feature). When you update the Library item, every page that uses it is updated. A time-saving feature, for sure, but since a Library item is only *part* of a page it doesn't include the <head> portion needed to either store styles or attach an external style sheet. So when designing a Library item, you're working in the dark (or at least, without any style). But using Design Time style sheets, you can access all the styles in an external style sheet and even preview the effects directly in Design view.

You'll also turn to this feature when working with Dreamweaver 8's new XML tools, which let you add an *XSLT fragment* to a complete Web page—essentially letting you convert XML (like you'd find in an RSS news feed) into a chunk of HTML. But to accurately design these components, you'll need to use Design Time style sheets.

By the way, Design Time works only with external style sheets. You can't use it to prevent Dreamweaver from displaying internal styles.

To apply a Design Time style sheet to your Web page, choose Text → CSS Styles → Design Time. The Design Time Style Sheets window appears. Click the top + button to select an external style sheet to display in Dreamweaver. Note that clicking this button doesn't attach the style sheet to the page; it merely selects a .css file to use when viewing the page inside Dreamweaver.

To properly view your page with this new style sheet, you may need to get an attached external style sheet out of the way. To do that, use the bottom + button to add it to the Hide list.

Design Time style sheets apply only when you're working in Dreamweaver. They have no effect on how the page looks in an actual Web browser. That's both the good news and the bad news. Although Dreamweaver lets you apply class styles that you take from a Design Time style sheet to your Web page, it doesn't actually attach the external style sheet to the page. You have to attach it yourself when design time is over, or else your visitors will never see your intended result.

Editing in the Properties Pane

The CSS Rule Definition window (Figure B-3) is a rather tedious way of editing CSS properties. It's easy to use, but the categories and menus may slow down experienced CSS folks. Dreamweaver 8 introduces a new tool—the Properties pane—to streamline the process of editing styles. The Properties pane displays a selected style's currently defined properties, as well as a list of other not-yet set CSS properties.

Note: MX 2004 veterans: The Properties pane is nearly identical to the Rule Inspector which has been spruced up a little and moved into the CSS panel.

Select the style you wish to edit in the CSS Styles panel, and the Property pane displays CSS properties in one of three different views: a "set properties" view which

Help, My Styles Don't Work!

I've just edited a CSS style, but the changes I made don't appear when I preview the page. Why?

When you edit a style located in an external style sheet, Dreamweaver opens the .css file—in the background, where it then surreptitiously makes the change to the style. Unfortunately, the program doesn't save the file when it's done, so while the changes exist in the still-open .css file, the file safely saved on your hard drive doesn't yet contain the changes.

Therefore, if you preview a page on your site, and merrily click away to see how the newly edited styles look on your site's pages, you'll be sadly disappointed. Those pages are loading the .css file on your hard drive; they don't have access to the open file in Dreamweaver.

The method to this apparent madness: Dreamweaver is giving you a chance to undo changes you made to the external style sheet. Because the program hasn't closed the .css file, you can use the Edit → Undo command to undo edits to the file. To do so, you must have that file open in front of you—but where is it? Just pull it forward by choosing from the list of all open files at the bottom of the Window menu.

If you find this arrangement more a nuisance than a benefit, you can turn it off. Open the Preferences window by choosing Edit → Preferences (Dreamweaver → Preferences on the Mac). Select the CSS Styles category and turn off the "Open CSS files when modified" box (see Figure B-10). Remember, though, if you turn this feature off, then you won't be able to use Edit → Undo to undo edits you make to external style sheets.

displays only the properties that have been defined for the selected style (Figure B-8); a category view, which groups the different CSS properties into the same seven categories used in the Rule Definition window (Figure B-9, left); and a list view which provides an alphabetical listing of *all* CSS properties (Figure B-9, right). Clicking the view buttons at the bottom-left corner of the CSS styles panel switches between these three displays (circled in both figures).

Property names are listed on the left, and their values are on the right. Figure B-8 shows an example of a style for the <h1> tag that lists 10 properties (such as *background-color*, *font-family*) and their corresponding settings (#FFFFCC, "Arial, Helvetica, sans-serif", and so on).

Tip: As you've read, CSS lets you use various shorthand methods for combining several CSS properties into a single property. You can turn on this feature in Dreamweaver as well, as described in Figure B-10.

To add a new property, click the Add Property link at the bottom of the list, and select the property name from the pop-up menu. You set (and can edit) the value of a particular property in the space to the right of the property name. Most of the time, you don't have to type in the value. Dreamweaver provides the tools you're likely to need for each property: the ubiquitous color box for any property that requires a color, like font color; a pop-up menu for properties that have a limited list of possible values, like *dashed* for the *border-top-style* property shown in Figure B-8; and the familiar "browse for file" folder icon for properties that require a path to a file.

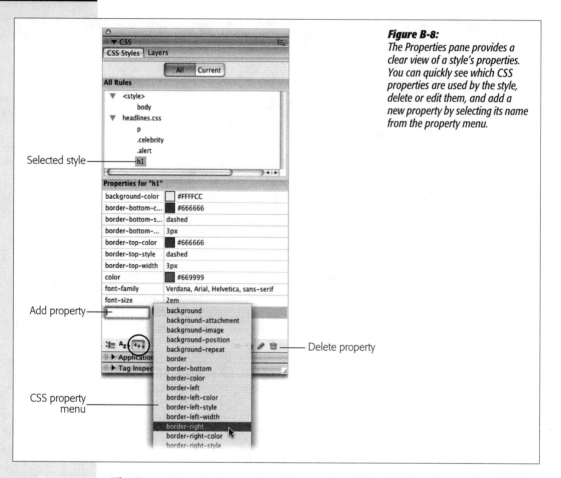

Figure B-8:
The Properties pane provides a clear view of a style's properties. You can quickly see which CSS properties are used by the style, delete or edit them, and add a new property by selecting its name from the property menu.

Selected style

Add property

CSS property menu

Delete property

The Properties pane is a great editing option if you have some experience typing your own CSS code, as you've learned throughout this book. Appendix A has a handy list of CSS properties. Also, Dreamweaver includes a built-in CSS reference so you can sharpen your CSS chops even further: choose Window → Reference to open the Reference panel, and then select O'Reilly CSS Reference from the Book menu.

Note: The Properties pane can only *edit* styles. You can add and remove properties with it, but you can't create, delete, or rename styles using it. For those maneuvers, see page 445.

Even those who are not-so-experienced will find the Properties pane helpful. First, it's the best way to get a bird's-eye view of a style's properties. Second, for really basic editing such as changing the colors used in a style or assigning it a different font, the Properties pane is as fast as it gets.

To remove a property from a style, just delete its value in the right column. Dreamweaver not only removes the value, but the property name from the style

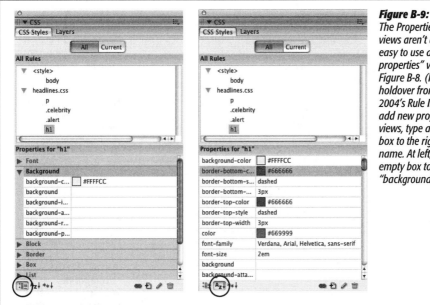

Figure B-9:
The Properties pane's two other views aren't as streamlined or as easy to use as the "set properties" view pictured in Figure B-8. (In fact, they're a holdover from Dreamweaver MX 2004's Rule Inspector panel.) To add new properties in these views, type a value in the empty box to the right of the property name. At left, you can type in the empty box to the right of "background."

sheet as well. In addition, you can right-click (Control-click) a property name and choose Delete from the shortcut menu, or click a property name followed by the trash can icon to banish it from your style sheet (see Figure B-8).

Managing Styles

Sometimes, instead of editing the properties of a style, you want to delete it and start over. Or you've come up with a way to better organize your Web site and you want to rename some styles according to your new system. Dreamweaver makes it easy to do both those things. It even lets you duplicate a style, so you can quickly create a new style that bears some similarities to one you've already built from scratch.

Deleting a Style

At some point, you may find you've created a style that you don't need after all. Maybe you redefined the HTML <code> tag and realize you haven't even used the tag in your site. There's no need to keep it around taking up precious space in the style sheet.

To delete a style, make sure the CSS Styles panel is open (Window → CSS Styles). Click the name of the style you wish to delete, and then click the Trash can at the bottom of the panel. You can also remove all of the styles in an internal style sheet (as well as the style sheet itself) by selecting the style sheet—indicated by "<style>" in the CSS Styles panel (see Figure B-10)—and clicking the Trash can. When you

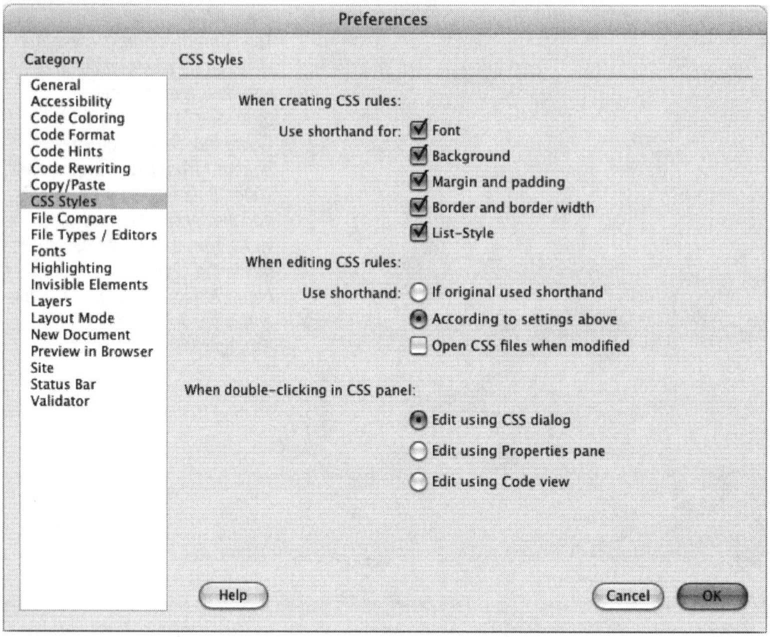

Figure B-10:
Some CSS properties can be condensed into a shorthand version. For example, the values for the background image, background-repeat, background-color, and background-position properties can be combined using the background property like this: background: #FFF url(images/bg.gif) no-repeat left top;. Normally, Dreamweaver creates a style using each individual property name, rather than the shorthand version. You can change that from the CSS Style category of the Preferences window (choose Edit → Preferences in Windows or Dreamweaver → Preferences on the Mac).

trash an *external* style sheet, you merely unlink it from the current document without actually deleting the .css file.

Tip: A faster way to delete a style is to right-click (Control-click) the name of the style in the CSS Styles panel and choose Delete from the shortcut menu.

Unfortunately, deleting a class style *doesn't* delete any references to the style in the pages of your site. If you've created a style called *.company* and applied it throughout your site, and you then delete that style from the style sheet, then Dreamweaver doesn't remove the <span> tags or class properties that refer to the style. Your pages will still be littered with orphaned code like this—*<span class="company">The National Exasperator</span>*—even though the text loses the styling. (You can use Dreamweaver's Find and Replace tool to locate and remove <span> tags with a particular class, or to locate a tag with a particular class and just remove the class attribute from the tag's HTML.)

Renaming a Class Style

While you have many ways to change the name of a style in a style sheet (open the .css file in Code view and edit the name, for example), just changing the name doesn't do much good if you've already applied a class style throughout your site. The *old* name still appears in each place you used it.

What you really need to do is rename the style and *then* perform a find-and-replace operation to change the name wherever it appears in your site. Dreamweaver includes a handy tool to simplify this process.

To rename a class style:

1. **In the Style menu (or Class menu) on the Property inspector (Figure B-6), choose Rename.**

   The Rename Style window appears (Figure B-11).

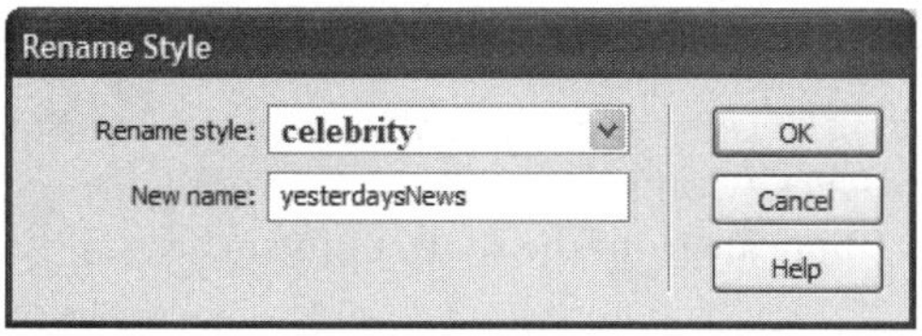

Figure B-11:
The Rename Style tool is a fast and easy way to change the name of a class style even if you've already used the style hundreds of times throughout your site.

2. **From the top menu, choose the name of the style you wish to rename.**

   This menu lists all class styles available on the current page, including external and internal styles.

3. **Type the new style name in the "New name" box.**

   You must follow the same rules for naming class styles described on page 45. But, just as when creating a new class, you don't need to precede the name with a period—Dreamweaver takes care of that.

4. **Click OK.**

   If the style whose name you're changing is an internal style, Dreamweaver makes the change. Your job is complete.

   If the style belongs to an external style sheet, Dreamweaver warns you that other pages on the site may also use this style. To successfully rename the style, Dreamweaver must use its Find and Replace tool to search the site and update all pages that use the old style name. In that case, continue to step 5.

5. **If you get cold feet, click Cancel to call off the name change, or click Yes to open the Find and Replace window, where you should click Replace All.**

   One last warning appears, reminding you that this action can't be undone.

Note: *If you click No in the warning box that appears after step 4, then Dreamweaver still renames the style in the external style sheet, but doesn't update your pages.*

6. **Click Yes.**

Dreamweaver goes through each page of your site, dutifully updating the name of the style in each place it appears. This hidden gem is a great tool, and is particularly useful if you use the Property Inspector to set font colors, types, and sizes. In that case, you can use this feature to rename the non-descriptive class names—Style1, Style2, and so on—that Dreamweaver starts you off with.

Duplicating a Style

Dreamweaver makes it easy to duplicate a CSS style, which is handy when you've created, say, an HTML tag style, and now decide you'd rather make it a class style. Or you may want to use the formatting options from one style as a starting-off point for a new style. Either way, you start by duplicating an existing style.

You can duplicate a style in two ways. The easiest method is to open the CSS Styles panel (Window → CSS Styles), right-click (Control-click) the name of the style you wish to duplicate, and then choose Duplicate from the shortcut menu.

The Duplicate CSS Rule dialog box appears (Figure B-12), where you can give the duplicated style a new name, reassign its Type setting, use the "Define in" menu to move it from an internal to an external style sheet, and so on.

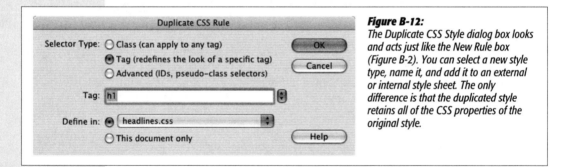

Figure B-12:
The Duplicate CSS Style dialog box looks and acts just like the New Rule box (Figure B-2). You can select a new style type, name it, and add it to an external or internal style sheet. The only difference is that the duplicated style retains all of the CSS properties of the original style.

When you click OK, Dreamweaver adds the duplicate style to the page or external style sheet. You can then edit the new style just as you would any other, as described earlier in this appendix.

Examining Your CSS in the Styles Panel

As you read in Chapters 4 and 5, inheritance and the cascade are two very important CSS concepts. Inheritance provides a way of passing on common properties like a font color to descendents of a styled tag. Giving the page's <body> tag a font color, causes other tags inside the page to use (inherit) that same font color. The cascade is a set of rules for determining what a Web browser should do if multiple styles apply to the same tag and there are conflicts between the two styles. The cascade helps decide what to do when one style dictates that a particular paragraph should be displayed in 24-pixel type, while another style dictates that the type should be 36 pixels tall.

Current Selection Mode

With all this inheritance and cascading going on, it's very easy for styles to collide in unpredictable ways. To help you discern how styles interact and ferret out possible style conflicts, Dreamweaver 8 includes another view of the CSS Styles Panel (see Figure B-13). When you click the Current button, the panel switches to Current Selection mode, which provides insight into how a selected item on a page—an image, a paragraph, a table—is affected by inherited styles.

Tip: You can also switch the CSS Styles Panel into Current Selection mode by selecting text on a page, and then clicking the new *CSS* button on the Property inspector. Doing so also opens the CSS panel, if it's closed—a nice shortcut. If the button's grayed out, then you're already in the right mode.

This is really an incredible tool that's invaluable in diagnosing weird CSS behavior associated with inheritance and cascading. But like any incredible tool, it requires a good manual to learn how it works. The panel crams in a lot of information; here's a quick overview of what it provides:

- **A summary of style properties for the currently selected item in the Summary for Selection pane.** Remember that whole thing about how parents pass on attributes to child tags, and how as styles cascade through a page, they accumulate (which means it's possible to have an <h1> tag formatted by multiple styles from multiple style sheets)? The Summary for Selection section is like the grand total at the bottom of a spreadsheet. It tells you, in essence, what the selected element—a paragraph, a picture, and so on—will look like when a Web browser tallies up all of the styles and displays the page.

- **The origin of a particular property is displayed in the About pane** (Figure B-13, top). If a headline is orange, but you never created an <h1> tag with an orange color, then you can find out which style from which style sheet is passing its hideous orangeness to the heading.

- **A list of styles that apply to the current selection appears in the Rules pane** (Figure B-13, bottom). Since any element can be on the receiving end of countless CSS properties handed down by parent tags, it's helpful to see a list of all the styles contributing to the current appearance of the selected object on the page.

- **The order of the cascade in the "Rules" pane** (Figure B-13, bottom). Not only are styles that apply to the current selection listed, they're also listed in a particular order, with the most general style at the top and the most specific ones at the bottom. This means that when the same property exists in two (or more) styles, the style listed last (furthest down the list) wins.

A few examples can help demonstrate how to read the CSS Style panel when it's in Current Selection mode. Figure B-13 shows the CSS properties affecting a selection of text (in this case, a paragraph) on a Web page. The Summary for Selection pane lets you know that if you viewed this page in a Web browser, this paragraph

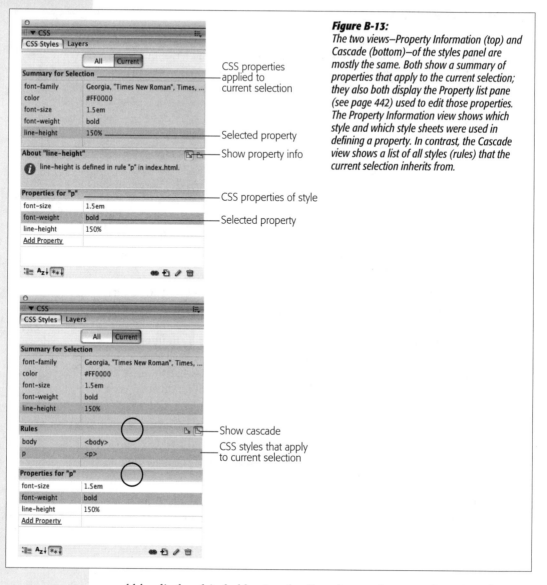

Figure B-13:
The two views—Property Information (top) and Cascade (bottom)—of the styles panel are mostly the same. Both show a summary of properties that apply to the current selection; they also both display the Property list pane (see page 442) used to edit those properties. The Property Information view shows which style and which style sheets were used in defining a property. In contrast, the Cascade view shows a list of all styles (rules) that the current selection inherits from.

would be displayed in bold using the Georgia type-face, at a font-size of 1.5ems with 150 percent line-height (space between each line of text). When you select a property from the Summary for Selection pane and then click the Show Property Information button (Figure B-13, top), the About pane displays where the property comes from—in this case, that property belongs to the <p> tag style which is defined in the internal style sheet of the file *index.html.*

You've seen the bottom pane before. It's the Properties pane, and it's used to delete, add, and edit the properties of a style (see page 442). You simply click in the area to the right of the property's name to change its value, or click the Add Property link to select a new property for the style. Notice that in this example, the Properties pane contains fewer properties than the summary view. That's because it displays only properties of a single style (the <p> tag style), while the Summary view shows all properties inherited by the current selection.

Tip: Sometimes one or more of the three panes are too small for you to be able to see the information displayed. You can use the gray bars containing the panes' names (circled in Figure B-13, bottom) as handles and drag them up or down to reveal more or less of each pane.

Deciphering the Cascade

Clicking the Show Cascade button (Figure B-13, bottom) reveals a list of all styles that affect the current selection. In this case, you can see that two tag styles—one for the body tag and one for the p tag—contribute to styling the selected paragraph of text. In addition, as mentioned above, the order in which the styles are listed is important. The lower the name appears in the list, the more "specific" that style is—in other words, when several styles contain the same property, the property belonging to the style *lower* on the list wins out (see page 84 for more on conflicts caused by cascading styles).

The Properties pane provides even more information about conflicting properties. Figure B-14 shows that four styles are affecting the formatting of a single paragraph of text: three tag styles (<body>, <p>, and <p>) and one class style (.sidebar). Why two <p> tag styles? One is in an external style sheet, while the other belongs to the page's internal style sheet.

Clicking a style name in the Rules pane reveals that style's properties in the pane below. In the bottom-left image in Figure B-14, notice the *sidebar* class style has properties such as background color, text color, and so on. When a line appears through a property name (see the circled areas in Figure B-14, bottom middle and bottom right) that property isn't applied to the current selection. Either it's overridden by a more specific style, or it's not an inherited property.

The second-to-last style in the list in Figure B-14—a <p> tag style—shows that it has a setting for the *font-family* property. In addition, there's a line through the property name, indicating that it doesn't apply to the current selection. Because the more specific .sidebar class style also has the *font-family* property set, in the battle of cascading style properties, *.sidebar* wins (see Chapters 4 and 5 for more on inheritance and cascading).

Tip: When you hover over a property name that's crossed out in the Properties pane, a pop-up window explains why the property doesn't apply. This is a big help, when a certain property setting (such as a font color) from a style isn't being applied to your selection. The pop-up window will explain which style it's in conflict with, providing you with the diagnostic information you need to go fix the problem.

If your Web pages are elegantly simple and use only a couple of styles, you may not find much need for this aspect of the CSS Styles panel. But as you become more proficient (and adventurous) with CSS, you'll find that this panel is a great way to untangle masses of colliding and conflicting styles.

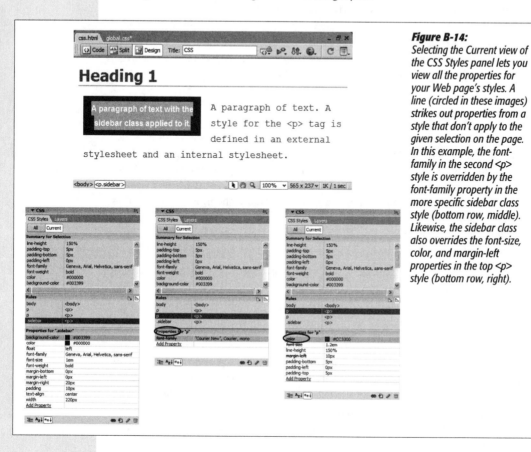

Figure B-14:
Selecting the Current view of the CSS Styles panel lets you view all the properties for your Web page's styles. A line (circled in these images) strikes out properties from a style that don't apply to the given selection on the page. In this example, the font-family in the second <p> style is overridden by the font-family property in the more specific sidebar class style (bottom row, middle). Likewise, the sidebar class also overrides the font-size, color, and margin-left properties in the top <p> style (bottom row, right).

CSS Properties

For the most part, the Dreamweaver's CSS Rule Definition window lists CSS properties using nearly the same language as the actual property names; the *color* property, for example, is listed in the Type category as Color. But sometimes Dreamweaver uses very different names for CSS properties. Table B-1 shows each category of the CSS Rule Definition window, and lists the actual CSS property name and a page reference where you can learn more about the property. In addition, Appendix A contains a complete list of CSS 2.1 properties.

Table B-1. *Dreamweaver property names and their CSS equivalents*

Dreamweaver Property Name	Actual CSS Property Name
Category: Type	
Font	*font-family* (page 101)
Size	*font-size* (page 104)
Weight	*font-weight* (page 109)
Style	*font-style* (page 109)
Variant	*font-variant* (page 110)
Line height	*line-height* (page 112)
Case	*text-transform* (page 109)
Decoration (underline, overline, line-through, blink, none)	*text-decoration* (page 110)
Color	*color* (page 102)
Category: Background	
Background color	*background-color* (page 145)
Background image	*background-image* (page 172)
Repeat	*background-repeat* (page 175)
Attachment	*background-attachment* (page 181)
Horizontal position/Vertical position	*background-position* (page 176)
Category: Block	
Word spacing	*word-spacing* (page 111)
Letter spacing	*letter-spacing* (page 111)
Vertical alignment	*vertical-alignment* (page 254)
Text align	*text-align* (page 114)
Whitespace	*white-space* (page 413)
Display	*display* (page 140)
Category: Box	
Width	*width* (page 146)
Height	*height* (page 146)
Float	*float* (page 152)
Clear	*clear* (page 155)
Padding	*padding* (page 135)
Top	*padding-top* (page 135)
Right	*padding-right* (page 135)
Bottom	*padding-bottom* (page 135)
Left	*padding-left* (page 135)
Margin	*margin* (page 135)
Top	*margin-top* (page 135)
Right	*margin-right* (page 135)
Bottom	*margin-bottom* (page 135)
Left	*margin-left* (page 135)

Table B-1. Dreamweaver property names and their CSS equivalents (continued)

Dreamweaver Property Name	Actual CSS Property Name
Category: Border*	
Style	border-style (page 141)
Width	border-width (page 141)
Color	border-color (page 141)
Category: List	
Type	list-style-type (page 117)
Bullet Image	list-style-image (page 121)
Position	list-style-position (page 120)
Category: Positioning	
Type:	position (page 326)
Width	width (page 146)
Height	height (page 146)
Visibility	visibility (page 337)
Z-Index	z-index (page 336)
Overflow	overflow (page 148)
Placement Top	top (page 328)
Placement Right	right (page 328)
Placement Bottom	bottom (page 328)
Placement Left	left (page 328)
Clip Top, Right, Bottom, Left	clip (page 421)
Category: Extensions	
Before	page-break-before (page 374)
After	page-break-after (page 374)
Cursor	cursor (page 429)
Filter	Filter is an Internet Explorer for Windows only property. For more information go to: http://msdn. microsoft.com/workshop/author/ filter/reference/reference.asp

*There are many different border properties, all of which provide different ways to specify the same thing (see page 141). Dreamweaver's CSS Styles Preferences determine exactly how Dreamweaver writes the CSS code for borders (page 446). You can't set the very useful border-collapse property in the Rule Definition window (see page 256).

CSS Resources

Unfortunately, one book can't answer all of your CSS questions. (We did try, however.) Thankfully, there are many CSS resources available for both the beginning and expert Web designer. Below you'll find resources to help you with general CSS concepts as well as resources to help with specific CSS tasks such as building a navigation bar or laying out a Web page.

References

References that cover CSS properties range from the official to the obscure. There are Web sites and online tutorials, of course, but you don't have to be on the Web to learn about CSS. Some of these guides come on good old-fashioned paper.

World Wide Web Consortium (W3C)

- *CSS 2.1 Specification: www.w3c.org/TR/CSS21/.* For the official word, go to the source—the W3C—and read the actual set of rules that make up the most widely supported version of CSS, version 2.1.

- *CSS 3 Current Work: www.w3.org/Style/CSS/current-work.* If you want to take a look at what the future holds, check out the current work being done on the CSS 3 specification. It promises some very major enhancements to CSS. Just note that it's probably going to take a few years before these innovations are finalized and even longer before Web browsers understand them. But it's fun to dream.

Books and PDFs

- *Cascading Style Sheets: The Definitive Guide* by Eric Meyer (O'Reilly). For comprehensive technical (yet readable) coverage of CSS, check out this guide.

- *CSS Cheat Sheet (www.ilovejackdaniels.com/css_cheat_sheet.pdf).* Don't let the URL put you off. This one-page PDF document lists every CSS property, covers every type of CSS selector under the sun, and includes a handy diagram of the box model (page 133). Print it out, fold it up, and carry it in your back pocket.

Online Tutorial

- *WesternCiv's Complete CSS Guide: www.westciv.com/style_master/academy/css_tutorial/index.html.* A detailed online guide to CSS.

CSS Help

Even with the best references (like this book), sometimes you need to ask an expert. You can join a discussion list where CSS-heads answer questions by email, or peruse a wealth of information in an online forum.

Email List

- *CSS-Discuss: http://css-discuss.org/.* The longest living mailing list dedicated to just CSS. You'll find CSS masters willing to help get you out of your CSS troubles.

Note: Before pestering the *CSS-Discuss* list with a question that 47,000 people have previously asked, check out their *wiki*—a collaborative Web site where group members freely add, edit, and update each other's articles. This wiki has evolved into a terrifically convenient index of tips and tricks, best practices, and in-depth treatment of CSS topics. Visit *http://css-discuss.incutio.com/.*

Discussion Boards

- *CSSCreator Forum: www.csscreator.com/css-forum/.* A very active online forum offering help and advice for everything from basic CSS to advanced layout.

- *SitePoint.com's CSS Forum: www.sitepoint.com/forums/forumdisplay.php?f=53.* Another helpful group of CSS addicts.

CSS Navigation

Chapter 9 shows you how to create navigation buttons for your Web site from scratch. But online tutorials are a great way to solidify your knowledge. Also, once you understand the process in detail, you don't have to do it yourself every single time. On the Web you can find examples of navigation features for inspiration.

Tutorials

- *http://tutorials.alsacreations.com/rollover_unique/*. How to create a graphical menu with a single image. Includes rollovers!

- *Listutorial: http://css.maxdesign.com.au/listutorial/*. Step-by-step tutorials on building navigation systems from unordered lists.

Online Examples

- *Pure CSS Pop-ups: www.meyerweb.com/eric/css/edge/popups/demo.html*. Pop-up effects, purely with CSS.

- *CSS Tab Designer: www.highdots.com/css-list/*. Windows-only software for quickly generating tabbed CSS menus.

- *CSS Showcase: www.alvit.de/css-showcase/*. A gallery of navigation menus, tabs and CSS navigation techniques.

- *Listamatic: http://css.maxdesign.com.au/listamatic/*. Showcase of CSS-based navigation systems. Also lots of links to related Web sites.

- *Listamatic2: http://css.maxdesign.com.au/listamatic2/*. More CSS-menus, including nested lists with submenus.

- *Horizontal Pop-Out Menus: www.alistapart.com/articles/horizdropdowns/*. The name's a little deceiving. This tutorial actually creates a vertical menu, with submenus that pop up next to the main menu.

- *Free Vertical Menu Designs: http://exploding-boy.com/images/EBmenus/menus.html*. A handful of cool designs.

- *CSS Play Menu Showcase: www.cssplay.co.uk/menus/index.html*. Lots of cool menus, many useful techniques. A must see.

CSS and Graphics

Once you've tried the photo gallery in Chapter 8, you're ready to get even more creative. Here are some Web sites that showcase CSS graphics tricks.

- *CSS Slideshow: www.cssplay.co.uk/menu/slide_show.html*. CSS-only slideshow from the creative mind of Stu Nicholls.

- *Sliding PhotoGalleries: www.cssplay.co.uk/menu/gallery3l.html*. Dynamic, CSS-driven gallery.

- *Multi-page Photo Gallery: /www.cssplay.co.uk/menu/lightbox.html#tree1*. Yet another image gallery from Stu Nicholls.

- *CSS Star Rating: komodomedia.com/blog/index.php/2006/01/09/css-star-rating-part-deux*. Create a very cool, Netflix-like star rating system.

- *CSS Image Maps: www.frankmanno.com/ideas/css-imagemap/.* Create pop-up labels for your photos.

- *CSS Photo Caption Zoom: http://randsco.com/_miscPgs/cssZoomPZ3.html.* Make a ginormous version of a photo appear just by mousing over a thumbnail image.

- *Revised Image Replacement: www.mezzoblue.com/tests/revised-image-replacement/.* Overview of different ways to swap out HTML headlines with stylish graphics.

CSS Layout

CSS layout is so flexible you could spend a lifetime exploring the possibilities. And some people seem to be doing just that. You can gain from their labors by reading articles, checking out online examples, and experimenting with tools that can do some of the CSS work for you.

Box Model Information

- *Interactive CSS Box Model: www.redmelon.net/tstme/box_model/.* Fun, interactive tool for visualizing the box model.

- *On Having Layout: www.satzansatz.de/cssd/onhavinglayout.html.* Not for the faint of heart, this highly technical analysis of Internet Explorer explains the main cause (and some solutions) for many of the CSS bugs that plague Windows Internet Explorer 6 and earlier.

- *CSS Grid Calculator: www.gwhite.us/downloads/css_grid_calc.html.* A Flash application (now that's ironic) that asks for some basic properties of the layout you want—number of columns, gutter width, page width, and so on—and generates the CSS to make it happen.

Float Layouts

- *In search of the one true layout: www.positioniseverything.net/articles/onetruelayout/.* Interesting—if slightly mind-bending—presentation on how to create a float-based layout that overcomes most of the limitations of floats.

- *Any Order Columns: http://bitesizestandards.com/bites/understanding-any-order-columns.* A simple introduction to using negative margins for positioning columns regardless of their position in the HTML source code.

- *CSS Discuss Wiki page on float-based layouts: http://css-discuss.incutio.com/?page=FloatLayouts.* Even more links to float-based layout resources.

Absolute Position Layouts

- *CSS-Discuss Wiki on Absolute Layouts: http://css-discuss.incutio.com/?page=AbsoluteLayouts.* Good resources with some helpful background information.

- *Learn CSS Positioning in Ten Steps: www.barelyfitz.com/screencast/html-training/css/positioning/.* Quick, hands-on overview of CSS positioning.

- *Making the Absolute, Relative: www.stopdesign.com/articles/absolute/.* Guide to using absolute positioning for subtle design effects.

Layout Examples

- *Mollio Templates: www.mollio.org.* Great set of free CSS-layout templates. Very nice design.

- *Layout Gala: http://blog.html.it/layoutgala/.* Forty different CSS designs, running the gambit from two-column to three-column, fixed-width to liquid. (All have been tested in IE, Firefox, and Safari.)

- *Intensivstation Templates: http://intensivstation.ch/en/templates/.* Cool templates, weird domain name.

Miscellaneous Layout Resources

- *One clean HTML markup, many layouts: http://tjkdesign.com/articles/one_html_markup_many_css_layouts.asp.* Great blog post that takes a single HTML page and demonstrates eight different ways to lay it out with just CSS.

- *Variable fixed width layout: www.clagnut.com/blog/1663/.* Short blog post about a technique for adjusting the number of columns on a page, based on the width of the browser window.

- *3-Column Layout Index: http://css-discuss.incutio.com/?page=ThreeColumnLayouts.* A nearly exhaustive (or at least exhausting) list of different 3-column layouts.

- *Site in an Hour: http://leftjustified.net/site-in-an-hour/.* Slide presentation on how to build a CSS Web site.

Browser Bugs

CSS is the best way to format Web pages, and Internet Explorer 6 for Windows is the world's most popular browser…so why doesn't IE 6 do a better job displaying CSS? That's a question for the ages, but one thing's for sure: You'd be holding a thinner book if it didn't have to devote so much paper to IE workarounds. (And the following Web sites would go out of business.)

Windows Internet Explorer

- *How to Attack an Internet Explorer (Win) Display Bug: www.communitymx.com/content/article.cfm?page=1&cid=C37E0.* A great introduction to debugging Internet Explorer CSS problems.

- *RichInStyle's guide to IE 5/5.5 Bugs: www.richinstyle.com/bugs/ie5.html.* That pesky browser is still around, and still causing Web designers trouble. If you need help making your pages work for IE 5, check this page out.

- *Explorer Exposed! www.positioniseverything.net/explorer.html.* Information on the most common Internet Explorer bugs and how to fix them.

Mac Internet Explorer 5

- *Mac IE 5: Problems with CSS Rendering: www.l-c-n.com/IE5tests.* This book doesn't cover Internet Explorer 5 for the Mac, since it's just about a dead browser. Microsoft is no longer updating it or even providing technical support, giving Mac fans a perfect excuse to switch to the superior Safari and Firefox browsers. However, if you still need to accommodate IE 5 for the Mac, check out this site for helpful tips on Mac IE-only CSS bugs.

Showcase Sites

Knowing the CSS standard inside out is no help when your imagination's running dry. A great source of inspiration is the creative work of others, so here's a bunch of sites where you can appreciate and study beautiful CSS designs.

- *CSS ZenGarden: www.csszengarden.com.* The mother of all CSS showcase sites: many different designs for the exact same HTML.

- *CSS Beauty: www.cssbeauty.com/.* A wonderful gallery of inspirational CSS designs.

- *CSS Vault: http://cssvault.com/.* More cool designs.

- *CSS Mania: http://cssmania.com/.* Yet another showcase site, whose non-grammatical claim to fame is "Since March 2004, the most updated CSS showcase all over the globe."

- *Showcase of Showcases: http://css-discuss.incutio.com/?page=ShowCase.* The CSS-Discuss wiki presents a list of showcase sites, and great examples of CSS design.

CSS Books

Hey, not even this book can tell you *everything* there is to know about CSS!

- *Web Standards Solutions* by Dan Cederholm (Friends of Ed). Though not strictly about CSS, this book provides an excellent presentation on how to write good HTML. If you have any doubts about what tags you should use to create a navigation bar, how to best create HTML forms, or what's the best method for making your HTML code as simple as possible, this book is a must read.

- *Bulletproof Web Design* by Dan Cederholm (New Riders). A great book covering how best to create CSS styles that can withstand the pressure of visitors changing text sizes, resizing their browser windows, and the general instability of the browser environment. Great tips on building layouts, navigation bars and more.

- *CSS Mastery: Advanced Web Standards Solutions* by Andy Budd (Friends of Ed). Many advanced tips for using CSS, including good examples of CSS-based layouts, and techniques for streamlining your CSS and HTML code.

- *Head First HTML with CSS & XHTML* by Elisabeth Freeman and Eric Freeman (O'Reilly). A lively, highly illustrated introduction to Web sites integrating HTML and CSS.

Must-Have RSS Feeds

RSS lets the Web come to you in the form of summaries of posts from your favorite bloggers or instant notification of updates to the sites you follow. You can use the free Google Reader (*www.google.com/reader/*), Firefox's built-in RSS Reader, or Safari's reader if you're on a Mac. If you're not plugged into RSS, you should be, especially if you'd like to keep on top of the latest in CSS news. Check out these feeds:

- *456 Berea St: www.456bereastreet.com/feed.xml.* Great tidbits on CSS, accessibility and general best practices of Web design.

- *And All That Malarkey: www.stuffandnonsense.co.uk/atom.xml.* Fun, irreverent Web design info.

- *Collylogic: http://www.collylogic.com/index.php?/weblog/rss_2.0/.* Great commentary on CSS, Web design, and the Web in general.

- *TJKDesign: www.tjkdesign.com/xml/TJKFeed.xml.* Lots of good stuff, including tutorials and deeply researched information on CSS.

CSS Software

There are lots of different ways to create Cascading Style Sheets. Keeping it simple, you can stick with the free text editors that come with Windows and Macintosh like Notepad or TextEdit. There are also CSS-only editors, as well as full-fledged Web page development programs like Dreamweaver that include CSS creation tools.

- *CSS-Discuss list of CSS Editors: http://css-discuss.incutio.com/?page=CssEditors.* A long list of many different programs available for editing CSS.

Windows and Mac

- *Style Master: www.westciv.com/style_master/product_info/.* This is a powerful CSS editor with a long history which includes many tools, including simple wizards to get you started, sample templates, tutorials, and a complete CSS guide.

- *Dreamweaver 8: www.adobe.com/dreamweaver/.* Definitely not just for CSS, this premium Web development tool includes everything you need to build complete Web sites. Visual editing tools make it easier to see the effect of CSS on your Web pages as you work.

Windows Only

- *Top Style: www.newsgator.com/NGOLProduct.aspx?ProdID=TopStyle.* The venerable CSS editor that also lets you edit your HTML documents—a one-stop shop for Web page building. Includes many tools to increase your productivity. There's also a free "lite" version.

Mac Only

- *CSSEdit: www.macrabbit.com/cssedit/.* Simple, inexpensive CSS editor.

- *BBEdit: www.barebones.com/products/bbedit/.* Not a CSS-editor per se, BBEdit is a complete Web-page editing program. A slimmed-down version, called Text-Wrangler, doesn't include as many features but is free.

Index

CSS: The Missing Manual

CSS: THE MISSING MANUAL

Colophon

Philip Dangler was the production editor and proofreader for *CSS: The Missing Manual*. Dawn Mann wrote the index. Genevieve d'Entremont and Marlowe Shaeffer provided quality control.

The cover of this book is based on a series design by David Freedman. Karen Montgomery produced the cover layout with Adobe InDesign CS using Adobe's Minion and Gill Sans fonts.

David Futato designed the interior layout, based on a series design by Phil Simpson. This book was converted by Abby Fox to FrameMaker 5.5.6. The text font is Adobe Minion; the heading font is Adobe Formata Condensed; and the code font is LucasFont's TheSans Mono Condensed. The illustrations that appear in the book were produced by Robert Romano and Jessamyn Read using Macromedia FreeHand MX and Adobe Photoshop CS.